PARIS
AND ITS
PROVINCES
1792–1802

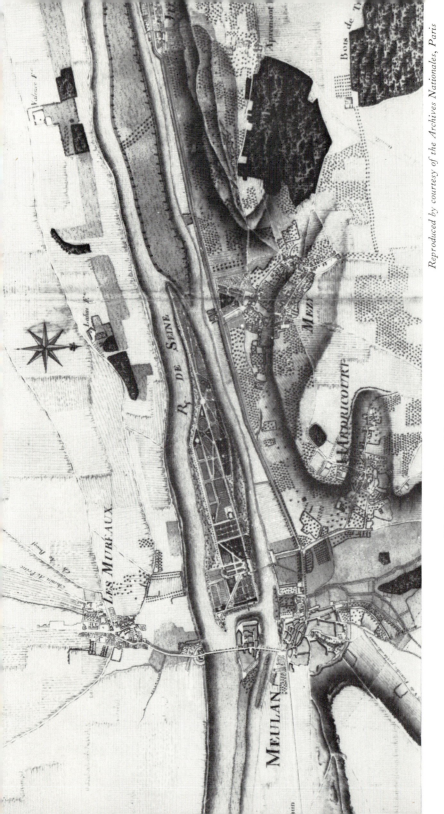

The Seine above Mantes: the port of Meulan
From the Trudaine road map, see p. 40.

PARIS
AND ITS
PROVINCES
1792–1802

RICHARD COBB

LONDON
OXFORD UNIVERSITY PRESS
NEW YORK   TORONTO
1975

Oxford University Press, Ely House, London W. 1

GLASGOW NEW YORK TORONTO MELBOURNE WELLINGTON
CAPE TOWN IBADAN NAIROBI DAR ES SALAAM LUSAKA ADDIS ABABA
DELHI BOMBAY CALCUTTA MADRAS KARACHI LAHORE DACCA
KUALA LUMPUR SINGAPORE HONG KONG TOKYO

ISBN 0 19 212195 2

© *Oxford University Press 1975*

*Printed in Great Britain by
Richard Clay (The Chaucer Press), Ltd.,
Bungay, Suffolk*

This book is for my friend Jane Heseltine, co-editor of *The Oxford Companion to French Literature*, editor of *The Oxford Book of French Prose*, who loves and respects the French language and who has known Paris for many years longer than I have, in token of gratitude and esteem

Contents

Introduction

'... La butte Montmartre avait représenté pendant des siècles un but très visible, planté au Nord, presque provocant. Pour une ville restée jeune, il était difficile de résister au désir de l'atteindre. D'abord par des pélérinages, des promenades du dimanche. Peu à peu des cabarets s'installent le long de la route. Une traînée de maisons joint la barrière de Paris aux guinguettes dans les jardins de la colline, et aux moulins où des ânes vous portent par des sentiers. Quand la basilique du Sacré-Coeur commença de s'élever, énorme, bombée de toutes parts, et d'une pierre merveilleusement blanche ... il y avait plus de mille ans que Paris rêvait de s'installer là-haut, et de marquer son occupation par quelque trophée qu'on verrait du bout des plaines de l'Ile-de-France, comme la trophée de la Turbie se voit des navires en mer.

... C'est ce trophée de Montmartre que regardait l'ouvrier agricole qui rentrait des champs à bicyclette par la route de Gonesse au Tremblay. Il avait de la peine à maintenir sur les pédales ses semelles empâtées de terre glaise. Mais quand tout à l'heure il serait assis au cabaret, l'horizon de Montmartre n'aurait pas tout à fait disparu de sa tête. La salle, les tables, les verres prendraient un peu de ce faste, de cette gloire qui entourent les loisirs de l'ouvrier parisien. ...'

Jules Romains, *Le 6 octobre*, 1932.

THEODORE ZELDIN, in his recent book,[1] makes the point that *compagnonnages* disappeared with the advent of the railways, which 'made travel less of an adventure and destroyed the practice of the *tour de France.* . . .' One could add that the construction of the railways, while destroying other forms too of the sociability of walking, by no means eliminated the more unpredictable elements of travel. Some years ago I was travelling by train from Turin to Modane. In the same compartment, there was an elderly man wearing a deerstalker's hat with a pheasant feather in it—it was in fact somewhat reminiscent of the headgear favoured by the Alpini—and dressed in a Sherlock Holmes style coat of the kind that the French used to describe as *un macfarlane.* Above his head, in the luggage carrier, there were three rucksacks. My companion appeared to be either a hunter or a mountaineer, or both. As the train climbed slowly out of the valley of the Po, we got into conversation, in French, mostly on the subject of Turin, of the Piedmontese, and of the famous café, decorated with superbly ornate eighteenth-century furniture, situated on the twin-churched Piazza San Carlo, and that unkind Torinese have sometimes called *il caffè della mennapausa,* owing to its afternoon frequentation by ladies of the upper bourgeoisie in their 50s and over, who come there to eat cream cakes and to drink minuscule cups of coffee. My vis-à-vis, I gradually gathered, was not a hunter, but a man of letters.

A few weeks earlier, I had acquired, from a second-hand bookstall in the rue de Gergovie—all one's best reading seems to have come from such places—a French translation of a novel by Mario Soldati, *Lettre de Capri,* a story which opens at the Porta Nova station: a young barrister, who is to meet his fiancée at the other end, is about to take the train to the coast, before crossing over to Capri. After going through the ticket-barrier, he walks the full length of the train, looking into all the first- and second-class compartments—he has taken a first-class ticket in order to allow himself a greater range of choice—to see if any of them contains an attractive girl travelling alone. He hesitates for some time between five different possibilities, but, as the train is about to leave, he eventually plumps for a compartment in which a girl with long auburn hair, wearing a low-cut multi-coloured blouse, is travelling. He seats himself opposite *la Primavera.* But, as the train pulls out, two hefty youths, wearing climbing boots, jump into the carriage,

[1] *France 1848–1945, vol. i: Ambition, Love, and Politics,* Oxford, 1973.

placing huge bundles of some smelly material in the rack. Already, as the first suburbs gather speed before the windows, the two louts engage the auburn beauty in the coarsest Torinese, a dialect in which the rustic girl proves to be equally proficient and as sumptuously earthy. The barrister is left to his gloom; his companions all get out at a country station, somewhere before Chivasso. At Savona, the young man walks once more the full length of the train, eventually choosing another compartment that appears to offer a more promising prospect. I cannot remember how things turn out after that; but I think at least that the conversation went quite well, once engaged. Also I seem to recollect that the young man never reaches Capri.

Anyhow, I told my companion how much I had been attracted by the acuteness of this observation of eternal, unquenchable masculine optimism, an optimism always stimulated by the unknown possibilities offered by a long train journey, and as much related to a romantic view of love as to a concern for the more banal possibilities of seduction. I went on to say how much I had enjoyed a story that had about it a certain haunting melancholy, as well as a very gentle irony. My companion became very attentive and seemed delighted by my comments; he asked me if I had read any of Soldati's other novels. I said that I had and explained why I had enjoyed them. I had struck lucky, for the old man's pleasure was now visible. Just as the train went into the long tunnel leading to Modane and France, he got up to prepare to leave; I helped him down with his rucksacks. After shaking hands, he handed me a visiting card, telling me how much he had enjoyed travelling with me. The card carried addresses in Turin and Rome—my new friend told me that he would be delighted to entertain me in either place— and the name, in embossed italics, *Mario Soldati*. It was my only encounter with the novelist.

Another time, I travelled from Marseille to Bandol; opposite was perhaps the most beautiful French girl I have ever seen, and, though this was in 1945, I can still recall her. We were alone in the compartment; the girl, with a smooth, pale face, like that of a *pénitente*, was plunged in the magazine *Pour lire à deux*. Was she too riveted by some story in which a *midinette* meets a *Duc*, who introduces her to his *vieille mère* who calls her *ma chère enfant*; the eventual wedding, followed by a *dîner aux chandelles*, served by domestic personnel dressed in *l'habit à la française*, taking place in the magnificent Gothic refectory of the ancestral castle? Pernicious nonsense, perhaps, a literature designed to perpetuate the slavery of the shop-girl; yet it appealed to the humble fantasies of the *pénitente*. I could only watch the rapt attention of the wonderful face. The girl got out a few stations beyond Aubagne, sweeping my face, as she opened the carriage door, with a smile of simple warmth. I had had plenty of time, I supposed unobserved, but from her smile it occurred to me that this may not have been so, to watch her serene eyes, caught in the reflection of the window, as the train had gone into the tunnel at the exit from Saint-Charles. So, on another occasion, in the tram from Stupinigi to Turin, in the growing darkness, had I studied the eyes, enormous and full of love, of the Italian girl with whom I had had a day's outing to the hunting lodge of the House of Savoy, as they were caught, in the swerving panes lit up by the street lights and the glare of the endless *La Fiat* buildings of the suburbs of the approaching city.

On the occasion of my first leave in Marseille, well supplied with Belgian cigarettes and francs, I headed downhill from the Gare Saint-Charles, impelled, both by the gradient and the awareness of sea, towards the Canebière and the Vieux-Port. On the quai des Belges, later on the same day, I was drawn into conversation with two *légionnaires*, whom I had met, after lunch, in a Greek café on the quays. After several rounds of *pastis*, the three of us were induced to take on a series of bets from some of the Greek customers that we would swim across the Vieux-Port, from the side of the Hôtel de Ville, to that of Endoum, without our tunics, but with our boots and trousers. Where armies are concerned, it is difficult to evade such an invitation: I could hardly hope to compete with the Foreign Legion, but I would none the less try. It was August and very hot, so we all took up the bets, all reached the other side, on which a small crowd had collected, and then returned, dripping, on foot. There must, I think, have been a great many more rounds after this; and there was certainly a lot of Greek music and slow dancing, with the men clapping their hands. I cannot remember what happened to the two *légionnaires*; perhaps they had to report somewhere. Nor can I recollect what happened to myself. The next morning, I woke up in a very light room, the walls freshly whitewashed, a cool floor of dark red tiles, a still room into which the sun was streaming. I knew that I could not be far from the scene of our swim, because I could hear the regular beat of the engine of the ferry that, every few minutes, crossed from the Hôtel de Ville to Endoum. Otherwise, I had no idea where I was or how I had got there. But as I turned over on my right side, I noticed that the bedclothes, under a red eiderdown, undulated in the gentle rise and fall of the Stretton hills or the Long-mynd: the undulation did not in fact move, and it was only after some prodding that I was confronted with a sleepy girl, long-legged, naked, with very dark hair and a brown skin, long eye-lashes and extremely pretty. *Dieu protège les ivrognes* and some Greek god of Marseille had certainly protected me. I asked her how we came to be where we were; she said we were in her place and told me to look under my pillow, where, to my immense relief, I found all the money for my leave, in a large number of Belgian notes; on the side table, there were fifteen packets of *Aros Jaunes* and *Bastos* and my pay book. My socks and trousers had been hung up to dry, on a line from the window; the trousers blew in the hot wind, like a flag announcing the presence of the British Army. I noticed that my shirt, placed over a chair, had been ironed. The girl, who told me that she was the wife of a Greek seaman —hastening to add, to my relief, that her husband was not due back in port for another week—and that she was Greek herself, explained to me that it was thanks to her care that *ma petite fortune*, which I had been brandishing imprudently in several cafés on the quays, had been saved. Later that morning, she allowed me to ask her out to lunch at a Greek restaurant. I never saw her again.

It was the sort of luck that, very occasionally, perhaps only once or twice in a lifetime, one encounters the first time in a strange city. I have been to Marseille many times since then, and nothing of the kind has ever happened to me. Yet the memory of that first encounter has lingered on, so that, each time I have walked down the many steps of the Gare Saint-Charles, taken the Boulevard d'Athènes, then the rue du Petit-Saint-Jean, always thick with noisy prostitutes (protected perhaps by the Petit-Saint-Jean) perched on their amazing heels, eventually to reach the quai des Belges, at the level of a little black Counter-Reformation church, I have been filled with a vague expectancy that always seemed to be stimulated by the unique smell of the Mediterranean, by the noise of ships' engines, by the brilliant oranges of the pale blue Catalan boats moored off the Hôtel de Ville, and by the shouted offers of the fishermen competing for passengers anxious to do the trip to the Château-d'If.

In October 1944, on the strength of a non-existent uncle whom I had invented and whom I had had interned, as a British subject, in the barracks of Saint-Denis, I obtained compassionate leave for Paris, then in the American Zone. I was by then stationed in Malines. There were no trains and I had to rely on British Army transport for as near as it would take me. I was, predictably, picked up at the exit from Brussels, near Hal, on the road to Tournai and Lille; and I had myself put down, at dusk, in the small market town of Aumale, which I reckoned was the nearest point to the capital on the British military supply lines between the Dutch frontier and the old beach-head at Arromanches (I was pretty confident of my route, as I was myself attached to the Head-quarters of the Lines of Communication). At Aumale, almost as soon as I had climbed down from the back of the lorry, I was accosted by a French farmer, who offered me a lift, in his gas-driven van, to Marseille-en-Beauvaisis—no wives of Greek fishermen here, in the depths of Picardy—where he lived and where I spent the next three days. I was not unwelcome because, as well as my sten, webbing, and full equipment, rolled up blanket, ground sheet, overcoat, tin helmet, and so on, I was carrying full rations. I was also not unduly hurried, was, on the contrary, quite prepared to let the winding country road take charge of me, as my leave did not start technically till I had re-ported, with my pass, to the military attaché at the Canadian Embassy in Paris. I was given the best bedroom, sleeping in a magnificent feather bed, facing on to photographs of the farmer and his wife at their wed-ding and of the *première communion* of their three children. Over my head were a crucifix and a cross in palm leaves. During my stay, I went to the village hairdresser and had my hair cut for nothing; the *coiffeur* drew my attention to a woman in the village who had had all *her* hair shaved off; he seemed to be pleased with what he had done to her. He explained to me that she had been a *collaboratrice horizontale*. To me her sin seemed as nothing compared to those of people, mostly men, who had collaborated standing up. She might even have *loved* her German soldier. And I could not see anything wrong in that.

Then the farmer, after delivering sacks of beet and potatoes in half a dozen places, with leisurely pauses for drinks at each, drove me to Beauvais, dropping me at a level-crossing, saying that it was the like-liest place for a lift, as, being now in the American Zone, I was entirely dependent on what civilian traffic there was to be had. There was even some rail traffic, for I remember a huge black engine, with a driver, his face covered in grease and wearing a grimy black bérêt, like a majestic mechanised messenger of Death, clanking slowly through a cloud of steam between the gates. About fifty French people, carrying fibre suitcases held shut with rope, or weighed down with shapeless bundles and parcels, were also waiting, evidently with the same idea. We did not in fact have long to wait, all of us being picked up by a wheezing, asthmatic, gas-propelled lorry, with a wood-burning stove fixed to its side. We all got on, sitting as best we could on the top of a load of peat, getting off at each small hill as the lorry struggled upwards. And, every now and then, we had to stop and fill the stove with branches, twigs, bits of wood, and fencing.

We drove through the night, huddled together to keep warm in the windy flat lands of the Beauvaisis and the Pays de France, talking or singing the whole way. There was a wild sort of hilarity about the whole company; people displayed their acquisitions: potatoes, eggs, cheese, hams, Belgian cigarettes and tobacco, telling me where they had come from and where they were heading. Some were going south of the Loire and were wondering how they would get across that great frontier, with all the bridges down. Some had been on the move for the previous two months; everywhere, in fact, people seemed to be on the move, as if to prove, at least to themselves, that their country had recovered its horizons and that the internal frontiers of the four years of Occupation had disappeared with the German occupying forces. It was a sort of *Exode*, in reverse, fraught with as much uncertainty and adventure as the previous one. Now, too, I supposed, odd friendships might be struck up, while the husband, on the move and out of reach of family ties, might head into the entirely new life of a chance liaison. Simenon had written something of the sort about a man who had become separated from his family in the chaos of June 1940 and who had met a young Jewish girl on a commandeered train.

The driver dropped me at the Porte de la Chapelle just after dawn, and I walked into Paris, with my arms and equipment, reaching the monumental Porte Saint-Denis, the point of entry of real conquerors, of proper soldiers, at about seven in the morning. I remember wondering whether the oyster stalls would be out and then realising that they would not be. I waited for an hour, in a café on the Boulevard Bonne-Nouvelle, listening to the rumbling of the Métro. The smell was still the same. Then I climbed up five storeys and rang the bell of a flat that belonged to a French family that I had not seen since the end of 1939. I had managed to get word to them once, from Bayeux, through a Parisian *marché-noiriste* I had met in a café and who was heading back to the city with two enormous suitcases full of butter and eggs. They were all in and were quite astonished to see me; but they were even more astonished by my appearance, as well they might be, for I was a most improbable-looking soldier. *Mais, Richard, te voilà déguisé.* I had always felt that myself. But disguise has, in exceptional times, some advantages. The next day I drew ten days' full rations from the Canadian Embassy. Everywhere I went, I was the object of amazement, for not only was I carrying a wealth of tins and packets, bread and flour; my chevrons were the wrong way up. There were no British soldiers in Paris at the time. Complete strangers would stop me in the

Métro to ask me questions and to tell me about themselves. It had been worth waiting nearly five years for this.

In 1972, I was invited by the President of the Royal Historical Society to take part in a colloquium on urban history to be held in St. John's College, Oxford, in September. The paper I read on this occasion which was chaired by Dame Lucy Sutherland, was entitled 'Paris and its neighbourhood in the late eighteenth century' and is the immediate origin of the present study, though little of it has survived in its original form. In the course of revising my notes, I found that I had accumulated a great deal of archival material that I had not previously used, both from the Série F7 (*Série alphabétique*) and from the minutes and correspondence of the Revolutionary Committees of the *communes* of the two rural Districts that, together with the capital, formed the Département de Paris, a series that follows that of the *Série alphabétique*, in the Archives Nationales, and from the records of the Seine-et-Oise, the Seine-et-Marne, the Oise, and the Seine-Inférieure, fifteen or twenty years previously. As a result of moving house, I also unearthed notes from the Archives de la Seine, many of them concerning Belleville, Bagnolet, and Sceaux, as well as the Paris Sections, that I had taken in 1947 and 1948. More recently, I had acquired further material, mostly from the Série BB 18 (*Justice*) and from the Archives départementales (*Tribunaux*) on Paris, the Eure-et-Loir, the Somme, the Eure, the Orne, and the Nord.

I had long wanted to write a history of *Paris et son pourtoir*—there is no such telling phrase in English—during the revolutionary period, mainly because I tended to identify myself with places on the Seine or the Marne, or a little further afield, in which I had spent weekends, or to which I had gone by *les cars Citroën* or by train, in search of material concerning the Paris Revolutionary Army, and would no doubt eventually have done so in French, with a view to publication in the *Mémoires*, had I not been induced to return to England in 1955. My talk at St. John's seemed an excellent opportunity to return to the project. So I later expanded the original paper, in the form of lectures, given in the Michaelmas and Hilary Terms, 1972–3. As suited to a subject so wandering, so constantly on the move, though perhaps in no very certain direction, the lectures were given first in Balliol, then, after the New Year, in Worcester. It would be interesting to see if the change of environment has brought any change of tone. My audience, at least, remained constant, a fact that made my own translation in the direction of Oxford canal and Oxford railway station, less perceptible to myself. Finally, in the course of two visits to Paris in 1973, I acquired additional material, mostly concerning the Nord and the nine Belgian Departments; and this I first used, in the form of two papers read to my graduate seminar, the one on Salambier, the other on the so-called '*bande juive*'.

Setting out on a lecture course, at the opening of the academic year, is not unlike that theme of walking that is one of the main threads of the present study. One sees for the first time an audience composed of people mostly unknown. Very rapidly, the audience thins and is reduced to a few faces soon familiar, the sturdy and true *compagnons de route*. And it is with these that I travelled, from October to April. As time went on, I came to know them individually and to appreciate their presence more and more; and it is thanks to their fidelity, even amidst rain and sleet, that I have found joy, at every stage, in completing a study that will perhaps compensate in part for their inevitable absence in the future, one of the sad facts of university life; for audiences come and go, while the lecturer, like a man walking against a moving staircase, talks year after year to similar age groups. So I would like to thank, both for their persistence and for their friendliness, Miss Heather Fenby and Miss Patsy Tapping, both of St. Anne's College, Mr. Gavin Farley, of Corpus Christi College, Mr. Justin Wigoder, of Wolfson, Mr. Richard Maltby, of Magdalen, Mr. Jonathan Mandelbaum and Mr. Nigel Bryant, of Balliol, and Mr. Jo Mandel, of Worcester. I am indebted to them because, as my lectures had no conceivable relationship to the requirements of Schools, I can only presume that they continued to come to them out of pleasure or from a sense of curiosity. I have also profited from the criticisms of two more of my Balliol pupils, Mr. Bertrand Bailey and Mr. Peter Gilbert; some of my suppositions were rather too much for the former, who, no doubt rightly, suggested that I was often attempting to push my evidence too far.

Mr. Maltby and Mr. Wigoder, both of whom have read papers to my seminar, have been generous with advice and criticism, drawn from their own already considerable knowledge of French criminality at the end of the eighteenth century and from their understanding of the various penal codes. I have also profited greatly from Mr. Michael Shepherd's encyclopaedic research on Jewish communities in France. As a result of his observations, I have made considerable modifications to the section devoted to the so-called '*bande juive*' at the end of this study. Mr. Shepherd, who is a lecturer at the Centre of Social Studies in the University of Warwick, is about to complete a thesis on Jewish groups in late-eighteenth-century France. Mr. Simon Schama, Fellow of Christ's College, Cambridge, has translated for me phrases in eighteenth-century Lithuanian Yiddish and has applied his unique expertise to guide me through the tidal inlets and lost rivers of the waterlogged frontier between the isle of Axel and East Flanders. My old friend, Bill Fishman, attached to the research centre on Jewish studies at Queen Mary College, London, has also given me sound and expert advice on the subject of Jewish banditry, as well as encouragement to venture into an area of social history with which I had previously been entirely unfamiliar. Miss Marianne Burns, of Lady Margaret Hall, who is engaged on research on the relations between the Directory and the United Irishmen, has reminded me that historical research can be amusing as well as learned: her description of the personality of General Arthur O'Connor, in the course of a paper to my seminar, has left me envious of her literary gifts and acute imagination. Two more of my graduate students, Mr. Peter Jones, now of the University of Leicester, and Mr. James MacMillan, of the University of York, have been generous with information, Mr. Jones on the subject of the Aveyron during the Terror, Mr. MacMillan, on that of French feminism in the early years of the present century, a topic that is not unrelated to some of the themes of the present book. Miss Wendy von Wehrstedt Mann, of Lady Margaret Hall, has put me right on a number of points concerning criminality in the former Papal States of the Comtat.

As on so many previous occasions, I have relied heavily on advice and criticism readily supplied by my old friend Olwen Hufton, Reader in History at the University of Reading. I would never venture to make any statement on such subjects as female poverty or the crimes of women or the structure of the family without first having recourse to her immense fund of detailed knowledge, as well as to her ever-sensitive intuition. I would also like to thank Alan Forrest, of the University of Stirling, for having offered me the benefit of his understanding of problems of masculine poverty. Dr. Forrest is a particularly sensitive urban historian who has already produced a remarkable study of Bordelais society during the federalist crisis. I have, over the last few years, greatly profited from his company, his immense reserve of common sense and his friendship. I have indeed been extremely fortunate to have had research graduates of his quality.

I have derived much encouragement, too, over the years, from my former pupil, Dai Smith, now a lecturer at the University College of Swansea, and a leading member of a team carrying out research on the history of the South Wales Miners' Federation. Mr. Smith is a man of most unusual gifts, combining acute literary awareness with deep insight into human behaviour and popular culture. He is an admirable historian of the communities of the valleys and the paper that he read to my seminar on the subject of Arthur Horner and of other leaders was so full of life, so revealing of the assumptions of a closely-integrated and very proud community that it served as an example both of research methods and of the sort of human questions to be asked on such subjects as the employment of leisure, clothing, status, furniture, appearances, community relationships and inter-village rivalries. I have also been heartened by Mr. Smith's approval of my own methods of approach to my 'dead souls', as a recent reviewer, who has also called me a *poète maudit*, has described some of those whom I have attempted to rescue from total oblivion, not so much because of their contribution to events, great or small, but rather because they were so often by-passed by them. Mr. Smith has the Welshman's peculiar capacity to describe people caught unawares, to puncture solemnity, and to blend an alert malice with gentle humour. Any historian has a great deal to learn from the Welsh and, at the same time, it has always seemed to me that only a Welshman can write Welsh history, because only a Welshman can perceive the multiple ties of 'cousinage' that so much dominate Welsh society.

This would be an appropriate occasion to try to say how much I owe to another inhabitant of South Wales, one of my first pupils in Aberystwyth, my first researcher, Gwynne Lewis, lecturer at the University of Warwick. It is not just a matter of shared interests, especially in the history of French Protestantism: we have behind us more than fifteen years of shared experiences, enlivening companionship, and narrow escapes from difficult situations, generally brought about by our own imprudence and provocativeness and by our common intolerance of pretence and grandeur.

For the final emergence of this study in a vaguely coherent form, as for the completion of my previous book, *Reactions to the French Revolution*, my readers should thank Miss Susan Lermon, of the Oxford University Press. Miss Lermon has done her best, with patience and persistence and frequent references to the map, to keep up with me, at each stage of this galloping account. An author gets the publisher that he deserves: I do not know whether I deserve the Oxford University Press, but I at least am certainly very happy and very lucky in an association which has now reached a fourth book. (There is a fifth in gestation.)

I would like to thank the Provost and Lady Franks and the Fellows of Worcester College for having made me so very happy in my new and serene eighteenth-century home and for having made my wife so very welcome there. I have not often felt that I belonged to any institution; most I have strongly reacted against, and Shrewsbury has seemed pleasant mainly in retrospect, with the benefit of nostalgia for years when I was discovering both Thomas Hardy and Housman and of gratitude for the marvellous teaching of my history master, J. R. M. Senior. But now I feel that perhaps I do have a place in an institution. Of course, I may be quite alone in this conviction.

Georges Lefebvre used to tell Albert Soboul and myself that marriage was the enemy of research and that historians should remain single, while satisfying their basic biological needs by recourse to prostitutes. (He was talking of a period when these were still in the financial range of the poor scholar.) My own experience has been entirely different. I have found serenity and joy in my family as well as the ideal conditions for pursuing, from the relative quiet of an attic, a regular routine of work and writing. This book owes much more to my wife Margaret, and to my children, Nicolas (*le petit Parisien*, for he was born in the XIVme and so earns a place in his own right in this study of his ancestors and their neighbours), Lucy Jane, and little Richard than anyone of them would ever imagine. The debt is perhaps so obvious that it had never occurred to me to acknowledge it sooner. But I do so now with gratitude and tenderness.

Worcester College, January 1974

I

La Montée à Paris

'. . . Marie-Chantal Fosseuse, une valise à chaque main, resta immobile quelques minutes devant la gare. C'est de ce tremplin—quatre ou cinq marches à sauter—qu'elle devait faire le premier bond en avant, vers l'ennemi.

Elle entra dans un café pour boire quelque chose de chaud et demanda le Bottin.

Elle trouva l'adresse d'un petit hôtel, avenue du Maine, loin de la gare de l'Est. Cet hôtel s'appellait: l'*hôtel du Séjour*. Ce nom qui indiquait une certaine mesure dans la pensée de celui qui l'avait baptisé, lui plut pour cette raison. La jeune fille héla un taxi et donna l'adresse du domicile qu'elle venait de choisir. La première soirée qu'elle passa sur le boulevard du Montparnasse l'aida à rompre toutes les traditions familiales. Elle se jugea seule, bien seule, avec une certaine satisfaction. Elle se trouvait chez elle dans cette étroite chambre de l'*hôtel du Séjour*. Elle n'avait jamais éprouvé cette impression réconfortante quand elle habitait le domicile de ses parents. Sur le billet de mille francs, que lui avait donné son jeune ami de Nancy, il lui restait, sa chambre payée, un peu moins de cinq cents francs. A la terrasse d'un café célèbre du boulevard du Montparnasse, Marie-Chantal méditait des hypothèses de son avenir. Personne ne prêtait attention à sa présence. Elle était simplement vêtue d'un petit tailleur gris. Son genre, assez jeune fille, n'était pas celui du quartier. . . .'

Pierre MacOrlan, *La Tradition de minuit*, 1930.

I n the late eighteenth century, to walk to Paris would be an adventure.[1] There was no telling what companions, male or female, one might encounter *en cours de route* or at the tables, darkened by constant use, of roadside inns, or what rewards, or what perils, would be awaiting one, either in those welcoming wine-shops placed just outside the principal points of entry—barrière de Vincennes, barrière de Choisy, barrière du Faubourg Saint-Martin, barrière du Faubourg Saint-Denis, barrière de Montreuil, barrière de Chaillot, barrière d'Enfer—or, on arrival in the capital itself. The traveller, whether on his first trip, or on a weekly or a monthly assignment, would probably be more likely to dwell agreeably on the possible rewards rather than on the more obvious or hidden perils. The journey *up* would be laced with optimism, whatever disappointment or humiliation might accompany the journey *down*; *that*, in any case, lay in the future.[2] There was at least about the whole operation an agreeable element of unpredictability, as well as of danger, an element that might be expected to add extra spice to the whole undertaking and that would, to the male walker at least, appear in some way flattering to his self-esteem, to his resourcefulness in facing up to unexpected situations and to unlikely opportunities, as well as providing him with any number of occasions of impressing others with his courage, strength, and physical prowess. It was, too, an occasion for sociability, for the exchange of news, gossip, provincial origin, for talk about hard times. One did not walk alone, nor in silence, and so the operation would put a premium on the resourceful liar, rather than on the truthful dullard. The married man, the father of a large family would be likely to conceal the fact, if he

---

[1] It could, of course, be an agreeable one; but it could also be dangerous. There are plenty of instances, when one examines the 'murder map' of the Paris area, of persons being killed on the roads by their walking companions, some of them already known to them, others with whom they had struck up an acquaintance *en cours de route* and whom, perhaps, they had told that they had just carried out a successful sale of livestock or of grain at the nearest market. Thus on Saturday 6 October 1798, a murder was committed on the highroad at one league from Melun. The victim was a carter, who had been killed by his servant. Robbery seems to have been the motive (A.N. BB 18 824, juge de paix de l'arrondissement de Melun, au Ministre, 21 vendémiaire an VII). On 25 November 1796, Haillot, *marchand de dentelles*, was murdered by two travellers with whom he had been walking, on the main road near Château-Thierry. His two murderers were condemned to death in Ventôse year VI [March 1798] (A.N. BB 18 824).

[2] See note A, p. 214.

found himself walking in pleasing mixed company, just as the provincial girl would prefer to put out a doctored version of her family status and origin.

For the male, the long road might appear to offer an unforseeable number of opportunities for seduction. For the entirely unscrupulous, almost professional womaniser, each *étape* could offer promise as the point of departure of eventual bigamy or of the seduction, gained at less risk to oneself, of a *fille de salle* working in a roadside inn. The bigamist was most at home thus on the move, especially on the military highways leading from Paris to the garrison towns of the north-east and the east. There was a regular *route de la séduction* leading from Paris to Lille, while the road of the military bigamist would lead through Châlons and beyond, towards frontier areas that, in this respect, might appear to be full of promise.[1]

The *route du Nord*, of Aragon's *La Semaine Sainte*, especially after the incorporation, in 1795, of the Belgian Provinces, extended further, beyond the old frontier, the network of crime and escape, linking the capital to a new, very highly populated, redoubtable area. The Committee of Public Safety, when, in May 1794, it had formed the well-named *comité d'extraction*, had looked to the Provinces Belgiques, as a limitless source of supply, in cattle, in wheat, and in sheep. But it does not seem to have considered for one moment that the population of the penal settlements of Brest, Rochefort, Lorient, and Toulon would now be supplemented by violent, able, and fearless recruits from Flanders and from the Walloon areas. With the monthly passage of the *chaîne*, from Ghent, from Antwerp, from Tournai, from Courtrai, and from Brussels, the road from the north was now to witness the frequent escape of some fearful bandit from the Deux-Nèthes or the Escaut, the Dyle, or the Sambre-et-Meuse, providing an additional source of alarm to the harassed authorities of the Nord, the Pas-de-Calais, and the Somme.[2]

Military travel, furthermore, provided, especially in time of war, endless opportunities for graft, embezzlement, and fraud: the misuse of travel warrants, the abuse of *fausses étapes* form the commonest of military crimes, providing, once more, close links between the officer or the soldier on the move and the not over-scrupulous innkeepers and employees of the postal services placed along their route. Throughout the Terror of the year 11, there were endless complaints on the subject of the venality, the unreliability, and the political shortcomings of the *employés des Postes*, while the personnel of military transport was said

[1] See note B, p. 215.   [2] See note C, p. 216.

to have been shot through with agents of the Princes and with active counter-revolutionaries.[1] These accusations may have been exaggerated; but they are indicative of the detestable reputation enjoyed by both services, both under the old régime and during the revolutionary years. *Postillon* was a nickname much in demand with professional bandits. When they did not take it for themselves, they often had it foisted upon them, either by witnesses or by repressive authorities anxious to prove their point or to give some sort of identity to a man as elusive as quicksilver. Indeed, in some cases, *Postillon* was not even a nickname, but an accurate description. No good, it would now seem, could ever come southwards, in the direction of Paris, from the plains and forests of the old *barrière* between France and the Austrian Netherlands. After 1795, Parisian authorities and those of the interlying Departments began to display towards the *route du Nord* the same almost manic suspiciousness as did the inhabitants of Avignon to anything or anybody that came floating down the Rhône, from the direction of Lyon.[2]

Referring again to those employed on the fringes of the army, in the north-east and the frontier region, there is an extremely interesting comment from a retired *homme de loi* of Saint-Quentin, Colliette, on the subject of the particular dangers offered by demobilisation, after a long period of war, especially on the part of employees of military transport or clothing (*habillement militaire*) and who, thanks to their war situation, had grown into the habit of eating and drinking at the expense of the Republic (or earlier, of the King: it would make no difference). At the beginning of the Directory, when a general amnesty had been adopted in Brumaire year IV, it had also been decided that with the advent of general peace, the death penalty should be abolished. Commenting on the proposed legislation, Colliette wrote to the Minister of Justice on 24 Germinal of the same year [13 April 1796]:

. . . La loi qui abolit la peine de mort à la paix générale ne présente-t-elle pas les conséquences les plus dangereuses?

Je ne saurois m'empêcher de répondre: Oui. A l'époque de la paix générale dont l'Europe a grand besoin, il faudroit licencier plus ou moins de mili-

---

[1] A.D. Seine VD 989 (extrait du procès-verbal de la société populaire de la Section Poissonnière, séance du 2 frimaire an II): '. . . Un membre dénoncé les bureaux de la Marine. . . . un autre a dénoncé l'administration des postes pour le même objet . . . [that is as institutions containing many suspects].' See also Arnaud de Lestapis, 'Gentilshommes charretiers', *Revue des deux mondes*, 1 September 1953.

[2] *The Police and the People*, pp. 31–3.

taires et d'employés à la suite des armées. Ce licenciement, telles mesures que puisse prendre le gouvernement, ne pourra se faire sans mouvemens, sans donner naissance à de crimes nouveaux. Après la Guerre de Sept Ans, à la suite des réformes, plusieurs provinces furent infestées de voleurs et d'assassins. Cependant alors existait une loi terrible, tout voleur de grand chemin était rompu vif, et la loi était inflexible. Les militaires licenciés ne seront pas dangereux . . . les individus qui doivent faire naître des inquiétudes, ce sont tous les employés dans les charrois, les fourrages, les vivres &ca de l'armée, presque tous gens accoutumés à manger le dindon, à boire le bon vin, par conséquent à voler . . . en cessant de voler la république, ils voleront les particuliers sur les chemins, dans les bois; et si la peine de mort est abolie, il est à craindre qu'ils ne soient assassins toutes les fois qu'ils croiront avoir le moindre intérêt de le devenir. Qui sait même si, après avoir assassiné quelques voyageurs, ils ne s'habitueront point tellement au meurtre qu'ils osent devenir rebelles à la république? Une étincelle peut devenir un embrasement. . . .[1]

Colliette, who seems to have been something of a crank—he bombarded a succession of Ministers of Justice, always favoured recipients of the lengthy lucubrations of crackpots on a variety of subjects— living in an area always on the edge of the war zone, clearly spoke from some experience. For instance, at the period at which he was writing, it was reasonable to express fears that hardened criminals and bandits might soon become members of politically-motivated murder gangs and might actively take up arms against the Republic. Similar fears were being expressed, at much the same time, and *en connaissance de cause*, by the authorities, French and Belgian, responsible for the maintenance of public order in the *Départements Réunis*.[2] Like so many people in authority, Colliette was also obsessed by the connection between *lieux de passage* (*sur les chemins et dans les bois*) and the development of widespread criminality, especially robbery with murder.

Nor is this all. For it would be interesting to take a closer look at some of his suggestions, by examining the patterns and the statistics of highway and woodland crimes, in such areas as the Aisne, the Ardennes, and Flanders, first of all for the period 1763–5, the two years following the Peace of Paris, and, again, for that of 1813–17. Both would appear to offer worthwhile lines of inquiry on the subject of *les routes dangereuses*. Mr. Justin Wigoder, in his work on criminality in the Departments of the former Province of Champagne, has already unearthed important indications on this subject for the town of Chaumont, at the

---

[1] A.N. BB 18 92 (Justice, Aisne, Colliette, homme de loi de Saint-Quentin, au Ministre, 24 germinal an IV).

[2] See below, chapter 5.

time of the advance of the Russian troops, the first action of whom, on
their arrival in the *chef-lieu* of the Haute-Marne, was to open the local
gaol and release all its inmates.[1] Colliette was perhaps, over-optimistic
on the subject of ordinary soldiers, as opposed to employees of the
transport services. As we will see later, when dealing with military
violence and with the activities of Salambier and of the so-called '*bande
juive*' in this frontier area between France and Belgium, there was little
to choose between them. We even find former officers, especially those
of Belgian corps, re-enlisting in the active armies of crime.[2]

For the girl, there was always the faintest chance of a profitable encounter with a wealthy cattle dealer or grain merchant. But these, too,
would be careful to conceal their resources, not to display the cash that
they were carrying, and to put on their most unobtrusive clothes. It
was probably as well to be fairly vague both about one's point of departure and one's provincial origin—though there were certain things
that could not be hidden, owing to tell-tale clothing or accent. But
there was no need to be precise: *des environs de Lyon* would be better
than from Lyon itself, while 'Flanders' could cover a multitude of
places, large and small, pronounceable or scarcely so. *Du Berry* seems
to have been a much favoured designation by those travelling northwards towards Paris: it had at least the great merit both of probability
and of familiarity.

Coming to Paris to sell one's produce was not just a matter of
making money; it could also be the occasion for a great deal of
vicarious pleasure and enjoyment, as well as of heavy spending. Clearly
not *all* itinerants were ill-thought of by the resident population of the
city. Those who had effected many profitable sales would themselves
bring profit to a host of publicans, keepers of lodging-houses, wine-
shops, and others whose skills and occupations were dependent on the
constant coming and going of such visitors. In this last category, one
could place, for instance, the wholesale fish merchants of Dieppe,
Saint-Valéry-en-Caux, Honfleur, Fécamp, Saint-Valéry-sur-Somme,
and the other Channel ports, who came to Paris regularly with the
chasse-marée and who were consequently known as *mareyeurs*. The
high-ranking police agent, Limodin, has an interesting report on their
leisure habits, in a memorandum addressed to the Minister of Police,
and dated 23 Fructidor year V [9 September 1797]. The *mareyeurs* were

---

[1] I owe this information to the kindness of Mr. Wigoder, who is at present
engaged in research in the Archives départementales of the Haute-Marne and in
the Archives communales of Chaumont.

[2] See below, chapter 5, pp. 141–210.

in the habit of parking their very long and cumbersome carts in the rue Montorgueil, adjoining the fish market, thereby causing terrible traffic blocks. The police were anxious to clear their carts off the street, after the market had closed, but the fish merchants had zealous allies among the tradesmen of that and adjoining streets:

... Vous ne serez pas surpris de leur opposition [to police regulations forbidding parking at night of any vehicles in streets that were not culs-de-sac] quand vous saurez que tous ces individus sont aubergistes, logeurs, marchands de vin ou limonadiers, intéressés par conséquent à retenir autant qu'ils peuvent les marchands forains, qui, accoutumés à faire de gros bénéfices, en dépensent une partie dans leurs maisons et s'oublient souvent jusqu'à 10 et 11 heures du soir dans les cabarets, les cafés et autres endroits publics, sans s'inquiéter si leurs voitures nuisent ou non à la circulation. La plupart d'entr'eux même cherchant à se procurer un chargement en retour, passent quelquefois la nuit à Paris et ne partent que le lendemain. ...[1]

The *mareyeurs* were primarily summer visitors and were thus tempted to stop off in the city to enjoy the long summer nights.

Whatever one's sex or one's trade, it was certainly wise to be discreet about the purpose of one's journey, and, above all, about one's precise destination. However much one enjoyed company, if one had anything to lose, whether in the form of the contents of pockets, or bundles, or of urban prospects, there came a point at which it was advisable, even urgent, to take leave of it, preferably with expressions of regret, if necessary by laying a false scent. Like accents, there were some things that could not well be concealed: just as there was no mistaking a *mareyeur*, whether from his Cauchois accent or from the smell of his clothing, there was also no mistaking a horse dealer, and it might be assumed that, while the former was heading for the rue Montorgueil, the latter was making for the Faubourg Saint-Marceau.[2] Nor would there be any mistaking a corn merchant, set on a predictable course in the direction of the new Halle au bled. But as all three were surrounded by numerous lodging-houses, wine-shops, and restaurants, there would always be plenty of opportunity later to go to ground.[3]

[1] A.N. F11 1185 (Limodin au Ministre, 23 fructidor an V).

[2] See note D, p. 216.

[3] There is a good example of the importance of concealing the address of the place in which one is staying in Paris in my *Reactions to the French Revolution*, p. 107. Chartrey had taken the additional precaution, when travelling from Dijon to Paris, of hiring a gig, in order to avoid using public transport, a method so expensive as to be beyond the reach of anyone other than a successful international crook.

The great advantage of walking over other forms of travel, was that it gave the walker as wide a possible choice of points of entry, as well as limitless opportunities, even once beyond the *barrières*, of shaking off pursuit.[1] One did not necessarily have to take the shortest possible route and it was easy enough to keep to oneself the address of a *logeur* already familiar, though, in certain cases, such an address might be rapidly guessed at. It was reasonable to assume, as we shall see, that the wife of a Jewish merchant from Dunkirk would go, on arrival in Paris, straight to a lodging-house in the rue Notre-Dame-de-Nazareth, a place that seems to have been familiar to Jewish travellers from all over western Europe. Even so, as the journey neared its end, many walkers must have regretted the slips of loquacity provoked earlier along the route, by the easy companionability of the wayside wine-shop. It was all a matter of careful calculation: not to tell too much, and yet to let out enough to be sociable and interesting. Jacques, in Diderot's novel, *Jacques le Fataliste*, was, of course, a past master at this kind of game; but then he was a servant with an endless store of patter for all occasions. *Son bon Maître* would have to be more careful, more reticent.

At a more prosperous level, travel by stage-coach might likewise offer its own rewards, especially to the well-dressed, the plausible, the well-spoken, and the amusing. A recent and perceptive article on Casanova[2] is a reminder that the actual physical environment offered by the diligence, with travellers inside tightly packed together, for hours on end, and frequently thrown across one another, with each bump in the road, provided conditions especially favourable to the early stages of seduction; the later stages could be completed, following a blaze of conversational inventiveness at the *table-d'hôte*, after the meal in a posting inn. The eighteenth and early nineteenth centuries had thus a great deal to offer the accomplished *amuseur public*, even if he

---

[1] We read, for instance, in a petition to the Minister of Justice dated 20 Brumaire year VI [10 November 1797] the following account of the possible dangers of public transport: '. . . Négotiants et domiciliés à Paris, nous partîmes de cette commune pour des affaires que nous avions à traiter dans ce pays-ci [Jemappes]. Nous voyageâmes avec deux citoyens nommés Lefebvre et Gilbert, nous n'avions avec eux d'autres liaisons que celles de co-voyageurs dans une voiture publique, bref nous logeâmes dans la même auberge, *A la Couronne*, à Mons . . . on procède à leur arrestation, notre chambre étant à côté de la leur, on présume que nous faisons partie de leur société, on procède à l'examen de notre chambre . . .' (A.N. BB 18 401, Jemappes 20 brumaire an VI). The disclaimers of these two travellers appear unconvincing, for all four were to be accused of having formed part of the so-called '*bande juive*'. See below, pp. 181–3, 188, 201.

[2] 'The picaresque phallus', *The Times Literary Supplement*, 1 September 1972.

were *not* concerned with seduction, were *not* attempting to sell his own particular brand of patent medicine or line of fraud, and merely wanted a readily captive audience. The elderly military gentleman, travelling from Paris, by stages, to Niort, had plenty of time, both in the coach and at meals, to complete that wonderful period piece of the life of a young cavalry officer in a provincial garrison town, where he had been billeted *chez l'habitant*, in Barbey d'Aurevilly's short story, *Le Rideau cramoisi*.

This is not to suggest that such chance encounters were always agreeable, enjoyable, and rewarding. They could also be acrimonious, highly embarrassing, and politically explosive. The fixed routes of the diligence, with their predictable *points de chute* and their single point of arrival within the capital, exposed the traveller to the alert attention of all those who lay in wait of the provincial bumpkin, the wealthy foreign gentleman; Russian noblemen and their numerous retinue of servants seem to have been particularly fair game in this respect, as one may judge from the activities of an ingenious artisan from Versailles, a natural producer of people with sharpened wits, under the Empire, a régime which would of course produce a wider range than ever of travellers. Putting on a foreign accent, and gabbling away in a strange jargon, he succeeded in capturing the attention of unwary servants of grand dukes (this was after Tilsit) and putting them at their ease before inviting them to try their hands at cards.[1] The well-dressed girl, travelling with her maids, would be likewise exposed, the maids being the weak point in the armour of upper-class impregnability; it was from them that most could be learnt, including the address at which their

[1] A.N. F7 7012 (rapport à Dubois, 30 thermidor an XII): '. . . Jean-Louis Alexis Pitois . . . 28 ans, natif de Toul, se disant professeur de mathématiques . . . Pierre-Joseph Toussaint Poidevin . . . 37 ans, natif de Béthune . . . se disant coiffeur, et Louis Jolivet . . . 34 ans, natif de Versailles, se disant sellier, ont été arrêtés déjà dix fois comme escrocs de jeux où ils ne cessent de faire des dupes. . . . Ils se disposaient à exercer leurs dangereux talens envers le nommé Wainouski, valet de chambre de Mr. le comte de Strocnowsky, seigneur russe.

Poidevin aborda ce valet de chambre, et à l'aide d'un jargon qui lui est propre, se présenta comme étranger, causa avec lui, le pressa et le détermina enfin à entrer avec lui chez Duclos, limonadier, rue du Champ-Fleury, repaire ordinaire de cette espèce de voleurs.

Poidevin à peine entré chez Duclos avec (ce qu'ils appellent entre eux *le Simple*), il le pressa de jouer avec Jolivet & Pitois qui se trouvaient déjà dans ce billard où ils attendaient le retour de Poidevin, leur émissaire. . . .' The Minister ordered that all three should be confined to Bicêtre for six months; but no attempt was made to close the establishment of Duclos, the continued existence of which no doubt served the interests of the repressive authorities.

mistress would be staying. Brissot, in his Grub Street days before the Revolution, made most of his political and social contacts by hanging about the *bureau des diligences*; and he was only a minor crook. The stage-coach terminus and the *messageries* might be described as traps for the socially unwary, as well as for those on the journey *out* and who, for good reasons, wished to leave Paris as quickly and as unobtrusively as they could: speed they might achieve, but they would not be unobtrusive. When an old-clothes' merchant decided to abandon her shop near the Invalides and head south, she went to another quarter, and took out a passport for Nîmes. But she travelled, under her own name, by diligence; the *commissaire de police* merely had to look up the list of travellers to learn that she had left on the Lyon mail-coach. A courier was sent in pursuit, to warn the Lyon *bureau central*.[1] This was the danger of public transport, whether by road or by river; for the *coche-d'eau* followed a course even more predictable.

Let us take the case, for instance, of a journey that by all accounts— and these were totally conflicting—cannot have been enjoyable or profitable for any of the travellers concerned and that, for one at least, resulted in derision and acute social humiliation. Here is what happened on a journey by public transport from Fontainebleau to Paris, on 25 Prairial year V [Tuesday 13 June 1797], that is, a little before the *coup d'état* of Fructidor. The first version is taken from a letter addressed to the Minister of Justice by the *directeur du jury d'accusation* of the *arrondissement* of Fontainebleau:

... étant dans une voiture de messageries de Fontainebleau à Paris avec différens voyageurs du nombre desquels étaient la citoyenne Fiquet et son mari [two well-known neo-jacobins who after operating on the Paris scene in the course of the Terror, had taken refuge, along with a number of other Parisians in similar circumstances, either in Fontainebleau or in Melun[2]], un citoyen qu'ils appelaient leur beau-frère et un autre individu qu'on leur a dit s'appeller Senez fils, les particuliers avaient tenu les propos les plus incendi-aires. ...

As a result of their remarks, one of the other travellers, Molongny, is said to have replied to Fiquet:

'Vous êtes donc terroriste,' qu'alors Fiquet, sa femme et un autre de la soci-été répondirent: 'Oui, nous le sommes et nous nous en faisons honneur, si nous avons le dessous aujourd'hui, nous ne serons pas longtems sans nous relever et chacun aura son tour', qu'après ce propos, la femme Fiquet se mit

---

[1] A.N. BB 18 751 (Ministère de la Justice, Seine, 5 germinal an V). The case concerns *la femme* Ballancet, *fripière*.

[2] See note E, p. 217.

à rire, que sa camarade lui ayant demandé le sujet de son rire, elle lui dit qu'elle pensait à la lessive, qu'il lui fut répliqué: 'de quelle lessive entends-tu parler?', qu'alors la femme Fiquet répondit: 'c'est d'une lessive qui ne plaira pas à tout le monde, j'aime beaucoup à laver mes mains dans le sang', que son mari ajouta 'cette lessive ne sera pas longue, elle ne durera que 3 jours, il faudrait que les femmes lèvent leurs jupons pour passer dedans', que le C. Molongny lui dit: 'vous n'êtes donc pas content de ce qui s'est passé, il n'y a donc pas eu assez de sang répandu et d'honnêtes gens égorgés', que la femme Fiquet se leva spontanément de son siège, les yeux étincelans de colère et, arrachant son bonnet, répliqua: 'Oui, l'égorgement, le re-égorgement reviendra. Je me laverai les mains dans le sang et chacun aura son tour'. Sur quoi Fiquet, son frère, et autres de leur société, applaudirent vivement par des claquements de mains.

Le 3 messidor l'administration municipale de Fontainebleau dénonça ces propos et leurs auteurs au juge de paix de cette commune. . . .

The woman Fiquet was arrested on 24 Thermidor [11 August]. But, as a result no doubt of Fructidor, Sotin, the new Minister of Police, who appears to have been favourable to the surviving neo-jacobins, ordered her release on 15 Vendémiaire year VI [6 October 1797]. The matter did not, however, end there; for, after the explosion of the Infernal Machine, a new investigation was ordered.[1]

From prison, the woman Fiquet wrote, on 4 Fructidor year V [21 August 1797] to Fouché, giving *her* account of the conversation and of what had happened on the virulent and no doubt extremely stuffy journey—June 1797 was the hot opening of one of those stifling summers that seem always to have accompanied the violence and the *coups d'état* of the revolutionary period—across the broad cornfields of the Brie, a route more usually associated with the activities of bandits and highwaymen and of individual murderers, than with a discussion about contemporary politics:

. . . il y avait dans la voiture la femme d'un capitaine de hussards . . . [and others] . . . tous 5 rien moins que républicains, vous allez en juger. La

[1] '. . . Les journaux m'ont appris qu'au nombre des gens arrêtés par suite de l'événement du 3 nivôse et soupçonnés d'y avoir eu part est un nommé Fiquet . . . je crois devoir vous rappeler qu'ayant été nommé directeur du jury à Fontainebleau au mois de fructidor an V, j'ai trouvé une procédure commencée contre un nommé Fiquet, sa femme et plusieurs autres personnes de leur société pour raison de propos atroces . . . je reçus une lettre du Ministre de la Justice du 3 vendémiaire an VI qui m'interdisait de donner suite à cette affaire en marquant *qu'il n'y avait pas lieu à instruction de procédure* . . .' (le juge suppléant au tribunal civil de Fontainebleau, au Ministre, 8 pluviôse an IX, A.N. BB 18 823, Ministère de la Justice, Seine-et-Marne).

conversation s'engagea sur Bonaparte, ses talens militaires, sa bravoure, sa conduite politique dans les événements d'Italie &ca . . . l'illustre descendante de Noailles [the wife of the Captain, who, according to the Fiquets, claimed to belong to an ancient family], à cet éloge mérité . . . dit qu'il fallait être coquins scélérats pour applaudir aux succès de pareils brigands, alors guerre ouverte entre la femme Noailles et nous, et ses honnêtes partisans; le C. Senez ayant quitté la voiture à Ponthierry, nous fûmes, mon amie et moi, assaillies d'injures les plus grossières par cette aimable société, traitées de tricoteuses à 300 sols, de fumier de guillotine, de coquines, voleuses, bonnes à faire compagnie à ceux que le Rhône avait engloutis [a reference to the numerous victims of the White Terror in Lyon and the Rhône valley], de femmes bonnes à être traînées du faubourg Antoine au faubourg du nom comme des moines, ils poussèrent l'audace jusqu'à nous dire que tout ce que nous avions sur le corps était volé, que c'étaient les dépouilles des illustres victimes, mais, ne pouvant contenir mon indignation je dis: *je voudrais que l'on donne l'émétique à tout le monde, nous verrions ceux qui n'égorgeraient le plus*, à cette réponse de ma part, ils s'écrièrent que je demandais l'égorge-ment, je répondis, *on [n'] égorge point avec de l'émétique, on ne fait que vomir*, la femme Noailles me saute à la tête, déchire mon bonnet, tombe en syncope, criant *du sang, du sang*; je descends de la voiture avec mon fils, marche à pied et monte ensuite sur le siège du cocher. . . . Mon frère . . . se rend de la voiture pour m'accompagner et faire le reste de la route à pied pour ne pas m'exposer. . . . la voiture arrivée à la Vieille Poste, le soi-disant commandant de Choisy-le-Roi (sans uniforme) et son digne beau-frère firent arrêter la voiture . . . vinrent sur mon frère et sur moi, accompagnés de 2 hommes du lieu et de 2 très gros chiens, disant *je vous arrête au nom de la loi* (qu'il n'exhiba pas) *je suis commandant du canton, ma femme a mes pouvoirs, cela suffit, vous ne nous échapperez pas, la justice est à l'ordre du jour, le nouveau tiers, composé d'honnêtes gens, saura la faire triompher toute entière, et va enfin nous délivrer de brigands comme vous, marchons, ou sinon —— . . .* mon mari . . . leur dit *résistance à l'oppression, vous ne nous conduirez pas à Choisy, mon domicile est à Paris, je n'obéis pas à des actes arbitraires* . . . nous mon-tâmes tous dans la voiture exceptée la fine Noailles, qui avait pris un cabriolet pour arriver plus tôt et obtenir, disait-elle, notre arrestation, mais quelle fut notre surprise, en arrivant au bureau des voitures, de trouver l'illustre mar-quise donner son adresse à ceux qui l'avaient si bien soutenue dans un hôtel garni, rue Victor, quartier et maison très honnêtes pour des personnes de cette caste. C'est, Citoyen, au bout de 7 semaines, le 15 thermidor, que nous recevons des mandats d'amener. . . .[1]

Match nul, I would say, but with plenty of points to both sides. However, I feel that *la femme* Fiquet, at least in her letter to Fouché—

[1] A.N. BB 18 823 (directeur du jury d'accusation de l'arrondissement de Fontainebleau, au Ministre de la Justice, 3me jour complémentaire an V; femme Fiquet, détenue à Fontainebleau, au Ministre, 4 fructidor an V).

she may have thought of it then—if not in the course of the row—
manages to get in the last word. She was certainly a neo-terrorist, and
it is altogether credible that, in the heated conditions of 1797, she may
well have indulged in the sort of sanguinary metaphors that survivors
of the Terror were so imprudently prone to bandy about—and the
allusion to washing could only come from a woman. She might have
been described as an *exclusive*, her brother was certainly a *babouviste*—
but she also knew what was what, her prejudices were those of a petit-
bourgeois: *no* person of good condition would stay in a lodging-house,
much less one situated in the malodorous Faubourg Saint-Victor, on
the left bank, the home of tanners and *décrotteurs*, *savetiers* and poor
weavers, of horse dealers and horse thieves.

The incident might also be taken as a dramatic illustration of some
of the more general themes concerning the relationship between Paris
and the rural *communes* on its perimeter that form the subject of the
present study. The authorities of Fontainebleau, especially those,
royalist-inclined, of the year V, were notoriously ill-disposed towards
the capital—as, indeed, were those of Provins, and of most of the rural
areas of the Brie. The Fiquet couple, on the other hand, seem to have
acted as typical Paris-imperialists,[1] and with characteristic Parisian
arrogance, especially in their encounter with the captain, the officers,
and the soldiers of the national guard of la Vieille Poste and of Choisy.
It is quite deliberately that, in her letter to Fouché, the woman refers
to the latter *commune* as Choisy-le-Roi, that is by its *pre*-revolutionary
name, when, as she was perfectly aware, it had, ever since 1792, been
called Choisy-sur-Seine. This is not the last we will hear of the place,
of what other Parisians thought of Choisy, as well as of Fontainebleau
and Provins, and of what the villagers of Choisy, with or without a
King, thought of the Parisians: at which point we can take leave, not

---

[1] As a study of provincial attitudes to Paris and of Paris contempt for provincials, the present work is not merely of historical interest. At a recent trial
before the *Cour de Sûreté*, of a group of Breton separatists, one of them, as
reported in *Le Monde*, in October 1972, read out a written statement in which,
among many other idiocies, he complained of the 'colonisation' of Brittany by
Paris and of the 'alienation' of Breton children, forced to live in Paris, far from
their parents and deprived of the opportunity to learn Breton. He would no doubt
have subscribed to the demands often made by eighteenth century Physiocrats
that Paris should be destroyed! I cannot, however, carry the parallel any farther
as, before the construction of railways—presumably another anti-Breton measure
thought up in Paris—very few Bretons ever came to the capital or settled there.
In the eighteenth century they were largely able to enjoy the freedom to remain
in their own wretched province and to profit from the opportunity of dying there
young.

without a tinge of admiration for the sheer venom of female invective, of the so-called Marquise de Noailles and of the incandescent *femme* Fiquet. Travel clearly, especially in the hot summer months of 1797, a period of acute political tension, could produce quite variable forms of sociability. Fontainebleau was a small place; and one suspects that members of both teams knew one another by sight and by name, before ever setting out on this bloody-minded journey. In 1797, *l'amabilité* would seem as far removed from the realities of life, as the conversation of *salons*, the grottoes, waterfalls, sea-monsters, and Negro pages of the *style Louis XVI*.

My subject is, literally as well as mentally, a two-way one: after *la montée, la descente* (for one always comes *up* to the capital, even if, in fact, one lives on the heights above it, in Sèvres, in Clamart, in Chaillot, on the Butte Montmartre, or in Belleville). My purpose then is to map out the channels of this constant coming and going, an enterprise of no great difficulty, at least in geographical terms, for Trudaine and his successors had supplied the later ones; the pilgrims to Saint-Denis, and beyond, to Étampes, on the long road to Compostella, the earlier ones, cutting right through Paris from north to south when routes had not already been supplied by nature in the form of the extensive river network of which Paris, even then the most important port of northern France, is the centre.

A two-way traffic that is much more difficult to analyse is a mental one, based on a mixture of experience, observation, memory, fear, prejudice, and myth, in its most dramatic manifestation, almost a permanent form of a *grande peur*: how Paris weighed on the attitudes of the underprivileged *communes*,[1] both on the perimeter and those situated on the great highroads leading out of the capital, in every direction, especially the *route du Nord*, and those placed on the network of rivers and canals that play such a decisive rôle in the environment of the city and in the conditioning of mentalities that face in opposite directions: inwards towards the capital, and outwards, towards *le pourtoir de Paris*, the dark, alarming tribal lands, some of them visible to the naked eye from the heights of the Butte and of Belleville and from the outer bulwarks and customs posts of the great city.

All these *communes* are places best described as *lieux de passage*: villages, *bourgs*, and towns through which people are constantly passing, at least during the hours of daylight or at dusk, on foot, in carts, or by water, or on horseback—the most prestigious form of personal

[1] See note F, p. 217.

transport, the horse being the most ostentatious, and, in times of near-famine, the most insulting form of wealth, placing the rider as a lonely, proud figure, well above the heads of his fellow-citizens[1] (the poor man would have to make do with a donkey, or, at best, with some old nag that could still pull a cart or carry pouches[2]). A great many provisioners of Paris would have to walk through the night, often from as far away as Gisors or Aumale, in order to reach the markets at the early hour, just before dawn, at which they opened; all such people could be taken to be thus about their business, whether legitimate or illegitimate. For it was a very general assumption that people on the move, like people, of either sex or any trade, congregated together in large numbers, were up to no good, could be up to no good, an assumption that had a pretty sound basis in fact, in both cases.[3] It is with such *lieux de passage* that this study is most concerned, for it is through them that not only people pass,[4] constantly and in clusters of small groups; it is also through them that radiate the shock waves of popular fears and prejudices, news and rumours of great events, of violent political changes, of great disasters, natural and human.

The late Marcel Reinhard,[5] in his study of the period intervening

[1] '. . . C'est que le gros cultivateur qui a des écus en bourse ne veut vendre qu'à ce prix . . . son luxe augmente, il n'hésite pas à faire l'emplette de 3 ou 4 chevaux de 50 louis ou plus et fait ainsi nargue au malheureux dont il a épuisé les ressources. . . . Ne serait-il pas à propos d'exiger des gros cultivateurs un certain nombre de ces chevaux vigoureux dont ils étalent le faste et qui seraient très propres à remonter notre artillerie et nos charrois? . . .' (an inhabitant of a village of the Eure, to the Minister, 22 December 1812, A.N. F11 709).

[2] For him the loss of a horse could be utterly disastrous. Lardot, *blanchisseur*, who had formerly lived in Fontenay-aux-Roses, 'il a continué son état de blanchisseur pour ses pratiques de la ville *jusqu'au moment où il a perdu un cheval et un âne* qui lui servaient pour transporter le linge . . . il a pris le parti de venir résider à Paris . . .' (A.N. F11 1182, germinal an IV).

[3] See note G, p. 219.

[4] On the occasion of the widespread bread riots that took place in Saint-Denis on 3 Prairial year III, once news of events in the Faubourg Saint-Antoine had reached the town, two of the rioters addressed the municipality in the following terms: 'Pourquoi la municipalité ne fait-elle pas donner une livre de pain, puisque les soldats l'ont? Et pourquoi n'aurons-nous pas comme ces Savoyards qui passent dans notre commune, qui l'ont ainsi que leur ration de viande? . . .' The inhabitants of Saint-Denis, a *commune* that was the meeting place of seven roads and that was also an important port on the Seine, would be familiar with the appearance of *Savoyard* street musicians, pedlars, and chimney-sweeps, while those of a village in the *plat pays* might go through life without ever seeing one of these characteristic figures of the highroads (A.C. Saint-Denis 1D1 4, municipalité de Saint-Denis, séance du 3 prairial an III).

[5] Marcel Reinhard, *La Chute de la royauté. 10 août 1792*, Paris, 1969.

between the Flight to Varennes and the 10 Août, has been particularly
concerned, with the help of a series of maps, to illustrate the chain of
reactions, on the part of municipal bodies, to the news of these two
stupendous events in the east and north-east. Once the King's Flight
was known, the belief in the imminence of invasion and foreign war
led to the adoption of a series of defensive measures, the manning of
the guard posts, the dispatch of couriers to neighbouring towns and
villages to apprise them of what had been done, to urge them to act
with similar rapidity, to watch out for suspicious strangers, and to
carry out a rapid, preferably nocturnal, check on lodging-houses. The
King, it might be said, in his vast *berline*, weighed down with hampers
of cold pheasant, truffles, consommé, paté, burgundy—a rumbling,
barely mobile Fortnum and Mason—had killed travel for almost everyone else, during that critical period between Easter, the *Fête-Dieu*, and
the evidence, on the ground, of the state of the new harvest, always a
time of acute anxiety and alarm; and hence the fate of the unfortunate
comte de Dampierre, lynched by the local peasantry because he appeared to be riding too close to the King's vehicle.[1] Vigilance in the
east and north-east and all along the frontiers, including those with
Piedmont and Spain, compared with a slowness to react, even an indifference, on the part of many localities in the centre and the west.
This was characteristic of local attitudes not only at the time of the
King's Flight. Later, throughout the revolutionary period, all the *communes* of the Seine valley were particularly sensitive to news and
rumours emanating from Paris, and the nearer that one got to the
Channel coast, the more insistent and the more fantastic were the
forms these took, especially at a time when English frigates were daily
to be spotted within sight of the cliffs. There was apparently no limit to
the credulity of the inhabitants of the Channel ports, not only during
the crisis of 1793–6, but again in 1800 and in 1812. The authorities
themselves did much to stimulate such popular fancies by spreading or
lending credence to reports of the mysterious activities of English
agents, of well-dressed men travelling in closed carriages.[2] As if to give
body to such rumours, coastguards and members of the *garde nationale*
occupying coastal forts gave frequent reports of the flashing of lights
and of coloured signals seawards in the night sky.[3]

[1] Georges Lefebvre, 'Le meurtre du comte de Dampierre', republished in
Études sur la Révolution française, 1952.

[2] See note H, p. 220.

[3] A.C. Ingouville Registre 3, séance du 9 septembre 1793. On this occasion,
the *maire*, the extraordinary Musquinet-Lapagne, spoke of lights and rockets

On the whole, local reactions to the news of the King's Flight offer an impressive tribute to the solidity of municipal institutions, most of them only recently created (a point made by Lefebvre in his lectures entitled *La Fuite du roi*) and to the ability displayed by local communities to look after themselves, while at the same time keeping neighbouring places informed of what they were doing. What emerges from an account of these dramatic hours, the roads fanning out to the east and west made dusty by the galloping couriers in national uniform, is that, when put to it, France, or large areas of it, could breath *without* the capital.

We find a similar reaction to immediate events, as soon as they were known, and this time very much in the *presence* of Paris, at a much later date. On 10 or 11 Thermidor year II, according to the distance from Paris, the authorities of most villages of the immediate perimeter were to call out the *garde nationale* and man the guard posts at night, with the rather confused, but utterly respectable, motive of preventing the survivors of the 'conspiracy' from escaping from the capital;[1] in actual fact, very few did, most being rounded up within Paris, and, indeed, they would have been extraordinarily ill-advised to have attempted even to have passed through the *barrières*, much less to have appeared, in the very early hours, in some small village in which their presence would have been at once noticed and reported, countrymen being afoot and about their business before daylight, at any season. Of course, much of this display of zeal may merely have been designed to convince the Convention and the other Parisian authorities of their own vigilance. But the panic often seems to have been quite genuine. Local authorities must also have felt a certain satisfaction at such a long-awaited opportunity to get even with politicians and officials from the big city who, in the previous months, had often been particularly objectionable towards the country people beyond the limits of the city.

Less than a year later, at a time when in Paris the former terrorists were being exposed to the first wave of arrests and disarmament, following the Germinal rising of the year III, a locksmith from Passy, faced with the prospect of being deprived of his arms, threw himself

---

from the sea, suggesting that some influential inhabitants of le Havre were in close touch with the English frigates off the coast, and referring to attempts on the part of the Havrais to invade the territory of Ingouville and carry off by force its *maire*. On Musquinet, see my *Reactions to the French Revolution*, pp. 107–15.

[1] A.D. Vincennes 1 D 2; A.D. Saint-Denis 1 D 1 2; A.D. Choisy D 4; A.D. Saint-Germain-en-Laye D 15.

into the Seine, and was drowned, or drowned himself;[1] a gesture that
was rarely imitated by the former militants in Paris itself, though we do
hear of one, a carpenter from the Section Popincourt, who killed his
wife and three of his four children, before attempting to take his own
life.[2] His case was quite exceptional. No doubt it was more damaging
thus to be deprived, through disarmament, of the visible emblems of
citizenship, in a small, closed rural community, like Passy, than in the
relative anonymity of a Parisian *arrondissement*. Residents of Paris,
exposed to a similar threat, would probably merely have moved to
another quarter. In Paris, a man's past did not necessarily follow him
around from Section to Section; often he could shed it merely by
crossing the river. In country villages, the past weighed heavily on all
the inhabitants; it was a *shared* past, even if it was the only thing that
was shared. And it was visible in the shape of white hairs, of ancestry,
of physical resemblances, and of inherited deformities and diseases.

A month after this incident in Passy, the Prairial Days set off a
further chain of reactions on the perimeter; and these were naturally the
most marked in the *communes* to the east of Paris that were nearest to
the three Sections of the faubourg Saint-Antoine: Vincennes, Saint-
Mandé, Montreuil. But measures equally indicative of panic were taken
also to the north of Paris, in Saint-Denis and in La Chapelle; in the
former, it is true, there had been a minor popular uprising that seems to
have been set off by the example of the faubourg. Predictably, the
authorities of villages close to the other faubourg: Ivry, Choisy,
Gentilly, were likewise quick to act, as soon as they had heard of events
in the capital.

Places *off* the main routes of communication need concern us less,
just as they were often ignored by contemporaries. A village or a small
town well away from the highroad or river valley would suffer a
number of economic disadvantages as it would attract few travellers
and traders; it would probably contain no *auberge*, and in the absence
of an *aubergiste*, who was there to spread news and rumours of the big
city?[3] Such places were not in a position to blackmail Parisian author-

---

[1] A.N. F7 4784 (17 floréal an III): '. . . On peut conclure de là,' writes the
municipality of Passy, 'que dans cette commune les terroristes d'aujourd'hui sont
les mêmes qu'autrefois. La terreur qu'ils inspirent est si grande que Joseph Leroux,
serrurier de la manufacture [de Milne] a disparu de chez lui la veille du désarme-
ment et qu'on l'a trouvé noyé dans la Seine. . . .' The only case of a political
suicide within Paris itself, apart from those of Rühl and the *Martyrs de Prairial*,
is that of Denis Denelle (*The Police and the People*, pp. 158–60).

[2] *The Police and the People*, p. 267.

[3] On 2 Germinal year II, the authorities of Le Pré-Saint-Gervais report:

ities, or indeed any other important city officials, as so few supplies for
the city markets would pass their way. There were, of course, some
negative advantages, too, in such obscurity, especially in time of
revolution and terror; the inhabitants of such places would probably be
left to their own devices, and even a régime as authoritarian as the First
Empire would find itself powerless when confronted with the inertia
and the ill-will of the *maire* of some isolated village, hidden in the vast
enfolding cornlands of the Beauce.[1] They might starve;[2] but no one
would mind very much whether they had formed a club or a revolutionary committee, whether their church was open or shut, whether the
great religious feast days were still being celebrated or not. It did not
really matter; and even if it had done, there was not much that the distant city authorities could have done about it. Colin Lucas, in his
pioneering study of the implementation of the Terror and of its
characteristic institutions in the Département de la Loire,[3] has shown
that in this desolate part of France (yet so near the great city of Lyon)
in the mountain villages, under snow for five or six months of the year,
that formed perhaps as much as a third of the localities contained in this
bizarre and accidentally-formed Department, revolutionary legislation
remained unapplied, because unknown (or so it was claimed). The
gendarmes and the *porteurs d'ordres* could not reach such places; one
does not expect to encounter country *gendarmes* attempting to force
their way through snowdrifts, and, as they owned their horses, they
would have been unlikely thus to risk such a precious capital, in an
effort to apprise the illiterate inhabitants of a tiny village perched on the
top of an extinct volcano that the Golden Age was about to begin with

---

'. . . Notre commune n'étant pas un passage, il n'existe aucune auberge loge-
ante . . .' (A.N. F7 4783, rapport de Rousseville). The revolutionary history of
this *commune* was relatively untroubled.

[1] See note I, p. 220.

[2] The penalties of isolation are brought out in a report on the small town of
Châteaulandon, by a doctor from Nemours (A.N. F8 79, rapport de Goupil,
2 octobre 1815): '. . . La population est de 1,800 habitans . . . il y a 6 à 7 ans elle
montait à 1,820, & les vieillards attestent l'avoir vue porter à 1,900 & plus . . .
on peut donner comme cause certaine de sa dépopulation actuellement 1. le
changement de la grand'route de Paris à Lyon qui passait autrefois par cette ville &
qui maintenant passe à une lieue d'elle. . . . Les pertes que le changement de
route a fait éprouver à cette ville dans sa population, en déterminant des marchands, des fabricants, des ouvriers de toutes espèces, des aubergistes &ca à
porter dans une ville de passage & par conséquent plus fréquentée des étrangers,
leurs capitaux & leurs industries sont aujourd'hui consommées. . . .'

[3] Colin Lucas, *The Structure of the Terror. The Example of Javogues and the
Loire*, Oxford, 1973.

the introduction of the worship of the Supreme Being: one could well imagine their bewilderment had they been informed of the new god.

And even when revolutionary decrees and the *Bulletin des lois* did somehow reach such places, the semi-literate members of local municipalities and revolutionary committees were as often as not quite incapable of interpreting them. The Terror, which proliferated its own parallel institutions, often without any reference to central authority, was not, at the best of times, easy to interpret. If the local authorities of Charlieu, a place of some importance, with a market and good communications between Roanne and La Clayette, were unable to distinguish between the Committee of General Security in Paris and the *Commission Temporaire* of *Commune-Affranchie* which sat in Lyon and constituted the effective government of the disgraced city—a government peopled by strangers: Parisians, Nivernais, and Bourbonnais—reporting to the latter when they should have done to the former,[1] what then could be expected of the *notables* of a place like Saint-Laurent-de-Chamousse, cut off in the mountains?

There was some advantage in thus being either in the middle of *le plat pays* or on a high, inaccessible escarpment, far from interfering strangers and left to one's own devices. In the matter of food supply, whether in normal times or in those of dearth, such isolated *communes* generally managed to get by, thanks to some alternative form of subsistence.[2] Even in terms of disease, there was perhaps something to be said for a situation such as that existing in certain mountain villages of the Mont-Blanc, in which virtually *all* the inhabitants were either mentally deficient or suffering from some nutritional complaint.[3] They were at least all in the same boat, in a sort of community of disaster, like those villagers of the Pays de Caux who, owing to the prevalence of damp winds, are said to have been chronically exposed to pulmonary diseases and to have developed a fatalistic lethargy and an apathy that caused them to await with resignation an early death.[4] Isolated or

---

[1] R. C. Cobb, *Terreur et subsistances*, Paris, 1965, p. 55.

[2] *The Police and the People*, p. 259.

[3] A.N. F10 242 (Agriculture, rapport de Villat, médecin, sur le Mont-Blanc, 21 nivôse an IV): '. . . L'imbécilité se trouve répandue dans la majeure partie des enfants des 2 sexes . . . depuis Aiguebelle jusqu'à La Chambre inclusivement . . . c'est là un malheur local qui prive cette partie du territoire de toute industrie et les retient dans une misère d'où ces misérables familles ne peuvent se tirer qu'un moment où un homme mieux constituée vient de se marier à une demi-imbécile en soutenant l'agriculture, mais quel qu'il soit et tant bien constitué qu'il puisse être, il ne tardera pas à se voir père d'imbéciles. . . .'

[4] A.N. F8 78 (Hygiène et épidémies, rapport de Lucas et de Riolle, médecins

semi-isolated communities of this kind—and isolation could be as much the result of inter-breeding, of collective alcoholism, and of common exposure to disease, as of poor communications—had their own ways of dealing with the offender, their own collective code of discipline and a very long experience of concealing from the stranger what it was inconvenient for him to discover.[1] It should here be emphasised that such places constituted the majority of the *communes* of revolutionary France, *lieux de passage* being the exception rather than the rule, even in the Paris area. One might insist, for instance, on the relative impermeability of such Departments as the Seine-et-Oise and the Seine-et-Marne to the spread throughout their territories of revolutionary institutions like *sociétés populaires* and *comités de surveillance*. In the District de Melun, for instance, out of a total of 116 *communes*, there were clubs only in 10 places. The canton de Versailles had 7 clubs; the whole District, 17.[2] It might be easy enough to walk from such places as Puiseux-en-France or Fontenay-en-Parisis to Paris; but,

---

dieppois, sur l'épidémie de Bacqueville, 9 nivôse an IV): '. . . Parmi le grand nombre de malades que nous avons vu à Bacqueville et à Pierreville, il nous a paru que l'épidémie attaquait indifféremment tous les âges, mais qu'elle affectionnait les femmes . . . depuis six mois les vents y ont toujours soufflé sud sud-ouest, les pluies ont été très fréquentes. . . la constitution pluvieuse de l'année . . . a favorisé la prédominance de la diathèse pituiteuse. . . . La crainte, les autres affections de l'âme y disposent d'autant plus les habitans, qu'à peine alités, ils perdent tout espoir et se regardent comme victimes assurés de cette maladie, aussi nos plus grands soins ont-ils été de relever le courage abattu des habitants. . . .'

Bacqueville was a large village. According to the census of the year III, the total population in 1792 had been 2,370, with 55 births, 17 marriages, and 58 deaths (A.N. F20 19, Population, recensement de l'an III, Seine-Inférieure).

[1] See for instance A.N. F7 7010 (Bureau Central au Ministre de la Police générale, s.d. an XIII) on the subject of the small town of Bazas (Gironde) the Sub-Prefect of which had been denounced by the leading *notables*: '. . . C'est une petite ville où les passions, les commérages et les intrigues qui signalent les bourgades sont exaltés au-delà du dégré ordinaire; la haine pour l'étranger y naît de *l'envie*, la haine pour l'étranger investi du pouvoir y tient de *la rage*. . . .'

But woe betide the inhabitant of a small *commune* if the community were unprepared to vouch for him. The *juge de paix* of Montdidier, in the Somme, writes to the Minister of Police, 24 Pluviôse year IV [15 February 1796]: 'L'agent national de Mortemer d'où est Lhuille, déclare qu'il ne peut répondre des moeurs, de la vie, ni de la personne de cet homme. *Sa commune est très peu peuplée*, et vous concevez qu'en s'exprimant ainsi sur son compte, c'est qu'il ne le croit pas un honnête homme, qu'il le regarde comme un homme suspect.' Lhuille, who lived in this village, was suspected of having committed a series of thefts in the neighbourhood (A.N. BB 18 846, Somme).

[2] See note J, p. 221.

mentally, the distance between them and the capital was vast, separated as they were by different time-scales amounting to several centuries.

For, to the inhabitants of such villages, well off the beaten track, the sense of the past, or, to put it more grandly, history, could be measured in the wrinkles of the local aged, in the different coloured stone of the various levels of the church tower, in ancient disasters like that which, apparently overcame, two centuries before the Revolution, the small village of Champdeuil once called, so it was said, Champ d'Or, until most of its inhabitants perished in a pestilence. I suppose most of the inhabitants of such places had never met a Parisian. Parisians might have been pointed out to them, when they went to the market, at a centre like Brie-Comte-Robert or Guignes: but they would be merely objects of an almost zoological curiosity. Yet their history is not indifferent, even if it is difficult to write, for, even in the Seine-et-Oise, the majority of the population would be living, *à l'ombre du clocher*, in almost total ignorance of the capital and of its inhabitants.

So much then for the isolated villages that did not impinge even on the awareness of Parisians, both native-born and those more recently converted to the pride and prejudices of the inhabitants of the capital. Parisians were, however, fully aware of the existence of the villages of *le pourtoir*, as well as of those, *lieux de passage*, situated on their supply routes. And their attitudes displayed towards these places revealed a mixture of arrogance, contempt, mistrust, and fear. The Parisians would, one feels, readily have subscribed to the more fanciful passages of Godard's unpleasant film, *Weekend*, depicting the sudden emergence of cannibalism among the woods and streams of what had once been the Seine-et-Oise. Where, indeed, was one more likely, in the late eighteenth century, to encounter *anthropophages*, the whole tribal wonderland of the explorer, the navigator, and the writer of adventures? The Hottentots, the Sioux, the Iroquois began at the very gates; indeed, on occasion, they might be perceived within them, *le teint basané*, their brilliant white teeth filed down, prowling on the outer fringes of the *foire de Saint-Laurent* and the *marché Saint-Germain*, looking hungrily at little Parisians dressed in nankeen waistcoats and velvet blouses.

In conditions in which Parisian soldiers were frequently stabbed to death, in brawls in rural inns, on the occasion of a christening or a wedding, and after the good name of the regiment had been besmirched by drunken village dancers;[1] in which a soldier from Mantes had been

[1] See note K, p. 222.

beaten to death in a village quite near, and only just off the highroad on
the south bank from Paris to Vernon, *à l'orée du bois*, because quite
unwittingly, he had sinned against rural tribal *mores*, by initially re-
fusing to drink out of a glass offered him by a countryman who had
already drunk out of it, *selon l'usage de la campagne*;[1] in which a young
man of fifteen, thought to have been from a village near Lyon, and who
had walked in the company of three soldiers, from Paris, via Pontoise,
to Rouen, and thence on the road to Évreux, had been hacked to death
by sabre thrusts, so that his face had been rendered unrecognisable (in
the unlikely event that, in this part of the world, there would have been
anyone who would have been able to recognise it, had it not been dis-
figured), by some inhabitants of a village in the Eure, apparently, so far
as the judicial inquiry could be made to reveal, because he could not
make out what the villagers were trying to say to him[2] (and the *parler
normand* would have been incomprehensible to an adolescent from the
Lyonnais), there might indeed be something to be said for the Parisian
view that most of the inhabitants of the rural periphery were really
nothing better than naked savages and cannibals, and that these people
were innately nasty, brutal, and bloody. Did not a young girl, from a
village near Senlis at 11.30 on a long winter night, come back into the
kitchen of a farmhouse screaming, because she had just seen a ghost,
clad in a blue and red uniform—a ghost then in the national colours—
in the courtyard outside?[3]

One did not even need to be a long-established Parisian to hold such
views, based on a mixture of observation and hearsay. Antoine
Descombes, a typically ambitious provincial in his twenties, who had
profited, like so many of his kind and of his age group, from the
opportunities offered by the Revolution to leave a fairly prosperous

---

[1] See note L, p. 223.

[2] A.N. BB 18 297 (Eure, directeur du jury d'accusation d'Évreux, au Ministre,
germinal an IV) '. . . Le 2 ventôse dernier [Sunday 21 February 1796] un jeune
homme de 15 à 16 ans, faisant route avec 3 volontaires, a été assassiné dans un
bois, proche le chemin qui conduit à Brionne. . . .Il n'a été trouvé sur lui aucuns
papiers indicatifs de son nom et du lieu de sa naissance. Il était tellement défiguré
par les coups de sabre, portés à la tête et sur le visage, qu'il n'a pas été possible de
prendre son signalement. Il a dit aux deux premiers volontaires qu'il a rencontrés
en sortant de Pontoise et qu'il a suivis par Rouen jusqu'au lieu de l'assassinat,
qu'il venait de Paris, et qu'il était des environs de Lyon. . . . Il avait aussi une
grosse montre . . . dans l'intérieur de la boîte, le no. 197—Nom de l'horloger—
Fieffé à Paris. . . . ce moyen pourra réussir pour apprendre à une famille, jusque-
là ignorée, la perte d'un enfant qui, errant sans papiers, sans passeport, paraît lui
être échappé. . . .'

[3] See note M, p. 223.

family and good local prospects in trade, in Besançon, to come up to
Paris in 1790, had, in the course of three years, so completely adopted
the point of view and the prejudices of the native-born inhabitant of the
capital, that, when he was appointed a food-commissioner of the Commune in the rich wheatfields of the Brie, he not only devoted himself
entirely, with a sort of missionary zeal—he was after all a convert to
Paris—to the interests of the great city, but came quite naturally to
describe the inhabitants of the Brie as selfish, perverse, traditionalist,
fanatical, and untruthful.[1] The Briards, it is true, got his number,
too, and in the political crisis of the spring of 1794, succeeded in
obtaining his head, as a prime mover in the 'food plot' contrived by
Hébert and his friends to starve the people of Paris into abject sub-
mission to a re-established monarchy, no doubt under the Duke of
York;[2] all of which proved that they might be all the things that
Descombes had said they were, but that they also possessed a grain of
humour, as did those inhabitants of Champs, in the Seine-et-Marne
who, at much the same time, accused Madame Dubarry, their local
representative of Parisian imperialism, of having participated in a
similar enterprise by having her fields placed under clover.

Of course, there might be something in these attitudes. On a summer
morning of 1795, a Parisian shop-keeper took his daughter, who was
tubercular, for a walk on the heights of Belleville (a village well-
known for its salubrity[3]) to enjoy the fresh air; in the course of a walk
that seems to have been idyllic—the air was clear and the fruit trees
were in bloom—the girl wrenched a branch off a red-currant tree, in

---

[1] See note N, p. 224.

[2] A.N. W1a 94 (Descombes, à sa soeur, 8 janvier 1793): '. . . Je ne suis pas allé
voir les parens de ma femme comme je vous l'avais marqué, attendu le jugement
de Louis Capet qui va se décider. . . . Je te dirai que j'ai acheté pour 400 l. de
meubles et linge et que depuis 3 mois j'ai vécu sur le reste de la somme de 600 l.
que mon père m'a envoyée. . . .' We learn more about Descombes' background
from a letter addressed to him in prison by Sales, an inhabitant of Besançon, on
8 Pluviôse year II [27 January 1794], a few weeks before his execution: '. . . toi
qui as mieux aimé quitter tes parens pour aller à Paris y puiser dans la source du
patriotisme . . . j'ai demandé la parole [à la société populaire de Besançon] et
j'ai dit que te connaissant plus particulièrement parce que dès l'enfance nous avons
été amis, je pouvois mieux que personne faire connaître à la société ton patriotisme. J'ai dit que pour te retenir auprès de nous, je t'avois proposé de t'associer
dans mon commerce, que tu m'avais répondu que si tu consultais ton intérêt,
tu ne pourrais mieux faire que d'accepter ma proposition, mais que ta patrie et
l'amour du bien étaient plus forts chez toi que ton intérêt. . . .'

[3] A.N. F11 1183 (pétition au Directoire d'un menuisier en retraite, germinal
an IV). '. . . il vous observe que sa femme ayant été malade plusieurs années, il a
été obligé de se retirer à Belleville pour la rétablir. . . .'

order to take the pretty blossom home to her small brothers and sisters
(who, the widow was to hasten to add, were *also* consumptive). On
their way back, they were met by the municipal *garde-chasse*, who,
after bursting into a torrent of coarse abuse, told the father that he was
going to shoot him, and, taking careful aim with his musket, shot him
dead through the head, carrying off the body, in triumph, accompanied
by the girl half-mad with terror, to the *juge de paix* of the *canton rural*
of Belleville[1]—no doubt that same zealous persecutor of Parisians
who, the year before, had charged two Parisian girls caught stealing
potatoes at night—who, after mildly admonishing the gamekeeper,
sent the girl away, saying that it was high time that something of the
kind should have happened, that he was fed up with Paris weekend
visitors who trampled on ripe corn, picked flowers, left behind them a
mess of papers and bottles, and started shouting every time a villager
attempted to remonstrate with them.[2] The widow never succeeded in
bringing the murderer before a court and never received any compensation. The family was presumably ruined as a result of the loss of the
breadwinner.

If one were indeed surrounded by cannibals, it made one's own sense
of refinement more pronounced. And if these *anthropophages* were inclined to eat the Parisian traveller unwary enough to stray into the
tribal areas, they were at least paying him a sort of back-handed compliment, because, in eating him, they were presumably desirous of
acquiring, in one vast meal, all his skills, his wisdom, his *savoir-vivre*,
and his secrets. What certainly never occurred to the Parisians was that
there existed a lot of people, even almost in sight of the golden domes,
who never gave Paris a thought.

But history has to contend with vast areas of non-involvement, of
many places that do not obligingly come up with dramatic or predictable events, that indeed do not witness for anything at all apart from
the dumb force of sleep. I am reminded in this respect, of the mis-
fortunes of an American historian who embarked on the study of a
small and isolated town in the Cevennes. It *should*, of course, have been
a most rewarding subject; for, in the course of the Wars of Religion, it
had been a Protestant stronghold and, at the beginning of the eighteenth century, it had been the main centre of Camisard defiance. What

[1] See note O, p. 225.
[2] See for instance, A. C. Ivry D1 (registre de la municipalité d'Ivry, séance du
10 floreal an III [29 April 1795]): '. . . un membre a observé que plusiurs habitants
des faubourgs de Paris se permettoient de couper des grains en verd et des luzernes
dans les champs, et ce pour la nourriture de leurs lapins. . . .'

splendid references! And yet, the history of this town during the revolutionary period turns out to be almost entirely uneventful. It certainly does not *prove* anything, save perhaps the naïveté of a historian who, having looked into the past, expected a present that would at least conform to some sort of pattern. It did not. And nothing much has ever happened in the place since then, save in a purely negative sense: more and more people have left it. Probably, soon, its history will indeed be definitively concluded, as there will be no one to write about.[1]

So I do not feel the need to apologise for an inconclusive excursion into the once forgotten villages of the Brie and the Gâtinais, the Pays de France, and the Vexin français; the fact that they did not impinge in any way on Paris, and that Parisian events did not impinge on them does not mean that they have no history, nor indeed that they have no relevance to the subject under discussion. For, even in the dim knowledge of such a vast hinterland of indifference and non-involvement, the Parisian *commissaire*, like the Napoleonic Prefect, must have felt a slight shiver, have spurred on his horse or hastened his pace, as he headed for the dim yellow lights of the *auberge*. It was as if, in the still distance of night, he could faintly hear the tribal calls, the sound of savage instruments, or the silence of years and years of deep sleep. Was, one wonders, the Pays de France called that to make it more reassuring to the literate French? Was the Parisis called that to cover the nakedness of the northern plains, unbroken by a distinguishing mark, and to make it faintly chartable to the inhabitant of Paris?

[1] Patrice L.-R. Higonnet, *Pont-de-Montvert. Social Structure and Politics in a French Village, 1700–1914*, Cambridge, Mass., 1971.

2

Forest and Woodland

'... *Péchette* est fille d'une femme violée par des voleurs, après avoir assassiné, ou emmené le mari, on ne sait lequel. L'homme & la femme étaient marchands forains. Ils traversaient un bois; ils furent attaqués. ...'

Restif de la Bretonne, *Le Palais-Royal*, p. 112.

L ET us then look at the geographical facts governing the surroundings of Paris. Most of them are self-evident from a glance at the map or from the often alarming accounts of journeys to and from the capital left by eighteenth-century travellers; for the *dangers de la ville*, such a favoured theme with novelists of the period, were more likely to be met with on the way there, or on the way back, than within the metropolis itself. Perhaps more than any other European capital, with the possible exception of Brussels, which, for the purposes of this study, may be taken to form part, and an important one, of the outlying region of Paris—though I cannot speak with any knowledge of Warsaw and St. Petersburg—Paris was closed in, on almost all sides, by extensive forest and woodland, some of which touched on the border of the city limits and nearly all of which enclosed, at points within less than two leagues of the city, the great roads leading out of it in all directions. A superficial glance at any of the beautifully coloured pen-and-wash maps drawn up, mostly in the 1760s and 1770s, by the disciples of Trudaine, *ingénieurs des Ponts et Chaussées*, emphasises the sweeping patches of dark green that spread around the outer flanks of the liver-shaped city, itself touched out in a delicate pink, with light lime greens for the extensive parks and gardens, lilac grey for the network of streets, and with the Seine a blue ribbon winding through the centre in a great south-westerly curve, before heading once more towards the north. The patches of dark green ride ahead of the deeply marked paved highways, like alarming outriders, as the roads fan out towards the corners of the kingdom. Yet this embracing patchwork of dark greens is as reassuring in its delicacy and in its neat everydayness, as the delightfully-drawn squares and rectangles indicating vineyards and orchards that also crowd in a confused medley of colours on the perimeter of the coloured city.

But nothing could in fact have been *less* reassuring, once these conventional colours had been translated into the reality of stark winter forest, the branches cracking like alarming reports in the deep frost, or of thick summer coverage, the foliage threatening the prudent traveller, as he walked or rode, preferably in company, well to the middle of the road, with the almost felt presence of those who watched through thickets and branches. The highroads were but uncertain, fragile frontiers between huge areas of primeval jungle; and the pretty colours of the cartographer's palette tell us nothing of the snakes lurking within, of the wild pigs and wolves, of ancient trees, covered in stifling ivy or magic mistletoe, of the mutilated, half-devoured bodies lying in thickets, sometimes a few paces from the King's military roads.

For instance, to do the six-hour walk from Paris to Versailles, it was necessary first to traverse the bois de Boulogne and then to cross the Seine by the pont de Saint-Cloud, passing through the extensive woodlands that surrounded that *commune*. The bois was the rendez-vous, we hear, in the summer of 1794, that is, in the middle of the Reign of Virtue, of hordes of walking prostitutes, of the lowest type, for they had come on foot. An agent of the Committee of Public Safety expressed fears for the impressionable cadets of the near-by École de Mars, Saint-Just's experimental Sparta, situated in the plaine des Sablons; it was perhaps just as well that the school did not long survive the fall of Robespierre and of its commandant, Le Bas.[1] Another, slightly quicker, way would be through Vaugirard and Issy, to Sèvres, and then through the forests of Meudon and Ville-d'Avray. Neither route was particularly inviting and it was, perhaps, hardly surprising that these highroads, best known to anecdotal history by the bets taken up by English equestrian friends of the comte d'Artois, that they could cover the ground in under the hour, or as a result of the October Days, were more familiar to contemporaries, especially to those who had to travel regularly between the old capital and the new, as the most prolific and most sanguinary murder routes on the perimeter of Paris. For the traveller coming the other way, the worst part of the journey would be the last: the bois de Boulogne contained a shifting population that was not only alarming to morals; many poor female pedlars, on their return from a fair or a market in Versailles, would find themselves robbed, and, more occasionally, raped and then murdered, on this last lap of their walk through the late afternoon and the dusk.[2] It was with a great sense of relief that the traveller, walking to Paris, must have reached the highest point of Sèvres—a spot still dominated by the watch-tower on the top of an old posting inn from which an observer

---

[1] A.N. F7 4783 (rapport de l'observateur Rousseville du 30 messidor an II): '. . . des membres de comité . . . de Neuilly . . . m'avaient instruit . . . que le bois de Boulogne [était] infecté comme de coutume de femmes perdues. . . .'

See also, for more recent times, Claude Néron's novel, *Max et les ferrailleurs*, Paris, 1967, under the section 'Le Mont Valérien': 'Le fort, très agréable, très vaste, très accueillant, est situé aux limites de Suresnes, Nanterre, Rueil-Malmaison. Il comporte une partie boisée, rendez-vous de prostitués des deux sexes sitôt la nuit tombée. . . .'

[2] *Quelques aspects de la criminalité parisienne pendant le Directoire* (sept leçons données au Collège de France, mars–avril 1971; forthcoming).

could announce the imminent arrival of the stage-coach from the west
—and look down on the at least apparently reassuring white mass of
Paris and its outlying *communes*; for the most dangerous part of the
journey would then be over.[1]

To the east of the capital lay the bois de Vincennes, to the south-
east, on the highroad to Melun and, ultimately, to Lyon, the notorious
forêt de Sénart, commemorated in song and popular memory by the
ill-named Lieusaint, a favourite murder spot in these years, at its
southern tip—this was where the Paris to Lyon mail-coach was to be
so regularly attacked, during the Terror, the Thermidorian Reaction,
the Directory, the Consulate, and even the Empire.[2] Beyond Melun,
over a huge extent, spread the alarming forêt de Fontainebleau; in the
eighteenth century an object of dread rather than a haven of rousseauite
bucolic bliss. When it was proposed to site a court in Fontainebleau,
during the Directory, the authorities of Nemours—not unbiased witnesses, it is true, as they were concerned to retain for themselves the
court and the trade that it provided their town[3]—pointed out that it
would be highly unfair both to witnesses and to jurors to expose them
thus to the possibly murderous attacks of the friends, relatives, and
accomplices of those who were to be judged or who, worse still, had
been:

Ajoutez à cela la position de Fontainebleau, qui, placé au milieu d'une forêt,
est d'un abord difficile & dangereux, ce qui exposerait les témoins & les
jurés à la vengeance de ceux qui auraient nécessité leur déplacement . . .[4]

---

[1] The building with the look-out post, a sort of campanile, was still in existence
in the mid-1950s.

[2] A.N. BB 18 831 (Justice, Seine-et-Marne, 11 pluviôse an IV) and *Quelques
aspects de la criminalité parisienne*. On Sunday 31 January 1796, the body of a girl
aged about 25 was discovered in the Bois de Saint-Jean, territory of Lieusaint.
She had been killed by a dozen or more sabre thrusts; the authorities were of the
opinion that the murderer was a soldier and that she had been killed on the way
back from a dance, late on the Saturday night. They were to add that this was the
fifth murder in this area in the previous seven months.

Writing to the District de Corbeil, the District de Melun forwarded 'copie de
la lettre de la municipalité de Lieusaint qui nous informe que le courrier de la
malle de Lyon a été arrêté pendant la nuit du 11 au 12 [floréal an III: 30 April–1
May 1795] dans la forêt de Sénart et que le postillon a été tué, nous avons recom-
mandé au capitaine de la gendarmerie à la résidence de Melun de faire accompagner
par deux gendarmes toutes les malles qui iront de nuit de Melun à Lieusaint et de
Lieusaint à Villeneuve-Saint-Georges ou à Melun, nous vous invitons à donner
les mêmes ordres au commandant de la brigade de Villeneuve-Saint-Georges. . . .'
(A.D. Seine-et-Marne L 567).

[3] A.N. BB 18 822 (Justice, Seine-et-Marne).   [4] Ibid.

Nemours, at this time, enjoyed the support of a powerful advocate, Dupont, who was to put much the same argument, further supported by historical precedent, in a memorandum addressed to the Minister of Justice.[1] One just did not put a *tribunal criminel* in a town situated in the middle of a vast forest. The authorities of Château-Landon voiced similar complaints on the subject of the transfer of *their* former court to Nemours.

The road to the important market town of Brie-Comte-Robert passed through le Gros-Bois; Milly-la-Forêt, Dourdan, Étampes, Montfort, and Dreux were all enclosed in thick woodland, while Rambouillet was surrounded by a forest that extended from the valley of the Chévreuse, over the highroad, northwards to the lakes and ponds of Saint-Léger. Much of the valley of the Seine, between Rouen and Paris, and between Rouen and le Havre, went through forest land: forêt de Marly, forêt de Saint-Germain, bois de Verneuil,[2] forêt de Rosny, forêt de Moisson (in the great bend of the river opposite Bonnières), forêt de Bizy (the former estates of the duc de Penthièvre, behind Vernon), and the forêt de Vernon on the north bank opposite that important river port, forêt des Andelys, an extension of that of Vernon, bois de la Tremblaie, behind la Garenne, forêt de Louviers, reaching down to the river near Pont-de l'Arche, forêt de Roumare, forêt de la Londe, and forêt de Mauny, in the immense bends of the river just beyond Rouen, thence to the gigantic forêt de la Brotonne in the southern bend of the Seine opposite Caudebec, a port itself enclosed by the forêt de Maulévrier, while the northern road from le Havre to Gonneville passed through the forêt de Montgeon.

It was hardly surprising that, in the favourable conditions prevailing under the Directory, the whole of the Rouen area and much of the hinterland of le Havre should have become, along with wide sections of the Eure, on the other bank, the persistent stronghold of *chauffage*.[3] The population of the whole area of the valley of the lower Seine was extremely poor and lived habitually just above subsistence level. In times of dearth, the inhabitants of these riverside towns and villages would be the first to feel the effects of scarcity and would take advantage of their position to hold up and pillage grain and wood convoys

[1] Ibid.

[2] Vacher, *cultivateur* of the *commune* of Saint-Nicolas, near Verneuil, was murdered in the course of the year V (A.N. BB 18 298, Accusateur public au Ministre, 30 thermidor an VI). The village was Saint-Nicolas-du-Bosc-l'Abbé. On 12 June 1799, the municipal pay-chest of Verneuil was taken by a group of bandits, who killed four members of the escort.

[3] *Reactions to the French Revolution*, pp. 257-9, 278.

passing up or down the river. These were, in fact, some of the habitual locations of *arrêts*.[1] If we leave the valley, the overland *route haute* through the two Vexins, from Paris to Rouen via Pontoise, the route of the mail-coach between the capital and the Norman city, passed through the forêt de Lyons, itself the scene of a number of brutal murders in the last decade of the century,[2] and the forêt de Bacqueville, at the level of the old border between the Île de France and the Duchy, at Fleury-sur-Andelle.

But it was worse still to the north, on the roads to the Pays de France, the Soissonnais, the Vermandois, the Sangterre, and the Argonne, and up to and beyond the old frontier with the Austrian Netherlands, the southern tip of which was enclosed, on both sides, by what is still the largest remaining forest area of north-western Europe, the ancient forêt des Ardennes, still teeming with wild boar and, at the end of the eighteenth century, the point of departure, during the *grands froids* of 1788–9, 1795–6, and 1800–1, of hordes of wolves.[3]

Due north of the capital were the forests of Montmorency and L'Île-Adam (to which, in the course of the famine of 1795–6, school-masters took their pupils, during school hours, to gather acorns, bark, mushrooms, and *cèpes*);[4] the road to Senlis traversed the immense forest of Chantilly, that to Noyon, the forest of Compiègne, that to Soissons, the forest of Retz. The roads from Soissons to la Fère and Soissons to Chauny passed through the two forests of Coucy, the home of the Prémontrés, while Laon was skirted by an equally extensive wooded area to the south, on the road from Fismes.[5] The eastern military highroad from Paris to Metz, via Châlons-sur-Marne, passed through the forest of the Argonne between Sainte-Ménehould and Verdun.

It is self-evident that bandit groups, of which there were many pro-

---

[1] 'La Question des arrivages' in *Disette et subsistances*, Paris, 1965, pp. 211–19.

[2] A.N. BB 18 297. There was a murder in La Bosse, canton de Lyons-la-Forêt on a Sunday, in Frimaire year IV [Nov.–Dec. 1795]. On 17 June 1796 [29 Prairial year IV] a farmer from Puchay, in the same canton, shot *la femme* Niel, who had started a lawsuit against him (ibid.).

[3] On the subject of the proliferation of wolves in the Paris area, especially in the forêt de Compiègne and in that of Chantilly, as a result of the destruction of the wolf traps, that had been decorated with fleurs de lys, see my article, 'Le Mouvement revendicatif parmi les bateliers de l'Oise et de la Marne au cours de l'hiver 1793–4', *Revue d'histoire économique et sociale*, no. 4, 1954.

[4] *Les Armées révolutionnaires, instruments de la Terreur dans les départements*, 2 vols., Paris and The Hague, 1961 and 1963, p. 404 (130).

[5] 'L'Armée révolutionnaire parisienne dans le département de l'Aisne', *Revue du nord*, nos. 132, 133, and 134, June–October 1952.

liferating on the northern, eastern, and southern outskirts of Paris twenty years before the Revolution, throughout the revolutionary period itself and, above all, during the anarchical years of the Directory and the Consulate should have favoured forest and woodland that offered them cover and ready means of escape, just as, on the *route du Nord*, which passed through almost continuous forested areas, they enabled the convicts of the *chaîne* and the steady stream of deserters from the annexionist Republic to go underground, secure for a time in the silent jungles of the frontier area.

It was highly dangerous, to say the least of it, to walk or ride on any of the highroads leading from or to Paris at dusk, and, of course, during the night. Olwen Hufton, in her recent book on the poor of eighteenth-century France, has produced detailed evidence concerning the activities of the *bande* commanded by François Bridat, in the wooded areas of rolling hills separating the valleys of the upper Seine and the Aube, south and east of Troyes, twenty years before the outbreak of the Revolution. Bridat appears to have operated primarily in the thick woodlands between Bar-sur-Seine, Châtillon, and Sainte-Seine-l'Abbaye, near the source of the river, taking for cover to the forests of Aumont and of Châtillon, and, in the valley of the Aube, to that of Clairvaux.[1]

A murder map drawn up for the period 1793 to 1799 both indicates the importance, in respect of crimes of violence, of *lieux de passage* like Lieusaint, Saint-Denis, Sermaise, Asnières, Longjumeau, Argenteuil, Antony, Saint-Pierre-lès-Nemours, Neufmoutiers-lès-Meaux, Pantin, Belleville, Sucy-en-Brie, and, on the roads to the north, Amiens, Cambrai, and Fresnes, and the dense forest areas of the Nièvre, in the neighbourhood of Château-Chinon,[2] and the frequency of weekend murders. The roads east and north-east of Paris appear to have been particularly dangerous. Compared to the last twenty years of the ancien régime, the situation in respect of highroad murders in the vicinity of Paris undoubtedly worsened during the revolutionary period, and especially after Thermidor. There were a number of reasons for this: with mobilisation, there would be more people on the roads, more people, too, like deserters, who had no legitimate business to be on them at all and who would, therefore, resent being asked questions about their destination and might be tempted to solve that

[1] See Olwen Hufton, *The Poor of Ancien Régime France: A Social Study*, Oxford, 1974.

[2] A.N. BB 18 578 (Justice, Nièvre, procureur général de Nevers au Grand Juge, 31 mars 1809).

particular problem in the simplest manner, by killing the questioner. Also, with the collapse of the *assignat*, the temptation to rob and then kill travellers likely to be carrying large sums of money in hard cash, such as cattle merchants, farmers, millers, grain merchants, and even carters, would become more insistent.[1]

Much of this forest land had been the hunting preserve of the Princes of the Blood; and these *apanages* were duly confiscated and became, nominally at least, the property of the Nation. The inhabitants of woodland areas were liable to interpret this change quite literally. Were *they* not the Nation? Was the wood then not common property? Did not the produce of the forest come to them by right? Even during the Terror of the year II, we hear of armies of villagers making it a family outing, even carrying babes in arms, armed with axes, knives, and sabres, setting out for the woods, each taking to his own: father sawing through the trunk of a tree, mother getting to work on the larger branches, children breaking or tearing off twigs and gathering faggots.[2] At dusk, the passer-by might be confronted by silently-moving lines of shadowy figures, their backs bent under the weight of trunks and piled-up wood, as they headed for home. Whole communities, living *à la lisière des bois*, were involved in this type of collective pillage.

Un autre fléau nous menace, les bois sont impunément volés, saccagés hautement, publiquement, on les enlève par voitures, par bateaux. . . . Tandis que les hommes portent d'un bras nerveux la hache sur les gros arbres, leurs femmes, leurs enfans s'amusent avec la serpe à faire des fagots avec ceux qui sont plantés depuis 3 ou 4 ans. . . . ils y vont presque toujours attroupés et menacent de tuer ceux qui veulent s'opposer à leurs délits, ils ont même poursuivi la gendarmerie nationale de Corbeil qui a failli être victime de leur fureur. . . . Je dois aussi observer que ce sont les Maires et municipaux de village qui vont à la tête de leurs communes faire le ravage, il en est qui sont charpentiers et qui remplissent leurs chantiers avec les plus beaux bois qu'ils vont couper. . . .[3]

---

[1] See note A, p. 225.

[2] See also Claude Néron, *Max et les ferrailleurs*: '. . . On est les voleurs de cuivre et on est là, comme des cloches et on a plus un radis et on attend au milieu du chantier, dans la tôle et dans la ferraille, et le soleil tape salement dur, et vous pouvez toujours chercher un arbre dans la Plaine, et il y a longtemps qu'on a coupé le dernier pour faire du feu. . . .'

[3] A.N. F10 210 (Commission d'Agriculture, Simon, de Corbeil, à la Convention, 23 avril 1793).

This from an inhabitant of Corbeil in April 1793, at the beginning of the Terror! Later, the Paris Revolutionary Army was to use up much of its time and energy in unsuccessful house searches for stolen wood, in the forest of Rambouillet, in the woodlands around Nemours and Montereau. Among all its economic activities, directed towards the preservation and the mobilisation of the resources of the Republic, its attempts to prevent *la dilapidation des bois de la Nation* were to be the most completely ineffective. What could, in fact, small groups of Parisian artisans and shop-keepers do, when faced with the collective solidarity of woodland village communities, often, one suspects, protected by complaisant *comités de surveillance*, eager to keep a wary eye out for strangers and travellers, but strangely blind to the existence of piles of stolen wood in the yards of their neighbours?[1]

And if this were the position in the middle of the Terror, what would the position be after Thermidor, after two terrible winters of extreme cold and privation? The answer is not hard to come by. Already, in the course of the year IV, public prosecutors frequently complain to the Minister about the impunity accorded by local *juges de paix* to those known to have devastated woodland and forest in such places as Saint-Denis, Bourg-la-Reine (much of the parc de Sceaux went up literally in smoke), Boulogne, Marly, Saint-Cloud, Sèvres, Compiègne, Chantilly, Senlis.[2] All over the area, from Paris to Brussels, the higher-ranking judicial authorities give expression to their sense of hopelessness. The loquacious Colliette, ever ready with helpful suggestions for the Minister's ear, has, as usual, an answer to the problem, writing, in January 1796:

... Nos forêts nationales sont dévastées: pour quoi? Parce que nos lois forestières ne renferment aucune mesure suffisament répressive. On a déjà annoncé l'abolition de la peine de mort à la paix générale. Si une pareille loi pouvait exister, *en moins d'un an la république ne seroit plus qu'une forêt de Bondy* [Colliette, however much of a nuisance he may have been, has a certain talent for the striking catch-phrase.]. ... En 1787 [he goes on] une ordonnance abolit la peine de mort dans tous les cas contre les déserteurs, en 1788, on comptait 10,000 déserteurs: l'état en fut envoyé aux Grands Prévôts des maréchaussées; en 1788, il fallut abolit les galères de terre et rétablir la peine de mort. ...[3]

Whatever the problem, Colliette at least could always propose a simple

---

[1] *Les Armées révolutionnaires*, vol. ii, p. 416.

[2] A.N. BB 18 742, 743, 748, 750, 755.

[3] A.N. BB 18 92 (Colliette au Ministre de la Justice, 25 nivôse an IV, Justice, Aisne).

solution: more repression, a severer code, the automatic recourse to the death sentence. Some of his colleagues could only express their sense of hopelessness and bewilderment:

Le pays est réduit à la misère; il sera bien difficile de mettre fin aux dilapidations de bois nationaux, sans le secours d'une force armée, et j'ai la douleur de vous apprendre que tous les efforts que j'ai faits jusqu'à ce jour pour les arrêter sont nuls. C'est le seul article qui m'occasionne des peines en matière de délits. . . .[1]

complains the *commissaire* attached to the municipality of Marchiennes, in a letter sent to the Minister in February 1797. Late in the previous year, he had already concluded on a similar note of helplessness: 'Les dilapidations dans les bois continuent et surtout depuis les grands froids.'[2]

The *commissaire* attached to the Hazebrouck court has exactly the same story to tell:

Je ne puis, sans me rendre coupable, tenir le silence sur les dévastations qui se commettent journellement en la forêt de Nieppe, une des plus belles propriétés nationales existantes en ce Département, les particuliers tant de Saint-Venant, département du Pas-de-Calais, que de Morville et autres communes environnantes et contigues à cette forêt, . . . envisagent cette forêt, parce qu'elle est nationale, comme une propriété à eux appartenante et sous ce point de vue y commettent journellement des dévastations et dégradations qu'il n'est point possible de vous peindre . . . ce tribunal . . . se trouve encore actuellement chargé au moins de 200 procès-verbaux de ces délits forestiers . . . .ceux qui commettent ces délits n'ont rien à risquer.... les receveurs du droit d'enregistrement négligent le recouvrement des amendes. . . . les autorités constituées semblent enhardir et soutenir ces individus. . . .[3]

Some authorities, no doubt closer than these public prosecutors to the realities of rural poverty, particularly during the catastrophic winters of 1795 and 1796, were to show a little more sympathy to a type of law-breaking that witnessed above all to the solidarity bred of extreme hardship. A petition from the Somme, in March 1797, stated, in the name of the petitioners, 'tous manouvriers demeurant en la commune de Juval, canton d'Oisemont':

[1] A.N. BB 18 580 (commissaire près l'administration municipale de Marchiennes, au Ministre de la Justice, 28 pluviôse an V).

[2] A.N. BB 18 580 (ibid., 17 fructidor an IV).

[3] A.N. BB 18 581 (commissaire près le tribunal d'Hazebrouck, au Ministre de la Justice, 2 floréal an V).

que lors du verglas qui a eu lieu au mois de nivôse dernier ils ont été dans la forêt d'Arques ramasser du bois qui étoit tombé des arbres, dans la confiance que ce bois seroit destiné aux pauvres, ils eurent d'autant plus lieu de s'affermir dans cette idée que, les premiers jours, ils ne virent personne qui s'opposât à leur intention. Quelques jours se passèrent ainsi. Mais les gardes de cette forêt ayant eu ordre de s'opposer à l'enlèvement des bois brisés, ils se mirent en activité et firent ensuite perquisition chez les exposans, qu'ils trouvèrent munis, les uns de fagots, les autres de branches de bois éclatés. ... Or la plupart de ces bois ont été consommés pendant les rigueurs de l'hiver, ce qui rend leur restitution impossible. ... Dans cette circonstance malheureuse, ils ne peuvent éviter la prison & leurs femmes & leurs enfans vont gémir dans l'indigence. ... [1]

Immense damage was thus done to state forests and woodlands all over the Paris region. Furthermore, after the incorporation into the Republic of the nine *Départements Réunis* that had previously formed the Austrian Netherlands, the habit of collective indiscipline and open defiance of law and authority was to spread across the old border, further adding to the many problems of the hard-pressed judicial and repressive authorities in areas in which perhaps the majority of the rural population, Walloon as well as Flemish, was opposed to the new régime, remaining attached to their priests and old nobility, if not to the Austrian connection. South-west of Brussels, the immense forest of Soignies, as well as harbouring for a time groups of deserters and brigands,[2] offered a standing temptation to the inhabitants of the capital and of the woodland villages due south of the city, especially during the crisis years 1794, 1795, and 1796.

The rather unpleasing Charles Jaubert, a Walloon from Ath who, during the Terror, had been one of Fouquier-Tinville's principal informers on the subject of alleged 'prison plots'[3]—and he made himself so useful that he was to do the rounds of the Paris prisons—on returning to his home country in the course of the Thermidorian Reaction, proceeded to bombard the newly-formed authorities with endless denunciations, on every imaginable subject, but all of them concerning the inhabitants of the Département de Jemappes, of which Mons was the *chef-lieu*. Woodland offences were among the objects of his insistent solicitude. Jaubert, who, during the Terror, had contracted the habit of always addressing himself to those at the very top

[1] A.N. BB 18 846 (pétition au Directoire, 22 ventôse an V).
[2] See note B, p. 226.
[3] R. C. Cobb, 'Jaubert et le procès des hébertistes', *A.H.R.F.*, no. 147, avril-juin 1957.

of the hierarchy of repression, now proceeded to subject the Minister of Justice, as well as Boutteville, the principal *commissaire* of the Directory in the new Departments, to his usual litany of complaints on the subject of the dishonesty, lawlessness, and 'fanaticism' of his compatriots; he was fond, too, of giving the Minister and his subordinates lectures on the 'Belgian character'. (It was hardly surprising that, on a number of occasions, mostly in week-end fracas, he should have been set upon by some of the more unruly and louder citizens of the small town of Ath, apparently unappreciative of the unwinking zeal of the informer in their midst.[1]) In a letter to the Minister dated 11 Prairial year V [30 May 1796] he reported gloomily:

... Dans le courant de germinal dernier le garde-forestier de la commune d'Arbre, canton de Chièvres, département dé Jemappes, a dénoncé à l'agent national de cette commune que des habitants de la ville d'Ath étoient venus couper plus de 50 chênes blancs dans le bois du Renard, qui fait partie du domaine, ces arbres abattus ayant depuis 10 pouces jusqu'à 15 pouces de circonférence, l'agent est resté dans l'inaction, il n'a dressé aucun procès-verbal du délit qui est resté impoursuivi, de plus les arbres ont été vendus publiquement à Ath en présence de cet agent. . . .[2]

Later the same year, the *commissaire* attached to the municipal administration of Ath—perhaps the official denounced by Jaubert, replied to an inquiry from the Minister:

Le fait est, Citoyen Ministre, que ce bois [du Renard] a été presque entièrement détruit pendant l'hiver rigoureux de l'an III. Depuis germinal an IV que j'exerce ici, il n'a été commis dans ce canton que des délits forestiers peu graves et les auteurs ont été traduits devant les tribunaux.[3]

This is in contradiction with what Jaubert had written a month or so earlier; the official may have been trying to allay the fears of the Minister. Equally, Jaubert, an almost professional *prophète du malheur*, may, as usual, have been attempting to curry favour with the French by blackening the reputation of the inhabitants of the former Hainaut.

Much of the damage was no doubt irreparable, many saplings having

---

[1] A.N. BB 18 401 (accusateur public du tribunal de Mons, au Ministre, 7 pluviôse an VI [26 January 1798]) '. . . Le tribunal correctionnel s'occupe de la plainte du C. Charles Jaubert. . . . vous verrez que ce n'est qu'une querelle de cabaret qui n'est pas de nature à ce qu'on en occupe les premiers magistrats de la République, il paraît que tous les querelleurs avaient passablement bu, de tems en tems, au reste, la petite commune d'Ath nous rappelle qu'elle renferme dans son sein quelques citoyens un peu bruyans. . . .'

[2] A.N. BB 18 400 (Jemappes, Charles Jaubert au Ministre, 11 prairial an V).

[3] A.N. BB 18 400 (commissaire au Ministre, 28 thermidor an V).

been pulled up during these collective invasions of woodland and forest that are one of the most characteristic features of the anarchy of the Thermidorian period and of the early years of the Directory. Nor was the lesson lost to the poor. During the rigorous winter of 1801, there are once more complaints on the subject of the collective indiscipline of village communities living on the edge of woodlands, an indiscipline which, as in the case noted for Marchiennes, tended to involve the inhabitants of *communes* coming from just the other side of a Departmental border. It was, in fact, to have just the same divisive effect, as between neighbouring communities, as the grabbing for markets and the invasion, by rival *commissaires aux subsistances*, of provisioning areas, that characterise the troubled inter-urban relations of years of dearth and famine.

Indeed the habit of impunity had been so well established that almost throughout the Directory, the *garde-forestier* who made the mistake of taking his functions seriously came to be regarded as sinning against the whole community. Such zeal was probably rare, but, when displayed, it was liable to be fatal. The villagers would see to it that there would be no second occasion for its display. Jaubert, in the letter to the Minister already quoted, went on to inform him:

Il y a un mois, un garde-forestier a été assassiné en plein jour sur la place de Lezelles, canton de Lezelles . . . d'un coup de couteau, l'assassin est connu, et on n'ose ni l'arrêter ni le mettre en jugement parce que dans ce pays personne n'ose témoigner et dire la vérité. . . .[1]

This, of course, brought a rapid inquiry from the Minister, who wrote to the public prosecutor of the Mons court, a few days after receiving the letter:

Je suis informé qu'il y a environ 4 décades un garde-forestier a été assassiné en plein jour d'un coup de couteau sur la place de la commune de Lezelles; on m'assure que l'assassin est connu; mais qu'on n'ose ni l'arrêter, ni le mettre en jugement, parce que la crainte enchaîne les témoins et qu'ils n'auroient pas, dit-on, le courage de déposer la vérité. . . . je ne puis imaginer que les

---

[1] A.N. BB 18 400 (Jaubert au Ministre, 11 prairial an V). See also BB 18 402 (Administration générale des Forêts, Jemappes, au Ministre, 23 novembre 1807): 'Le nommé Salmon, garde des bois communaux de la commune de Saint-Rémy, arrondissement de Charleroi . . . a été assassiné et enterré dans les bois confiés à sa surveillance le 6 août dernier. Je prie V.E. d'écrire à M. le procureur général impérial . . . de ce Département et de lui recommander les poursuites les plus actives pour découvrir les auteurs de ce crime, afin que leur punition puisse servir d'exemple aux délinquans, et mettre s'il est possible un terme aux assassinats des gardes forestiers qui se renouvellent d'une manière effrayante. . . .'

dépositaires de l'autorité publique partagent ces craintes pusillanimes et laissent jouir d'une impunité scandaleuse l'auteur d'un attentat aussi public. . . .[1]

Fine words, but then the Minister lived in Paris, not in Lezelles. For a *garde-forestier* to be assassinated by daylight and on the principal square of a village, it was clear that the murderer had little to fear from the numerous witnesses of his gesture in favour of the unstated laws of rural solidarity.

Even under the Empire and as late as 1809, the areas of France containing the most extensive woodlands were to be those that posed the major problems to those responsible for public order. Nothing, it would seem, according to the agitated reports of the unfortunate Sub-Prefect of Château-Chinon, would ever 'civilise' and discipline the savage inhabitants of the forest villages of the Morvan. And such was the popular loathing for the *garde-forestier* that, even at this time, he remained a favourite target for the hedgeside murderer:

. . . Sur la prévention de l'assassinat ou du meurtre du garde-forestier de la commune de Saint-Sulpice dans laquelle était impliqué le nommé Jean Joly, déserteur, et plusieurs de ses frères, 2 de ces derniers seulement avaient été mis en accusation. . . . Sébastien Joly . . . a été condamné à 20 années de fers. Gilbert Joly, son frère . . . a été déchargé. . . . La cour criminelle va bientôt être saisie de l'accusation de l'assassinat d'un garde des forêts aussi de l'arrondissement de Clamecy. Je veille à l'instruction. . . .[2]

a characteristic example of a family crime, that is a crime that would probably have been widely acceptable to a whole rural community, particularly in the brutal and lawless Morvan, an area of France that appears to have lived permanently under successive eighteenth- and early-nineteenth-century régimes, largely outside the law, conforming to its own secret customs and collective taboos.

One might well ask how, here, or indeed, anywhere else in the forest lands of France and the *Départements Réunis*, anyone could ever have been induced to take up an employment so obviously hazardous, so clearly exposed to family or collective vengeance, as that of a *garde-forestier*. The answer may be sought both in terms of prestige—always especially insistent in a small community—and of power—we have noted elsewhere how, in a village in the Saône-et-Loire—a triumvirate

---

[1] A.N. BB 18 400 (Ministre de la Justice à l'accusateur public du département de Jemappes, 18 prairial an V).

[2] A.N. BB 18 578 (Nièvre, procureur-général de Nevers, au Grand Juge, 31 mars 1809).

consisting of a gamekeeper, a *garde-forestier*, and a *gendarme*, dominated the whole community, terrorising their neighbours into silent and
trembling acquiescence, and reserving for themselves the exclusive
enjoyment of *la chasse*, the most prized privilege of the French
peasant, and one all the more appreciated in that it had been so recently
acquired: in other words, no conduct could have appeared, to the late-
eighteenth-century countryman, more despotic.[1]

The *gardes-forestiers* were themselves men of extreme brutality. In
one of the murders committed during this period in the Brie, the murderer was a *garde-forestier*, while the victim had a brother who occupied
the same function.[2] Entrusted with a weapon and the prestige of a
uniform, gamekeepers and *gardes-forestiers* often seem to have displayed the same ferocity, the same readiness to kill, almost without
thought, in the context of rural society, as the soldier of the Gardes
Françaises in that of the city.

The woodsman and the inhabitant of the woodland village, however
illiterate either might be, were as capable as the native-born Parisian of
drawing their own interpretation of the history of a recent and, to
them, visible, Revolution. For them, the Revolution would mean a
very desirable change in their relationship, both as individuals and as
members of a rural *commune*, with outside authority. In terms of day-
to-day justice, the new system would leave such people face to face
with the *juge de paix*, a man who was one of themselves and who could
be expected to share all the assumptions of a tight woodland community, turned in on itself and deeply suspicious of the outside world,
even of the village to the other side of the wood. Woodland villages
were as acutely individualistic as the lonely woodsman himself. After
all, a wood would offer a jungle of rural indiscipline and collective
anarchy, a temporary haven to the bandit and to the lonely wild man, as
well as, in spring and summer, a temptation to the rapist, to the sexual
violence of the forester, a bower, too, of physical love among ling and
fern. It would be, also, a source of supply to the village healer, and the
habitat of the mysterious *Chasseur Vert*, half man, half tree.[3] In the

---

[1] *Reactions to the French Revolution*, pp. 218–19.

[2] On 4 April 1797, Vié, *cuiseur de charbon*, was killed by Petit, *garde-forestier*, in
a wood near Neufmoutiers-lès-Meaux. The victim's brother was also a *garde-
forestier*; the murder seems to have been the result of a quarrel between rival
groups of woodlanders on the subject of the theft of wood (A.N. BB 18 703–4).

[3] For an extraordinarily dramatic, sensitive, and eloquent evocation of the
immense forested area of East Prussia and of the Mazurian lakes, of its population
of hunters and hunted, one should read Michel Tournier's prize-winning novel,
Le Roi des aulnes, Paris, 1971, which has recently been translated.

depths of winter, it might be a refuge to the girl who had sinned and who looked to the forest as a place in which discreetly to give birth and to dispose of the *fruits de sa faiblesse*, perhaps discovered, months later, as a little pile of tiny bones, by the flair of a hunting dog. In the year III, we hear of the wife of a former terrorist from Sedan taking to the forest of the Ardennes, in the terrible cold of December 1794, in order to give birth, unmolested, and safe from the cruelty of neighbours, to her child, while her husband was in prison; both mother and child are stated as having died of cold.

The memory of the past would dictate what forms of collective defiance were legitimate, in terms of local custom, and what were not. *Délits forestiers* no doubt go back into the night of time. The main effect of the Revolution was to make them easier and more profitable to commit, and to render them far more extensive than they had ever been previously. The recurrence of exceptionally bitter winters in 1793, 1794, and 1795 probably completed the process. From November 1794, the cold seems to have been the principal preoccupation of most local authorities within the vast Paris area. On 26 November, the municipality of Saint-Denis had announced hopefully: 'la gelée s'est relâchée cette nuit', adding, however, prudently: 'mais il y a à craindre dans ce moment-ci que la neige ne tombe avec plus d'abondance', fears that were to be fully justified, for, on 13 January 1795, the same authority was to add, sadly: 'la gelée a fait glacer la petite rivière de Croux.'[1] And when, at last, in the north of France, the winter did come to an end, almost suddenly, at least as far as the snow and ice were concerned, for temperatures remained exceptionally low well into April, the long-expected release brought new disasters. On 26 January 1795, the hard-pressed municipality of Versailles was to note: 'le verglas, suite inévitable d'un degel désiré, a rendu depuis hier les chemins impracticables et toutes les farines attendues sont restées en route. . . .'[2] Two days later, on the twenty-eighth, the District d'Amiens was still referring to 'le mauvais temps et la grande quantité de neige'[3] and on 1 February, the authorities of Saint-Denis were calling attention to the plight of the inhabitants of the neighbouring village of l'Ile-Saint-Denis, whose homes were being swept away by the disastrous floods that had followed the break-up of the ice.[4] There seems to have been a return of the offensive of the cold, in some areas of the Paris region, in

---

[1] A. C. Saint-Denis 1 D 1 4 (séances du conseil général de 6 et 24 nivôse an III).
[2] A. C. Versailles 1 D 1 79 (séance du conseil général du 8 pluviôse an III).
[3] A.D. Somme L 1441 (district d'Amiens, séance du 10 pluviôse an III).
[4] A. C. Saint-Denis (séance du conseil général du 13 pluviôse an III).

June and July 1795, with consequences disastrous to the crops.[1] The
following winter was again very severe, and, according to observers
from the Yonne, there was a second return of the cold in the same
summer months of 1796.[2] In short, *le Grand Froid*, far from having
been confined to the notorious Nonante-Cinq, had been spread over a
cycle of three years.

The insistent need to acquire wood, in order to combat such extreme
cold, would thus fall on countryman and townsman alike, further increasing the gulf between them, while undoubtedly offering a few
advantages to the woodlander who at least lived within sight of the
means of salvation. The exceptional climatic conditions, then, that
prevailed from 1793 to 1796 clearly offered a stimulus, in all forest and
woodland areas, both to collective crime covered by the complicity of
whole communities and by the tacit acquiescence of local *juges de paix*,
and even of local forest officials, and to individual or group banditry.
As a result of the formation of the nine Belgian Departments, at the
beginning of the Directory, the French authorities in Paris and in
Brussels created the very conditions that were to favour the extension
of such disorder far beyond the normal *pourtoir de Paris*, by adding to
that undefinable area the thick, extensive, and impenetrable forest zones
of the new territories while at the same time placing further emphasis
on the *route du Nord*. In military terms, the *reculement des barrières*
certainly made Paris far more secure from external attack. But some of
these advantages were offset in the changing forms of law-breaking and
banditry, for, in criminal terms, an ex-frontier is probably more
dangerous than an existing one.[3] The former *frontalier*, so often himself

[1] A.N. F10 242 (Commission d'Agriculture, Mayenne, vendémiaire an IV):
'. . . Les froids de juin et de juillet ont beaucoup nui à la granaison et la récolte des
froments et seigles est au-dessous de la récolte ordinaire. . . .'

[2] A.N. F1b 11 Yonne 1 (rapport du Département de l'Yonne, 21 frimaire an
IV): '. . . Pendant deux années de suite les vignes ont été ravagées par la grêle et
par les gelées d'hiver et d'été. . . .'

[3] A.N. F10 210 (Agriculture, un habitant d'Issoudun, à la Convention, 5
fructidor an III): '. . . Lorsque j'habitais la Russie, j'ai eu la disgrâce d'entendre
dire par des spéculateurs, de différentes nations, à Saint-Pétersbourg, que le
Berry est la Sibérie de la France relativement à l'agriculture et au commerce . . . la
disgrâce de voir dans l'Argentonois le long de la Creuse, dans les Ardentes, à
Prunières, Bonnier, Saint-Oust Chesalbenois, L'Eperce, Lépinasse, et dans toutes
nos campagnes, des milliers de logis, dont la plus grande partie est remplie de
familles vagabondes qui, à pied et à cheval, fesoient autrefois, la contrebande du
sel et qui, depuis la révolution, font celle du bled. . . . L'autre partie est remplie
de familles indigentes qui ne peuvent se procurer leurs foibles besoins l'hiver
qu'en mendiant et en cherchant le bois nécessaire pour rechauffer des innocens

a woodlander, a man who, for years, had used woodland paths known only to those in his trade as channels of smuggling, was now put, as it were, *sur la place de Paris*, the latest, eager, and dangerous convert to the metropolis. At the same time, the inhabitant of Paris had now to take into his calculations not only the familiar and ever-feared forêt de Sénart, the jungle at the city's eastern approaches, but also a less familiar, and so even more alarming territory, most of the inhabitants of which, including the jurors, could not speak a word of French.[1] He would now have to reckon with the immense forest of the Ardennes and with the sweet-sounding Groenendael, a hamlet in the forest of Soignies, at a point where the ancient trees grew highest, the grave of so many imprudent and drunken French soldiers, some of course from Paris, as they sought their way back to the relative safety of Brussels.

---

dont une partie est conduite au tombeau par la misère avant de connoître ceux qui les ont mis au monde. . . .'

[1] A.N. BB 18 293 (Justice, Escaut, Administration du Département de l'Escaut, au Ministre, 3 messidor an IV): '. . . En effet . . . il est des cantons de ce Département et entr'autres ceux de la ci-devant Flandre hollandaise, où il est impossible de former un jury, sans qu'il aît besoin d'interprète, sur une population de 30,000 âmes que contient la ci-devant Flandre hollandaise, on ne trouveroit peut-être pas 200 personnes qui soient versées dans cette langue [French], encore ceux-ci ne la connaissent-ils qu'imparfaitement. . . .'

3

The Seine

'. . . Alors les lycéens, dans les salles d'étude, mordillant leur porte-plume ou fourrageant leurs cheveux, suivaient les derniers reflets du jour chassés par la lumière du gaz sur la courbature miroitante des grandes cartes de géographie. Ils voyaient la France tout entière; Paris posé comme une grosse goutte visqueuse sur le quarante-huitième parallèle, et le faisant fléchir sous son poids: ils voyaient Paris bizarrement accroché à son fleuve, arrêté par une boucle, coincé comme une perle sur un fil tordu. On avait envie de détordre le fil, de faire glisser Paris en amont jusqu'au confluent de la Marne, ou en aval, aussi loin que possible vers la mer. . . . '

Jules Romains, Le 6 octobre.

'. . . Dans la matinée, il ficela avec du fil de fer ses vêtements de femme maculés autour d'un poids de cent livres qu'il laissa tomber dans la Seine, comme il se trouvait seul à l'arrière d'un bateau-mouche. . . .'

MacOrlan, La Tradition de minuit.

THE second, and equally obvious fact concerning Paris and its environment is the Seine. It divided the city, divided even the mentality of the city, provided it with its principal channels of supply, in grain, in wood, in wine, and in coal. The *coches-d'eau* also offered the cheapest form of collective human transport between Paris and the towns and villages of the upper and lower Seine valleys, of the Oise, the Aisne, the two Morin, the Marne, the Yonne, the Loing, the Ourcq, the Essonne, and the Bièvre. They made of Auxerre, in mental terms at least, a faubourg of Paris[1] and of Rouen, the foreport of the capital.

The *coches* were also favoured by the humbler sort of seducer, who used the long slow hours of the journey *en aval* to prepare the terrain for the exercise of his verbal and physical talents on arrival in the metropolis. But he might equally fall victim to the apparent naïveté of young girls from the Morvan and the Avallonnais who were seeking to exercise *their* talents on a more promising and varied clientèle, after having gained their first experience in the provinces. In such mixed company, it would be hard to distinguish between deceiver and deceived. The police, however, made few such distinctions; the *coches* provided them with an admirable, regular, and entirely predictable opportunity to filter the potentially more doubtful elements of an unsettled population, on arrival or on departure. For they formed a natural trap for the less intelligent malefactor and for the unimaginative deserter. There might, for instance, be nineteen such water-coaches in operation each day between Paris and Rouen, in the early years of the nineteenth century but there was only one route that they could follow.[2]

---

[1] When, that is, the *coches* actually reached the capital. There seem to have been frequent accidents to this popular form of transport. Thus, on 3 Floréal year III [22 April 1795] the *commissaire de police* of the Section du Muséum, which was situated on the river, reports the discovery of the body of a woman of about 28 which had been recovered from the Seine. He concluded that it must have been that of one of the passengers who had been drowned, 18 Ventôse [Sunday 8 March 1795] when the *coche* had capsized near Montereau, always a dangerous spot, especially at the time of the spring high waters, as the point of entry of the fast-flowing Yonne into the more sluggish Seine. Many Sunday travellers seem to have been drowned in this particular disaster (A.P.P. A/A 187, commissaire de police de la Section du Muséum, 3 floréal an III). See also *The Police and the People*, p. 229 (1).

[2] A.N. F11 1177, s.d. an IV. 'Les entrepreneurs des Messageries par eau de Rouen à Paris et retour, sous-propriétaires de 19 bateaux, bons et solides en état

In a very different part of the world and at the height of the Counter-Terror, the police authorities of the Directory had succeeded in rounding up the leaders of a dangerous group of highwaymen who, after operating on the mountain roads of the Loire, had decided that the place had become too hot for them and had taken this public form of transport from Lyon to the royalist stronghold of Chalon-sur-Saône: as if further to draw attention to themselves, they had chosen to travel fully armed. They were thus noticed by the navigator, who discreetly denounced them at one of the stops, so that the police were awaiting them at the following one, up river.[1] The *coches*, too, like the Seine itself, would provide a rapid and convenient receptacle for the disposal of compromising objects, including unwanted wives or mistresses.

It was probably by the Yonne and the Seine and the canal de Briare that the dialect of the Berry had become, by the end of the eighteenth century, the principal component of Paris slang and the provider of much of the secret or semi-secret vocabulary of the argot.[2] It would be impossible, too, to exaggerate the enormous importance of the river network in the provision of the more recent and younger elements of the population of the city. Marie-Chantal Fosseuse had arrived from Nancy by way of the Gare de l'Est.[3] Eighteenth-century Lorraines, Champenoises, and Alsatian girls were to reach Paris by the Aisne, the Seine, the Meuse, and the Marne, and, as Jean Vidalenc has shown in his most recent book, the river network continued to assure the arrival of such recruits to the capital throughout the first half of the nineteenth century, and, indeed, until the construction of the railway network altered the whole balance of recent intake.[4]

---

de faire le service desdites messageries jusqu'à l'an VIII . . . sans réparation, à moins de force majeure. . . .'

[1] *Reactions to the French Revolution*, p. 231. A.D. Côte-d'Or L 2658* (comité de surveillance de Dijon, séance du 18 ventôse an III): '. . . Reçu . . . du Comité de sûreté générale . . . du 13 . . .: "nous vous prévenons . . . que Dominique Allier . . . vient de partir par le coche et passera vraisemblablement à Dijon . . . taille de 5 pieds 6 pouces, visage plat et long, très gravé de petite vérole, habillé en veste chamois usé, un grand chapeau dont l'aile de derrière rabattu, cheveux blonds, sourcils & barbe de même, en marchant tenant toujours la main ouverte, les doigts très écartés. . . ." ' Allier was believed to be the leader of the murder gangs of the Ardèche and the Rhône valley.

[2] Louis Chevalier, *Les Parisiens*, Paris, 1967, p. 199. The Berrichons were also driven towards Paris by the extreme poverty of the Sologne.

[3] Pierre MacOrlan, *La Tradition de minuit*.

[4] Jean Vidalenc, *La Société française de 1815 à 1848*, ii, *Le Peuple des villes et des bourgs*, Paris, 1973. Referring to the origins of Paris prostitution during these years, Jean Vidalenc notes, p. 450: '. . . L'apport des départements du bassin

It also dictated the calendar of much of the seasonal intake of casual labour or of permanent settlement. The *flotteurs*, for instance, would come down from the woodlands of the Morvan on the high spring waters, in late February or early March; very hot summers would immobilise them in the upper reaches of the smaller, shallower rivers, like the Loing, the Cure, the Essonne, and the Ourcq. By December most river traffic would be interrupted, the Seine freezing hard two or three months most winters, and even longer in the exceptional crisis of 1794 and 1795.[1]

Within Paris, the Seine, from having been a channel of work and supply, would become the principal terrain of winter leisure, with armies of young people and children taking to its frozen surface, to slide and to skate:[2] a poor compensation, but a compensation even so for the terrible hardships caused by such winters, as well as an opportunity for the malefactor to avoid the dangerous filter of the bridges and to pass unnoticed by the police and their watchful agents among the crouching artisans who plied on the Pont-Neuf[3] and the Pont-au-Change.

In the hot summer months, it might similarly tempt the imprudent swimmer and bather, taking its toll of the drowned, as well as offering an easy magnet to suicide.[4] It was one of the few open spaces, at least

---

parisien était ensuite toujours prépondérant, comme si les facilités de transport par voie navigable, sur les radeaux de bois en particulier, avaient constitué un facteur favorable à ces migrations vers la capitale: plus de 300 de l'Oise, de l'Aisne, de la Somme, et aussi du Nord, relié par les canaux et rivières. . . .' The same author states elsewhere, p. 71: '. . . L'attraction de la capitale ne s'exerçait pas de façon uniforme sur l'ensemble du pays. En fait, la majeure partie des Parisiens de fraîche date venaient de Seine-et-Oise ou des départements qui la bordaient; on trouvait encore un nombre important d'originaires de Normandie, de Bourgogne, des Picards, des gens du Nord et des Lorrains, mais le nombre des provinciaux d'origine plus éloignée devenait vite dérisoire. . . .'

[1] See the previous chapter, p. 55.

[2] A.C. Vernon D1/6 (Conseil général de la commune de Vernon, séance du 11 nivôse an III) and A.C. Saint-Germain-en-Laye D 15 (Conseil général de la commune de Saint-Germain, séance du 21 nivôse an II).

[3] Cognacq, the founder of *La Samaritaine*, had started his commercial life as a pedlar on the Pont-Neuf. In 1870, he bought a shop on the quay, at the northern end of the bridge, on what was to be the site of *La Samaritaine*. It was as if he could not bear to be out of sight of the bridge and the river. In his recent book, Dr. Zeldin comments: '. . . Cognacq really loved the theatre, where declamation recalled to him his own successes as pedlar on the Pont-Neuf. . . .' op. cit. p. 110. Thus eighteenth-century habits and locations persisted well into the late nineteenth century.

[4] *The Police and the People*, p. 158.

before the Revolution (which created more of these, by opening up to the public the gardens of the Luxembourg and the Tuileries and those of some convents and monasteries, though it did little else for the poor), freely available to the common people. Judging from the almost daily reports, by the *commissaires de police* of the riverside Sections, of bodies fished out of the river during heat waves, bathing, though forbidden, must have been very widespread. In a period when cleanliness was a luxury denied to the general mass of the inhabitants, the river, too, would at least offer a ready form of personal ablution, as well as the means to avoid the expense of recourse to the laundry boats: the frequent repetition of seventeenth-century ordinances forbidding both —and goodness knows what diseases the turgid river must thus have carried in its swirling waters—would suggest that it was in fact widely used for both purposes, especially in the shallow waters just off the quai du Louvre.

Throughout the revolutionary period, the Seine valley was to be the most persistent, often the most rapid, always the most unreliable, channel of news and rumour. There is, in this respect, a constant interchange between Paris and Bray, Paris, Nogent, and Troyes, on the one hand, and between Paris, Vernon, Rouen, and Le Havre, on the other. The Parisians did not need to be reminded, by journalists like Hébert, or by the officials of the *Commission des Subsistances*, that the inhabitants of Vernon, or, for that matter, of Pontoise or Le Pecq, did not look favourably on the interests of the capital. And one should not really be surprised that a semi-lunatic *poissarde*, from one of the riverside Sections, should have been readily believed, even by quite literate *sans-culotte* militants, when, as a result of overhearing a conversation between grain merchants in a wine-shop near the Halle au bled, she had discovered the entrance of an underground tunnel which ran the whole way, alongside the Seine, from Rouen to Le Havre, to enable the enemies of the people to export the grain set aside for Paris, to M. Pitt, on the other side of the Channel. An exactly similar story was given equally wide credence during the Siege of Paris, in the winter of 1870–1.[1]

A slightly more credible version appears in an anonymous report addressed to the Minister of the Interior, some time in the course of the year II:

Je préviens le C. Ministre qu'il existe encore une autre classe de scélérats au Pecq et à Saint-Germain-en-Laye. Ceux-ci sont des accapareurs de denrées

---

[1] Alastair Horne, *The Fall of Paris*, London, 1965.

de toutes espèces qui journellement mettent le peuple qui environne ce port de la Seine dans l'impossibilité de se procurer à prix d'argent ce qui lui est de toute nécessité, ils font transporter leurs denrées et ils les emmagasinent. Puis ils les font refouler vers *Triel* où dans cette commune les aristocrates qui les habitent les envoyent dans les départements en insurrection. . . . Cette commune [Triel] est le séjour de tous les ci-devants Conseillers du Châtelet et de Parlement, de quantité de ci-devant Colonels et capitaines et de toutes les femmes des émigrés, depuis Le Pecq et Marly jusqu'à Dieppe, il n'y a pas une maison qui n'en récèle. . . .[1]

This time, it is true, the secret route abandoned the valley of the Seine, at Rouen, to continue overland, via Tôtes, to the port of Dieppe. It was a legend that would at least have suited the much-repeated appeals of the Dieppois in favour of the construction of a canal linking their town to Paris via Forges-les-Eaux and the valley of the Oise. A little later, in the same year, Épone, which had been the ancestral home of the family of Hérault de Séchelles—the *parlementaires* seem to have had a pre-dilection for the Seine valley—was to become an object of as much suspicion in the eyes of various Parisian authorities, including the officers and soldiers of detachments of the Paris Revolutionary Army, as Triel.[2]

In Germinal year III, it was as much the arrival of the *coche* as that of the mail-coach that imposed the date of the popular uprising, two days behind Paris, in Rouen[3] and in Évreux, as well as dictating the times of similar events in Saint-Denis and Saint-Germain-en-Laye.[4] If both the *hébertiste* and the *dantoniste* crises had such immediate repercussions in Troyes, it was not only because both Hébert and Danton were known to have close friends there. The population of Troyes had always looked to Paris, to which it was directly connected by the river life-line.[5] And no 'plot' set in Paris could have been considered complete without its ramifications in Charenton-le-Pont, in Carrières-sous-Charenton,[6] or,

[1] A.N. W 151 (tribunaux révolutionnaires, Mémoire s.d.).

[2] *Les Armées révolutionnaires*, p. 506.

[3] *Terreur et subsistances*, pp. 257–305.

[4] Ibid., pp. 257–305.

[5] *Les Armées révolutionnaires*, p. 759.

[6] Primarily, I suppose, because of its name. Nothing good could be expected of a place that contained a quarry. Charenton itself was very ill-thought of. Furthermore, it was noted that on Sunday 8 December 1793, mass in the church of Carrières was widely attended, not only by the local inhabitants, but also by those of half-a-dozen neighbouring villages (A.N. F7 4782, rapport de la municipalité de Carrières du 19 frimaire an II). Antony enjoyed a similar reputation, partly owing to the existence there of important quarries. (A.N. F11 1182, 7 germinal an IV).

for that matter, in Conflans-Sainte-Honorine,[1] or Moret.[2]

The Seine made itself felt at regular intervals, in other ways too. While the right bank had been well protected by the end of the eighteenth century, with the construction of paved quays surmounted by a high stone wall,[3] the riverside areas of the left bank were exposed to seasonal flooding in February–March, the wood and wine ports of Bercy and areas of the faubourg Saint-Marceau being the most affected. The Bièvre, which ran through the Gobelins—indeed, there would have been no Gobelins without it—was a constant source of infection; and the marshland around Saint-Lazare, also annually flooded, prevented urban development in this direction, and long made the quartier Saint-Honoré and the Roule one of the most unhealthy of the city.[4]

It was much worse on the periphery. For the Parisian, the eighteenth century might have been spelled out in terms of the exceptional *crues de la Seine*—a calendar as memorable as and more visible than that of dearth and famine, and one that can still be recalled, in old picture postcards, obtainable from the *bouquinistes*, of the floods of 1910; Restif, by carving with his penknife the dates of successful seductions on the quays of the Île-Saint-Louis was no doubt trying to prove to himself that he really had become a Parisian *à part entière*. But for those living above and below the city, flooding was an annual, though terrible, occurrence, so inevitable, in fact, as scarcely to qualify for a place in the calendar of disaster that, in this great valley, a mental as well as a geographical unit, would weigh so insistently on popular memory, above all in the stark chronicle of the *années disetteuses*.[5]

The valley of the Seine conditioned the lives of the *riverains*, above and below Paris, in less dramatic, but equally dangerous ways. Night fishing on the river, with the employment of lights and the use of certain types of tackle, had been specifically forbidden by a series of

---

[1] '. . . La justice de paix a été demandée ici . . . par rapport à sa grande population & son port qui est le plus considérable des environs de Paris . . . servant de point de ralliement & de séjour à tous les bateaux montans, descendans la Haute & Basse-Seine, l'Oise et l'Aisne . . .' (A.N. BB 18 831, 9 frimaire an IV).

[2] A.C. Moret Registre IV, séance de la municipalité du 18 frimaire an II): '. . . que journellement plus de 200 mariniers qui conduisent des marchandises et denrées . . . à Paris étaient obligés de se fournir de pain en cette commune. . . .'

[3] Germain Brice, *Description de la ville de Paris et de tout ce qu'elle contient de plus remarquable*, 1752 ed., edited by Pierre Codet, Paris and Geneva 1972, pp. 117, 518.

[4] Ibid., p. 314.

[5] See note A, p. 227.

royal ordinances on the *Eaux & Forêts* dating back to the second decade of the reign of Louis XIV; these were still enforced, like most of the repressive legislation most likely to be directed against the poor and the disinherited, throughout the revolutionary period, though, under the Directory, such regulations were to become increasingly difficult to make into deterrents in any way effective. *Communes* like Gennevilliers, la Briche, Saint-Cloud, Sèvres, Argenteuil, and Colombes, situated in the great bends of the river, were to derive a sense of solidarity, as well as the habit of successfully defying any prohibition that came from Paris, in the massive, collective infractions of these ordinances. As a result, their inhabitants developed the mentality of *fraudeurs*, of people who lived habitually, and with impunity, outside the law. No local *juge de paix* could be expected to act in these cases; he looked the other way, failing even to report such offences.

The Revolution decentralised justice, to the advantage of local, elected authorities, just as it tended to fractionalise the forces of repression, so that the new régime, in this respect at least, tended to make things much better for all those who felt that they had a vested interest in the continuous defiance of the law, whether royal or revolutionary. It might, meanwhile, be objected, that such offences were insignificant and that they were only comparable to the sort of collective lawbreaking that one associates with rural *communes*, especially those situated on the borders of two or three Departments and, even more, those placed on the frontiers of the Republic. But these were *not* really rural villages; they were mostly heavily populated with a large proportion of people in real need, even at the best of times.[1] They were *lieux de passages*, some of them actually touching the *barrières* of the capital, and the inhabitants of which had in fact half a foot in Paris itself; for we hear that many of the fishermen of Gennevilliers, for instance, would come to fish in Paris during the day, coming into contact with the *gens de rivière* and with all the most unruly elements of the quay-side population, reserving the nights for the more lucrative fishing by lantern offshore from their own *commune*.

The example of their comparative impunity would speak eloquently to many of the fringe elements of the population of the capital. Equally important, from the point of view of the inhabitants of Paris, by fishing throughout the year their activities would naturally greatly reduce the total number of fish spawning in the valley of the lower Seine in its Parisian reaches. What they caught and either ate themselves or sold locally to fishmongers or, more probably, to innkeepers and *restaura-*

[1] See note B, p. 227.

teurs catering for the wealthy week-end visitor,[1] was lost to the Paris fish market. This was only a short-term evil; but the habit of illegal night fishing, throughout the year—for even when the river was frozen, we hear that these ingenious people used to fish through holes in the ice—must also have compromised the future, by reducing the total fish population of the river and of its tributaries.[2]

Even during the Terror, the revolutionary authorities never showed themselves so powerless as when attempting to deal with fishermen—whether with those who went to sea, off the Channel coast, or with those who, from Thonon, regularly supplied the Swiss *communes* on the other side of the lake of Geneva, or with those, finally, who made nonsense of more than a century of regulations imposed in the interests of the Lent needs of the population, as well as of the everyday consumption of the Parisian in a foodstuff that was cheaper, more readily available, and less subject to seasonal disasters, than bread or meat. It was above all the nearness to Paris of such *communes* that made such examples of lawlessness dangerous to public order within the city itself.

Riverside communities in the proximity of Paris were subjected to other conflicts and tensions resulting both from the sheer complication of the river and canal networks in the area and from the gigantic needs of the city's bakeries. As most of the mills situated in the Paris area, in the valleys of the upper Seine, the Marne, the Oise and its tributaries, and the many other smaller rivers that connected with them, were operated by water power, constant attention had to be paid to the level of the water used to supply the motive power of the mill wheels. During long, dry summers, milling might be brought to a standstill, while, in the spring and autumn floods of any normal year, many mills would be swept away on the high waters: and, in 1793, the years II and III, conditions were far from normal. The competing needs of neighbouring millers were a source of bitter conflicts, litigation, appeals to the *juges de paix*, and personal violence, often involving whole communities, as one miller attempted to retain the waters for the use of his

[1] '. . . *Le Portier Anglois* a 2 auberges destinées de tout temps aux rendez-vous des ci-devant nobles et qui sont tenues par des hommes égoïstes et regrettant l'ancien régime: *on ne vend plus rien, on ne fait plus rien, le temps passé était bien meilleur*, etc, tels sont leurs discours . . .' (rapport de Rousseville sur Charenton, 16 prairial an II, A.N. F7 4746 d 1, Hugot). See also F11 1177 (14 thermidor an IV): '. . . Certains bouchers de Paris, connus sous la désignation de mercandiers, achètent les bestiaux à mesure qu'ils arrivent sur le marché de Poissy et les revendent avec usure sur les routes et dans les auberges. . . .'

[2] See my *Quelques aspects de la criminalité parisienne.*

own mill by constructing a dam that would thus deprive his rival downstream of motive power.

As a collectivity, the interests of the millers would also conflict with the many people like *mariniers*, *gens de rivière*, and *flotteurs* who, by the nature of their livelihood, were concerned to maintain the flow of traffic on rivers and canals, for, by diverting the course of a stream, they were likely to lower the water level to such an extent that the waterway would no longer be navigable, so that traffic would be interrupted. In the highly-charged atmosphere of 1793–5, millers, at the best of times the objects of ingrained popular hostility on the part of townsmen, were liable to find themselves accused of having plotted to prevent the arrival, at the Paris ports, of much-needed supplies of wood, grain, and coal.[1] The belief that the millers were deliberately exploiting their position in order to hold the inhabitants of the capital to ransom was a major factor in the deep suspicion in which Paris provisioning authorities at this time were to hold both the administrative personnel and the general mass of inhabitants of the District de Corbeil where many of the mills working for the capital were situated. The millers could, of course, reply that they too were doing their best and that the need to keep the mill wheels turning was as imperative as that, so often contradictory, of keeping the channels of communication in working order. It was the sort of conflict to which, in eighteenth-century conditions, there could be no obvious solution. Nor was it a straight conflict between millers and *gens de rivière*: the interests of farmers, carters, and itinerants were also certain to be involved, for, in their efforts to divert the course of waterways, the millers as often as not succeeded in flooding roads and fields, interrupting land communications, and destroying the crops, as well as damaging habitations. There were many complaints of this kind from the riverside *communes* of the District de Grandvilliers, in the Oise, in the course of the summer of 1794[2] and such complaints can undoubtedly witness for many others that have not been recorded, from similar areas.

Let us return a moment to the capital. The Seine had of course

[1] See note C, p. 228.

[2] A.D. Oise 1er registre du directoire du District de Grandvilliers (séance du 18 septembre 1793): '. . . Les administrateurs ont pris connoissance du mémoire présenté par les officiers municipaux de Thérines . . . expositif que la construction du moulin à bled de Jacques Bourdon situé sur la rivière de Thérines vers Epaty, faisant refluer l'eau dans la rue nommée à Cailloux, la seule qui communique du hameau de Montaubert à Thérines, de manière que la communication des gens de pied, de bestiaux et de voitures est interceptée [on décide d'envoyer des commissaires sur place faire l'examen des lieux].

dictated the original location of Lutetia, and the city had gradually spread out from the original island site, a fact commemorated pictorially in the coat of arms of the city of Paris. In the eighteenth century, the most important axis of communication within the city was from north to south (rather than, as it is now, from east to west) along the rues des faubourgs Saint-Martin and Saint-Denis, the rues Saint-Martin[1] and Saint-Denis and, on the left bank, the rue Saint-Jacques and the rue du Faubourg-Saint-Jacques. This put a maximum strain on three central bridges: the Pont-Neuf, the Pont-au-Change, and the Pont Notre-Dame. Congestion was worsened, at the northern end of the Pont-au-Change, by the sinister medieval bulk of the Grand Châtelet, which narrowed the rue Saint-Denis at the run-up to the bridge.[2] The result was that, at any time of the working day, the three bridges would be the scene of cursing and swearing carters, of endless and violent disputes, of spectacularly horrific accidents, as well as the meeting places of the idle, the ill-intentioned, the prophets of doom, and the mournful dirges of the street-singers, on the irresistible theme of the edifying or unedifying last minutes of such and such a bandit, as he was being broken on the wheel, place de Grêve, itself adjacent to the river and within easy reach of the Pont Notre-Dame.

I have suggested elsewhere that it was regarded as a particularly heinous offence *d'avoir parlé sur le Pont-Neuf*[3] (even more, to have *shouted* there). More recently, I came across the case of two girls in their twenties, both of them out of work and starving, in the terrible summer of 1795, who ran into each other while watching a traffic accident on the Pont-au-Change. There they struck up an acquaintance made easier, in this initial stage, by the fact that they were similarly clothed, discovered that they had many grievances in common, were about the same age, and decided to walk north, once it was dark, so as to reach the open fields on the heights of Belleville, where they would steal potatoes for their next meal, and where they were caught, early in the morning, by a municipal *garde-chasse*, who brought them before the *juge de paix* of the *canton rural* of Belleville, an official of whom we have already heard in the course of this study. As the girls had come

---

[1] Saint-Martin '. . . a donné son nom à un quartier très-peuplé, mais le plus sale peut-être de Paris, & du moins le plus lugubre du côté de la rue Grenéta. Il y a aux environs de Saint-Martin-des-Champs 2 ou 3 marchés très incommodes, qui entretiennent sur le pavé l'humidité & l'infection: une boue noire & fétide ne sèche jamais là, même pendant l'été . . .' (Mercier, *Le Tableau de Paris*, X, p. 199).

[2] Germain Brice, op. cit., p. 512.

[3] *The Police and the People*, p. 21(4).

from Paris, though it seems that they lived in lodging-houses there, the *juge de paix* was able, for once, to indulge in the luxury of extreme severity, in the interest, of course, of those who had elected him.[1] In the study of the sociability of the poor, of how people establish a relationship, albeit a criminal one, the location of bridges can be a very important indication, as the *point de départ* of so many adventures that ended up happily or, more often, badly. In Lyon I have found that bridges, especially those, more familiar and much shorter, over the Saône, were a favourite point of departure in the simple, ancient, and persistent manoeuvres of the seducer, full or part-time.[2]

The Seine was not only thus an encouragement to sociability and to petty crime. Its bridges offered a valuable source of information to police spies. An *officier de police*, provided with the detailed description of the personal appearance of a wanted person, would, almost as a first thought, take up his post on one of these three bridges. Sooner or later, his client, Parisian or stranger, would be forced across, on business or in search of pleasure. The left bank, after all, was not a wilderness, and it contained its own professional skills and specialities.

Finally, as a further, and indeed convincing, tribute to the importance of these bridges, it is worth recalling that army recruiters, *raccoleurs*, those intelligent and eloquent witnesses of popular habit and popular conceits, in fact social historians before their time, were prone to seek out promising material by stationing themselves prominently— and they could not be anything other than that, thanks to the plumes and feathers that they wore in their hats and that gave them something of the appearance of the eighteenth-century vision of the Noble Savage —either on the Pont-Neuf or on the neighbouring quay:

. . . Un grand nombre, travestis en brillans domestiques, gardaient toutes les avenues de la capitale, et allaient au-devant des rustres inexpérimentés, qui, fuyant les ingrats travaux de la campagne . . . venaient chercher un maître opulent. . . . *Le quai de la Féraille* est encore le Champ de Mars où les successeurs de ces *habiles* se promènent avec de hautes plumes sur la tête. . . .[3]

I have never really believed in that hardy annual, the old story about the aged *concierge* in the XVIIIme or the XXme, who told a reporter that, in a lifetime in Paris, she had never seen the Tour Eiffel. Nonsense! In the eighteenth century, in any case, people would be con-

[1] See note D, p. 228.
[2] See chapter III, 'A View on the Street: Work and Leisure in Revolutionary Lyon', in my *A Sense of Place*, London, 1975.
[3] *Le Tableau de Paris*, x, p. 273.

stantly impelled towards the banks of the Seine, by need, by the indulgence of a fantasy, or to watch the fireworks on a royal, religious, or revolutionary state occasion, or, more prosaically, to buy wood, wine, flowers, old clothes, scrap-iron, locks and keys, a canary, a song-bird, or a child.

In Lyon, the Rhône acted as a real frontier between the old city on the peninsular, *entre Rhône et Saône*, and the semi-rural badlands of les Brotteaux and la Guillotière, and to cross the pont de la Guillotière, even in pursuit of week-end entertainment and relaxation, was to move into another social unit.[1] The Seine, on the other hand, did not divide Paris at all in the same way.[2] The lower one goes down in the social scale, the more frequent is the transfer from one bank to another. A laundrywoman might live in Grenelle, Vaugirard, or Issy, or in le Gros Caillou, and even work there, for these were all places, like Saint-Denis to the north, in which large-scale laundries were heavily concentrated,[3] and yet spend much of the time picking up or delivering packages in the neighbourhood of the Palais-Royal, the Roule, or the Blancs-Manteaux, in the Marais, where both the marché du Temple and the Mont-de-Piété were situated, and which, under any régime, were the object of special attention from the police. It was always as well to put at least the river between the scene of the crime and the temporary dis-posal of the goods that had been gained from it, thanks to the inter-vention of an innkeeper, an old-clothes' merchant, a *revendeuse*, or some other go-between. A family group, including a mother and her two daughters and her son-in-law, after killing a merchant at dusk, as he was making his way from Paris to Saint-Denis, sold his watch to a publican in the Section des Invalides, while hiding his clothes, kept for eventual sale, in three rooms that they had leased in the same area, and in which as it turned out, they were themselves living, although they had addresses on the right bank.[4]

[1] See my chapter on Lyon in *A Sense of Place*.

[2] At the level of skilled trades, however, the river appears to have remained a frontier between two separate worlds well into the middle of the nineteenth century. Referring to the partial revival of *compagnonnages* during the Restora-tion, Theodore Zeldin notes: '. . . Artisans of different orders refused to work together. In Paris the river was a strict dividing line, and rival orders of carpenters, for example, each had a monopoly of employment on the left and right banks. . . .' op. cit., p. 214.

[3] A.C. Saint-Denis 1D 1 4 (séance de la municipalité du 8 brumaire an III). The municipality points out 'que les blanchisseurs de cette commune sont dans l'usage de faire le blanchissage du linge pour les citoyens de la commune de Paris. . . .'

[4] See note E, p. 229.

In revolutionary conditions, the former *noble* faubourg would have obvious attractions to anyone trying to dispose rapidly of stolen goods; not only was it less carefully watched by the police than the Marais or the quartier Saint-Honoré, it was itself the centre of a brisk trade in the furniture, silver, and pictures of the *hôtels particuliers* of *émigrés* and suspects. Equally, those concerned in one of the many murders to have been committed in the bois de Boulogne or anywhere on the highroad from Versailles to Paris would generally have enough imagination not simply to move on into the area of the rue de Vaugirard, the rue Saint-Dominique, or the Gros Caillou, parts of the city that were nearest to the scene of the crime. A much better bet would be to cross the river and try one's luck around the Halles or the Hôtel-de-Ville, or among the numerous lodging-houses of the rue de la Verrerie. At least, there, one would be less likely to be known or recognised; for most of those who operated on the celebrated murder route between the old capital and the new, seem to have come from the western parts of the left bank, or to have moved there from the Versailles region.

Of course, I may be making too much of such obvious, elementary, native cunning. For instance, after committing a murder just beyond the barrière de Vincennes, those who had taken part made the fatal mistake of moving back into the city along the same route. And it is also true that some petty thieves—with one exception, all of them beginners—could display a quite unbelievable lack of imagination, eating, drinking, singing, shouting, and generally making themselves seen and heard by as many witnesses as possible, in a restaurant, the owner of which was, no doubt inevitably, a police informer, just around the corner from a house which they had broken into, a few hours earlier and in the course of which one of the thieves had been seen coming downstairs, loaded with stolen hats, whistling and singing, as joyful as a lark. What is more, their meal concluded, the men went back to the lodging-houses of their respective girl friends where, of course, they found a couple of *commissaires de police* waiting for them.[1] Such crass stupidity can often make nonsense of the most carefully contrived theory of the geography of theft and of the disposal of stolen goods. Even so, I think these people cannot really witness for most.

The vital thing was to cross the river, even if one ended up at the nearest, and so most obvious, point on the other bank.[2] Some will recall a Simenon plot at which the vantage point of observation for Maigret was a small café, several feet below the level of the pavement,

---

[1] *Quelques aspects de la criminalité parisienne.*
[2] See note F, p. 230.

quai des Grands-Augustins, that, in the 1930s—it no longer exists today[1]—was frequented almost exclusively by Flemish bargees—their boats were moored just below—and that served Stella-Artois, steak, and chips. It was from there that the *commissaire* could observe the lights in his own office, directly opposite, quai des Orfèvres. He could not have been better, or more obviously, placed; in this case, it was his intention to make himself as obvious as possible and his manoeuvre eventually produced the hoped-for results. Simenon's plot can be illustrated in reality in an event that occurred in July 1795. In the early hours of the morning of the ninth of that month [21 Messidor year III], after a very hot night, a lawyer of 45, named Tournay-Branchecoeur, a man of means, for he owned the appartment in the arcades of the Palais-Royal, no. 23 Maison-Égalité, in which the events occurred, murdered his wife in her bed. The murder must have taken place between four and four-thirty, for, at about five, a neighbour heard the lawyer, whose step he knew, opening the front door on to the arcades, to let himself out. The murder was discovered at about six, Comminges, the *commissaire de police* of the Section de la Butte-des-Moulins, and a doctor, called out in his night-shirt, making an official report of the death at six-forty: the woman had been strangled.

The couple had been living apart for some time and Tournay-Branchecoeur had started divorce proceedings, but, for some reason, the husband had decided to spend the night of the eighth to the ninth at his former home. In the course of the night, his wife had been visited by her lover (or by one of her lovers) who, while making love to her—we are not told whether the husband was in the same room or was sleeping in a neighbouring one—had been concerned to emphasise both his presence and his activities by singing, very loudly—some of the neighbours could recall the words—a popular operetta: *Nuit charmante, nuit, sois propice à l'amour*. It is not stated how long this went on for or whether there were repeat performances, but the lover must have eventually departed, for there is no mention of his presence in the morning in the report drawn up by the *commissaire*. For the husband, the night must have been anything but charming, even if he were *en instance de divorce* and might have been supposed inured to his wife's infidelities.

Anyhow, after strangling her—and the neighbours who had been kept awake by the operetta, had heard no sound of a struggle—he opened his bureau and wrote out a note for his father-in-law explaining that he had reached the end of the road and could take no more, and

[1] It was called *chez Jeff*.

asking him to look after the three children. After leaving the Palais-Royal, he had crossed the river by the nearest bridge—the old Pont-Royal—and had gone straight to a public bathing establishment, *les bains Poitevins*, on the quai d'Orsay, which, like all such places, remained open all night, hiring a *cabine* on the first floor. After he had been in the bath for over an hour, two bath attendants, who were cleaning out the bath in the next box, worried by his silence, looked through the gaps in the wooden slats and noticed that the water in the tub had turned a deep red. This was at eight o'clock, about four hours after the murder; the murderer had been dead for at least an hour, as his blood had darkened the tepid water. *Drame de jalousie*, though it seems unlikely, for the husband was in financial difficulties and may well have decided to kill himself and, only under the extreme provocation afforded by the sultry sociability of a summer night, to have been driven into this extra killing: we cannot know, so it does not really matter. The point about this episode, so worthy of Hitchcock's eager attention, is that it had to be the quai d'Orsay.[1]

It would be inappropriate, at this stage, to discuss the new judicial and administrative units created by the Revolution and to suggest some of their effects on the relationship between Paris, the *communes* on its perimeter, and those placed on the supply lines of the capital. But it is worth emphasising that the administrative changes thus brought about both within Paris, and in its Department, would greatly have increased the incentive to cross the river, especially if one had anything to hide; and there would be plenty of people who would be anxious to separate themselves from a recent past. Each *commissaire de police*, each *juge de paix* of the forty-eight Sections, enjoyed a considerable margin of freedom and initiative, while being extremely jealous of interference from outside: *commissaires* did, it is true, correspond with one another, even exchanging information, while they were supposed also to keep the *Bureau Central* and the Minister of Justice—and, later, the Minister of Police—informed of the daily happenings in the restricted areas for which they were responsible. But it is rather rare to find two *commissaires*, even from adjoining Sections, working together on the same case or co-operating in the same *enquête*. The *commissaire*, like the *juge de paix*, liked to be undisturbed in the exercise of his functions. If one were either a resident or a lodger in a given Section, it was often enough, even in the conditions of the Terror, to cross the river in order to begin afresh with a judicial life at least temporarily virgin.

The river did, inevitably, also provide a fairly clear line of differentia-

[1] See note G, p. 230.

tion between different types of trades and activities. The position of the Halle aux vins, the wood market, and the horse market confined to the left bank the many activities, legitimate and semi-legitimate, or wholly illegitimate, of those more or less directly attached to these trades and of the even more numerous hangers-on that lived, seasonally or constantly, on their fringes. The adulteration of the wine drunk by the majority of the unfortunate inhabitants of Paris began, of course, at source: that is, in Clamart, Issy, Choisy, Meudon, Suresnes, Puteaux, the chief suppliers of the *vin de Paris*. According to Brice, most of the wine used by Parisians came in either from the south, via the barrière de l'Enfer[1] and the faubourg Saint-Jacques, or, by river, to Bercy; but he had in mind the palatable wines of the well-to-do. Most of the *vin de Paris* would be brought by cart, through Grenelle and Vaugirard and the rue de Vaugirard. A further stage of adulteration was reached thus either *en cours de route*, in the south-western districts of the left bank, or on arrival at the Halle aux vins, in the faubourg Saint-Marceau and Bercy, and the process was completed at the level of each individual *marchand de vin*. Those of the right bank would probably receive wine that had already gone through several stages of adulteration; but this did not prevent them from adding a few more alien elements to what was to be consumed by their customers. Adulteration began outside the city, proceeded in transit within it, and was completed on arrival, on both sides of the river. It might, however, have been considered a speciality of the left bank.[2]

The words horse dealer and horse thief were largely interchangeable and, as we have seen,[3] the legislation concerning the purchase and sale of horses at a fair or a market was actually to facilitate the disposal of stolen horses. The horse market was thus to provide the most valuable links between the faubourg Saint-Marceau and the left bank in general and the various bandit groups that operated with such success in the rural *communes* south of Paris, in the neighbourhood of Montlhéry and Arpajon, during the Directory. It had perhaps been a wise move on the part of the *Lieutenant de Police* to have placed the horse market on the very edge of Paris, at a point where the faubourg bordered on the no-man's-land of the villages of Ivry and Choisy; at least such a location removed most of those directly concerned in the trade well away from the centre, though some of the advantages to be derived from this type of preventative planning must have been obviated by the fact that

---

[1] Brice, op. cit., p. 29.
[2] *Reactions to the French Revolution*, pp. 170–2.
[3] Chapter 1, p. 27.

stables were spread evenly throughout the city, with a maximum con-
centration in the faubourg Saint-Germain, where most of the riding
schools were situated, in the faubourg Saint-Honoré, in the Palais-
Royal area, and in the Marais.[1] Stables also provided a regular refuge to
adolescents and runaway children, as well as to persons who, for one
reason or another, preferred not to risk spending a night in a lodging-
house, or simply could not afford that relative luxury in a world of the
very poor. It was certainly dangerous, as we have seen, to risk bringing
a stolen horse across the river, as there would be plenty of people on
the look out for it on the bridges and their approaches. The physical
descriptions of stolen horses recur almost as frequently in the daily
reports of the *commissaires de police* as those of wanted persons; and
they must have been easier to trace, if only because they were much less
numerous. In the 1752 edition of Brice, the *abbé*'s editors calculate the
total horse population of Paris at about 100,000, that is, one horse to
about seven people[2] (a proportion made much more familiar as a result
of the experience of the First World War[3]). The number would, of
course, have been much less in time of war.

Stolen horses are constantly used as a means of guiding the police
towards the identification of those who had attempted to dispose of
them within Paris, thanks to the co-operation of blacksmiths and
ostlers, who, like *logeurs* and procurers at the human level, were
anxious to keep in with the authorities, and provided them with a chain
of informers spread throughout the city, but, like the latter, heavily
concentrated both in the faubourg Saint-Marceau and in the neighbourhood of the Palais-Royal. It will be recalled that, following the
attempt on the life of the First Consul, with the explosion of the Infernal Machine of the rue Nicaise, Fouché had the remains of the pony
that had been blown up, along with the small boy who had been in
charge of the cart, collected and stitched together by a taxidermist, so
that the stuffed animal could be shown to every blacksmith in Paris; it
was by this means that the royalist squires who had bought the pony
from a mews were eventually to be identified.[4]

---

[1] Brice, op. cit. p. 359.

[2] Ibid., p. 30.

[3] *40 Hommes 10 Chevaux*. In England, the proportion was rather more
generous to bi-peds. When I began in the army, during the Second World War,
we were housed four to a horsebox, on Chepstow race course.

[4] Marcel Le Clère, 'Comment opérait la police de Fouché', *Revue de crimino-
logie et de police technique*, Geneva, January–March 1951. See also my *Terreur et
subsistances*, p. 185. Nothing could be done about the small boy, who had literally
been blown to pieces by the bomb that he had, unknown to himself, been carry-

The horse market could then be peripheral; indeed, it was preferable that it should be, for some of the reasons that I have suggested. Horses in any case reached Paris from the south and the west, from the stock-breeding areas of the Perche, so that the trade further contributed to the activities of that dangerous south–north axis, from the barrière de l'Enfer to the faubourg and the rue Saint-Jacques, offering armies of carters, horse dealers, and drovers a last refuge, just before their entry to the city, or on their way back from it, in the numerous inns, taverns, and lodging-houses of the notorious *commune* of Montrouge, not nearly so heavily populated as the alarming plague-spot of Gentilly, its neighbour (which, according to the figures for the year III, had a population of 4,495, as compared to a total of 869 for Montrouge;[1] but both villages would count, in addition a highly mobile floating population which would remain unaccounted for in any analysis), but certainly quite as dangerous. So the horse market really *had* to be on the left bank.[2]

The grain market, on the other hand, *had* to be central, and *had* to be on the right bank, as the grain port was there, quai du Louvre. The new Halle au bled, so much admired, both for its practical elegance and for its utilitarian distinction, by Arthur Young, had been built very near the Seine, and, one would have thought, in rather dangerous proximity also to the Louvre and the Tuileries, though, of course, neither of these was occupied as a royal residence in the eighteenth century, the Revolution, in this respect, creating a new geography of perils. It was generally possible, in the event of turbulence, to block the bridges across the Seine, between the Pont-au-Change and the Pont Louis XV, as, indeed, was done on the morning of the execution of Louis XVI, place de la Révolution. It was the fact that it had *not* been done, on the 10 August, added to the passivity of the moderate

---

ing in the cart that had been hired along with himself and the pony. See also note H, p. 231.

[1] A.N. F20 19 (Population, recensement de l'an III, Département de Paris, District de Bourg-l'Egalité).

[2] Livestock, too, seem to have been more numerous on the left bank. This one would expect, as the *barrière de l'Enfer* would be the point of entry of most of the livestock coming from the meat market of Sceaux. For instance, 39 cows are enumerated, in Brumaire year V, in the Division du Panthéon-français, 15 of them with a single owner, Pévrier, 7, with Sonnet, 6, with Samson. There must have been plenty of fields in this very highly populated quarter (A.P.P. A/A 202, commissaire de police de la Section du Panthéon-français, 16 brumaire an V [6 November 1796]).

battalions of the National Guard from the western districts, that may
partly have accounted for the second event.[1]

On a very different occasion, on 6 February 1934, it was thanks to
the presence of solid ranks of mounted *gardes mobiles* on the Pont de la
Concorde that finally prevented those participating in this Fascist-
motivated riot from storming the Chambre des Députés in the Palais
Bourbon. But, just as the prostitutes of the Palais-Royal quarter, if
unduly harried by the police, would move *eastwards*, towards the rue
des Lombards and the rue de la Verrerie, so riot, in the last ten years of
the eighteenth century, would move *westwards*, from behind the
Hôtel-de-Ville towards the Tuileries, picking up, as it went on its
course, further recruits in the neighbourhood of the cornmarket. The
location of the new Halle au bled had not been dictated by considera-
tions of riot control; no one could have foreseen, when it was built,
that the royal family would once more be resident in the old royal
parish of Saint-Germain-l'Auxerrois. It could not have been put anywhere else. Most of the grain from the Vexin, from the Brie, the
Soissonnais, and the Bassigny, as well as the Baltic supplies of dearth
years, was brought by water and was unloaded at quai du Louvre. Most
of the rest would be brought in by road from the north, from the
grain-producing areas of the Pays de France, via the faubourg Saint-
Denis and the street of the same name. The cornmarket also had to be
near the Halles, in the parish of Saint-Eustache, as the provisioning
trade was minutely interrelated. Topographical convenience was
probably not, however, the only consideration, though, clearly, the
position of the Halle au bled would be likely to impose the location of
the cattle and fish markets, the latter placed very near, rue Montorgueil.[2]

All eighteenth-century French authorities, at least at the top level,
favoured Paris markets, as opposed to markets held outside the city
limits. For one thing, they were easier to watch over; furthermore,
being very large and dealing with goods in bulk, they were reassuring
(though hardly so in times of dearth) and would thus be likely to
produce lower prices. This preference in favour of the capital was an
additional grievance of the *communes* of the perimeter, which, with the
suppression of the *droits d'entrée*, had at first hoped for much from the
Revolution.[3] They were soon to be disappointed, though the new
régime did at least maintain Poissy and Sceaux as the two traditional

---

[1] Marcel Reinhard, *La Chute de la royauté*.
[2] See above, chapter 1, p. 19.
[3] See note I, p. 231.

sites for the sale of livestock, a decision, that in the conditions of the year II and the following year, was to offer dangerous hostages to the interests of the Parisian consumer, as it placed the inhabitants at the mercy of the fat-stock merchants and the authorities of these two *communes*.[1] Either way, in a period of crisis, the provisioning and repressive authorities of the capital were liable to lose out, because the presence *intra-muros* of huge, monopoly markets was bound to act as a magnet to riot, by gathering together in one place large numbers of people similarly motivated and often in the same trade.

Both the horse market and the grain market would attract to themselves a myriad of satellite occupations: *traiteurs, restaurateurs, gargotiers, cabaretiers, logeurs,* as well as the armies of prostitutes that plied within visible distance of either; these had to be *visible*, because horse dealers or grain merchants could not be expected to scour Paris in search of them. But they would in fact be different prostitutes, even different types of prostitutes. The *filles du Palais-Royal* did not normally cross the river; it did not occur to them to do so,[2] and, had they done so, their reception at the hands of those in their profession on the south bank would not have been friendly. When pressed, as I have said, they moved in the direction of the east-centre. It required more flair, more refinement, better clothes, a wider vocabulary, to chat up a well-to-do grain merchant or large farmer, from the Vermandois or the Beauvaisis, than to come to terms with some coarse and undemanding horse dealer or carter from the Perche or the Beauce.

Here, for instance, is what happened to three countrymen from the neighbourhood of Senlis, Charles Mercier, miller, Louis Bourée, and Philippe Rougeau, *gardes-moulin,* when they came up to Paris on business, in the course of the winter of 1796. Writing to the Minister of Justice from Brest—they had been condemned to twenty-four years in the galleys—on 11 Germinal year V [3 March 1797], they report:

... Dans le fait, nous étant trouvés à Paris, à la halle aux bleds, nous sommes entrés chez un traiteur sans autre intention que d'y prendre notre repas. Nous y fûmes abordés par 3 femmes du monde avec lesquelles nous avons ensuite passé la nuit. Elles nous prenaient certainement pour ce que nous n'étions pas, c'est-à-dire pour des riches fermiers.

En badinant, nous avons promis à chacune d'elles un deshabiller [*sic*]; elles nous ont alors pressés sur cette promesse qu'elles vouloient être effectuée à l'instant, mais nous avons dit que nous [ne] pouvions leur donner qu'après que nous aurions retiré dans un bois du ci-devant prince de Condé

---

[1] On the subject of the importance of Sceaux, see below, chapter 4, pp. 106–8.
[2] See note J, p. 231.

un trésor que nous savions y être caché. Elles nous ont tourmenté pour partir sur le champ. . . . En parlant ainsi, nous n'avions d'autre but que de nous retirer de la compagnie de ces 3 femmes et de leur affidé [a man to whom they had been introduced at the inn]; il nous était échappé de dire que notre route étoit par Senlis. A peine le lendemain étions-nous à la barrière du Faubourg Martin et entrés chez un marchand de vin pour y déjeuner que ce nommé Bryngdly [the friend of the three ladies] et 2 autres particuliers nous ont rejoints et ne nous ont point quittés d'un instant, ils ont fait tomber la conversation sur le prétendu trésor, nous leur répondimes que tout ce que nous en avions dit la veille étoit d'invention purement chimérique. Ils ne nous ont point quittés pour cela.

L'un de nous ayant dit qu'il savoit bien où il y avait de l'argent, mais que c'étoit dans une maison habitée, ils en ont demandé l'endroit & sur l'indication que c'étoit au moulin de Neuilly près Senlis dans un pot de terre . . . ils ont répondu: *tant mieux, nous allons directement à Senlis, nous savons où il y a une bonne pacotille chez un négotiant, venez avec nous, vous seriez des lâches et des poltrons si vous n'accédiez pas à notre demande.* Enfin ils ont dit qu'ils étoient sûrs de réussir et que d'un coup on en feroit deux, qu'ils sont accoutumés à ce métier et qu'ils en vivoient.

Ils ont payé à boire & nous ont forcés à les conduire à l'endroit indiqué, nous voulions les laisser entrer les premiers et nous esquiver, mais ils nous ont introduits de force, prenant l'un de nous au collet & le poussant dans la maison. . . . ils se sont jettés sur le maître de la maison & sur ses enfans, les ont liés et ont demandé où étoit leur argent. Dans le même instant la force armée s'est saisie de nous, laissant libres Bryngdly & ses deux associés. . . .[1]

Clearly their account is not entirely truthful; nor were they as innocent as they would have the Minister believe. But it is very easy to see what happened and not difficult to decide who had been fooling whom. Their business concluded, the miller and his two assistants had headed for a wine-shop within sight of the vast domed building, prepared to see what the city might have in store for them. They did not have long to wait, as is clear from their account, being very soon joined at their table by the three well-dressed ladies who appeared only too willing to make the strangers feel at home and to give them the benefit of their knowledge of Paris. The countrymen were no doubt impressed and wished in their turn to impress, directing their conversation to the subject of the purchase and sale of corn; the ladies were easily convinced, as they were meant to be, that they were in the presence of three important *blatiers* from the grainlands to the north of Paris. Their conversation, their clothing, and their accents—and anyone

---

[1] A.N. BB 18 602 (Ministère de la Justice, Oise, Mercier, Bourée & Rougeau, du bagne de Brest, au Ministre, 11 germinal an V).

frequenting the cornmarket would be familiar with the various dialects of the Pays de France, the Soissonnais, the Vermandois, the Vexin, and the Brie—all clearly indicated participation in that lucrative, and, in the conditions of 1796, unbelievably, scandalously profitable, trade.

It was hard to know, at this stage, who was deceiving whom; but the ladies' interest was sharpened by the promise of a complete new set of night clothing for each of them. This would have ensured the travellers of their company for the night. But the men then overplayed their hand, by referring to the hidden treasure; it was probably at this stage that a signal from one of the women brought to their table one of their male accomplices who, like his friends, seems to have believed the story. They also made the even more disastrous mistake of letting it be known to their companions that they would be up and on their way betimes on the following morning, as they needed to be back at their homes near Senlis that same evening. The next day, early, they seem to have been able to shake off the company of those with whom they had no wish at all to travel on the homeward journey. But not only did they, predictably, take the direction of the barrière du faubourg Saint-Martin; worse still, they stopped off for a drink in a wine-shop just outside it and there they had the extremely disagreeable surprise of finding three men awaiting them, including one of their friends of the night before. There was no hope now of shaking them off. Was there not strength in numbers? And what three could do, six could do better? And were they not all men of courage, not cowards who shrank back at the last moment? Did they not know their job as well as they did theirs?

And so, in dismay and outnumbered by their alarming fellow-walkers, self-proclaimed bandits with plenty of experience behind them, they set off, after their own admission that the treasure story was a pure invention had been casually brushed aside; after all, if there were no treasure, there was always money to be taken somewhere or other. For the three countrymen, it must have been an extremely gloomy journey, the gloom increasing as Senlis drew nearer. No doubt their discomfort was apparent, for, as we can see, the Parisians were not taking any chances, pushing them into the house ahead of them. It does seem rather unlikely that Mercier and his two companions were on the first operation of this kind; anyhow, it all ended up very badly for them. In the end, the joke was on the Parisians who, if denied the promised treasure, got clear away.

I quote this case at some length, not as an amusing anecdote, though it is not lacking in savour, but because the reasoning of the ladies and of their male friend should also be that of the historian, not so directly involved, not risking, for such a mixture of boastfulness and lack of discretion, a long term in the King's service, but equally concerned to suggest the probable, if not the absolutely self-evident. The ladies, with no doubt a pretty vast experience of grain merchants and their like, knew the many tenuous, yet obvious, links by which the capital was connected with its wide area of supply. When dealing with the Parisian proper, it was a matter of telling where he would be likely to be, judging by his occupation, during working hours or at leisure. When dealing with the visitor, especially if he appeared to be a man of good condition, with a stake in society and a purse full of hard cash, it was reasonable to assume that he would go out by the way he had come in. The miller and his assistants could not have followed a more predictable course in this respect. This is not so much historical guesswork as a matter of observation.

The repressive authorities make similar deductions as to the likeliest route to have been taken by malefactors or murderers, when confronted with two crimes that had been committed, both in 1804, in or on the borders of the Département de Jemappes. Writing on the subject of the first case: the murder of an old woman of seventy and of a girl of ten, in the village of Papignies, about two miles from the small town of Ath, a very important *lieu de passage* on the highroad from Lille to Brussels, at ten in the morning of Boxing Day 1803, during Mass, the Prefect informs the Minister:

... Les premières indications étaient qu'on avait remarqué les pas de deux hommes venant de la maison des personnes assassinées et deux hommes ont été en effet vus vers cette heure, venant du chemin de Tournai. ... ces deux hommes ont été vus au faubourg d'Ath, peu éloigné de Papignies, vers dix heures et demi du matin, de là dans un cabaret à Rebaix [at this stage, they must have turned back in their traces] d'où ils sont sortis vers une heure pour se rendre dans un endroit près de Grammont. ... ils ont paru émus, quoique s'apitoyant beaucoup sur le sort des victimes. ...

The two men seem in fact to have done everything humanly possible to draw attention to themselves, spending their money at an inn, going over the ground by which they had come, displaying their knowledge of the murder, and choosing a snowy day to carry out their operation.[1] The so-called '*bande juive*', as we shall see, at least had the elementary sense to stay at home when there was snow on the ground.

The other case is equally routine. Its interest lies in the fact that, on

---

[1] A.N. BB 18 402 (Préfet de Jemappes au Grand Juge, 21 nivôse an XII). The two men were perhaps not stupid. As it was Boxing Day, they may well have been drunk.

this occasion, the first thought of the police and judicial authorities was to keep a watchful eye on all persons using *des routes détournées et inusitées*, a deduction sensible enough when dealing with a group of people who had just carried out a large-scale robbery in a locality on the borders of a neighbouring Department, and which, in the event, completely paid off.[1]

The Seine imposed other distinctions, other differentiations between the activities of north and south banks. I have said that the faubourg Saint-Marceau was especially subjected to seasonal flooding from the Bièvre, which rose even more dramatically every time the Seine rose, leaving its bed and covering wide areas with pestilential mud. It was the principal source of the foul stench of the whole area around the Gobelins. But as the quarter was already malodorous, it might as well become even more so. The Gobelins were a very smelly industry, and the faubourg, which was heavily populated, but both poor and extensive, with plenty of open space for yards and workshops, could attract other trades that were equally stinking. Most of the tanneries were located there, while, on the southern tip of the perimeter, in the very poor and very populous *commune* of Gentilly, an enterprising entrepreneur had set up, in the early years of the Revolution, on a property that he had acquired from the purchase of church lands, a tripe factory (*boyauterie*). Gentilly had, up till then, been a place for Sunday walks for Parisian families and a village to which the urban artisan came to drink and to dance at week-ends. The owners of the local wine-shops, restaurants, and *guinguettes* were repeatedly to complain to the municipality that the tripe manufacturer was putting them out of business, but as he was a rich man, and they were comparatively poor, they did not succeed in having his establishment removed.[2]

---

[1] See note K, p. 232.

[2] A. C. Gentilly 1D1/1 (séance de la municipalité du 1er août 1793): '... depuis un mois ou environ il s'est établi sur le hameau de la Maison-blanche un marchand boyautier qui, par la putréfaction des matières servant à son commerce est cause d'une exhalaison forte qui se fait sentir non seulement dans les maisons voisines mais encore dans tout le hameau, ce qui nuît extraordinairement à leur commerce en détournant de leurs maisons les chalands et les citoyens qui sortent de Paris pour prendre l'air de la campagne. . . .' There is a further report on his activities on 2 Floréal year II, when a group of local innkeepers 'ont déclaré que ce commerce n'était pas supportable dans un hameau dont le principal commerce consiste à vendre de la viande et du vin et aussi à attirer un grand concours de monde. . . .'

Smells will recruit more smells, and the tripe manufacturer had not been the first in the field as far as Gentilly was concerned. The village had long been an object of concern to the well-to-do and settled Parisian as the location of the infamous maison de Bicêtre, to which sturdy beggars and children convicted of theft or of other crimes were confined, awaiting their transfer either to the penal settlements on the coast or, in the case of healthy boys under sixteen, to the Navy, as *mousses*. Bicêtre had been extended and largely rebuilt at the end of the seventeenth century, a period prolific in the formation of houses of correction and of lazarettos that were generally plague spots. The stench from the place spread over a wide area and could, in certain climatic conditions, be perceived in the faubourg Saint-Jacques. Nor was this all; for, every month, the *chaîne*, formed of convicted criminals from the various Departments, would arrive there, that from Belgium, Lille, and the north first crossing the whole of Paris, on the north–south axis of the faubourg Saint-Martin to the faubourg Saint-Jacques. This was no doubt alarming enough to the more peaceable and prosperous inhabitants of Gentilly and of its neighbouring *communes*; but what must have rendered the whole of the southern perimeter of the capital an area of intense anxiety and very justified fear was the biannual departure, for Brest, Lorient, Rochefort, and Toulon, of the national *chaîne*, formed of all the convicts who had previously arrived in Bicêtre from such centres as Troyes, Reims, Châlons, Évreux, Rouen, Amiens, Lille, Ghent, Brussels, and Antwerp, all plentiful suppliers of criminal talent. The *chaîne* was formed up and left the Paris area each year on 25 May and 10 September,[1] both dates dangerous enough in the normal process of things, especially in a period of real or feared shortage[2] and, during the Revolution, and more especially during the Terror of the year II, fraught with even more sinister political undertones of panic and uncertainty for the future. We will have occasion later to comment on the *Grande Peur* that swept all the perimeter of Paris, and above all its southern tip, at the time of the Admirat affair, at the beginning of Prairial year II; in that year, the *chaîne* left Bicêtre on 6 Prairial which, to make matters worse, was a Sunday.[3] In the following year, its departure almost coincided with the outbreak of the Prairial Days, their suppression, and the flight of many

---

[1] *Le Tableau de Paris*, x, p. 151.

[2] *The Police and the People*, pp. 263–9.

[3] *Concordance des Calendriers-Grégorien et Républicain*, Paris, 1963. The first departure in the year of *la chaîne* fell again on a Sunday in the years VIII, XI, XII, XIII, and XIV, on a Monday, in the years III, IX, and XV.

of those who had taken part in them to the sheltering *communes* to the south.

Each departure must have been a matter of considerable alarm not only to all concerned with the operation itself, but to all those who lived in the villages through which it would pass. The route of the *chaîne* to the three penal establishments situated on the Atlantic coast can hardly have made the highroads from Paris to Orléans, Paris to Dreux, and Paris to Chartres seem more reassuring. But during the Terror and the Thermidorian Reaction, and the anarchical years of the Directory, when escapes from the *chaîne* were extremely frequent,[1] Gentilly must have been the centre of a series of shock waves radiating all over the southern quarters of Paris and the whole of the countryside to the south and the west of the capital. Most quarters of Paris would have witnessed, at one time or another, the passage of groups of manacled and chained men; but the spectacle would be the most familiar to those who lived along the north–south axis. It was no more surprising that Bicêtre and Gentilly should have figured thus so constantly in the preoccupations of all who lived anywhere near the sinister building than that Gentilly should have had the highest mortality rate of any *commune* in the Département de Paris, with 40 births, 32 marriages, and 344 deaths in 1792.[2] One must assume that this was an exceptional year.

It was almost as if successive medical and repressive authorities had followed a deliberate policy in order to make the faubourg Saint-Marceau the most unhealthy, as well as the most alarming, area of Paris. For in the late seventeenth century, the same faubourg had been made the site of the Pitié and the Salpêtrière, the two principal hospitals for the female poor, incurable, and aged. Whether their location had been originally decided upon by the fact that they were far removed from the centres of wealth and fashion and that the Seine separated them from the Marais, I do not know. But their presence can only have further increased the degradation of this low-lying and underprivileged quarter; it may, of course, also have helped the task of the medical authorities by hastening these poor women on the road to death. They were, in any case, in good company. For on the neighbouring Montagne Sainte-Geneviève, alongside the Faculties of Law

---

[1] *Quelques aspects de la criminalité parisienne* and *Reactions to the French Revolution*.

[2] A.N. F20 19 (Population, recensement de l'an III, Département de Paris, District de Bourg-l'Egalité). The figure is so exceptionally high that it must indicate the existence of a devastating epidemic in the course of 1791 and 1792.

and Theology (the one concerned primarily with death, the other with
the life to come), and the Collèges that gave the Montagne its international reputation, were situated, in the late eighteenth century, the
Schools of Anatomy. There are frequent complaints, during the
Directory and the Empire, by householders and property-owners of
the stench caused by the rotting and dismembered corpses thrown out
in the street or piled up in open bins in courtyards, after Dupuytren
and his assistants had practised their skill on them.[1] As a result, rents
tended to be low on the Montagne, a quarter that people would be inclined to leave, as soon as they could afford to; but few could, for there
were few areas of Paris that were poorer than Maubert-Mouffetard,
and, none that counted so many elderly women, whether spinsters or
widows.[2]

The right bank, it is true, was not entirely immune in this respect,
owing to the presence of the municipal garbage heap of the notorious
Montfaucon. At the end of the eighteenth century it was used, along
with the Île des Cygnes, just outside the Paris boundaries, in the middle
of the Seine (hardly a feature likely to improve the river prospect), as
the charnel house of horses and dead animals. Whole areas of eastern
Paris were regularly subjected to the stench emanating from the place.
The Revolution, thanks to the tribal violence that it had released
among some sections of the Paris population, had further contributed
to these older miasmas; the authorities of the hôpital de l'Abbaye, in
the faubourg Saint-Antoine, were to complain, in 1797, of the effects
on their patients of the proximity of the newly-established cemetery in
which many of the less important victims of the September Massacres,
slaughtered in the Abbaye, had been given mass graves in the shallow,
sandy soil.[3] There was, in short, something of a blight on north-

---

[1] A.P.P. A/A 202 (Section du Panthéon-français, commissaire de police, 4
germinal an VII [24 March 1799]): '. . . Un mémoire de plusieurs habitans de la
rue des Carmes demandant la suppression de l'amphithéâtre de dissection y tenu
par le C. Bichat, officier de santé démonstrateur . . . pour les motifs de l'insalu-
brité de l'air, de l'indécence des cadavres de femmes et d'hommes, exposés nuds
aux yeux des jeunes personnes de l'un et de l'autre sexe, l'horreur qu'inspirent ces
cadavres et les dangers qu'ils font courir de la vie aux femmes, et particulièrement
à celles enceintes, enfin sur l'impossibilité des principaux locataires des maisons
voisines dudit amphithéâtre de payer leurs contributions, si leurs maisons restent
vides par un plus long séjour du C. Bichat. . . .'

[2] See note L, p. 233.

[3] A.N. F15 270 (Fay, économe de l'hospice de l'Est, au Minsitre de l'Intérieur, 18 germinal an IV): '. . . Je vous ai exposé de vive voix les . . . malheurs
qui pouvaient résulter du voisinage du cimetière de l'Abbaye, déjà nous en res-
sentons les effets. Une odeur cadavérique est répandue dans la bâtiment qui

eastern and eastern Paris, as well as on south-eastern areas of the city. At that end of the city, both banks had this in common, if little else.

So much for the Seine and its numerous tributaries, a river network that so deeply conditioned the attitudes of Parisians, both towards one another, in the context of their own city, and towards a perimeter which, in terms of provisioning, would extend, even in normal years, as far as le Havre, as far as Bray, Troyes, and the valley of the Aube, as far as Montereau, and beyond, to the wood ports of the Yonne and the Cure, and the small towns and villages of the Loing, as far as Château-Thierry, Épernay, and Châlons by the Marne, as far as Soissons[1] and Neufchâtel by the Aisne, as far as Noyon, Chauny, and la Fère by the valley of the Oise, as far as La Ferté-Milon by the Ourcq,[2] and La Ferté-Alais via the Essonne. This river network offered even the most untravelled Parisian an acute awareness of his environment, an environment that extended to the Channel coast, from Dunkirk to the Seine estuary, to Burgundy and Champagne, Artois and Picardy, to the valley of the Loire.

It also imposed fixed *lieux de passage*, localities conveniently placed on the lifelines of Paris, and that would thus form a permanent map of suspicion. *These* categories of suspects, unlike the human ones,[3] did not

l'avoisine, et lorsque les chaleurs vont augmenter, le reste de l'hospice en sera infecté, il est donc urgent d'arrêter sur le champ le transport des citoyens des trois Sections [du faubourg Saint-Antoine], la mortalité étant plus considérable dans ce quartier que dans les autres, vue sa population. . . .'

[1] '. . . Les moulins des environs de Soissons sont inaccessibles pour les voitures. . . . La rivière de l'Aisne [?] qui va à Pontoise doit y transporter les grains pour y être moulus . . . Les routes de Château-Thierry, de Reims, de Laon et de Paris ont des chemins ferrés ou pavés, mais il y a peu de moulins sur ces routes . . .' (A.N. F11 1177, Gilbert, commissaire à Soissons, au Ministre de l'Intérieur. 20 frimaire an IV).

[2] 'Les grains des magasins de Villers-Cotterets devront être dirigés par terre sur la Ferté-Milon où ils seront chargés sur des bateaux . . .' (A.N. F11 1177, rapport du 29 prairial an IV). See also A.N. F11 1185 (s.d. prairial an IV): '. . . à une lieue de Mary, lieu d'embarcation pour Paris de tout ce qui descend la rivière d'Ourcq sur laquelle est située la Ferté-Milon. . . .' Mary is opposite the port of Lizy-sur-Ourcq.

[3] And, of course, not only in 1793 and the year II. Pierre MacOrlan wrote his novel, *La Tradition de minuit*, in 1929. It centres on a *bal musette*, *le Bal des Papillons*, situated near the quai de Versailles, near the *viaduc d'Auteuil*, 'petite boutique qui sentait le port d'eau douce et les kermesses de mariniers; . . . le soleil animait gaiement une bande de Kabyles qui sortaient de chez un boulanger, les poches pleines de croissants chauds. . . .' The plot centres round the murder of the owner of the bar, Noël *le Caïd*; in the course of the investigation, one of the

change: river ports like Vernon, Mantes, Meulan, Pontoise, Beaumont, Pont-Saint-Maxence, Bray, Montereau, Moret, Chauny, Meaux, Lagny, Épernay, La Fère, Soissons, and, nearer still, Gennevilliers, Argentueil, and Saint-Germain, occupied a permanent place in the demonology of the Parisian, as he anxiously scrutinised the *mercuriales* or the height of his river.

---

characters, clearly au fait with the ingrained habits of the Paris police, makes the following comment: '. . . La police d'ailleurs est assez silencieuse. Elle prend le vent. . . . On va faire des rafles sur les quais et dans toutes les boîtes de Javel. Les uns pensent que l'assassin est un Kabyle ou un Chinois, et les autres pensent que c'est un affranchi du quartier. . . .'

4

Paris and Versailles: The Politics of Mistrust 1793—1798

'C'est le p'tit *Bal des Papillons*
La java que l'on chante;
C'est le râle d'un vieux couillon
Qui meurt dans la soupente.
Dansez, filles de Billancourt
Sur la berge gluante
Doux souvenirs du point du jour
        Serments d'amour
Dansez aux sons d'l'accordéon
Au p'tit *Bal des Papillons*.'

Une chanson de Marie-Chantal Fosseuse,
Pierre MacOrlan, *La Tradition de minuit.*

'... Les express qui venaient de Boulogne, de Clermont-Ferrand, de Belfort, avaient traversé sans s'y arrêter, avec un claquement d'air contre les verrières, les chefs-lieux des pays d'Île-de-France: bourgs cossus, marchés des campagnes à blé, bons nourrisseurs de bourgeois et de bestiaux; répondants des terroirs anciens qui ont gardé leur race et leur langue. Paris, qui les tolère et les emploie, les empêche depuis dix siècles de dépasser une certaine taille: cent rues, cinq cents notables, dix mille foyers ....

... chaque fois que Paris s'était débarrassé d'une enceinte, il s'était heurté aux Villages; un peu surpris chaque fois et décontenancé; car s'il n'ignorait pas leur existence, il avait omis d'en tenir compte dans ses rêves d'avenir ....

... En 1908, elle était remplie. Paris avait fini par venir à bout de sa campagne intérieure. Les chèvres ne paissaient plus aux flancs de la rue Caulaincourt. Les troupeaux de vaches quittaient les parages des Buttes-Chaumont, pour s'exiler au-delà de l'enceinte, vers Romainville. Le val de Bièvre dépouillait ses jardins, devenait le tracé d'un égout. ... Les villages capturés, qui portaient de si beaux noms: Clignancourt, Charonne, Grenelle—avaient laissé passer entre eux un épanchement de mornes quartiers grisâtres, une crue de maisons, rapide et triste, qui les avait soudés l'un à l'autre, noyés dans une même pâte. ...'

Jules Romains, *Le 6 octobre.*

'. . . Paris un seul jour sans subsistances anéantit la République, par les secousses et le bouleversement général qu'il communique à toute la France . . .' (Commission des Subsistances à Antoine Descombes, 4 brumaire an II [25 October 1793]).[1]

'. . . La loi reste sans force dans un pays où la force armée est dans les mains des gens qui ne se soumettent point à la loi et qui se tiennent tellement tous qu'il est impossible d'acquérir aucune preuve de leurs prévarications . . .' (comité de surveillance de Nanterre au Comité de sûreté générale, 22 nivôse an II [11 January 1794]).[2]

Parisian and Rural Rivalry: The Politics of Provisioning

THE two extracts quoted above both date from the period of the Terror; and they illustrate, in their somewhat brutal simplicity, the principal points of friction between a jealously affirmed Parisian food autonomy, and the equally strong sense of rural solidarity.[3] Paris, argues the *Commission des Subsistances*, a body directly responsible to the Commune, must be in sole control of its own food supplies. Certainly, few documents could have illustrated more dramatically what so many of the political conflicts of the year II were about: what exactly was the place of Paris to be within the Republic?[4]

---

[1] A.N. W1a 94 (tribunaux révolutionnaires, papiers d'Antoine Descombes condamné).

[2] A.N. F7 4784.

[3] '. . . Les campagnes sont exclusivement remplies de cultivateurs; celui qui ne l'est pas pour son compte l'est pour celui des autres, ou il travaille pour eux; après le propriétaire, ce sont les hommes de charrue, les moissonneurs, les batteurs, les charrons, les maréchaux, les bourreliers; tous ces gens-là travaillent durant toute l'année pour le laboureur; ils dépendent . . . de lui. Restent après cela les tailleurs et cordonniers . . . les maçons et charpentiers . . . et le cabaretier . . . tout le monde dans un hameau dépend donc du laboureur. Quand on dépend, on est dévoué . . .' (Lettre de la Commission des Subsistances de la Commune à Antoine Descombes, commissaire dans le District de Provins, 18 septembre 1793, A.N. W1a 94).

[4] '. . . Cependant le Ministre de l'Intérieur vient de nous écrire une lettre qui infirme l'intention par lui ministre de faire faire des réquisitions par des commissaires de sa nomination, et qui correspondraient avec lui. Ce seroit à proprement parler transporter l'administration des subsistances dans les mains du Ministre de l'Intérieur. Nous avons fait des observations là-dessus à notre concitoyen Paré

How was one to conciliate the interests of Paris with those of the Nation?[1] What were to be the relations between the Parisian authorities and a government that had its seat in the middle of the city, Section des Piques? How far was the respect of the autonomy of local municipal authorities, in the *communes* of the periphery, to be conciliated with the needs of the city's population in the vital matter of provisioning?[2] Was it right for the Sections on the edge of the city to interfere in the internal affairs of the villages almost within sight of the gates? Were the villagers to be their own masters in such important matters as the decision to keep their churches open and to allow the celebration of the old feast days? Was the local *garde nationale* the sole repository of armed force, or could Parisian soldiers be sent in to impose the will of the city? Were any limits to be set on the powers of local *maires*?

All these were conflicts, potential or real, that belonged almost exclusively to the period of the Terror, though some of them continued to be points of contention in the course of the five following years. The Sections themselves lost much of their importance in the spring of 1794; and, after Thermidor, as a result of the suppression of the forty-eight revolutionary committees and their replacement by the even more subservient twelve *comités d'arrondissement*, Paris lost its most effective means of intervention in the affairs of the neighbouring villages. At the same time, with the formation of the *Commune robespierriste*, provisioning was taken right out of the hands of any city authority, and was henceforth the exclusive concern of a government agency.

After Thermidor, provisioning and requisitioning were largely to be the responsibility of Boissy d'Anglas, who thereby incurred much of the popular odium attached to the famine conditions of the year III. In

---

. . . Cela a quelque liaison avec ce que tu nous écris hier que l'on travaille en tous sens pour que Paris ne se mêle plus de son approvisionnement. . . .' (La Commission à Descombes, 23 septembre 1793, ibid.).

[1] See for instance A.D. Seine D 4 AZ 626 (lettre de Guérin, Dessart et Cie, négotiants, 469, rue du Bac, au Département de Paris, à propos des huiles et du suif, 27 ventôse an II [17 March 1794]): '. . . On a mis en réquisition partout tout ce qu'on a trouvé de marchandises étrangères, cette mesure est bonne pour empêcher qu'on ne les tienne cachées et soustraites à la consommation, mais elles ne seront pas éternelles, que deviendroit-on ensuite? Est-ce pour l'approvisonnement de Paris qu'on les destine? Paris a certainement tout fait pour qu'on s'occupe de lui, *mais Paris n'est que le fils aîné de la grande famille républicaine, les autres Départements sont, si on le veut, les Cadets*. . . .'

[2] See note A, p. 234.

the year IV, provisioning and the administration of poor relief were to become the responsibilities of the Minister of the Interior, though both those of Justice and *Police générale* could also be involved. Throughout the Consulate and Empire, the administration and *police des marchés* were in the hands of the two Prefects. If Parisians did not starve in 1800 and in 1812, it was due primarily to their intervention.[1] Furthermore, after the spring of 1794, Parisians were not even to be allowed the small luxury of discussing the problem: it had become an affair of state, to be dealt with behind closed doors. The principal crime, in the eyes of the Thermidorian authorities, of the rioters of the spring and summer of 1795 was not to have called for the Constitution of 1793, or even to have said that things had been better in the time of Robespierre, but publicly to have claimed a share of responsibility in the distribution of cheap bread.

Again, in 1795, and throughout most of the Directory, Parisians were to be subjected to the summary justice of military courts, the *5me Division militaire* becoming as effective a power within the city as the Minister of Police. They were now to experience the insolence of garrison commanders, just as Lyon, Marseille, and many towns in the Midi had already done in the year II. After Thermidor, it is true, the Parisian press regained much of its vigour, but it was almost totally suppressed under the Consulate and Empire, so that the capital had no means of addressing itself to the rest of the country. At best, it was merely allowed to witness to the prestige of the new dynasty in much-publicised Court occasions.

It would be hard to say how the inhabitants of the periphery fared under these new conditions. For, after the end of 1795 and throughout the first fifteen years of the nineteenth century, village records are almost entirely mute on all matters of local, or indeed, national, interest.[2] The minutes of rural municipalities (*administrations cantonales*)

[1] Jean Tulard, *Nouvelle Histoire de Paris: le Consulat et l'Empire 1800–1815*, Paris, 1970, ch. vi, 'L'Approvisionnement de Paris', pp. 243–62.

[2] It is perhaps symptomatic of a change of emphasis in the relations between the villages and small towns of the Île de France and the central authorities that, as the imperial régime headed towards impending collapse and military defeat, the records of these municipalities become much more eloquent, and even critical. Higher authorities are blamed for the misbehaviour of passing troops and for massive requisitioning. As in all times of crisis, there is a visible return to the traditions of self-help. The *archives communales* of Moret, Montereau, and Dourdan, have much of interest to report on the subject of the drunkenness and disorderliness of the Cossack troops passing through in 1814 or garrisoned in these towns in the following year. With the return of normal conditions, the local records become once more almost entirely uninformative, though those of

palely reflect the great feast days of the régime: the Emperor's birth-day, the commemoration of victories, or, possibly, nearer home, the election of a *rosière*, for this was a régime which placed increasing emphasis on family solidarity and on the simple rural virtues. No doubt things remained much as they had always been, though, to judge from Jean Vidalenc's book on the rural population between 1815 and 1848,[1] life in the countryside, on the borders of Paris, as well as farther afield, became more uncomfortable, and poverty more insistent and degrading, as the rural population increased.

So much for the blacks and whites of opposing solidarities; the proud assertion of Parisian authority, the unity of the rural community.

The Formation of the Seine-et-Oise and the Containment of Paris

First of all, it is necessary to return to the new administrative and judicial units introduced by the Constituante. I have referred earlier to the fractionalisation of authority within the city itself, as a result of the increased importance of the Sections, as semi-autonomous bodies, deeply particularist, and satisfying varied and contrary collective interests, as well as illustrating a wide range of mental attitudes, dictated by topography, overcrowding, sociability, smell, and habit, and of the powers exercised within the Sections by the *juges de paix* and the *commissaires de police*. This process was, however, even more marked in the rural villages situated in the two Districts *extra-muros*, Franciade (Saint-Denis) and Bourg-l'Égalité (Bourg-la-Reine) that, with Paris itself, formed the Département de Paris. It was only during part of the Terror that a repressive body, the *comité de surveillance du Département de Paris*, possessed powers of intervention and arrest throughout the area, and these were only grudgingly recognised by the Committee of General Security, which, in the spring of 1794, intervened to remove altogether a body that might appear to exercise a rival political authority, and that contained, among its roving personnel, an alarming number of adherents of the Cordeliers club. It was indeed true that this committee had, along with the Ministry of War, been one of the most

Clichy, Colombes, and Vincennes report at length on the effects of the cholera epidemic of 1832. There is a return of interest in the early months of 1848, when, in some of the localities of the perimeter, clubs, formed in 1793, often resume their sittings, sometimes even using the same minute books, rescued from an attic or a cellar of the *mairie*.

[1] Jean Vidalenc, *La Société française de 1815 à 1848*, tome i, *Le Peuple des campagnes*.

successful areas of Cordelier penetration, even though people like Clemence and Marchand,[1] when the crisis came, were quite prepared to take an orthodox Jacobin line.

At the same time, the *Directoire du Département*, under Lulier, far from encouraging the implementation of the Terror in the *communes* of the periphery, seems, on the contrary, to have been more concerned to limit its effects, in the interest of their rural inhabitants. After Thermidor, effective authority within the two rural Districts, was to reside in the *juges de paix*, one to each *canton rural*, and in the *maires*—and, little was to be expected of them, in so far as the interests of Paris were concerned, when, as they nearly always would be, these would be in conflict with the preoccupations of their own *administrés*.

We have already had many occasions to refer to the apathy displayed by the *juges de paix* in matters of rural offences. A retired judge from the Oise, in a report to the Minister dated Prairial year VI [June 1798], put the case against them with considerable clarity and eloquence:

... Si les juges de paix dans les villes sont généralement bons, il en est bien peu dans les cantons ruraux qui soient au niveau de leurs fonctions. La rareté des sujets, la médiocrité de leurs traitements, l'inexactitude du paiement sont en partie cause de cet état fâcheux; mais la crainte de se compromettre, d'éprouver les funestes effets des vengeances, les liaisons de parenté et d'amitié, l'éloignement pour la plupart de la force armée m'ont paru les principaux motifs qui les retiennent dans la poursuite des délits, surtout s'ils sont connus dans les communes qu'ils habitent et par des domiciliés de leur arrondissement. ... Je me proposois une circulaire aux juges de paix. ... je les avois invités à prendre des renseignements sur les individus de leurs cantons dont les moyens d'existence sont inconnus; cette précaution m'avoit paru d'autant plus nécessaire qu'il m'avoit été démontré que les brigands connus sous le nom de *chauffeurs* étoient trop instruits des localités et des usages intérieurs des maisons où ils s'introduisirent pour n'avoir pas avec eux des hommes au fait de ces localités et de ces usages. ...[2]

Equally unreliable, in a similar rural setting, were the *jurys de jugement*, once it was a matter of bringing local people before the courts and exposing them to the full penalties contained in the Codes. No officials, complained another judicial official from the Oise to the Minister of Justice, in the year VII, were more likely to:

se laisser à leur tour entraîner par un sentiment d'humanité à acquitter de

---

[1] See my *Les Armées révolutionnaires*, pp. 528–32.

[2] A.N. BB 18 603 (Justice, Oise, directeur du jury d'accusation de l'arrondissement de Senlis, au Ministre, 19 vendémiaire an VI [10 October 1797]).

grands coupables; après avoir déclaré le délit constant, l'accusé convaincu, ils s'appésantissent sur la peine qu'il a méritée, et s'ils aperçoivent un moyen de la mitiger, ils le saisissent avec empressement. . . . il faut que le crime soit absolument dépourvu de tous moyens d'excuse, pour qu'ils se déterminent à déclarer la criminalité de l'intention. . . . Un homme s'étoit embusqué à la trouée d'une haie par laquelle passoit tous les soirs pour retourner chez lui un berger auquel il en vouloit depuis longtems, il tombe sur ce berger à l'improviste, il le mutile à la tête et le laisse pour mort, après trois mois du plus grand danger pour sa vie, ce malheureux paroît aux débats, un oeil absolument perdu et le visage rempli de cicatrices, il n'avoit échappé que par une espèce de miracle; deux témoins avoient vu l'accusé se cachant derrière la haie une heure avant l'assassinat, quatre avoient trouvé le berger baigné dans son sang, l'accusé auquel on demandoit où il étoit la nuit du délit, répondit qu'il étoit à chercher ses vaches, tout prouvoit contre lui! le jury de jugement déclare que le délit est constant, que l'accusé en est l'auteur, qu'il a agi dans des intentions criminelles, mais qu'il n'y a pas de guet à pans; en conséquence, le tribunal prononce six années de détention. Le coupable s'est bien gardé de se pourvoir en cassation, le jugement a été exécuté dans les 24 heures. . . .[1]

So much for the repressive zeal of a body that constituted an essential link in the chain of repression, in any rural area, whether in the Oise or in the exactly similar conditions offered by the two rural Districts of the Département de Paris, which, owing to the mere fact of their proximity to the capital, would be even more inclined to turn a blind eye to the crimes committed by their own neighbours. Even less was to be expected, in this respect, of the *garde nationale*: the comments made, in the course of the Terror, by the revolutionary committee of Nanterre: '. . . La loi reste sans force dans un pays où la force armée est dans les mains des gens qui ne se soumettent point à la loi et qui se tiennent tellement tous qu'il est impossible d'acquérir aucune preuve de leurs prévarications,' and that we quoted at the beginning of this chapter, on the subject of the total unreliability of armed force, in the context of a village within sight of Paris, could be applied to any rural locality in this Department or in near-by ones.[2]

Furthermore, the whole area formed by the Département de Paris was surrounded, and, indeed, contained—as it had been intended that

[1] A.N. BB 18 603 (Justice, Oise).

[2] A.N. BB 18 846 (Somme, commissaire près le tribunal d'Amiens au Ministre, 21 prairial an V): '. . . Je me plains de l'inactivité de la garde nationale. Tous les postes sont presque toujours vides; plus de patrouille, plus de surveillance, plus de frein. Les Brigands ne sont contenus ni intimidés. . . .'

it should be—within the bizarre, but effective, encircling embrace of the Département de Seine-et-Oise, surely one of the most peculiar administrative units ever to have been created, and the formation of which was perhaps the most anti-Parisian of a series of measures carried out by the decidedly physiocratic and federalist-inclined members of the Constituent Assembly, deeply suspicious of the capital and of its potentially dangerous inhabitants; it may have been significant that the moving light of the *comité de division* should have been Thouret, who was a deputy of Rouen. (He showed as much concern to promote the administrative interests of that city, at the expense of Le Havre, with results that have lasted to the present day, as he did to place a narrow limit on those of Paris; his physiocracy was clearly of the elastic kind, for him *les dangers de la ville* would be spelt out as *les dangers de la plus grande ville*; they apparently would not apply to the ninety thousand inhabitants of the Norman capital. But le Havre, with a population of only twenty thousand, was too dangerous to be allowed any say in the affairs of its hinterland.[1]) Later, from the Directory onwards, the Département de Paris became the Département de la Seine; the change of name is indicative of a deliberate effort to demote the capital.

The Seine-et-Oise was to embrace both banks of the upper and lower Seine, at their points of entry to and exit from the Paris area, as well as parts of the valleys of the Oise, the Marne, the Bièvre, and the Essonne; and most of the principal supply routes of the immense city passed through the *communes* under its administration, including the *chefs-lieux* of the nine Districts: Versailles itself, Montagne-Bon-Air (Saint-Germain-en-Laye), Mantes, Pontoise, Dourdan, Montfort-le-Brutus (Montfort-l'Amaury), Étampes, Corbeil, and Gonesse. The Department had been conceived by its creators as a check on Paris initiatives in the towns and villages of the whole vast perimeter: the inhabitants, for instance, of Étampes, Dourdan, Corbeil, Arpajon, Montlhéry, Gonesse, or Pontoise, took their orders from Versailles, although, in fact, Paris was much nearer, and although they thus often had to pass through the capital, from one end to the other, in order to put their grievances to the authorities of Versailles, or even to obtain one of the innumerable paper checks that the Revolution and the bureaucratic régimes that followed imposed, in increasing number, on the ordinary citizen. In this respect, at least, Paris was not the only victim of such discrimination; and it was not without reason that some of the leading inhabitants of such places as Corbeil, Pontoise, or Dourdan were, at various periods, to petition for the formation of

[1] See note B, p. 234.

Departments of their own that would remove them from the distant and, therefore, expensive, tutelage of the old royal capital.

The Seine-et-Oise was no doubt also thought of as the potential point of departure of repressive operations against the capital, a function that was to be given its most dramatic illustration, after the outbreak of the Commune, when the *chef-lieu* of this circular unit became the seat of the Provisional Government and the chosen haven of M. Thiers, as well as of the Prussian High Command, united at least, along with most of the Versaillais and of the many wealthy Parisians from the western districts who had sought refuge there, with their children and their servants, in their hatred and fear of the Communards. From the very outbreak of the Revolution, the relations between Paris and Versailles had been extremely unhappy, embittered as they were by mutual fears, and, on the part of the Parisians, by contempt for a 'population of lackeys', and on that of the Versaillais, by a sense of deprivation, rendered tangible by the widespread unemployment caused by emigration and by the closing down of the houses of the great. Indeed, by the time of the Terror, a great many Versaillais, of both sexes, had themselves emigrated to Paris in search of work; by the year II, it was estimated that the population of Versailles had dropped by as much as 20,000, though this was certainly an exaggeration. But as a great many of these neo-Parisians were either domestic servants or other kinds of hangers-on of the *ci-devants*, far from being welcomed as converts, and as victims of the Revolution—and this they certainly were—they were often treated with marked suspicion, especially in the western and south-western Sections, and their presence *intra-* rather than *extra-muros*, came to be regarded as an additional potential threat to the revolutionary régime. What made matters worse, as we shall see, was that, in the spring of 1794, their place was taken by a large number of former nobles who, on being expelled from Paris, naturally gravitated towards a town familiar to most of them, and in which some still possessed houses. Thus, mutual antipathies between the inhabitants of the two towns had a long history; it is indeed likely that they dated back to a period before a Revolution that lent them additional force. The scene depicted by Darien, in *Bas les coeurs !*, as the well-to-do and well-dressed Versaillaises set about the bedraggled Communardes, avenue de la Reine, as they were led, manacled, and chained, between the sailors and soldiers of the armies of repression, with their umbrellas, was merely the last, most dramatic, stage in a long history of what represented, in its most dramatic form, class, as well as Paris versus the Rest, antipathies. Perhaps Darien too, who was a native-born Parisian, as well as a Protestant, had grown up with inherited prejudices on the subject of the *chef-lieu* of the Seine-et-Oise![1]

Be this as it may, at all times, even in electoral terms, the function of the Seine-et-Oise was to surround Paris by a *cordon sanitaire*—or, to parody a more current expression, a *ceinture verte*—of a very conservative rural vote, dominated by *notables*, big farmers, and grain merchants (especially in the rich grain-producing areas of the Pays de France and the Vexin Français), and, after the Revolution, by people who had successfully speculated in the acquisition of *biens nationaux*, or who had bought themselves country seats or farms; these were to prove providential to many wealthy Parisian families from the western districts, during the three famine years of 1794, 1795, and 1796: the *notaire* and his family with whom the young Duval[2] lodged, during his period as a *clerc* under the Thermidorian Reaction, ate pure white bread (in the presence of the poor young man who had to make do with the indigestible substance obtainable on a ration card) provided by their estate near Corbeil. People who had thus invested in rural properties and had themselves become producers of grain, would have rapidly shed any commitment they may have previously felt towards the collective interests of the resident Parisian and would have readily become recruits to rural egoism. When, under the Directory, their country houses were the object of nightly attacks, during the winter months, while they were back in the capital, from groups of *chauffeurs* and malefactors, it was typical that they should have attributed these attacks to the activities of marauding groups coming *out* of Paris before the *barrières* had closed, and returning to the relative anonymity of the peripheral Divisions before dawn, whereas, in fact, all the evidence points to the fact that they were the work of countrymen recruited locally and generally protected by the local judicial authorities. It was difficult to have it both ways and to divide the year between the summer salubrity of the countryside and the winter comforts of the capital. The fate of such people illustrates how difficult it was to cross the great divide.

The *Constituants* at least obtained most of the safeguards that they had sought, but, of course, at a price; for they had given powerful hostages to the forces of entrenched rural immobilism and economic 'communalism'. They were also over-optimistic in their belief that such areas could be placed entirely beyond Parisian interference. During the

---

[1] R. C. Cobb, 'Indignant Patriot', *A Second Identity*, London, 1969, pp. 242–55.

[2] Duval, *Souvenirs thermidoriens*, quoted in *The Police and the People*.

conditions prevailing under the Terror—conditions, it is true, that they could hardly have foreseen, so exceptional were they—the District de Gonesse, above all, was to be the scene of bitter class conflict, with village artisans and landless labourers walking to Paris to enlist the help of the Revolutionary Committees of the northernmost Sections: Bondy, faubourg du Nord, faubourg Poissonnière, areas themselves both exceedingly poor and inhabited largely by *jardiniers, maraîchers, éleveurs de lapins, nourrisseurs de bestiaux*, and other artisans in country pursuits; and this help was generally eagerly accorded. The *commissaires* of such Sections either wrote to the Committee of General Security, or dispatched one of their members to put the case of the *frères opprimés des campagnes* to it in person. Vadier and his colleagues were especially sensitive to events in the Pays de France or the Brie, and, as a result of direct intervention of this kind, a company of the Paris Revolutionary Army, headed by a *commissaire révolutionnaire*, would soon be on its way on the road northwards. During the months of the *Grande Terreur*, the District de Gonesse was thus massively subjected to Parisian penetration, at all levels, from that of rival groups of *Représentants en mission*—at one time there were eight of them in the District at the same time—to that, much more effective, of members of Revolutionary Committees acting in conjunction with local artisans.[1]

Local Demagogues and the Grande Peur of Ventôse-Germinal year II

This brings us to the great political crisis, one of the most important of the Revolution, that enveloped the whole of France, including the villages of the perimeter, in the early months of 1794. *Le pourtoir de Paris* was especially vulnerable in this respect, for once many of the *notables* had been temporarily, or permanently, removed from positions of influence, in the late summer and autumn of 1793—and some of them were sent before the Revolutionary Tribunal, the District of Gonesse providing Fouquier-Tinville with a number of his more eminent victims[2]—the inhabitants of these small rural *communes*, most of them illiterate, were readily to fall under the influence of strangers who had but recently settled in such places. Often these were people who hoped to escape from the witnesses of an unsavoury past, or to make a break with a life previously marked by economic failure or by personal unhappiness—Musquinet-Lapagne was one of many who, in 1792 or in 1793, took this sort of opportunity *pour se refaire une virginité*

[1] *Les Armées révolutionnaires*, pp. 190, 377(26), 466, 467, 477, 478, 493–4.
[2] Ibid., p. 505 (136).

républicaine[1]—and who were able rapidly to acquire considerable local influence, whether *à la force du poumon*, or as a result of measures that were sometimes distinctly demagogic, or again as a result of a charity both ostensible and well-placed as an investment in future political successes.[2] The Chevalier de Valmont in *Les Liaisons dangereuses* had used a timely charitable intervention, through the medium of one of his servants—anonymous, of course, but none the less identifiable as he was wearing the Chevalier's livery—as a leap forward in the siege and eventual seduction—a long-term and carefully planned military operation (Laclos was not an artillery officer for nothing)—of the virtuous *Présidente*: in the summer château-season, potential beneficiaries would never be lacking, and one would not have to look far to discover some wretched *chaumière* the thatch roof of which had caught fire.

Charity, similarly well-employed, could be used, in the very different conditions of the Terror, when seduction was no longer a primary concern—though of course it continued to have its full-time devotees —to build up political influence, often in a matter of months. Rural people might be suspicious of strangers; but if the latter spent enough, brought enough custom, and succeeded in getting some local grievance remedied at the level of *chef-lieu* de District, or with a court, suspicion might easily turn to unstinted trust and gratitude. Henri Rousseville seems to have had a nose for detecting such people and there are frequent references to them in his reports to the Committees of Government, in the summer of 1794.

J'ai acquis des données sur Benoît et le Noir, qui se dénoncent mutuellement [he wrote, on 28 Floréal [17 May] on the subject of two residents of Choisy-le-Roi], le premier jouit de l'estime de tous les patriotes. . . . le second est un de ces nouveaux installés dans les communes rurales qui a flatté les habitants des campagnes, s'est servi de leur confiance pour surprendre une place d'agent national et n'a aucun moyen d'existence. . . .[3]

Later, he was to accuse Le Noir of having saved a local aristocrat, Sanville, from arrest, and of having acted as a go-between for Danton when the latter was negotiating the purchase of his house there.

In the following month, on 11 Prairial, at the height of the scare following the Admirat attempt, he reports, in similar terms, on a

---

[1] *Reactions to the French Revolution*, pp. 107–14. See also n. B, p. 234.

[2] A good example is that of Marc Dolle, who, in the course of the Terror, set up in the *commune* of la Guillotière. See my *L'Armée révolutionnaire parisienne à Lyon et dans la région lyonnaise*, Lyon, 1952.

[3] A.N. F7 4631 d 2 (Caille, Rousseville au Comité de salut public, 28 floréal an II). See also note C, p. 235.

wealthy inhabitant of Neuilly, Bonnard, a retired barrister who, before
the Revolution, had acted as agent in France for the duc des Deux-
Ponts, and who had succeeded, in the course of the winter of 1793, in
building up for himself a considerable following among the poorer inhabitants of the village; these included a carpenter, Darud, 'son homme-
lige', a laundryman, Fournier, a water-carrier, Dumay, L'Héritier
'sans état', Jouvain, *nourrisseur de bestiaux*, and Royer, *facteur à la poste
aux lettres*, a group that Rousseville would have us believe represented
the 'hébertistes de Neuilly' and that totally dominated the local club.
Bonnard, who was to survive the Terror, was a very rich man, with
house property and land in Neuilly, Montmorency, and Samois-sur-
Seine, near Fontainebleau.[1] His principal crime appears to have been
the total support that he received from the *société populaire* that, on
8 Germinal—the date could not have been more ill-chosen—had petitioned for his release.

Rousseville, himself a former priest, was even more knowledgeable,
and far more condemnatory, on the subject of the leading figure in the
village of Vaugirard, Gilbert Bourdeaux, the founder and secretary of
the local club; Bourdeaux had originally come to Vaugirard, according
to Rousseville, in December 1791, as a juror priest. He had previously
been *vicaire* at Poissy, then at le Tremblay. Suspected of having been
the father of a baby girl who had been sent to Paris as a foundling, he
had been stoned by a group of women, after celebrating mass. It was at
this stage that he had decided to leave Vaugirard, taking up, this time,
the *cure* at Antony (he stuck consistently to the villages of the perimeter); but later he returned. In June 1793, he had organised a procession through the village for the *Fête-Dieu*; but he had handed in his
lettres de prêtrise to Chaumette, ahead of Gobel. Later, he is said to
have invited Momoro to talk to the local club. He was arrested on 17
Germinal year II in Paris where he had taken refuge, 17 rue des Lombards, an address that would suggest a lodging-house (Bourdeaux,
who, like Rousseville, had spent most of his life in the villages of the
Paris region, appears to have been unacquainted with this particular
aspect of *les dangers de la ville*, for a lodging-house was the last place
in which anyone in his senses would hide). He was charged with
having attempted to raise up the Vaugirard club, which had been the
instrument of his ambition, against the *autorités constituées*, that
is, the municipality. He had accused them of failing to provide the
inhabitants with adequate food supplies, and of fiendishly conceived
schemes to starve out the capital. In this instance his attacks against the

[1] A.N. F7 4607 d 4 (Bonnard), and see note D, p. 236.

municipality misfired, for, less fortunate than Bonnard, the local
demagogue of Vaugirard, who like so many ultra-revolutionaries of
his type, had attempted to set the local club against the municipality,
composed of inhabitants of longer standing—and many of these
conflicts could be described as ranging the older residents against the
newcomers, themselves backed by the poorer elements of the population—was condemned to death by the Revolutionary Tribunal on 27
Prairial year II [15 June 1794]. Bourdeaux was executed on the same
day.[1]

Another locality on the perimeter, Belleville, though it does not
figure specifically in the reports of Rousseville on the subject of local
demagogues (he was, however, to give the place plenty of attention
later in the summer, in the context of colonies of nobles present there),
seems at least to have been the terrain of bitter personal feuds, especially
within the local club, from the early winter of 1793,[2] right up to and
indeed beyond the spring crisis of 1794. From Frimaire to late Ventôse,
the appeals in favour of union and harmony are so numerous and so
pressing that it is clear that the *société* was becoming the object of
faction fights, all the worse for the fact that they were being fought out
within a small, tight community, *entre gens de connaissance,* and no
doubt between the established inhabitants and those who had arrived
more recently. There are repeated mutual accusations of demagoguery,
of false patriotism. The leading personalities of the club may offer some
clue as to what these incessant disputes were in fact about.

We have already referred to Huet,[3] who, although apparently a

---

[1] A.N. F7 4609 d 1 (Bourdeaux) and F7 4612 d 2. His second arrest had been
ordered by an *arrêté* of the Committee of Public Safety, dated 4 Prairial [23
May] and signed by Robespierre, Carnot, and Couthon. Again, the Committee
of General Security does not appear to have been consulted in a matter that was
clearly in its province, all the more so because Bourdeaux was arrested in Paris
itself.

Being on one of the roads from Versailles to Paris, Vaugirard was naturally
extremely suspect in Parisian eyes, especially in those of the militants of the Section des Invalides and that of Bonnet-Rouge. Similar suspicions may be detected
in a remark made, in Brumaire year III [Oct.–Nov. 1794], on the subject of the
club that had been set up in the village of Sèvres in 1791: '. . . la société de Sèvres
. . . a eu le courage (et il en falloit alors) [in 1791] de s'installer au centre de
Saint-Cloud, Bellevue, Meudon, et sur la route de Versailles à Paris . . .' (A.D.
Seine-et-Oise L 11m Versailles 70, sociétés populaires du district de Versailles).

[2] See note E, p. 236.

[3] See note A, this chapter, p. 234. See also A.D. Seine D 4AZ 590 (détails
biographiques des membres de la société populaire de Belleville) '. . . *Huet,* 41
ans, droguiste, reçu le 14 avril 1791. . . .'

founder member of the club, and thus anything but a newcomer, had drawn attention to himself, in the course of the early winter, by raising with the Département de Paris a number of awkward questions on the ticklish subject of the privileges enjoyed by the capital, in contrast to the rural *communes* of the perimeter, in the matter of provisioning. He seems to have been busily engaged in stirring the pot of class jealousy throughout this period. In the session of 8 Nivôse [Saturday 28 December 1793], for instance, another member, Jean-Antoine Gay-Astier, refers to these disputes:

... Citoyens, dans notre dernière séance, le C. Huet a fait une motion qui tendoit à inculper les citoyens qu'il nomme bourgeois, en les accusant de ne pas se faire connaître dans leurs Sections (ou Communes) que parce qu'ils sentoient qu'ils en étoient nécessaires, et qu'à cet effet ils cherchoient à s'introduire dans les Sociétés populaires, pour s'y faire la réputation de bons Citoyens.

Mais j'ai dit, Citoyens, qu'ils n'y avoient pas de bourgeois parmi nous, que nous étions tous des sans-culottes et que nous ne devions former qu'une même famille ... qu'il ne fallait pas intimider par des dénonciations vagues des citoyens sans reproche, ni attaquer en particulier les gens aisés, en les supposant d'être des égoïstes, et enfin qu'en cherchant à les éloigner de l'enceinte de la Commune, c'étoit faire un tort général à tous les Etats, et qu'étant tous subordonnés des uns aux autres, que la classe des gens aisés devenoit utile; j'ai ajouté que si l'on fesoit des motions tendantes à éloigner les citoyens aisés de la Commune, je ne saurois à qui vendre mes maisons, et que par ce moyen je me trouverois dans l'impossibilité de faire honneur à mes engagemens. ... Je suis descendu de la tribune aux bruits des applaudissemens, et dans le moment trois de nos frères n'ont pas craint de me dire avec un air menaçant que ma motion mettoit le trouble et le désordre dans l'assemblée. Vous avez entendu les calomnies atroces du C. Huet qui ... a fini par dire que j'étois un Marchand d'argent. ... J'ai encore entendu dire que ma motion étoit une cabale montée et préparée, et que j'avois un parti dans l'assemblée. ...[1]

From the *Tableau des membres*, we learn that Gay-Astier *père* was a comparatively recent inhabitant of Belleville. Born in Romans and aged forty, 'négotiant demeurant à Lyon à l'époque du 14 juillet 1789, depuis à Bordeaux, et en 1790 à Paris, rue neuve eustache no 7, jusqu'au mois de juillet 1792, qu'il a fixé son domicile à Belleville, admis à la Société le 28 frimaire l'an 2 [18 December 1793]'.[2] He was thus a personality who would fulfil most of the conditions that suspicious observers like

[1] A.D. Seine 4 AZ 590 (société populaire de Belleville, séance du 8 nivôse an II).

[2] A.D. Seine 4 AZ 590 ('142. Gay-Astier, Jean-Antoine ...').

Rousseville would detect in the formation of local demagogues, able, thanks to their wealth, to swing opinion and to form a party among the poorer and less educated sections of the community. On the other hand, according to another interpretation, especially at this time, it would have been equally easy to describe Huet as a trouble-maker and as an *hébertiste de banlieue*.

The quarrels went on, and there are further references to false patriots and demagogues. On 12 Pluviôse [31 January 1794] the *société* passed a resolution:

La Société populaire de Belleville . . . excluoit d'avance ces hommes hypocrites, qui ne se couvrent du manteau de patriotisme que pour déchirer plus sûrement la Patrie, ces aristocrates déguisés, que la crainte de passer pour suspects force à un langage simulé, qui prennent le Bonnet de l'homme libre pour couvrir leur amour de l'esclavage, qui s'habillent avec la carmagnole du sans-culotte, pour faire oublier avec l'or qu'ils enfouissent les vices et l'orgueil qui les dominent. . . .[1]

Is this then a reference to Gay-Astier, or to one of the other well-to-do householders who had come up to live in Belleville since the beginning of the Revolution? He would certainly fit the book. But there were other late-comers to the *société*: '109. *Fulchic, Noël-Antoine*, né à Paris, âgé de 40 ans, prêtre demeurant à Belleville avant et depuis le 14 juillet 1789; il est employé depuis l'année 1793 dans les Bureaux de la Commission du Commerce et il est toujours résident à Belleville. . . .'[2] had only been admitted on 18 Frimaire, that is ten days before Gay-Astier. In the following month, Fulchic declared that he was giving up his functions as a priest.[3]

---

[1] A.D. Seine D 4AZ 590 (séance de la société populaire de Belleville du 12 pluviôse an II).

[2] A.D. Seine D 4AZ 590 (détails biographiques de quelques membres de la société populaire de Belleville, tirés du tableau dressé en exécution de la loi du 25 vendémiaire an III). Other late-comers to the club were: *Thévet*, 34, *peintre en paysage*, admitted in February 1793; *Lenfumé*, in July 1793; *Dargent père*, 62, *cultivateur*, and his son, admitted on 22 Brumaire year II [12 November 1793]; *Saint-Paul*, 47, *receveur de rentes*, on 2 Frimaire [22 November]; *Chevet*, 31, *marchand de vin*, on 25 Frimaire [15 December].

[3] 'Le motif qui m'a déterminé à renoncer aux fonctions du ministère du culte que j'exerçois parmi mes concitoyens est trop louable pour que je ne désire pas qu'il soit inséré dans le procès-verbal, je demande qu'après ces mots *renoncé à son état* il soit ajouté *qu'il sacrifie par amour pour ses concitoyens, à la tranquillité publique*. Fulchic.' In Nivôse, we gather, Fulchic was asking the club for its support in order to obtain a post in the extensive bureaucracy of the Ministry of War, *2me Division, partie des subsistances militaires*. This the club readily accorded him. Fulchic was thus being recommended to one of the strongholds of *hébertisme*.

Nor was this the end of the faction fights within the club and the *commune*. Lenfumé, a leading member of the club, aged forty-three, described as 'entrepreneur à l'illumination de Paris', a member since July 1793, made a passionate appeal in favour of unity, in the meeting that took place on 5 Ventôse [Sunday 23 February 1794]:

Je viens à cette tribune, le coeur navré, vous entretenir un instant de l'esprit de discorde et de parti qui cherche à se propager dans cette société. . . . Quelles sont donc les intentions criminelles de ceux qui se disent si hautement patriotes, pour oser souffler le venin de l'aristocratie parmi tous les citoyens de cette commune, en cherchant en même temps à jeter de la défaveur sur les fondateurs de cette société . . .? J'ai vu avec peine nos dernières séances se passer dans un prouat [sic] affreux. J'ai vu avec peine *un certain parti* se lever parmi nous, on veut nous désunir, serrons nous de plus près, on voudrait nous diviser. . . . aujourd'hui nous aurions la lâcheté de nous abandonner à des querelles particulières. . . .[1]

To any outside observer, especially in these early days of Ventôse, the allusion would be clear. *Un certain parti* had set up its tents on the heights of Belleville, overlooking Paris. The village was about to become the prey of demagogues and ultra-revolutionaries, anxious to discredit those who had founded the club and who had long enjoyed the confidence of their fellow-citizens. Any reference to internal disputes in the course of Ventôse must necessarily have more than a local significance, and the Belleville club, which was affiliated to the Jacobins rather than to the Cordeliers[2]—it was exceptional in this respect— seems to have been particularly well-informed of the course of events in the capital. On 22 Ventôse [12 March], the day before the leaders of

We do not know whether he obtained this new post (A.D. Seine 4 AZ 590, Ozéré au président de la société de Belleville, 22 nivôse an II).

[1] A.D. Seine D 4AZ 590 (séance de la société populaire de Belleville du 5 ventôse an II). He went on to suggest that the danger, if it existed, would come from outside, presumably from Paris or from those who had settled recently in the *commune*: '. . . Mais hors de ce temple sacré de la raison et de la philosophie, Citoyens, méfiez-vous que quelque génie malfaisant ne veuille vous tromper par d'horribles mensonges en cherchant à vous égarer de vos devoirs envers la patrie. . . .'

[2] The *société* was clearly well-established in the hierarchy of the more respectable clubs, for, on 27 Frimaire year II [17 December 1793], the *société populaire dite de Marat séante à Vanves* received the report of a member 'que d'après les ouvertures à lui faites par plusieurs membres de la Société populaire de Belleville *affiliée aux Jacobins de Paris*, il croit pouvoir assurer que lad. société donnera son affiliation à celle de Vanves. . . .' (A.D. Seine 4 AZ 590). The club agreed to this request on 8 Pluviôse [27 January 1794].

the so-called *hébertiste* faction were arrested, the wife of Sibillot, the *agent national*, then in prison—he was, it will be recalled, later to be guillotined—wrote to the club to ask for its support in favour of her husband; but the *société* appears to have maintained a prudent silence in answer to the poor woman's timid appeal.[1] On 14 Germinal [3 April 1794], no doubt on learning of the fate of the *dantonistes*, the club once more showed its concern to keep apace with events, writing to the Jacobins:

Citoyens frères et amis, dans ces circonstances allarmantes nous vous députons trois de nos frères, les Citoyens Louvain, Ozeré et Bouy, chargés de vous demander ce qui se passe, quelles mesures vous prenez dans ces crises, afin de nous y conformer, en vous assurant que notre société est en permanence et que chacun des membres est prêt à voler où le devoir de bon citoyen l'appelle. . . . Bodson, président. . . .[2]

With its *agent national* in prison and accused of a counter-revolutionary initiative, the *société* would be particularly anxious to display its orthodoxy.[3] But it is also clear, from a peculiar incident that occurred a few days later in the same month, that the panic that was sweeping the whole of *le pourtoir* during the Ventôse-Germinal crisis, had enveloped the terrified inhabitants of Belleville. For, on 19 Germinal [8 April 1794] the Directoire of the District de Franciade wrote to the *société*:

Nous apprenons, Citoyens, que la malveillance se plaît à répandre des bruits allarmans sur la destination des machines du C. Chappe élevées dans la commune de Belleville. Ils ne peuvent qu'entraver des opérations dont la Convention et le comité de salut public ont reconnu l'utilité. Nous vous invitons à prendre toutes les mesures qui seront en votre pouvoir pour découvrir les auteurs de ces bruits, à nous les dénoncer, et à veiller par tous les moyens possibles à la conservation de ces machines télégraphiques. Nous écrivons aussi au Comité de Surveillance et à la Municipalité de votre commune pour qu'ils ayent, ainsi que vous, une surveillance active sur les malveillans qui cherchent à semer des inquiétudes et à préjudicier à la chose publique.[4]

Thus, in the highly-charged atmosphere of the spring of 1794, even Chappe's sun telegraph—commemorated to this day in the name of the rue du Télégraphe in what had once formed the *commune* of Belleville —was enlisted as an element in the politics of panic and mistrust

---

[1] See note F, p. 237.   [2] See note G, p. 237.   [3] See note H, p. 237.
[4] A.D. Seine D 4AZ 690 (Directoire du District de Franciade, à la société populaire de Belleville, 19 germinal an II).

dividing Paris from the inhabitants of its immediate periphery. The sun telegraph must have appeared to the peasants and artisans of Belleville as some mysterious instrument directed both against themselves and the capital.

We are particularly well informed of events in Belleville, thanks to the existence of many of the minutes of its club, perhaps the only one of the two rural Districts some of the records of which have survived.[1] For the other localities, we are forced back on to the testimony of outside observers, and, above all, of Rousseville.

Another prominent personality who was to figure in repeated denunciations by the former priest during the spring and summer of the same year was a temporary resident—he, too, was a newcomer—of the always alarming village of Gentilly. If that were not in itself bad enough, in addition, the man in question, Julien Leroy, occupied the important and influential post of *économe* of the *maison nationale* of Bicêtre. In 1793, he had taken on the more acceptable, though rather baroque name of *Églator*; and one feels that to the suspicious Rousseville, who seems to have been especially uncharitable towards those who attempted to move with the times, although he himself had effected a much more difficult transition, with perfect success, this was a further indication of guilt.[2] *Églator* seems in fact to have been more imprudent than villainous; as second in command of such an alarming institution, at the head of a potential army of vagrants, convicts awaiting the departure of the *chaîne*, and delinquent boys, he should have stepped with care. This he certainly did not do; a member of the Cordeliers, like so many of these *apprentis-démagogues* of the suburban *communes* (no doubt because, in their inability to gain admission to the Jacobins, possibly on account of certain gaps that stood out in their pre-revolutionary and revolutionary past, they had to make do with the second best), he is said to have invited Ronsin and Momoro to visit him and to have taken the former on a conducted tour of the *cabanons*. What could they have been up to, coming to harangue the lost souls who were confined to that awful place? To people like Rousseville and, indeed, Fouquier-Tinville, the implication was clear: it was all part of the *complot des prisons*. And Ronsin, in the last fortnight of his life, seems to have made a regular tour of inspection of some of the more sinister buildings on the edge of Paris, appearing, on

[1] There are a few scattered minutes of the Bagnolet club in A.D. Seine 4 AZ 652.

[2] Rousseville, as has been stated, had been a priest: *vicaire* of Bagnolet and *curé constitutionnel* of Bercy.

10 Ventôse at the fort of Vincennes, allegedly hunting in the woods of
Bois-d'Arcy, while Mazuel remained at his lodging-house in Versailles.[1] He and the military commandant of Bicêtre, Vassard, were
denounced to the Revolutionary Tribunal, on 5 Germinal year II; of
the latter, it was stated, characteristically: 'Vassard cherchait à se
captiver tous les pauvres.'

Églator was himself arrested in Prairial year II, at the direct instiga-
tion of Rousseville, and on the orders of Robespierre and Couthon; the
pretext for his arrest was that he had allowed two *forçats* to escape; but
this happened so often that one suspects he was really being victimised
for political reasons, as yet another adventurer who had attempted to
form a party among the poor. He was still in prison, awaiting trial, at
the time of Thermidor, a fact which probably saved his life, as it did
those of a great many 'ultras', likewise victims of the spring 'purge'.
But he seems to have remained in confinement throughout the Thermidorian Reaction; for he bombarded the new Committee of General
Security and the *comité de législation* with letters and petitions, all
couched in hysterically violent and utterly confused terms—and which
he signed *Julien Leroy* (*Églator* had met a quiet death sometime after
the *hébertiste* trials). He was finally released under the amnesty of
Brumaire year IV and was re-armed as a result of an *arrêté* of the expir-
ing Committee of General Security, the last measures of which nearly
always tended to favour 'ultras' of this kind, dated 10 Brumaire
[Sunday 1 November 1795].[2] He then returned to Bicêtre; and from the
year IV to the end of the Directory, he was to bombard successive
Ministers of Justice with endless complaints about the state of the institution for the running of which he took administrative responsibility.[3] He was probably something of a crank. But he had been
lucky. So had Vassard.

So had his near neighbour, the architect and building contractor,
Palloy, who, throughout the Revolution, had traded in stones from the
Bastille (these he obtained easily as he had been entrusted by the
municipality with the task of removing the remains of the old prison),
and who, in 1793 and the year II, but not in the year III, always signed
his letters—and he too was a great letter-writer and a great nuisance—
le Patriote Palloy, with a capital P, as if he were the only one, enjoying
a monopoly of this virtue as well as of Bastille stones. Palloy had built

---

[1] *Les Armées révolutionnaires*, ii, pp. 813, 817.
[2] A.N. W1a 27 (tribunaux révolutionnaires, papiers de Fouquier-Tinville)
and A.N. AF II 279 (arrêté du Comité de sûreté générale du 10 brumaire an IV).
[3] A.N. BB 18 739–763 (Justice, Seine).

himself a great reputation as a public benefactor and a friend to the poor
—he was a very rich man—in the important market town of Sceaux.
Like Bourdeaux, Vassard, and *Églator*, he seems to have dominated his
local club, the *société républicaine de Sceaux-l'Unité*; like them too, he
affected demagogic attitudes. But he had been lucky enough to have
fallen into political disfavour at a much earlier date, at the end of
Frimaire [November–December 1793]. Palloy was arrested a fortnight
after Vincent and Ronsin, on 8 Nivôse year II [28 December 1793], and
remained in La Force till his release on 25 Ventôse [15 March 1794], as
a result of a decree of the Convention.

During his detention, he had written to his wife:

N'allez pas surtout chez Robespierre, car je ne le puis croire vertueux.
Avec de l'esprit, s'il est vertueux, il n'est qu'une bête, car il souffre que l'on
mette des hommes en place qui font tant de mal. C'est enfin lui (ou de son
aveu) qui a coopéré à la nomination de ce tartuffe Fleuriot. Raison de plus
de ne pas avoir confiance en Robespierre, c'est que les aristocrates dans la
prison en font leur dieu. Toutes les permissions de sortir ne sont que de lui.
Les intrigans nouveaux le pionnent et semblent être [. . .?] de son nom.
Plusieurs lettres . . . en sont la preuve. . . .[1]

This highly imprudent letter was sent sometime early in Ventôse. On
the fourth of the same month, he wrote to the Sceaux club, asking for
its support. He seems to have organised his campaign effectively,
obtaining his release at the very time that the *hébertiste* leaders were
being arrested, a fact that he and his family were quick to point out, in
an address to the Convention dated 26 Ventôse, the day after his
release. The address begins with the words: 'La cabale qui m'avait
plongé dans les fers est encore à bas, votre justice vient de les briser.
. . . votre décret qui m'a mis en liberté me donne le droit de poursuivre
en dommages-intérêts les auteurs de mon arrestation illégale. . . .'[2] The
address is signed: 'Palloy, Patriote; N. femme Palloy; B. Palloy fils;
D. fille Palloy, républicaine pour la vie'. It was then something of a
family business.

He was denounced on several occasions, during the summer, by
Henri Rousseville, who had no difficulty in identifying him as a local
demagogue. Indeed, he was much more than this, for, unlike people
such as Vassard and *Églator*, his influence was not confined to a single
commune: in October 1793, he seems to have enjoyed the support both

---

[1] A.D. Seine D 4AZ 719 (note autographe de Palloy à sa femme lors de sa
détention frimaire-germinal an II [These dates are in fact incorrect]).

[2] A.D. Seine D 4AZ 719 ('Adresse à la Convention nationale par la famille
Palloy le 26 ventôse').

of the Section Brutus and of a group of refugee Liégeois,[1] no doubt the *Comité des Belges et Liégeois Réunis*, a body that had an unerring eye for vociferous adventurers and noisy windbags.[2] At the time of his release, he was congratulated by the doubtful Delaunay.[3] Perhaps he may be placed at this time in the ranks of the *pourris*. But he managed to avoid a second arrest for the remaining months of the Revolutionary Government, despite the attentions of Rousseville, who may have been vaguely aware of his strongly-expressed hostility to Robespierre. In any case, after Thermidor, he was naturally to make the most of this, posing as a victim of *l'infâme Robespierre*.[4]

He re-emerged, then, in the year III, shorn of *le Patriote*, and lived long enough to compose welcoming odes to the Emperor of the French, to Louis XVIII, 'de la branche légitime des Bourbon', and to the King of the French, on their successive visits to the château de Sceaux, which, before the Revolution, had belonged to the duc de Penthièvre, the father-in-law of the duc d'Orléans. All these verses have been preserved in his dossier in the Archives de la Seine.

Many other Parisian witnesses of the events of the villages *sur le pourtoir* and of the activities of their public officials, whether of recent transplantation or long established, clearly shared the opinions so bluntly expressed by Rousseville. There is, for instance, an anonymous denunciation, in the papers of the Committee of General Security, of the *maire* of Clamart, Morel:

... à présent il empêche que le vin ne sorte de cette municipalité, disant que puisque Paris ne leur laisse pas rendre des subsistances comme savon, eau-de-vie, sucre, café et soude, ils ne laisseraient pas sortir leurs vins; et c'est toujours M. Morel qui est derrière le rideau. . . .[5]

Rousseville himself, writing on 30 Floréal [19 May 1794], reports to much the same effect:

... Le citoyen Bourdais [a Parisian police inspector] ... m'a confirmé ... que Charenton étoit un entrepôt d'agiotage et d'accaparement sur les vins, le poivre et diverses autres denrées. .... Il y a eu des motions dans les communes de Bobigny et de Drancy tendantes à ce que les municipalités empêchâssent l'exportation de toute la crême et de la moitié du lait à Paris. . . .[6]

---

[1] See note I, p. 238.

[2] Orient Lee, *Le Comité des Belges et Liégeois Réunis*, Paris, 1929.

[3] See note J, p. 238.   [4] A. D. Seine D 4AZ 719.

[5] A.N. F7 4774 52 pl. 1 (Morel).

[6] A.N. F7 4603 pl. 9 (Blot, Rousseville au Comité de salut public, le 30 floréal an II).

And there was plenty more of this sort of thing, especially concerning these villages on the southern tip of Paris. Writing this time on the subject of Thiais, Orly, Villejuif, Gentilly, and Montrouge, the Committee's favourite informant was to add: '. . . dans toutes ces communes, qui forment le pourtoir de Paris depuis la Barrière Charenton jusqu'à celle d'Enfer, l'esprit public, sans être mauvais, me paraît moins bon que dans les autres environs de Paris. . . .'[1]

In Fructidor, after the fall of Rousseville's patron, Robespierre, the emphasis is once more placed on the evil influence of local bigwigs, who attempt thus to pander to *l'égoïsme communal*,[2] in order to make themselves readily popular with their *administrés*. On this occasion, the report concerns Billoré, the Thermidorian *agent national* of Fontenay-aux-Roses. Billoré is alleged to have made a speech to the *assemblée générale* of the *commune*:

. . . c'était disgracieux de voir sortir le vin de la commune, n'en ayant presque plus. . . . je leur dis: bien, Citoyens, n'est-il pas bien douloureux pour la municipalité de voir partir tout le vin du pays et qu'un citoyen ne veuille pas vendre du vin aux cabaretiers du pays, qu'il aime mieux le vendre aux citoyens du dehors, que nous avons beaucoup d'ouvriers, même des citoyens qui vont en journée, qu'ils ne peuvent pas en avoir un demi-septier de vin pour leurs besoins. . . .[3]

A last example of this readiness, on the part of Parisian observers, to attribute the defence of local interests and a concern for the poor, and, more especially, an anxiety to meet the needs of local consumers, to the intrigues of demagogues and adventurers and to the presence in these villages to the south and south-east of Paris of those *qui s'y sont fait parachuter*, of *inconnus, venus on ne sait d'où* (and, like the Représentant Crassous, so long active in the Seine-et-Oise during the height of the Terror, this might be from Martinique), comes from Carrières-sous-Charenton. In this instance, the man is not a victim of Rousseville who had been sacked by this time, perhaps to resume his priestly functions. The incident is of more than local interest, even in the context of the difficult supply relations between the capital and its perimeter. It is also significant of the brief revival, as a direct consequence of 9 Thermidor and of the sudden and unexpected end of Jacobin centralisation, of the activities of local clubs, both within and outside Paris. On 10 Ventôse

---

[1] A.N. F7 4775 pl. 5 (Rousseville au Comité de salut public, le 2 floréal an II).
[2] See note K, p. 239.
[3] A.N. F7 4627 d 1 (Billoré).

year III [28 February 1795], almost a year after the *Grande Peur* of the spring of 1794, the municipality of Carrières had called a general meeting of all the inhabitants to whom it had put the desperate plight of the village: there was no more grain to be had 'et que le peuple n'avait qu'à aviser aux moyens de s'en procurer et que c'est une des principales raisons qui a provoqué l'ouverture de la société populaire.'[1]

The *société* met on the following day, 11 Ventôse, which characteristically, was a Sunday. (In these rural communes, one can hardly distinguish between a *société populaire*, of apparently impeccable revolutionary lineage, and an ancient village assembly, held by the menfolk, in the *cabaret, à la sortie de la messe.*) The meeting took place—and again the choice of locale is hardly fortuitous—'chez Louis-Michel Royer, 36 ans, marchand de vin', and it was decided—such was the naïveté of these poor countrymen and rivermen—to send a petition, in the name of the *société* (the *société*, by the mere fact of its recreation, exposed those who attended it to the terrible consequences of outlawry, as they were acting in defiance of a decree of the Convention which, at the beginning of the month, had suppressed all such clubs) to the Convention asking for supplies of grain to meet the immediate needs of a starving population.

Apart from Royer, who, as a *marchand de vin* admirably fits the bill as a perfect demagogue-designate, the man behind the decision to call the meeting is said to have been Philippe Bourdois, forty-one, 'menuisier blanchisseur aux Carrières', no doubt a deceptive description, for he seems to have been a *notable* of importance and wealth, as he was still, in the year III, an *électeur* of the Département de Paris. The Thermidorian authorities acted rapidly and with vigour; Bourdois and Royer were arrested on the twelfth, a Monday, and were cross-examined by the Committee of General Security on the Tuesday. They were still in prison on the twentieth, when a *démarche* in their favour on the part of their counsel to Merlin de Douai, the Minister of Justice, elicited the reply that he was unable to do anything to help them, as they were held on political charges, and as their fate lay with the Committee of General Security. I do not in fact know what became of them. But their initiative had been particularly ill-timed from their point of view, for they had been arrested within a month of the Germinal Days, when the Thermidorians really began to harden their hearts both towards popular agitation and neo-Jacobin efforts to exploit popular grievances. Carrières, as we know, had had a bad reputation under the

---

[1] A.N. F7 4612 d 2 (Bourdois).

Jacobin dictatorship, and it was unlikely to have earned a better one with the Thermidorians, quite as suspicious of the villages of the *pourtoir* as Rousseville and his kind had been.

Furthermore, people like Boissy d'Anglas, unwilling to admit that they themselves had largely contributed to the development of a famine situation in the early months of 1795, would naturally tend to attribute initiatives of this kind, as well as the outbreak of the *journée* of 12 Germinal, to the political machinations of *la Crête*, rather than to genuine popular fears of famine. Bourdois, in particular, clearly had some powerful protectors, and he was in a position to afford the employment of counsel. But he could easily be presented as a troublemaker and a demagogue, anxious to stir up the notoriously explosive population of a village composed almost entirely of bargees, sawyers, *flotteurs*, and *portefaix*, the inns of which were reputed to be the noisiest, the most violent, and the most disorderly of anywhere in the Paris region outside Montrouge. In fact, in this discussion of the possible rôle of adventurers, and doubtful newcomers in the village affairs of the periphery, Carrières-sous-Charenton offers a most convincing, most suitable, concluding note.

Our purpose, in this section, has not been to decide whether men like Bourdeaux, Leroy, and so on, were or were not demagogues, though one is inclined to think that some displayed most of the signs of the trade; we are not trying to set ourselves up in political judgement on them, for that would be impudent and unfair. What we have tried to demonstrate is how, given a certain set of circumstances, a certain period, and a certain place—and the place is most important—a man with a ready and devoted local following may suddenly emerge and may appear, especially in the eyes of the staider, more conservative-minded Parisian observer, himself probably drawing his information from such moderate bodies as the *Directoires de District*, or even from local landowners, wealthy *acquéreurs de biens nationaux*—it would be quite wrong to think that the voice of wealth had been in any way stifled during the Jacobin dictatorship—as a dangerous interloper, and an adventurer, specialising in the politics of exaggeration, in order to raise himself up on the shoulders of his poorer, more ignorant, and generally illiterate fellow-citizens. Such suspicions would be further confirmed by the fact that such people tended to work through the parallel institutions that had grown out of the Revolution, often using them as a weapon against a municipality or even a Revolutionary Committee (and some of the Revolutionary Committees of the periphery were as eager as were the *autorités constituées* to denounce to the

Committee of General Security the 'demagogic' initiatives of this type
of activist, especially during the spring crisis of 1794).

Some of these local leaders, it is true, were to act through their
municipalities and one or two even succeeded in being appointed
agents nationaux. But more generally, they might have been described
as *clubistes*; and, what is more, the clubs, which some of them had even
founded and had then continued either to preside over or to dominate
through *aboyeurs* and *hommes de paille*, were nearly all affiliated to the
Cordeliers,[1] rather than to the much grander, much more demanding
Jacobins, whose noses were too high in the air for them to be able to
perceive the existence of the small rural communities that crouched on
their doorstep, craving for even the humblest form of political recognition, much less to hear their cries of distress. The Jacobins, after all,
were grand people who, like Robespierre, had little time to give to the
always insistent claims of the *problème des subsistances*; they were ready
to extend *le baiser fraternel* to clubs in places like Nantes, Rouen, or
Strasbourg, but not to those in Clamart, Montrouge, or Issy-les-
Moulineaux. Jacobinism, apparently, was to be rationed; like the
statues on the place de la Révolution, it was to be limited to towns of a
certain importance.

Of course, the government-inspired thesis may not have been
entirely an invention of centralist propaganda on the part of the Committees and of their subordinate agents like Rousseville, Dugard, and
the other *commissaires observateurs*. One should certainly not entirely
exclude the element of political intrigue to which situations and
localities such as we have been describing must have offered at least a
tempting premium. For there did at least exist, on the very borders of
Paris, a situation that was ready to be exploited. The Cordelier leaders
—a small enough group in fact, as events were to reveal (but that was
also because events went against them): hardly more than a dozen in
all, out of a club of some hundreds of members—were very much in
need of a widening potential political clientèle, if they were ever to have
any chance of achieving political power at the government level: and,
in Ventôse, people like Momoro, Ronsin, Vincent, and even the
normally cautious Hébert spoke often enough as if this had been their
aim. Without new elections—and after Brumaire year II this possibility was excluded—they were unlikely to command any parlia-
mentary support. In the crisis of Ventôse-Germinal, their potential
support in the Convention amounted to about four people: Collot,

[1] See note L, p. 239.

Fouché, Châles, and Carrier, and all proved broken reeds when the crisis developed. Nor was it enough to control—or believe that they controlled—an army of bureaucrats at the level of the *Bureaux de la Guerre*. For most of these—*commissaires du pouvoir exécutif, commissaires civils, hommes de liaison, apôtres civiques*—were, for most or all of the time, out of Paris and very far away indeed. In the spring of 1794, the so-called Cordelier group was well on the way to becoming a power minority based on the garrisons. But it was not much use enjoying some support in Perpignan, Nice, Strasbourg, or Briançon, when one had one's eyes on Paris. In this respect, the situation of this group of men frustrated in their ambitions was similar to that of the white terrorists of the Directory period, who were able to look to a great deal of potential support in the south-east and, indeed, like the so-called *hébertistes*, in Lyon itself. As long as Paris remained a force to be reckoned with, the conquest of power could hardly come from Lyon. *Le Père Duchesne* was a highly successful newspaper, with a wide, but mainly negative, appeal. But the *marchand des fourneaux* hardly had the makings of a generalissimo, or even of a staff officer.

Within the capital, they could count, at the most, on fairly effective support in three left bank Sections: Marat, Unité, and Luxembourg. But even in these Sections, the Revolutionary Committees escaped their control, and, like their forty-five counterparts in the rest of the city, were likely to remain the docile instruments of the Committee of General Security, in the event of a political crisis. And, indeed, in the course of the Revolution, and of the nineteenth and twentieth centuries, Parisian issues were never decided by the left bank alone: the failure, for instance, in May 1968, was above all a failure to extend riot and barricade to the important side of the river. Even the Commune remained in fact impenetrable. Chaumette was not an *hébertiste* agent—far from it—even if it suited Fouquier and the Committees to imply that he was, by trying him alongside some of the survivors of the first *fournée*.

Thus village *sociétés*, most of them inexperienced, many of them only recently formed, often at a time when militancy was losing its momentum within the Paris Sections themselves, on the very edge of Paris, could have presented an inviting clientèle to a group whose possibilities of expansion had been checked effectively *intra-muros*. For all their foolish talk about the right of insurrection, Ronsin and his friends must have thought that they still had plenty of time to play with (though they made the terrible mistake of giving the Committees the impression that time was in fact running out) and it might have seemed excellent tactics to start on the periphery as a base for a future attempt to regain the capital. Thiers was to reason in much this way eighty years later. And there is plenty of good evidence that, in such places as Passy, Issy, or Vaugirard, people like Momoro—the general factotum and the only intelligent member of the group, the only one indeed whose ideas could be said to go beyond the contemplation of a massive blood bath—and Ronsin, were actually called in, by local *meneurs*, as *conseillers-ès-révolution*, to advise them as to the best means of checking or toppling the local *autorités constituées*. Of course, many of these visits may have been entirely harmless; people with horses are likely to use them, and, as the spring of 1794 advanced, in the wake of a bitter winter, it was natural to want to ride out to the heights of Meudon, Clamart, Suresnes, or Passy. Nor was it necessarily a crime to have friends in these places. It may well be that *Églator* had invited Ronsin and Momoro to visit him in Bicêtre because he found them good company; they seem to have been quite jolly people, Ronsin was an ex-soldier and a good drinking man, and the *econome* of Bicêtre would have plenty of local wine at his disposal. Certainly when Ronsin went hunting in the woods of Bois-d'Arcy, it was to hunt, and for no fell purpose.

But what made matters worse, at least in the eyes of a suspicious government, was the additional fact that in what appeared to be the key places along the perimeter: Versailles, Vincennes, Gentilly, Gonesse, Lagny, Meaux, Pontoise, Conflans, Montrouge, Saint-Denis, Arpajon, Étampes, Sèvres, Meudon, Ronsin and Mazuel appeared to control the armed forces, in the shape of the scattered detachments of the Paris Revolutionary Army. Towards the end of Ventôse, when Fouquier was preparing that section of the indictment concerned with the *complot pour affamer* Paris, he sent out *commissions rogatoires* to the following places: Belleville, Bagnolet, Grande Charonne, Vincennes, Saint-Mandé, Charenton-le-Pont (of course), Bercy, Grand Montrouge, Châtillon, and Fontenay-aux-Roses;[1] it was almost as if

---

[1] A.N. W1a 116 (tribunaux révolutionnaires, commissions rogatoires, fin-ventôse an II). Already, on 16 Ventôse [6 March], the two Committees of Government had ordered Fouquier, who had been called before them, to extend his inquiries to about thirty *communes* of the periphery; these included nearly all the places on the edge of Paris that have figured in this chapter: Antony, Arcueil, Arpajon, Asnières, Belleville, Bercy, Bourg-la-Reine, Chanteloup, Chantilly, Charenton, Clichy, Colombes, Creil, Dammartin, Écouen, Étampes, Franciade, Gennevilliers, Gonesse, Linas, Marly, Le Mesnil-Amelot, Montlhéry, Nanterre, Nanteuil, Passy, Poissy, Pont-Saint-Maxence, Provins, Roissy, Saint-Germain, Senlis, Sèvres, Versailles, Villeneuve-sous-Dammartin, and Vitry. *Les Armées révolutionnaires*, p. 818(32).

Rousseville himself had dictated the choice, though it is unlikely that he in fact did, as he does not seem to have begun his mission till early in Floréal.

In a period of acute political uncertainty, everything would appear to hang together; the hidden enemies *intra-muros* would link up with the hidden enemies *extra-muros*, and a more careful watch would have to be placed on the *barrières* and on the *maisons garnies*. In its daily Bulletin for 1er Germinal, in the middle of the *hébertiste* trial, the *comité révolutionnaire* of the Section de la Montagne, always the most sensitive Section of the capital in times of political crisis, was to report characteristically:

. . . Il y a une infinité de nouvelles figures dans les maisons garnies, nous les surveillons, et nous arrêterons tous les ennemis du peuple, tous ceux qui, n'ayant aucune mission, ni moyens d'existence prouvés, seront arrêtés. Il est certain que des figures cachées se sont montrées dans ces moments de crise, ils rentreront dans la poussière avant que nous nous reposions. . . .[1]

Bourdeaux, it will be recalled, was picked up a little later in the same month, in a *garni* of the rue des Lombards.

At much the same period, a local *comité* reported an unusual assembly of valid beggars and vagrants in and around the village of Fresnes, to the south of Paris.[2] We can then easily guess at the identity of the *figures inconnues* mentioned by the *comité* of the Montagne; they would be the usual stock-in-trade of the very sophisticated *commissaire de police* of that Section, the printer Comminges: adolescents on the run from Marly and Vaucresson, pedlars, *blanchisseuses*, *marchandes de nouvelles*, from Versailles, Saint-Cloud, Meudon, and Sèvres.[3] Indeed the reaction of the authorities on this occasion was entirely predictable: in time of trouble, keep a wary eye out for the *gens sans aveu*. Let it never be said that the revolutionary régime was particularly original.

It did not really matter that there would *always* be runaway boys and girls,[4] and that *blanchisseuses* and *marchandes de nouvelles* were always coming to and going from Paris. It did not really matter that troops nominally in the control of Ronsin and Mazuel neither amounted to very much, were not much good, could generally be kept happy with a few bottles of wine—and their loyalty to the Convention thrived

---

[1] A.N. F7 4616 d 2 (Bresson, Bulletin du comité révolutionnaire de la Section de la Montagne, du 1er germinal an II).

[2] 'Le Complot militaire', *Terreur et subsistances*, p. 145.

[3] See note M, p. 240.

[4] See note N, p. 241.

especially on such liquid encouragement—and that they were to prove quite indifferent to the fate of their largely absentee and unpopular officers. All that was, in any case, in the future. The government and the subordinate repressive authorities had had a severe fright, there is no doubt at all about that. And even once the crisis was over and the so-called *conjurés* had been executed without fuss, no one would be prepared to admit that such fears had been the product, to a large extent at least, of a mixture of tradition and fantasy. It was not even just a matter of the Département de Paris; Mazuel had been taken in Versailles (What had he been doing there? Why had he resisted repeated orders to leave the place and to take up his assigned command in Lyon?[1]), Ronsin, in le Bois-d'Arcy, Vincent had gone on a mysterious journey to the village of Neufchelles, at the far end of the Seine-et-Marne, and on the borders of the Somme. What is more, on his return, round about 19 Ventôse, he had torn up his passport, while drinking in a café near the Ministry of War. The *marchand de vin* had picked up the bits and taken them round to the local Revolutionary Committee, which had sent on the document to Fouquier-Tinville.[2]

It may be understood from the preceding section that what I have endeavoured to illustrate is the reasons that may have persuaded normally sane and sober men like Jagot, Dubarran, Vadier, or Amar, members of the police committee, that the capital was surrounded by a hidden army of demagogues, *affidés*, responding to *mots d'ordre* coming from within the city and transmitted preferably by word of mouth by men on foot or, better still, on horseback; for a mounted conspirator is a more convincing one than a walking one. The Committee of General Security was suspicious of such people, both because they could not readily control and discipline them, because they did not know much about them, had no *fiches* on them—how could there be *fiches* on people who possessed no chartable past?—and, above all, because they, rightly, believed that such people, by an astute mixture of largesse, charity, and demagogic promises—and demagogic references to the economic and food privileges enjoyed by the Parisians—could rapidly acquire a devoted and credulous clientèle among the local poor.

---

[1] *L'Armée révolutionnaire parisienne à Lyon et dans la région lyonnaise.*

[2] Vincent's passport is to be found, for some reason, in the personal dossier of the Cordelier militant, Chéneaux, in the *série alphabétique* F7, papers of the Committee of General Security (A.N. F7 4645). I first discovered the fragments of the passport, that had subsequently been stuck together no doubt by the methodical Fouquier, while working on Vincent in 1939. See also my *Armées révolutionnaires*, pp. 844–5.

Most of the so-called *affidés* were, it goes without saying, perfectly harmless, the sort of people who, a century later, would have been content with the *palmes académiques*, and the presidency of the *Société historique, archéologique, philosophique et littéraire de l'Hurepoix*, or of the *Société d'émulation de Roissy-en-France et de sa région*. They wanted power and recognition, they wanted a platform and a tribune; and they too may have wanted to acquire a nice house or a lush pasture, a quiet mill by a stream, in the valley of the Yvette, or even the gothic remains of a modest château, especially if it also had the remains of a *pigeonnier*. It is very doubtful indeed if their vision extended any further than that, though, no doubt, they would have been flattered to entertain Ronsin, Momoro, or Mazuel. It was not everyone who could aspire to the heights enjoyed by a family we will encounter later,[1] in Choisy-le-Roi, and who could boast the presence of Robespierre at their table, under the trellis of roses. One made good with what one could get.

Of course, most of this is pure supposition; but what is one to do, other than to suppose, when dealing in these nether areas of the history of panic fears, myths, fantasies, and unstated suspicions? I do not really know what many Parisians thought about the Versaillais; but I do know that one Parisian at least described them as a population of lackeys.[2] I do not know what the authorities of Fontenay-aux-Roses thought of the Parisians; I do know that the *agent national*, at a public meeting, stated that they were unduly privileged, that it was not fair, and that the inhabitants should look to their own interests. And if he said this, I think it is likely that other *agents nationaux* would have thought, if not said, much the same. Is not the fear felt by the inhabitants of the capital, in the spring of 1794, of the *gens sans aveu*, the fear of what the really poor might get up to?[3] And does not poverty lay out its wretched bed in the *garnis* of the rue des Lombards, the rue de la Verrerie, and the rue de la Lune?[4] What the Parisian householder feared, both in Ventôse-Germinal, and, again, following the Admirat attempt in Prairial, was a *new* Revolution, a mighty uprising of the rural disinherited, that, from its entrenched heights, would engulf the capital and produce a bloody social massacre.

The task of the historian, especially if he is a specialist of social

---

[1] See below, p. 134, on the subject of the Vaugeois family, in Choisy, and the Laviron family, in Créteil, both, it was alleged, regular hosts to Robespierre, Couthon, and Le Bas.

[2] *Terreur et subsistances*, p. 124.

[3] See note O, p. 242.

[4] See note P, p. 243.

history, is very much akin to that of a novelist. There must be a wide element of guesswork. It is like attempting to sound the unsoundable and to penetrate the secrets of the human heart. I do not know, for instance, to put it on a practical level, why *brodeuses* from *entre Saône-et-Rhône*, in central Lyon, so often became pregnant, often as a result of a single, but never of a chance, encounter. I can only guess at a mixture of ignorance, naïveté, the readiness to listen to promise and blandishment, and, above all, the frenetic quality of the leisure of the very poor; many of these girls, one feels, would succumb at their very first outing, the first time that they drank in large quantities, that they attended a christening, or went to a dance. When the working day is extremely long, monotonous, and exhausting the pattern of leisure has to be accelerated. That is what Restif and Mercier mean when they describe the boisterous, riotous, unsophisticated bacchanales of the *bals* in the *guinguettes*, at the weekend, on the slopes above Paris. They put this boisterousness down to popular crudity; but Mercier at least was a middle-class observer, and he did not understand how much energy and pleasure had to be crammed into a very small space of time.

Ex-nobles on the Outskirts of Paris

It was suggested earlier in this book that Parisian events could be exploited by provincial manipulators for purposes quite of their own. But this was a two-way process, because Parisians, so convinced were they of the prime importance of the squabbles and jockeying that were going on ceaselessly within the confines of Section, Commune, or Convention, were prone to find reflections of these everywhere they went in the provinces. We will return later to the repercussions of the *hébertiste* affair, and of 9 Thermidor, on the imagination of Parisian observers so far as the localities of *le pourtoir de Paris* were concerned.[1] But we encounter similar attitudes and fears, a little after the great political crisis of the spring, this time in the summer of 1794, on the subject of the multiple repercussions of the *affaire Admirat* on the villages of the perimeter. It cannot have been merely a coincidence that most of Rousseville's visits to the localities of the two Districts should have taken place between the beginning of Floréal and the middle of Messidor—there are no reports extant from the former priest after the twentieth of that month, though some may have been lost—and that they should have become much more numerous in the second *décade* of Prairial. His presence in the area throughout Floréal

---

[1] See below, the section entitled 'The Geography of Mistrust'.

can be explained in terms of the implementation of the Law of 27
Germinal that ordered the expulsion from the Paris area of all former
nobles and their families. But in the following month, he appears much
more preoccupied with the presence and the activities of 'demagogues'
and of persons who could not offer a good account of themselves. In
Floréal, Rousseville contented himself mainly with reporting on the
numbers and the qualities of the *ci-devants* who had been forced to take
up residence in these villages. Nor was he alone in such preoccupations.
Thus, on 15 Floréal [Sunday 4 May 1794] the commandant of the *force
armée* of the canton of Belleville reports to the Committee of General
Security:

... qu'environ 110 ex-nobles ou étrangers se sont retirés dans la commune
de Belleville, que même quelques-uns d'entr'eux ont pris un domicile qui
n'est éloigné des murs de Paris de plus que la portée de pistolet ... que
plusieurs de ces individus, principalement les femmes, se promènent sur le
boulevard extérieur, et communiquent aisément avec les citoyens de l'intérieur. . . .[1]

and it followed, of course, that such communications could not have
been of an innocent nature. It was rather as if the revolutionary
authorities of the year II had sought to construct round Paris a sort of
Berlin wall, not so much to keep the Parisians in, as to prevent those
outside from communicating with them.

Rousseville has a very similar report, dated the twenty-second of the
same month:

Ceux des ci-devant nobles qui ont quitté Paris à l'occasion du décret du 27
germinal ont choisi de préférence les lieux les plus voisins des barrières
et ceux où l'esprit public étoit le moins prononcé. Il y en a à 155 à Belleville,
autant à Passy, 50 à Vaugirard, autant à Clichy, à Auteuil, à Vitry, à Montmartre, à Vincennes ... le tout ne me paraît pas être de moins de 2,000
personnes dans le cas de la loi, y compris les étrangers. ... à Vaugirard,
Auteuil et Passy ... ils paraissent assez bien vus par les municipalités. . . .[2]

The list might be described as the Gotha of suspected villages, all the
more dangerous, it may be noted, because they were all situated on
the very edge of the capital, from which they were often divided only
by the width of a boulevard.

On 26 Floréal, the same observer, who on this occasion, had moved

---

[1] A.N. F7 4781 (commandant de la force armée du canton de Belleville, au
Comité de sûreté générale, 15 floréal an II).

[2] A.N. F7 4775 2 pl. 5 (Rousseville, au Comité de salut public, 22 floréal an
II).

beyond the limits of his normal parish, sent the following report from Versailles:

Cette commune n'est point du lieu de ma mission, mais y étant allé prendre un cheval, j'ai eu occasion d'apprendre, qu'il y avoit jusqu'à 400 ci-devant nobles et étrangers, dont un assez grand nombre avec des moyens de nuire par ses richesses; et il m'a semblé que beaucoup d'habitants regardoient leur sejour comme un avantage. . . . [1]

On the twenty-eighth, we hear of twelve former nuns living in Rungis, as well as of a group of noblemen, all of them well-to-do, who are in the habit of eating well in the inns and restaurants of Châtenay and who make their orders in the neighbouring village of Antony.[2] But by no means all were so well set-up, for, on 3 Prairial, Rousseville sends in a long report on all those who have taken up residence in Vincennes. Included in this very comprehensive list are: '. . . 6. Anne-Marie-Xavier Duplessis, 27 ans, ouvrière en linge depuis la Révolution, née à Paris, avant la Révolution au couvent de Montfort-L'Amaury, pour se faire religieuse; est restée à Paris jusqu'en mai 1793, allée de là à Saint-Maur comme institutrice, vit de son travail. . . .' an interesting enough case history of adjustment to new circumstances. There is the similar case of '7. Anne-Marie-Angélique Fay, 58 ans, ouvrière en linge, née à Souspins (Oise), habitant de Paris', also then resident in Vincennes, as well as of: '56. Alexandre-Louis Marolles, 53 ans, en 1789 aux armées russes, ensuite capitaine dans le 43e Régiment d'infanterie. . . . sa femme n'est pas noble . . . elle vend à la halle sous des parasoles, en qualité de fripière. . . .'[3]

Hardly people, one would have thought, who should have caused alarm even to the most suspicious of authorities, for, far from being in a position to buy themselves *une popularité factice* among local tradesmen and *traiteurs*, by the extent of their custom, they had been driven to eke out an uncertain living, competing, at the very lowest level of society, with local pedlars and laundrywomen.

On 16 Prairial, an *arrêté* of the Committee of Public Safety, signed by Saint-Just and Carnot, entrusted Rousseville with the task of arresting three refugees living in Bercy, of whom one, Michel, had been the

---

[1] A.N. F7 4631 d 2 (Caille, Rousseville, au Comité de salut public, 26 floréal an II).

[2] A.N. F7 4631 d 2 (Caille, Rousseville au Comité de salut public, 28 floréal an II).

[3] A.N. F7 4784 (rapport du comité de surveillance de Vincennes au Comité de sûreté générale, le 3 prairial an II).

former coachman of Marie-Antoinette, and thus clearly a dangerous man.[1]

A few days earlier, Rousseville had been ordered, again by the Committee of Public Safety, to arrest a group of refugees who had settled in the village of Fontenay-sous-Bois, which, as we shall see (p. 127), was also marked down as a *centre de fanatisme*; these included the comte de Bontems, the former *curé*, a retired *agent de change*, and an officer of the *gardes-du-corps*, all of them living together in the house of the *Minimes*.[2]

The other Fontenay (aux-Roses), so often denounced by Parisian observers as an example of *égoïsme communal*, had also come under Rousseville's scrutiny, in Floréal, as having been the chosen residence of Thérèse Cabarrus, on her return from Bordeaux, where she had been denounced by Jullien *le jeune*.[3] She had clearly shown her usual discrimination in her choice of a refuge in which to sit out the last months of the Terror, until such time as her lover, Tallien, was able to secure her a place of influence, wealth, and comfort in Thermidorian society, for this particular municipality appears to have been especially ill-disposed towards Paris.

Late in Messidor, that is towards the end of his mission, he has a bad word for Saint-Denis: 'On voit toujours dans Franciade', he writes on the thirtieth, 'une des villes qui sont comme neutres en Révolution. . . . 50 ci-devant nobles, 40 ci-devant religieuses, 12 ou 16 ci-devant moines ou prêtres y sont toujours'.[4]

It was natural enough for the expelled noblemen and noblewomen to have settled as close to Paris as they could.[5] There does not seem to

[1] A.N. F7 4746 d I (Hugot, arrêté du Comité de salut public signé Saint-Just et Carnot, 16 prairial an II).

[2] A.N. F7 4608 d 4 (Bontems). The order for their arrest was signed by Carnot, Robespierre and Couthon.

[3] A.N. F7 4631 d 2 (Caille, Rousseville au Comité de salut public, 26 floréal an II).

[4] A.N. F7 4783 (rapport de Rousseville du 30 messidor an II [18 July 1794]).

[5] A little earlier, in Frimaire year II [Nov.–Dec. 1793], the former General, Biron, was stated to have been living in the *commune* of Montrouge. It was about this time that he was denounced to Fouquier-Tinville by Grammont and Momoro, as having been the enemy of Rossignol. According to Grammont, a former actor and a high-ranking officer in the Paris Revolutionary Army—he was to be guillotined with the *hébertistes*—'les crimes [de Rossignol] à ses yeux étaient 1. d'être Vainqueur de la Bastille; 2. d'être Parisien'. (Toulouze et Maugarny, *Histoire de Montrouge*, n.d.) Rossignol was indeed an authentic Parisian, having been born in the Faubourg Saint-Antoine, where he was later to practise the trade of goldsmith. His 'crime' would be that of most of the inhabitants of the capital in the eyes of provincials.

have been anything at all sinister in this desire to remain almost within calling distance of the capital, dictated as it no doubt was by the very understandable and legitimate wish to remain within easy contact of the friends and neighbours that they had possessed in their previous places of residence, as well as to maintain daily communication with their servants and *intendants* who would thus have no difficulty in keeping them regularly informed of what was happening to their town houses. But, of course, this would not be the view of a suspicious government.

All these places had already been *mal-notés*, for one reason or another, first of all in the course of the winter, and especially around Christmas, because many of their churches had remained open—we will return later to this particular subject—then at the time of the Spring crisis, either as making difficulties about supplying the Paris markets, or for allowing themselves to come under the influence of newcomers, most of them members of the Cordeliers. And now here they were, once more, offering hospitality (which had, it is true, been forced upon them by the Law of 27 Germinal) to all manner of *ci-devants*, former priests and nuns, many of whom were soon made welcome by the local inhabitants, providing them with both trade and, in some cases, employment. And in this respect it is worth remembering that one of the principal economic and, indeed, social, functions of these villages had been not only to provide the Parisians with dairy produce, fruit, vegetables, eggs, and rabbits, but also to act as centres of leisure and enjoyment. It was too much to expect of a *traiteur* in Charenton or in Belleville that he should make a distinction between his well-to-do middle-class customer who turned up, even at the height of the Terror, at the week-end, to enjoy a meal provided from black market transactions, and an equally well-to-do and better-spoken, more considerate nobleman who was dependent on such local facilities throughout the week.

As so often during the Terror, the Committees had in fact given body to their own panic fears by forming, through punitive legislation, these 'colonies' of potential suspects that encircled the capital. The *ci-devants* would have been far less dangerous had they been left alone and allowed to remain in their own quarters where they would have been constantly subjected to the rigorous scrutiny of the *comités révolution-naires*, especially when these, as was the case in the Section du Bonnet-Rouge, were composed largely of their own former servants and *gens de maison*. Indeed, at first, during Floréal, the two Committees do not seem to have been unduly concerned by this new category of enforced emigration, confining themselves to requiring the local *comités* to

provide them with complete lists of the new arrivals. They merely
wanted to know who was where, the usual, overriding preoccupation
of any French police authority during the latter part of the eighteenth
century. But, judging from the instructions given to Rousseville, their
relative complacency turned into suspicion and alarm as a result of the
revelation of the full extent of the Admirat affair. Now Rousseville was
ordered to carry out arrests, as well as to continue his surveillance. It
was then probably as an afterthought that these government-created
refugees were to be connected, in the obsessively vigilant minds of the
twenty-four members of the Revolutionary Government, with the
agents of the elusive baron de Batz believed to be active within the
city. Admirat might have come from the Auvergne; indeed, it has been
amply proved that he did.[1] But he must surely have had friends, even
relatives, on the perimeter.

The Survival of Rural Catholicism

Four or five months earlier, at the turn of the year, during Nivôse and
Pluviôse, at the time of Christmas and the New Year, both the Committees in Paris, those of the peripheral Sections and, in some cases, the
more zealous of the local *comités de surveillance*, had been giving increasing attention to the many, almost weekly manifestations of the
survival of Catholicism, often in the form of massive attendance at
Sunday services or at midnight mass on Christmas Eve [4 Nivôse year
II] in parishes within walking distance of Paris. Indeed, it was suspected, probably wrongly, that many Parisians themselves attended
these services. The Committees need not have worried so much about
what was going on *sur le pourtoir*, for, as Professor Reinhard has
shown, the more populous parishes of the capital itself—Saint-
Eustache, Saint-Sulpice, Saint-Médard, and Saint-Gervais—drew un-
precedented large crowds, of both sexes to mass during the three
Sundays preceding Christmas, while midnight mass also seems to have
been well attended. But, throughout the Terror, the Revolutionary
Government had shown much greater concern for examples of *fanatisme* in the rural villages along the city's supply routes than for what
was happening *intra-muros*, no doubt in the belief that, in small communities, the influence of the *curé* would be relatively greater and
would be more likely to become identified with the collective interests
of their parishioners than could happen in Paris itself, where those

[1] Arnaud de Lestapis, 'L'affaire Admirat et la conspiration du baron de Batz',
A.H.R.F., 1952–3.

sturdy Christians who insisted on still carrying out their duties after the *Fête-Dieu* of 1793, or after October of that year, could be subjected to the full glare of public scrutiny, whether through the press or through the *sociétés sectionnaires* or the Revolutionary Committees. Jacques Roux, for instance, had enjoyed wide support among the disinherited of the Section des Gravilliers and in the club of the rue du Vert-Bois; but he had eventually been destroyed by pressure from the *assemblée générale*, when, after June 1793, he refused to renounce his sacerdotal functions; this was, of course, merely a pretext to remove from public life an alarmingly eloquent witness of hunger, overcrowding, and of the wretched conditions suffered by the inhabitants of the *maisons garnies*. But the campaign begun, in August 1793, against the *prêtre* Roux had been entirely effective. He does not seem to have had any imitators within Paris itself.

An additional reason for such preoccupations on the part of the Parisian authorities would be the mere fact of the unequal distribution, throughout the two rural Districts, of churches that were still open at the time of the promulgation of the Law of 18 Frimaire on the *liberté des cultes*, and that, consequently continued to function throughout the rest of the revolutionary period, and those that had already been forcibly closed, generally as a result of outside intervention, by that date. The existence of one open and active church, among half a dozen parishes, would be likely to produce something on the scale of a pilgrimage, on the part of inhabitants from neighbouring villages, who had been deprived of the possibility of public worship within their own *communes*, either as a result of the closure of the church or of the removal of the *desservant* either as a *réfractaire* or as a suspect. For, from the autumn, it became increasingly difficult to replace non-jurors by *constitutionnels*, following Gobel's abjuration. Such occasions could thus easily take on the dangerous dimensions of an *attroupement*, each Sunday or feast day becoming the magnet for a spectacular form of public protest and an expression of lack of confidence in the new régime; and these in turn might produce open acts of hostility at the expense of the *meneurs* of local clubs, *cabaretiers*, and so on, known in their own communities to have been associated with campaigns of enforced dechristianisation, especially from the autumn onwards, for the *Fête-Dieu* of 1793 seems to have been widely celebrated, in these *communes*, in the preceding June.

Augustin Roussel, the former *curé* of Colombes, having handed in his *lettres de prêtrise* and closed the parish church, had been induced by a noisy delegation of his female parishioners, strengthened by an army of women from neighbouring villages, to unlock the church and celebrate midnight mass on 4 Nivôse [24 December]; arrested on the sixth, by agents of the Committee of General Security, which seems to have taken a special interest in the problem set by the persistence of *le culte*, he explained the reasons for his decision in terms which express, with great clarity, the dilemma in which these country priests, torn between the pressures placed upon them by parishioners whom they knew and the uncertain intentions of an alarming, but faceless government, opted for what appeared to be the lesser of two evils. As the Christmas season drew nearer, the strength of the traditional pattern of leisure and collective rejoicing would become increasingly hard to check. Furthermore, the law was by no means explicit as to what they could or could not do. Roussel wrote from prison, to the Committee of General Security:

le but de la loi du 18 frimaire était, en maintenant la croyance d'une divinité et la liberté des cultes, d'arrêter les ravages de l'athéisme. . . . Ce fut surtout dans les campagnes que cette loi . . . fut reçue avec transport. Elle leur redonnait Dieu qui féconde leurs champs et mûrit leurs moissons. Mais les campagnes la regardèrent en même temps comme un titre en faveur de l'antique solemnité de leur culte. . . . Je les exhortai à rendre désormais, chacun dans son coeur, leurs hommages à l'Eternel, et à ne plus se rassembler que pour les intérêts de la République . . . que c'étoit le moment de tenir la religion comme réléguée dans son âme, pour ne s'occuper que de la patrie, que les premiers chrétiens eux-mêmes avoient donné cet exemple de leur amour pour leur pays. . . .[1]

Such an orthodox language, that might have been gleaned from the edifying mish-mash of the *Lettres du vicaire savoyard*, would have little appeal to a rural congregation, determined above all to mark Christmas with accustomed pomp and fervour. The result was that Colombes witnessed an enormous afflux of worshippers on this occasion. Roussel had no doubt done his best to avoid such a confrontation. Fortunately, he was one of the luckier parish priests of the area, being released in Vendémiaire year III, at the beginning of the Thermidorian Reaction.

Colombes was no isolated example in this respect. The *Directoire* of the District de Bourg-l'Égalité, in its *Bulletin* for the first *décade* of Nivôse, reports: '. . . Le culte catholique a été rétabli dans la commune de Vincennes, un *te deum* a été chanté en action de grâces, et le citoyen

---

[1] A.N. F7 4775 2 pl. 3 (Roussel, Roussel au Comité de sûreté générale, s.d. nivôse an II).

Sue (the former *curé*) a prononcé un long discours à cette occasion.'[1]
In Créteil, again in Nivôse, there was a public meeting that voted in
favour of celebrating midnight mass; under pressure from his parishioners and from vast crowds from the surrounding villages, Gerdru,
the former priest, decided that, in order to avoid a riot, it would be
advisable to co-operate.[2] Again, on 6 Nivôse [Boxing Day] the Revolutionary Committee of Courbevoie wrote anxiously to the Committee
of General Security:

qu'il y avoit eu un rassemblement de plusieurs curés et vicaires des communes voisines à Colombes, chef-lieu, dont le curé [Roussel] a officié et
prêché dans le temple de la raison à minuit, suivant l'ancien régime, s'exprimant ainsi dans son sermon . . . qu'il ne fallait pas abandonner la religion, et
ne point écouter les fables qui régnent dans ce moment-ci; le jour de Noël,
il y a eu 9 messes, l'affluence des communes circonvoisines étoit immense et
le même soir nous [the members of the *comité de surveillance*] fûmes assaillis
par les femmes de Courbevoie qui avoient été auxdites messes demandant
un prêtre et la ci-devant église pour y célébrer, lesdits citoyens regardent la
conduite desdits prêtres comme très dangereuse et dans le cas d'occasionner
des émeutes. . . .[3]

A version, as we can see, somewhat different from that presented by
Roussel himself. In this instance, the members of the local *comité*, feeling themselves personally threatened, had called in the help of the
comité révolutionnaire of the Section des Champs-Élysées, only too
delighted to have the opportunity to 's'immiscer dans les affaires des
communes rurales'. It was hardly surprising, given these circumstances,
that, in the Ventôse crisis, Colombes was to figure prominently in the
'food plot', while the municipality was to be accused, later still, of
giving proof of a criminal indulgence towards the *ci-devants* who had
settled in the place.[4]

Already, on 18 Frimaire year II [Sunday 8 December, two Sundays
before Christmas] 'un membre [of the municipality of Conflans-
Charenton, in its session of the following Monday] 'a dit qu'il a été
facile de s'apercevoir d'une plus grande affluence de citoyens de
différentes communes des environs aux exercices du Culte catholique

---

[1] A.N. F7 4781 (Bulletin du District de Bourg-l'Égalité pour la première
décade de nivôse an II, envoyé le 22 nivôse).

[2] A.N. F7 4770 d 1 (Laviron).

[3] A.N. F7 4782 (Colombes, un membre du comité de surveillance de Courbevoie, au Comité de sûreté générale, 6 nivôse an II).

[4] ibid.

dans l'Eglise des Carrières-Charenton. . . .'[1] Charenton was no doubt a special place, in which Catholicism would be likely to be particularly tenacious, owing to the presence in the village of the only *temple réformé* permitted in the Paris area, as a result of the Edict of Toleration. The weekly presence in the *commune* of well-to-do Protestants coming from Paris can have been anything but welcome to the poor population of the port, and may have added further fuel to their sense of resentment with regard to the capital. Meanwhile, on 21 Frimaire [Wednesday 11 December 1793] the authorities of Fontenay-sous-Bois had reopened the parish church; and on Sunday 25 Frimaire [15 December] 'le curé a dit sa messe, bénissant avant l'intérieur et l'extérieur de l'église et le cimetière, disant que ces endroits avoient été souillés. . . .'[2] and, on this occasion, some members of the local club had been stoned by groups of women. It was no doubt as a result of these disorders that, on 14 Prairial year II [2 June 1794], Rousseville came to the village, with a warrant signed Couthon and Carnot, and arrested the former *curé*, Larivoire.[3] At much the same time, he also placed under arrest the former *curé* of the neighbouring *commune* of Champigny-sur-Marne, Pranville, a quarrelsome and difficult man, accused of having celebrated the Saint-Jean, both in 1793 and in 1794, with bonfires for the children.[4]

In many of these small villages, then, the advent of enforced dechristianisation, the interference of Parisian authorities in defence of local anti-clerical minorities, and the return of the festive season had brought in their wake disorders, denunciations, and counter-denunciations that did nothing to lessen the suspicions felt by the Committee of General Security in particular towards the inhabitants of the periphery, and that greatly increased the various tensions exacerbated, within these village communities, by the introduction of the *maximum*, the endless demands of Parisian food-commissioners, and the indifference displayed by the Parisian *garde nationale* to the needs of the suburban consumer when he came to the capital in the hope of taking away candles, soap, coffee, soda, or fat. The concluding note, in this respect, was sounded in the village of Fontenay-aux-Roses, the church of which was broken into, by persons unknown, on 30 Ventôse year II [20

[1] A.N. F7 4782 (Conflans, extrait du registre des délibérations de la municipalité de Conflans-Charenton, séance du 19 frimaire an II). See also note Q, p. 244.

[2] A.N. F7 4782 (comité de surveillance de Fontenay-sous-Bois, au Comité de sûreté générale, lettre reçue le 25 frimaire an II).

[3] A.N. F7 4765 d 4 (Larivoire) and F7 4608 d 4 (Bontems).

[4] A.N. F7 4652 d 4 (Contamine).

March 1794], at the height of the *hébertiste* scare, and put completely to sack, an action that Parisian observers were, not unnaturally, to attribute to the presence of agents of *la faction athée*.[1]

It was not just a matter of a personal attachment, on the part of a rural community, to a given priest. When it became imperative, one could do without a priest altogether. Thus, in its session of 26 Floréal year II [15 May 1794], the *comité de surveillance* of Brie-Comte-Robert was to question

Claude-Lazare Larue, natif de Grisy et demeurant à Moissy . . . 42 ans [qui] a répondu que le jour de pâques il s'est seulement revêtu d'un surplis et d'une chape pour chanter en latin . . . a chanté la messe à l'autel, en imitant [en ce qui concernait les chants usités] le ci-devant curé, qu'il a eu beaucoup de peine à se décider de faire cette office, mais qu'il y a été déterminé par plusieurs habitants [de Moissy] . . . que le jour de pâques le maire dudit Moissy fut le premier à solliciter le répondant à jouer le rôle de prêtre. . . .[2]

As a result of his initiative, villagers from Combes-la-Ville and Lieusaint had poured into Moissy, increasing the concern of the Brie committee. Nor was this by any means an isolated example. We hear of similar *magisters*, schoolmasters, *suisses*, gravediggers, and others thus administering the sacraments and celebrating Mass in villages of the Aisne and the Somme.[3]

[1] A.N. F7 4782 (Fontenay-aux-Roses, comité de surveillance; jugement rendu par le tribunal correctionnel et de police de Châtillon, le 24 floréal an II). The municipality, on sending details of the case to the Committee of Public Safety, was to observe: '. . . Vous verrez par les pièces . . . que la paix est loin de régner dans notre commune. . . .vous avez eu, Citoyens Représentants, plus d'un exemple que les patriotes exagérés ne sont pas ceux auxquels il faut le plus se fier, et qu'il y a aussi loin des vertus du Républicain dans l'exagération que dans le modérantisme. . . .' The municipality was in fact doing its best to toe the *robespierriste* line. It is clear from this letter that the lessons to be drawn from the trial of the *hébertistes* had percolated to most of the villages of the perimeter by the middle of Floréal.

It is also interesting to note that, while all the information regarding the celebration of Christmas on the periphery was sent to the Committee of General Security, clearly in the belief that *le fanatisme* was in some way the special province of this Committee, remarks concerning such incidents as those of Fontenay-aux-Roses should have been addressed to the Committee of Public Safety. It may, of course, simply mean that, while *comités de surveillance* would naturally report to the police committee, municipalities would be more likely to write to the Committee of Public Safety.

[2] A.D. Seine-et-Marne L 886 (registre de délibérations du comité de surveillance de Brie-Comte-Robert, séance du 26 floréal an II).

[3] R. C. Cobb, 'L'Armée révolutionnaire parisienne dans le département de l'Aisne', op. cit.

Perhaps, in this insistence on not missing the great feast days there is an element that is more than an attachment to habit and to the ancient calendar of leisure and seasonal celebration. The winter of 1793 and the spring of 1794 were a time of acute panic and fear, not only in Paris, but, perhaps even more, *sur le pourtoir*. Within the city, perhaps a third of the population would lie awake at night, listening for the early morning knock of the *commissaires* from the local Revolutionary Committee, who preferred thus to pounce in the uneasy hours just before dawn, when the citizen would be the most defenceless and when an administered Terror could take its relentless toll without fuss. The nights of the Terror, we may suppose, were still and silent ones, unrelieved by the reassuring clatter of the carriages of the gamblers, as they returned from the tables, unrelieved from those other welcoming night sounds that form a memorable descriptive passage in Mercier and to which he attributes the regular conception of many Parisians-to-be. But the *rural* night was even more silent and potentially more horrific and there was little to allay the panic fears of an isolated peasant family as its adult members tossed, listening to the shrieks of the owls and awaiting the crows of the cocks that would spell the end of the dark tunnel of nocturnal terror.

Even more dramatic, perhaps, is the account rendered by the *comité de surveillance* of Puteaux to the Committee of General Security, on 6 Nivôse year II [Boxing Day 1793] of the mysterious events that had taken place during Christmas night, between nine and ten o'clock, on the outskirts of the village, at a place appropriately called *la Demie-Lune* (a cross-roads) situated on the highroad to Paris. Three innkeepers had been knocked up, trembling in their nightshirts, by a group of armed men, who could not exhibit any powers of search or any

---

There were other ways, too, less conventional, but no doubt equally traditional, of celebrating the old feast days. The presiding judge of the Mons court, in a letter to the *Grand Juge*, dated 21 Nivôse year XII [11 January 1805] refers to the murder of a certain Joseph Rigault, a farmer from the village of Saint-Pierre-Capelle. The murder had been committed '*la veille [du] jour de Saint-Éloi, patron en ces contrées des cultivateurs*', during the night of 1–2 December 1804 (A.N. BB 18 402, Justice, Jemappes).

We have already referred earlier (p. 80) to the murder of a woman of seventy and of a girl of ten, on Boxing Day 1803, in the village of Papignies, near Tournai, at ten o'clock in the morning, at a time when most of the villagers were in church attending matins. The murderers had clearly counted on the fact that there would be no neighbours around to hear the screams of the victims. The old woman was presumably an invalid, being looked after by the girl, so that neither would have been able to attend the service (A.N. BB 18 402, Jemappes).

written orders. As a result of the panic that had ensued, several women and children 'sont tombés malades de frayeur', because, earlier in the year, a miller and his wife had been murdered, in similar nocturnal conditions, at a place in the neighbourhood known locally as *le Chant de Coq*, a pathetic expression of optimism, as if the name had been conjured up to drive away these nightmares and that had, in the circumstances, proved so completely inappropriate.[1] In all probability, the three innkeepers had been visited by a group of drunken National Guardsmen who had run out of drink and who had wished to end Christmas in a last blaze of festivity. The needs of the poor and the disinherited are doubly insistent on such occasions, and at such a time of night, on the road, some way from the town.

The incident might appear banal enough at first sight but the ensuing panic is more than of just local interest, and is indicative of something more than what happened on a dark Christmas night, on the road from Puteaux to Paris, serving as it does to remind us that, everywhere, but especially in the small villages on the edge of the capital, doubly alarming at night and itself dominated by men who talked incessantly of blood, ordinary people traversed the period so appropriately described as *la Grande Terreur*, in perspiring, shaking, sickening, physical fear: fear of what might come out of Paris during these night hours, fear of what might come walking stealthily over the frozen roads and tracks of the black countryside, fear of the night marauder, fear of the bandit disguised—and it was so easy to be so disguised, a couple of ribbons and a band of silk were all that were needed—as a *commissaire révolutionnaire*, fear of the order, loudly repeated: *Ouvrez au nom de la loi* that, to a family of farmers near Pontchâtrain, on the road from Versailles, was to spell out, round about this time, a hideous, mutilated death. In the nakedness of fear, might not recourse to the old guarantees of religion, the promise of Atonement, the hope of Salvation, and the everlasting lesson of Christ's sacrifice for ordinary men appear even more urgent and insistent than in more normal times?[2] To allow the great feast days that concluded the year to pass by without recognition would seem to invite the unknown dangers contained in the December nights of terror. These people had lived five years of

[1] A.N. F7 4783 (Puteaux, procès-verbal du comité de surveillance de Puteaux, 6 nivôse an II). It looks very much like the activities of one of the false *armées révolutionnaires* that, at this time, were given to operating, at night, in the villages on the outskirts of Paris. One of the witnesses reports that the officer at the head of the group 'étoit couvert d'une redingote bleue avec épaulettes. . . .' See also note R, p. 245.

[2] See note S, p. 245.

Revolution, each one more frightening than the previous one. And there seemed to be no end in sight. At least one could cling to Christmas, to Saint-Sylvester, to *la Chandeleur*, as to recognisable signals, lighting up the dark road, and reassuring with the memory of childhood. No wonder, then, that Rousseville was to report, long after this, in Messidor, in the full blaze of summer: 'Les signes du fanatisme, chassés de tous les lieux publics, semblent refugiés dans les maisons particulières des environs de Paris, chaque cultivateur a encore ce qu'on appelloit son christ, ses bonnes vierges, ses saintes-genièvres [*sic*]. . . .'[1]

The *ex-curé* of Bagnolet could perhaps afford to be contemptuous, though one rather doubts whether he would have used a similar language in the year III. The *pourtoir*, too, it was clear, possessed its vicars of Bray. But the countrymen were not taking any chances. The municipality of Villetaneuse writes for information, to the Committee of General Security, on 20 Nivôse [9 January 1794]:

Nous vous prions de nous expliquer en quoi consiste le fanatisme, pour nous, nous entendons par un fanatisme [*sic*] celui qui voudroit violenter les opinions et de forcer un autre citoyen de penser comme lui et d'adorer l'Être Suprême à sa manière. . . . Nous sommes autorisés . . . par le Représentant Crassous à qui nous avons fait part que la Commune avait confiance à un bon père de famille de 9 enfans et bon patriote pour faire les prières en français, le Représentant a répondu qu'il serait bien content si nous agissions ainsi. . . .[2]

Crassous was a man of sound sense, who seems to have been much appreciated in the course of his mission in the villages around Paris. The future at least was looked after. On 14 Ventôse [4 March], a week before the arrest of the *hébertistes*, the Committee of La Villette was to report:

. . . le Vicaire a rendu ses lettres de prêtrise, il vient d'être placé en qualité d'officier de santé dans les hôpitaux de l'armée. Le Curé est sollicité par les femmes enceintes pour baptiser leurs enfans chez elles, lui promettant la plus grande discrétion de femmes. Il va probablement consoler les malades. Ce qu'il y a de certain, c'est que le bedeau de la ci-devant paroisse a commencé à présenter de l'eau bénite aux parens et amis accompagnant l'enterrement d'un garde national de notre commune. . . .[3]

[1] A.N. F7 4784 (Franciade), and see note T, p. 246.
[2] A.N. F7 4784 (Villetaneuse, municipalité de Villetaneuse au comité de surveillance du District de Franciade, 20 nivôse an II).
[3] A.N. F7 4784 (comité de surveillance de la Villette, au Comité de sûreté générale, 14 ventôse an II).

The *comité de surveillance*, too, of this small village, gave proof of equally sound sense. It did not want to know too much; it was better to let people make their own arrangements. Thus, despite the Terror, death was accorded its ancient and everlasting importance, and birth was set on a road that would eventually defy the Revolution and those transient authorities who, for a time, had sought to shake the inhabitants of these rural *communes* out of their natural torpor and out of the framework of their accepted calendar of work and leisure, of suffering and rejoicing. No better testimony of the intractability of these small communities could be discovered than this successful attachment to the proper respect to be paid to Christmas, in the difficult and alarming winter of 1793.[1]

The Geography of Mistrust

It is now time to return once more to the angle of vision of the Parisian observer, hardly reassured, no doubt, by what he had witnessed of the attachment of the rural population encircling him to 'superstition' and 'fanaticism', when, faced with the series of political crises that mark the spring and summer of 1794, he set about transposing them on to what one would imagine to have been a rather recalcitrant terrain. Yet the Parisian would be firmly convinced of what was to him an almost sacred truth: the politics of Paris had to be those too of *le pourtoir*.

Thus, at the time of the Ventôse–Germinal crisis, one finds a variety of Parisian *commissaires* and other subordinate agents of the Commune, of the Committees, or of the Sections (especially those, like Finistère, Bondy, Popincourt, Invalides, Champs-Élysées, Faubourg du Nord, placed on the perimeter of the city), discovering *hébertistes* and *hébertiste* plots in a score or more of unlikely places, the inhabitants of which had probably never heard of the *Père Duchesne*, or, indeed, of any other Parisian journalist. There is some evidence that at least one article of *hébertiste* propaganda had reached Belleville and had been taken up by the member of the local club.[2] But Belleville was, after all, a communication centre, and with a population that could hardly be described as rural. Hébert was, like so many converts, a Paris imperialist. What had he to offer the inhabitants of *le plat pays*? Only threats so terrible that he, if no one else, might even have succeeded in re-establishing rural solidarity, for, with him, all countrymen were the children of Cain.

As we have suggested, the Cordeliers may have sought, and even

[1] See note U, p. 247.   [2] See note V, p. 248.

found, a few allies in some of the *meneurs* of the clubs of the periphery. But, according to many observers, we are asked to believe that a whole *hébertiste* network had sprung up, almost overnight, in the second half of Ventôse: a much bolder, more concrete assertion. Most claims of this kind were based on the simplest, and, therefore, the most convincing, of arguments: Hébert and his friends had been in the habit of dining out of doors, in the garden, for instance, of a house in Passy belonging to the Dutch banker, de Kock, the father of the rather lacrymose nineteenth-century novelist, Paul de Kock. Supper parties were bad enough, even *within* Paris, for they smelt of 'faction'. But to eat in a place like Passy, in a foreigner's country seat—and the foreigner a banker to boot—was rather like scoring a *tiercé* at the Grand Prix de Longchamp. It followed, of course, that Passy was a firm *hébertiste* outpost. Momoro had been to Vaugirard; Vaugirard was in the plot. Ronsin and Momoro had been to Bicêtre; Bicêtre was in the plot. Courbevoie, too, was in the plot, or had at least been contaminated. One of the last of Rousseville's reports, dated 2 Thermidor year II [20 July 1794] states:

. . . *Courbevoye.* Il y avait [le 30 messidor, 18 July] une fête à l'honneur de l'Être Suprême qui a attiré mon attention d'abord parce qu'elle ne se célé-brait que d'après un arrêté de la société populaire et des autorités de la Com-mune, ce qui est sujet à des abus [what Rousseville means is that this smacked too much of 'communalism' and 'direct democracy'], et ensuite parce qu'on y voyait deux chars dans l'un desquels étaient des blessés, mais comme présidés par deux femmes qu'on appelloit *déesses*, tandis que dans l'autre, qui était le plus honorablement placé, il n'y avait que des femmes traînées en triomphe, ce qui m'a eu l'air de sentir les restes de l'hébertisme. J'en ai fait la remarque à plusieurs membres de la commune. La foule des assistants était considérable. . . .[1]

It would thus seem that the unfortunate authorities of these villages could not win either way, that they must always be in the wrong in the demanding eyes of Parisian orthodoxy and vigilance. If they did not take the trouble to celebrate the Feast of the Supreme Being, this would be taken as proof of indifference. If they did take the trouble to cele-brate it, albeit rather late in the day—but the orthodoxy of the peri-meter necessarily drags two or three weeks behind that of the capital —and, if, in order to make the normally rather dreary occasion slightly more appetising, they enlisted the participation of a few pretty girls, shapely *déesses*, no doubt sparsely dressed in this hot month, they were teetering, perhaps without knowing it, on the brink of a *néo-hébertiste*

[1] A.N. F7 4783 (comité de surveillance de Neuilly, 2 thermidor an II).

heresy (for, in year II conditions, the heresy could always survive the heresiac).

Rousseville, as an ex-priest, may have been shocked by the spectacle of semi-nude girls. But perhaps his most astonishing comment is the suggestion that *hébertisme* (or at least the *néo* variety) was in some way connected with feminism. No revolutionary journalist had in fact been more boringly insistent on masculine virility than Hébert. Courbevoie, it is true, had been in trouble before. On 3 Germinal [22 March], a dangerous date, an inhabitant of Saint-Ouen, Bathe fils, had informed Fouquier-Tinville: 'qu'il existe une faction dans la société populaire de la commune de Courbevoie. . . . cette faction n'est composée que la plupart des voleurs des effets, bijoux, de la caserne de Courbevoie. . . .'[1] and he was to repeat this denunciation on 25 Messidor [13 July]. Finally, Ivry, too, was in the plot, though this was a different one. Danton had bought a house there, and was in the habit of eating in it, or in its garden, with some of his pleasure-loving friends.

We find very similar arguments employed a little later in the same year, this time on the subject of the spread of 'robespierriste' cells among the *communes* of the periphery, preferably in those that might constitute a convenient jumping-off place for an operation against the capital. Robespierre had friends in Choisy, he was in the habit of eating with them at weekends, they were related to the Duplay family; he had attended a christening there. Pin in a coloured flag for Choisy.[2] An official from the village of Clichy, on the northern tip of Paris, had been foolish enough, or ambitious enough, to have changed his name from Jean-Charles to Robespierre; that would no doubt earn Clichy a flag.[3] The Laviron family, grandmother, father and mother, two daughters, inhabitants of Créteil, are said to have been friends of Robespierre and of Couthon, who had visited them on Saturdays and Sundays; what is more, the grandmother was a cousin of Madame Duplay. Pin in a flag for Créteil.[4]

A woman from Lévignen, a *commune* on the main road from Paris to

---

[1] A.N. W 81(60) (tribunaux révolutionnaires, Bathe fils, à Fouquier-Tinville, 2 germinal et 25 messidor an II).

[2] A.N. W 79 (tribunaux révolutionnaires), Vaugeois père et fils. The father had been *maire* of the *commune* and was father-in-law of Duplay.

[3] A.N. W1a 80 (tribunaux révolutionnaires), Jean-Charles Legentil, *juge de paix* of the canton de Clichy, had changed his name to Robespierre on 16 Vendémiaire year II [7 October 1793]. He had been president of the *société populaire* of Montmartre. The Committee of General Security ordered his arrest on 14 Thermidor year II [1 August 1794].

[4] A.N. F7 4770 d 1 (Laviron).

Soissons, was in the habit of going to Paris two or three times a week, to sell dairy produce and poultry on the markets there; once back in the village, she liked to impress her neighbours with her Parisian lore; what she did was in fact what we would call name-dropping, but she dropped some dangerous names in Messidor year II, and these were of course remembered a month later, in Thermidor. She had said, among other things, that she had called on Robespierre, in his office at the Committee of Public Safety, and that he had received her almost immediately, and had listened politely, even making notes about what she had to tell him. It may well have been true, for it was in character, and Robespierre's accessibility is well established. But, a year or so earlier, the same woman had claimed to have had a chat with Marat, to whom she had delivered a package, Cour de Commerce.[1]

There must have been many people like her in these villages situated on the posting roads, local people, *porteurs de nouvelles de la capitale*; and it does not matter whether the news is good or bad—though disasters are perhaps preferable—as long as it is fresh. One is astonished, for instance, at the number of inhabitants of such places as Montgeron, Villemomble, Aumale, Gisors, Viroflay, Arpajon, Montlhéry, who, on their return home, claimed to have witnessed the events of 9–10 Thermidor: 'they were there,' right at the centre of things, in the Hôtel-de-Ville, at the very moment of the arrival of Barras, or on the place de Grève, in the early hours, after the famous downpour of thundery rain that altered the course of the Revolution by inducing the remaining artillery companies faithful to the Commune to return to their Sections. Such carriers of news from the big city enjoy a brief moment of triumph and then sink back into the obscurity and boredom of village life.

---

[1] A.D. Oise Grande Registre du comité de surveillance de Crépy-en-Valois (séance du 14 thermidor an II): '. . . [Il a été] arrêté que la fille Balon, marchande en la commune de Lévignen, qui a dit avoir des relations avec l'infâme Robespierre, qui souvent parlait de lui et se flattait de manger avec lui, sera amené au comité. . . .' Questioned, she told the *comité* that she had had a letter written for her by Torlé, *perruquier*, to Robespierre, on the subject of some soap that she had sent to Paris and that had been held up by the authorities of Nanteuil. She described herself as a *commissionnaire* who went to Paris once a month to return children who had been put out to wet nurses to their mothers. She stated that she had delivered parcels to Marat. The *comité* released her on 25 Thermidor [12 August]. It may be noted that the *société* of Lévignen contained a disproportionate number of *postillons* and *paveurs* among its members. The place was clearly very much a *lieu de passage* and very much open to any currents of news coming either from Paris or from Amiens and the Belgian frontier.

Other places that might be added to the list of suspects include Bercy, on the river, which, in 1796 and 1797, was said to be the rendez-vous and hiding place of a group of prominent *babouvistes*,[1] and Versailles, in yet another context, because it was the home of Félix Lepeletier, the rich brother of a Martyr of Liberty who was credited with having financed the Conspiracy for Equality and for having taken in a number of needy *exclusifs*.[2] In the year V and again in the following year, Clichy re-emerges, this time as the point of assembly of groups of moderate monarchists, at the time of the *assemblées primaires*, so that after *Grenelliens* or *Grenellistes*, neo-Jacobins and neo-terrorists, we now have the equally barbarous *Clichyens*.

The shock waves that spread from the explosion of the Infernal Machine of the rue Nicaise and that resulted in the rapid deportation of an important group of former terrorist militants, were not long in reaching the small town of Dourdan, the former *chef-lieu* of a District that had, in the year II, felt some of the impact of the so-called *hébertiste* conspiracy, thanks to the personality of Nutin.[3] A report addressed to the Minister of Police, and dated 24 Nivôse year IX [14 January 1801] states:

Le jour de l'explosion de la machine infernale, il s'est répandu dans la commune de Dourdan que le C. Lebrun, Consul, étoit tué, on découvrit l'auteur de cette nouvelle, distribuée et débitée par Supersac, dont le fils revenoit de Paris. Supersac est l'ennemi du C. Lebrun et de tout bon gouvernement. Il étoit revenu à Dourdan vendre son fonds de boutique et emmener à Alençon sa famille. Il étoit commissaire national à Dourdan, ses liaisons avec les anarchistes, avec les ennemis du repos public sont connues du C. Lebrun.

Il y avoit quelques jours avant l'explosion qu'il se promenoit d'un air sérieux, inquiet. Le coup manqué, il a disparu trois jours, et est ensuite revenu grand trait chercher ses meubles et sa famille, il était pâle, défait et comme au désespoir. Voilà des faits notoires à Dourdan. Mais il ne faut pas s'adresser aux deux juges de paix ses amis, ni sur son compte ni sur ceux des nommés Slat et Traversier. . . .[4]

---

[1] R. C. Cobb, 'Note sur la répression contre le personnel sans-culotte de 1795 à 1801', republished in *Disette et subsistances*.

[2] Ibid. See also A.N. F7 7011 (report to the *Ministre de la Police générale*, dated 13 November 1807), on the subject of meetings and *conciliabules* held in Versailles by a number of Parisian ex-terrorists, most of them members of former Revolutionary Committees, and including: Fournerot, Didier, Lécrivain, Planson, Guilleminet, Vélu, and Hivert. A few months later, in April 1808, the minister ordered the expulsion of all of them from Paris.

[3] See note W, p. 248.

[4] A.P.P. A/A 281 (198), rapport du 24 nivôse an IX.

We should likewise add Arcueil and le Petit-Bicêtre, the latter in such convenient proximity to le Grand-Bicêtre, the inns of which were said to be stopping-off places and recruiting grounds for the celebrated *bande d'Orgères*, when members of the gang came up to Paris to dispose of stolen goods, plan operations in the Brie, or merely to have a good time. Just as, at the present day, the cafés, boulevard Arago opposite the Santé, are frequented mostly by the friends and relatives of those who are living on the other side of the boulevard, and are kept by *indicateurs*, so one would expect that, in eighteenth-century conditions, the *cabaretiers* and the *logeurs* of le Petit-Bicêtre would have been in close touch with the inmates of the prison work-house of the adjoining *commune*.

One might, of course, add some of the villages that we have already mentioned, in the context of rationing, of the black market, and of the so-called 'food plot' of the spring of 1794: Puteaux, Belleville, Charenton,[1] Auteuil, Antony, Clamart-le-Vignoble (which was its revolutionary name), Suresnes, objects of suspicion during the Terror, as containing inns that served meals to wealthy Parisians and their ladies, including members of the Convention, who, it seems, tended to forget that Austerity was the watchword of the Sovereign People, once they had got past the *barrières*, places, therefore, that as well as being politically unsound and easily misled by local demagogues, were also morally wanting, sinning against Equality.[2] Les Porcherons, Clichy, Ménilmontant, Saint-Cloud, Meudon, Joinville, Antony, Asnières were also the sort of places to which the Parisian male, whether artisan or bourgeois, and whether married or single, might take a girl, whom he was anxious to impress, inebriate, and so seduce, on a Sunday or a

---

[1] Charenton, we learn from a report of Floréal year II, had other moral failings apart from housing black market butchers and *restaurateurs*. Its children used the most revolting language, no doubt picked up from their parents and from the numerous rivermen and sawyers of the village: '. . . Une dénonciation . . . nous a appris qu'il existait même parmi des enfans de 8, 9, 10 et 12 ans un libertinage révoltant. Ce libertinage a pour principe d'abord le défaut de surveillance de la plupart des pères et mères sur leurs enfans, ensuite les propos licencieux qui se tiennent en public en présence des jeunes gens de l'un et l'autre sexe par des citoyens que leur âge aurait dû rendre au moins circonspects . . .' (A.N. F7 4782, comité de surveillance de Charenton, au Comité de sûreté générale, 25 floréal an II).

[2] Rousseville, in one of his reports, writes: '. . . à Châtillon, à Clamart &ca., on a de la viande de boucherie toutes les semaines . . . plusieurs habitants de ces villages élèvent beaucoup de lapins et ils y sont dans ce moment de la plus grande ressource; le peuple n'y est donc pas dans une si grande pénurie qu'à Paris . . .' (A.N. F7 4782).

Monday outing—a complaisant *cocher* would be hired for the occasion
—either in a *guinguette* or in some riverside or wayside inn: any girl
who accepted an invitation so dangerous must in fact have done so with
her eyes open. The outward journey might be reassuring enough, but,
at some stage in the course of the afternoon, the *cocher* could be quietly
disposed of, sent off on the journey back to Paris, so that, in the
evening, a return would appear impossible. Those who ran the
guinguettes also provided rooms, and, for the more sophisticated,
cabinets particuliers.

Of course, there were many real grounds for Parisian suspicions.
These villages were hardly policed at all, and, when they did, as *chefs-
lieux de canton*, possess a company of the *gendarmerie*, it might have
been said of this force what a public prosecutor from one of the
Belgian Departments was to write of this particular arm: 'que loin
d'être surveillante, elle a besoin d'être surveillée'. In a place like Montrouge, the *logeurs* consistently failed to keep their books up to date, and
people could sleep in the inns there without having their names, even
false ones, recorded. It cannot have been at all difficult to induce
secretaries of rural *mairies* to fill in under dictation the blank forms of
baptismal entries. Guard duties were carried out very carelessly, and
with a great deal of absenteeism.

Parisians were, in any case, normally only momentarily concerned
with these places, and that was at weekends,[1] when they went there
with their families, to eat and to drink, and to marvel at the mental
image of themselves, as they walked along the banks of the Seine or the
Marne, admiring the weeping-willows, as late-eighteenth-century
promeneurs solitaires, even if they were staggering along, in uneven file.
Montmorency was, of course, a particular draw in this respect. One
could visit the abode of Jean-Jacques, reflect, with suitable emotion, on
the Virtues of that Friend of the Human Race, and then set to, with a
clear conscience, on a Sunday dinner in the *auberge*. It was *because* they
only came at week-ends that in the special circumstances of the Terror
period, many Parisians, not all of them like Rousseville, on official
business, discovered, to their affected horror and alarm, that, in a great
many of these places, churches remained open on Sundays and feast
days, and were extremely well attended, and that, in a village like
Courbevoie or Colombes, the four bells of the parish church had not

---

[1] Referring once more to Clamart and Châtillon, Rousseville goes on:
'... Quelques Parisiens qui se marient vont faire leurs noces dans les environs
de ces villages, soit par économie, soit pour y goûter l'air pur de la campagne ...'
(A.N. F7 4782).

only been kept, somehow escaping collection for melting-down, but were still calling the faithful, often from afar, to habitual forms of worship. Indeed, the bells must have often been heard from within Paris itself. Perhaps much of such horror was indeed simulated. For it was not unpleasant for a Paris shop-keeper or carpenter to reflect on his own superiority when confronted with such devastating examples of rural ignorance, superstition, and 'fanaticism'. *Il semble*, he might say, and often did, as he returned, slowly on his soporific way home back to the Elysium of Refinement, *que ces gens-là n'ont jamais connu les bienfaits de la Philosophie.* Well, *he* had.[1]

It took the régime of the Second Empire to effect a minor revolution in the relationship between Paris and its perimeter, by including in the city the former independent *communes* of Auteuil, Passy, Chaillot, Belleville, Montmartre (still nominally a *commune libre*, but only as a tourist attraction, involving the preservation of a fire brigade and a *musique municipale* in carnival uniforms), Vaugirard, and Grenelle. No other *commune* has been taken in since. The main result of these annexations was to increase the political and electoral importance, relatively to other more central areas of the city, of the two western *arrondissements*, the XVIme and the XVIIme. As they had the richest residents of any area of the city, once representation had been reintroduced under the Third Republic, they were constantly able to obtain for themselves a sizeable chunk of the annual municipal budget. It is perhaps the ultimate irony of the whole sad story of mutual misunderstanding, suspicion, and fear, that the one-time poor villages of Auteuil, Passy, and Chaillot, once they had been included, over a hundred years ago, within the boundaries of the city, should have become the favoured abodes of the very wealthy. There is perhaps more continuity in that other fact: that *most* of the poor *communes* of the periphery, including Saint-Denis, Pantin, Aubervilliers, Montreuil (where the *musée de la Révolution* is now situated), Villiers-le-Sec, Choisy, Ivry, Drancy, Montrouge, Vanves, Kremlin-Bicêtre (with such a name, how could it vote otherwise?) have, ever since the 1930s,

[1] In the following century, another of these riverside *communes* Gennevilliers, would have a further claim on the suspicions of the Parisian *petit peuple*, especially that from the north-eastern districts, for it was there that the *proscrits de juin*, after the collapse of the June Days, were marched under escort, to be embarked on barges on the first stage of the long and no doubt perilous journey to Algeria. I owe this information to M. Francis Ghillès, of Saint Antony's College, who is preparing a thesis on the colonisation of Algeria.

regularly voted Communist, and have thus come to constitute another girdle holding Parisians, or at least middle-class ones, in a ring of fear, the so-called *ceinture rouge*, this time a political no-man's-land encircling the city, and, on occasion, invading it.[1]

[1] As, for instance, at the time of the Clichy riots, in July 1936.

La Route du Nord

Banditry on the Border and in the
Belgian Departments 1795–1798

'. . . Tous les hommes et toutes les femmes du *Soleil noir* connais-saient la loi et une loi. On discutait la vie secrète de la ville et de quelques villes éparpillées dans le monde, sans même essayer de dissimuler ces propos. Au *Soleil noir* aboutissaient: Buenos-Ayres, Barcelone, Marseille, Tanger et Hambourg. Tous ces clients de la nuit monotone savaient retrouver dans l'une de ces villes un établissement semblable. Ils connaissaient des noms de femmes dont la célébrité était riche d'aventures et de complications exceptionnelles. On parlait d'Aline, de Fernande, d'Angèle la Marseillaise et de Ninon la Bre-tonne, comme en d'autres endroits on eût parlé d'industriels célèbres ou des princesses du haut commerce de luxe. Un nom, un tout petit nom de femme devenait à la fois un programme pour vivre un souvenir d'une qualité presque littéraire, un film facile à dérouler dans la solitude imposée par les mauvaises combinaisons . . .'

Pierre MacOrlan, *La Tradition de minuit.*

'. . . Et il racontait le Vieux, comment les Marseillais étaient montés à Paris et les règlements de comptes avec les Corses et la fusillade du cimetière de Thiais après l'assassinat de Stéfani, ce soir de Noël et comme ils se mitraillaient de tombe en tombe et il reste tout songeur, trente ans après.

"Il y avait quand même un certain romantisme, Max, à cette époque, même si c'était des crapules, comme une certaine honnêteté, un côté Cartouche, et vous voyez ce que je veux dire?"

C'est fini les Marseillais, et le train d'or, et Leca, et Stéfani, et Car-bone, et Spirito. C'est terminé les photos en belino dans *L'Intransig-eant.* Fini les chapeaux taupés. Il n'y a plus de bandits de grand chemin de Blanche à La Chapelle, et simplement des professionnels qui louent leurs services. . . .'

Claude Neron, *Max et les ferrailleurs.*

i Dinah Jacob and the *Bande Juive*

September 1795–March 1797

'. . . qu'il est à sa connaissance qu'il existe des bandes de brigands, savoir l'une dans les environs de Paris, la seconde en Hollande, la troisième dans les environs d'Amiens, la quatrième dans les environs de Bruxelles, la cinquième dans les environs d'Anvers, la sixième dans les environs de Lille, et la septième dans l'arrondissement du Tournésis . . . que de ces sept bandes, celle de Paris est la plus forte . . .'

'. . . elle lui fit part qu'il y avait 3 brigades de voleurs et assassins qui désolaient ce pays & lieux circonvoisins, qu'une de ces brigades était dans Paris & ses environs, la seconde à Bruxelles et environs, et la troisième en Hollande vers Midelbourg, que ces trois brigades formaient un total de plus de 600 personnes . . .'

'Dénonciation d'assassinats & brigandages s'extandans depuis Paris jusqu'en Hollande'

(from the statement made by Dinah Jacob to the public prosecutor of the criminal court of Tournai, on 6 Germinal year V [26 March 1797]).

'. . . Le mot d'ordre de la bande était conçu en ces termes, en frappant à la porte on demandait *qui va là?* La réponse était *Paris,* alors on ouvrit la porte . . .'

(from the statement made by Jean Frénay, a French *émigré,* to the same official, on the same date).[1]

---

[1] The three extracts concerning the so-called '*bande juive*' are all drawn from the *dossier* formed for the indictment of Kotzo-Picard and his alleged accomplices to be found in A.N. BB 18 400 (Justice, Jemappes, *affaire de la bande juive*). Unless otherwise stated, in order to avoid repetition, all the quotations in this section, including the massive testimony of the principal prosecution witness, Dinah Jacob, and those of Frénay and others of his alleged accomplices, as well as of his victims, are from the same box.

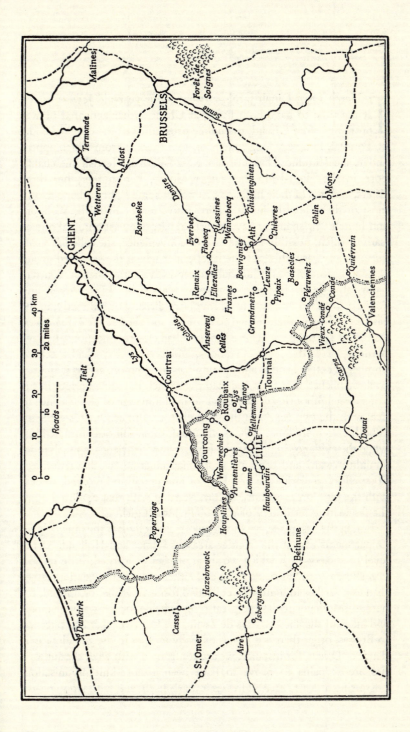

In March 1797, Dinah Jacob, a twenty-four-year-old Jewess, stated at the time to have been living at Ghent, either appeared or was brought before Giraud, the public prosecutor of the criminal court of Tournai. In a very long statement, two extracts from which appear above, she denounced her husband, Kotzo-Picard, a Jewish 'merchant', born in the Haut-Rhin, her father Moÿse, her mother, her three sisters, and two of their husbands, as well as some eighty other persons, most of them Jewish, but including also French, Flemish, Walloon, and Dutch Christians, as having formed part of a vast criminal organisation which, possibly for the sake of convenience, she called *la bande juive*. In any case, this was the label under which the so-called group came to be known to the judicial and repressive authorities of Tournai, Courtrai, Ghent, Brussels, Antwerp, Maastricht, Lille, Arras, and Amiens, all of whom were to be involved, directly or indirectly, in the case, as well as in that, related to it, of the so-called *bande à Salambier*. As the two groups are believed to have had close connections, to have participated in the same operations, and even to have had a certain number of active bandits and accomplices in common, and as it appears well established that they operated over much the same period, in the same or neighbouring areas, it has seemed a matter of convenience to deal with the two *bandes* in the same chapter. But as Dinah's evidence is both extremely long, very complicated, often full of contradictions, while the evidence implicating Salambier and his friends is much more straightforward and certainly more incriminating, we have decided, in an effort to clarify the problems of interpretation involved, to deal with the two 'organisations' in turn, starting with that conjured up in the fascinating testimony of the young Jewish girl.

But, in the first place, we should take a closer look at the nine Belgian Departments and at the frontier areas of France and Holland. At the level of society with which we are at present concerned, little respect was shown for man-made frontiers, either old or still existing, other than as a further invitation to collective forms of crime, or, indeed, for natural frontiers such as the great river Schelde, or the water channels and inlets of the ancient Pays de Zwijn, the lost river that had once led to Bruges, other than as a means of ready escape. In the garrulous evidence of Dinah, for instance, we are confronted with what the authorities are at pains to prove to have been a close-knit organisation, possessing at least three addresses in Paris itself, and with stopping-off

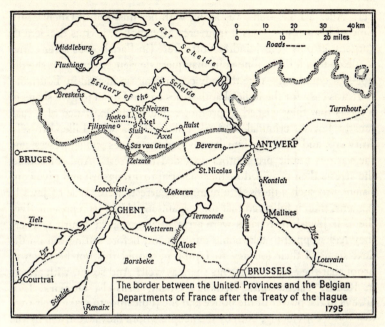

The border between the United Provinces and the Belgian
Departments of France after the Treaty of the Hague
1795

places in inns or in the shops of goldsmiths, engravers, old-clothes'
merchants, and printers, in Reims, Amiens, Béthune, Lille, Dunkirk,
Courtrai, Tournai, Ghent, Brussels, Antwerp, and, possibly, Maastricht.

There was no doubt, therefore, at this very practical level, in the
minds, for instance, of the officials of the Tournai court—and those of
Lille, Courtrai, Ghent, and Brussels would not have dissented from
this view—that Paris belonged to a network of crime spreading as far
as the Rhine and the Maas. According to Frénay, one of the prosecution witnesses against Kotzo-Picard and Dinah's relatives, Paris was so
much in the minds of some of the members of the 'Jewish organisation'
that, when attacking farms in the Ath-Leuze region, they were to
employ 'Paris' as a password, though this is indeed hard to believe, as
most of the men in this particular group were villagers from the neighbourhood, or inhabitants of Ghent. It is difficult to see why they should
have felt the need to invoke a city that few of them can ever have
visited. But the point is that the Jemappes judicial authorities clearly
wanted to bring in the French capital by hook or by crook; and this is
in itself of interest.

And, again, according to Dinah, when there was a general round-up
of suspected Jews, one of her relatives was to reassure the girl by telling

her: 'Allez à Lille'—she was living with her husband in Ghent at the time of his arrest—'vous y trouverez Monchoker, il vous donnera de l'argent, et puis vous joindrez votre frère [in Paris], vous serez entretenue de tout à Paris, il ne vous manquera de rien.' In any case she did not—or could not—take this advice, turning up instead in Tournai.

It was easy for the judicial authorities to use Dinah to give shape to a thesis that they wished to promote: that of the existence of a vast, mostly Jewish, criminal network linking Paris with Lille, Brussels, Antwerp, and Tournai. Dinah provided the names and addresses, and the various public prosecutors provided the arrests. And, of course, the arrests then provided further material to strengthen and give consistency to such a thesis. If a number of arrests were made of Jews in Amiens, then it followed that the 'organisation' had its representatives there. If Jewish merchants were arrested at an inn in Tournai, where they had stopped to take some refreshment, before setting out on the next stage of their journey to Limburg, would this not be taken as proof that the *bande* had agents there as well? And so on, with arrests in Reims, Valenciennes, Béthune, Ghent, Brussels, Dunkirk. It is always in the power of the police and the judicature to make their own case more convincing, both by the people whom they arrest, and by the places in which they are arrested. They are in effect the masters of whatever version of 'the geography of crime' they wish to promote. Much of the evidence for the actual existence, for instance, of a Jewish underworld network spreading from Paris to the Dutch border seems to have been based on this type of argument.

We do not know why these authorities should have been so visibly anxious to link Paris with such a network, said to be based in the nine new Departments, or, anyway, in five of them (Jemappes, the Lys, the Escaut, the Dyle, and the Deux-Nèthes). Perhaps they had reason to believe that much of what Dinah had to say was true. At least the map that she so obligingly and minutely produced seemed to correspond with what any policeman would know about the habits and movements of pedlars and merchants, whether Jewish or not. It would appeal to the authorities in its basic likelihood. For Dinah was certainly telling the truth on the subject of the comings and goings of her numerous relatives. The question is what all these amount to. Were they entirely innocent and normal, or were they, on the contrary, pointers indicating some vast criminal grand design? We should, then, proceed with care on a road that now has made Brussels and Ghent as much the faubourgs of Paris as Vanves and Gentilly.

It is with these new, extended, angles of vision, rather than with the reality of the existence of the *bande juive* that we are primarily concerned in the present chapter. In other words, the principal interest, at least to the historian, of the case of the so-called 'Jewish organisation' is that it poses redoubtable problems of interpretation, while at the same time throwing a mass of revealing light both on the assumptions of the judicial and repressive authorities, and of the habits, language, appearance, frequentations, and movements of groups of Jewish pedlars and merchants, as they ply their various activities between the mouths of the Rhine and the Schelde and the two banks of the Seine.

It is not for the historian to decide whether or not Kotzo-Picard was quite the man that he was said to be, nor whether he commanded the unstinted support of the armies of accomplices stated to have been in his service. These are matters of secondary importance, at least to us; for to Picard and his fellow-accused, they were indeed matters of life and death.

La Grande Nation, as we have noted earlier, might be thought to have brought mutual advantage to the populations of both sides of the old *barrière*: to Walloons and Flemings, the questionable benefits of a constitution imposed upon them, that of the year III, of the French system of justice, and the French instrument of death, the guillotine; and to the French, especially, as it was believed, to the *frontaliers*, the inhabitants of the Nord and the Ardennes, the promise of a decisive end to hardship and famine, with the dispatch, by canal, by river, by road, and by sea, of the varied products of the *richesses immenses des provinces belgiques*. For this is what the Committee of Public Safety had had in mind, when it had outlined the details of a pillage economy, with the formation in the early summer of 1794, a little before Fleurus, of the *comité d'extraction*, for once no euphemism, no misnomer, like those so generally affected by the rather prissy régime of the year II, but exactly what it said. The commissioners were to consult an impressive body of specialists: veterinary surgeons, industrialists, agronomes, engineers, artists, architects, dealers, jewellers, goldsmiths, who were given the task of drawing up detailed lists of what was considered worth stripping from the territories likely to be occupied by the end of the summer.

Immediately after Fleurus, the optimistic theme was taken up, both by the Paris authorities, especially the two Committees, and, above all, by the hard-pressed *Représentants en mission* in Lille and in Charleville-Mézières. Both Parisians and *frontaliers* were assured, almost daily, that they would not have long to wait, that their troubles would soon be over, with the arrival of immense stores of Belgian grain and cattle and horses, from the semi-mythical Pays de Waes, from the rich grainlands and stock-breeding areas of West and East Flanders, Brabant, the Tournésis, the Hainaut, Antwerp, and Limburg. The Ardennais were even given to expect that they might receive succour, presumably in the form of wood, from the wretchedly poor Luxembourg, as well as manufactured goods from Namur, Liége, and the valley of the Meuse.[1] The *frontaliers* naturally expected to be served first, because they were the nearest; in any case, they no doubt felt that they were well placed to see that they were, as the *immenses richesses* were bound to be passing across their territories, even if some of them were destined for the Paris markets. But a great many promises were made all round, so that the Parisians were also convinced that they, as always, would be given the first helping.

The inhabitants of the Nord and the Ardennes, as is generally the case with people who live in close, and sometimes profitable, proximity, to a foreign nation (even though many of the subjects of that nation did in fact speak French, especially in those areas that had the closest points of contact with Roubaix, Valenciennes, or Givet), regarded their neighbours to their immediate east with a mixture of contempt, loathing, and envy. The *kaiserlycks*, as they were generally described in the Ardennes, were known to be selfish, greedy, dishonest in business, 'fanatical' (dominated by their Gothic priests), attached to hierarchical values and to their old nobility, traditionalist, unworthy of liberty, uncouth in their eating habits—*les femmes belges*, French food chauvinists were to report, from the year III onwards, *ne savent cuisiner qu'une soupe grossière et une espèce de bouillie de pomme de terre.* Later, the French provisioning commissioners were to keep up endless lamentations on the subject of the eating and drinking habits of the liberated citizens, as bizarrely exotic no doubt as those attributed by Dinah to a Jewish merchant allegedly of *la bande:* 'qu'au surplus, lorsque son mari fut arrêté, il y a un an environ, led. Haÿman étoit chez lui et mangeoit du lait battu ainsi que du poisson avec des pommes de terre . . . étant avec plusieurs autres voleurs.' Furthermore, the Flemings in particular were known to be brutal, violent, quick to take offence, ever ready with knife and stick, a reputation that had in fact often been borne out in ugly weekend affrays in the *estaminets* of Lille, in the rough carters' inns of the faubourgs of that fortified city— Wazemmes-lès-Lille, faubourg de Béthune, faubourg Notre-Dame,

---

[1] R. C. Cobb, 'La Disette de l'an III en Belgique', republished in *Terreur et subsistances*, pp. 343–81. See note A, p. 249.

La Madeleine, Fives—between French smugglers, soldiers, and deserters and Flemish horse dealers, itinerants, and travelling salesmen.[1]

The Walloons can hardly have appeared more reassuring in French eyes. We hear, for instance, in 1798, of a girl of seventeen and her younger brother, both from the neighbourhood of Mons, who had been found guilty of parricide.[2] Of course, such things happened in France, too,[3] but, for a visiting Frenchman, some unwilling commissioner or judicial official, mouldering uncomfortably in the unfamiliar surroundings of one of the new Departments of the Republic, incest and parricide would be likely to witness to the crude tribalism of the new citizens. The Walloons at least were more or less understandable, at least when not talking the extraordinary *patois* of Liége. According to one report from Jemappes, their natural cruelty might find true expression in that taste for the bizarre, for dressing-up and for street-corner display and circus that one still finds characterised in les Gilles, the strange bellmen of Binche, as, clothed like Aztec warriors, they dance in a tremendous crash of sound; or in Mons' own dragon, the beloved and pampered Doudou, processed out at feast days and anniversaries as the collective emblem of civic pride and of the endurance of a city so often threatened by war and opened to the pillaging of cruel armies of dark men. For, in this frontier area, we are indeed in the land of genial giants—both Lille and Dunkirk possessed them—and of colourful pigmies, as well as of elaborately uniformed *musiques municipales*. The escort given to Christ in Ensor's famous picture, *L'entrée du Christ à Bruxelles*, contains all the elements of such a traditionalist and flamboyant *kermesse*.

In the course of the year V, one of the inmates of the Mons prison petitioned the Minister of Justice on the subject of the grotesque treatment to which he and some of his fellow-prisoners had been subjected by the local *gendarmes*:

[1] A.N. BB 18 400 (Jemappes, déposition de Dinah Jacob par devant le directeur du jury d'accusation du tribunal de Tournai, 5 fructidor an V).

[2] See note B, p. 251.

[3] The inhabitants of the Nord, both male and female, could, it appears, be equally brutal and violent. There is a report in the papers of the *commissaire de police* of the Section de la Butte-des-Moulins, dated 16 Brumaire year IV [7 November 1795] on the subject of a street accident. A child, standing in a queue in front of a butcher's shop, in order to draw his meat ration, had been pushed aside by a woman behind him who wanted to take his place. The child fell into the street and was run over by a cart and gravely wounded. The woman was a native of Valenciennes, aged 42, the wife of a printer (A.P.P. A/A 98, commissaire de police de la Section de la Butte-des-Moulins, 16 brumaire an IV).

. . . Nous fumes donc injuriés, maltraités, 2 d'entre nous furent grisés d'une telle façon qu'ils ne pouvoient articuler d'autres choses que ce que ces prétendus officiers de paix pouvoient et vouloient leur faire dire, ils eurent aussi la méchanceté de donner le jour même d'une interrogatoire à l'un d'eux 42 verres de genièvre. . . . ces gendarmes . . . eurent l'effronterie d'engager les habitants de Celmonbaix et les passagers à venir contempler leurs barbaries et leurs victimes. . . . ils mascaradèrent donc l'exposant en lui faisant de grosses moustaches, lui mettant des épaulettes rouges et sur son chapeau un pompom de grenadier, en joignant enfin des attributs militaires avec le costume du simple laboureur. C'est dans cet accoutrement bizarre qu'il fut injurié constamment, et montré comme une bête rare et curieuse à plus de mille personnes ingénieux dans leurs plaisirs . . . ils donnèrent à l'exposant, ainsi ridiculisé, le grand nom de *tigre marin*. . . . on réveilloit par des gentillesses prétendument révolutionnaires, par des récits fabuleux, la curiosité ordinaire du peuple, on le mettoit donc à contribution pour lui montrer le fameux *tigre marin*, un cabaretier nommé Jossain eut la bassesse même de prêter son ministère à de pareilles horreurs, puisqu'il avoit la sublime fonction de taxer les curieux et faire faire le recette par sa servante à la porte de ce magnifique spectacle. . . .[1]

All in good fun, no doubt, an expression perhaps of the rather rumbustious *bonhomie*, helped by extreme libations of *genièvre*, of the Walloon countryman, a scene indeed very reminiscent of certain pictures by the elder Breughel depicting collective rejoicings and gargantuan eatings in a countryside a little further to the west, almost at the gates of Brussels. But the victim would not see it thus; and a French traveller, had he passed that way and witnessed that strange fête, would no doubt have concluded that the Hainaut, like the Île de France or the Parisis, was indeed inhabited by wild animals, hyenas, and *tigres d'Afrique*, as well as by cannibals, even if this particular tiger were indeed made of paper and tinsel and paint, and belonged to a maritime breed. The sea, after all, was not far away.[2]

Other French witnesses were to complain of the lack of intelligence of the population of the Austrian Netherlands, of their slowness to grasp a point, of their *lourdeur*. 'Il y a une observation qu'il faut saisir,' wrote a French judicial official from Mons, to the Minister of Justice, in the summer of 1796, 'c'est qu'on ne peut pas encore exiger des individus de ce pays la même célérité, le même ensemble qu'on obtient ail-

---

[1] A.N. BB 18 400 (Hubert Dehay, détenu à Mons, au ministre de la Justice, s.d. an v).

[2] See note C, p. 252.

leurs. Le climat et le caractère se travaillent lentement pour parvenir au faire français . . .'[1]

In other words, French officials, at the time of the second conquest and the Directory, already adopted towards *les bons Belges* that rather condescending scorn later displayed in *Le Mariage de Mlle Beulemans* and that has tended ever since to stultify a proper understanding, *outre-Quiévrain*, of the quirks and virtues of the inhabitants of the neighbouring Kingdom. Jaubert, who could never keep his mouth shut, even when he was not denouncing people, and who could never resist an opportunity to lecture the French on the *mores* of his Walloon compatriots, had at least a wise word of warning on the subject of the dangers of French vanity in such a context: 'L'orgeuil est une sorte de brutalité qui est insupportable au peuple de ce pays . . .'[2] a message which, unfortunately, seems to have fallen on totally deaf ears. The inhabitants of the Nord, the Pas-de-Calais, and the Ardennes, in particular, as is the way with neighbours and *frontaliers*, had their minds made up on the subject of the many faults of the inhabitants of the *ci-devant provinces belgiques*. Nor were a great many of the new judicial authorities altogether convinced of the republican patriotism and pro-French sentiments of the new citizens of the French Republic. Many, as we shall see, suspected them, on the contrary, of remaining attached to the former Austrian rulers.

So it came naturally to the inhabitants of the Nord and of the other two French Departments to think that the new citizens should be exploited without mercy. Furthermore, the *frontaliers* had, in 1793 and in the course of the year II, been among the most underprivileged inhabitants of the Republic. Living in a war zone, often within the areas of Austrian, English, and Prussian cannon fire and bombardment, they had not only suffered all the horrors of war; owing to their proximity to the battle area, the inhabitants of the Departments to their west—Aisne, Marne, Somme, and so on—had invoked the fact in order to refuse to keep them supplied with grain, food supplies, livestock, and transport. What was the use of sending to the Ardennes or the Nord supplies much-needed inland when they were likely to fall into enemy hands when the *frontaliers* did not actually sell them to the enemy, which was all that could be expected of such habitual *fraudeurs*? This was an argument frequently put forward during the period of the *maximum* and requisitioning, as a pretext to fall behind on requisitions

---

[1] A.N. BB 18 400 (Giraud, directeur du jury d'accusation du tribunal de Mons, au Ministre, 24 prairial an V).

[2] A.N. BB 18 400 (Jaubert, d'Ath, au Ministre, 12 prairial an IV).

for the civil population of the two frontier Departments, as well as for
the voracious *armée du Nord*, the presence of which further diminished
the amount of supplies available to the unfortunate civilians of these
areas. In such circumstances, it was hardly surprising that in the weeks
following the fall of Robespierre, the needs of their own *administrés*
should have seemed so imperative to the *Représentants* in the Nord and
the Ardennes, and that the local population should have regarded the
apparently inexhaustible resources of the Austrian Netherlands as
coming to them in the first place by absolute right.

In fact, these hopes were to be rapidly and decisively shattered.
There is perhaps no need to describe once again the situation which
developed in this part of France and in the territories over the border,
in the course of the year III, as I have already done so in a previous
article.[1] In the first year of the second occupation, the integrity of the
former Austrian provinces was preserved, administration being placed
in the hands of a central authority, seated in Brussels, the *Commission
Centrale & Supérieure de la Belgique*, composed of French and Belgian
officials, as well as in those of the *Représentants* sent to the former
capital. Both had to reckon with the military authorities in the occupied
territories, as well as with the proconsuls still based on Lille and
Charleville. Briefly, there developed, in the course of 1795, an increasingly bitter three-cornered struggle between these groups. The
Commission was above all concerned to preserve the population of
Brussels and other Belgian cities from famine, and the military, it goes
without saying, raised enormous requisitions on local farmers, particularly in the Flemish-speaking areas.[2] Very little material ever reached
the Nord and the Ardennes. On the contrary, it was the French markets
that were invaded by Belgian speculators and black-marketeers who,
thanks to the plentiful supplies of hard currency—Austrian thalers and
florins—that were still in circulation on the Belgian side of the border,
were able to drive all before them. Very soon, a movement began in reverse, with French grain and livestock being drained away to hidden
markets in Belgium, while hordes of Belgian purchasing agents and
speculators appeared, at the same time as the first foreign tourists:
Prussians and Swiss, *sur la place de Paris*.

This then is the background to the growth of large-scale banditry
and brigandage in the Pas-de-Calais and the Nord, as well as in the
Lys, Jemappes, the Escaut, the Dyle, and the Deux-Nèthes, from the
early months of the year IV and throughout the year V. We have

---

[1] 'La Disette de l'an III en Belgique', *Terreur et subsistances*.
[2] See note D, p. 252.

already mentioned, in an earlier chapter, the extension of the *chaîne* to include, in its network of walking, manacled, and chained men, Courtrai, Tournai, Mons, Bruges, Ghent, Brussels,[1] Antwerp, Malines, Namur, Liége, and Hasselt. From the beginning of the Directory, Belgium, now annexed and divided into nine Departments, did at least provide, on an increasingly large scale, two articles of export to the French Republic: bandits and other hardened and experienced criminals, and prostitutes, for whom the *route du Nord* was soon to become the *route de Paris*; and indeed the prospect of Paris would appear singularly alluring to some Walloon peasant girl from the poor forest lands of the region of Namur. There had always been plenty of Belgians among the *filles du Palais-Royal* (Restif speaks of them with the approval of an expert) under the old régime; but now the appeal of the metropolis became far more insistent and, in the first two years of the Directory, there was something like an invasion of Bruxelloises, Luxembourgeoises, Liégeoises, Anversoises, Gantoises, and even Dutch girls *sur la place de Paris*; and they were soon followed by country girls and female inhabitants of these cities, in the humbler trades: *blanchisseuses*, domestic servants, *fileuses*, and so on, the presence of whom becomes increasingly noticeable in the cases of petty theft, burglary, and other specifically female crimes coming to the notice of the Paris judicial authorities, between 1796 and 1799.

Le pourtoir de Paris had indeed been extended, quite beyond the wildest dreams of partisans of *les frontières naturelles*, conquest, and military annexation. But it hardly took the form that they would have imagined, in the over-sanguine days preceding Fleurus. An entirely new national element had been added to current Parisian preoccupations on the subject of the presence of newcomers, itinerants, and *gens sans aveu*. A Belgian *mendiant valide* was quite as redoutable as a French one,[2] while Belgian prostitutes clearly had a lot to offer.

This new intake seems to have been confined, at least as far as women were concerned, to the Walloon section of the population. Flemish

---

[1] A.N. BB 18 283 (président du tribunal criminel de la Dyle au Ministre, 9 pluviôse an IV) '. . . 5 hommes condamnés aux fers sont également transférés, des maisons d'arrêt de notre commune, à celle de Bicêtre près Paris. . . .'

[2] The Fleming, Baelde, president of the Bruges court, writes to the Minister, 22 Ventôse year V [12 March 1797]: '. . . L'armée des Brigands qui infestoient naguère ces pays sont la plupart paresseux mendians ou prétendus marchands de vétilles de prétexte, rôdant de marché à autre et toujours en route, entretiennent et enrichissent nombre de petits cabarets sur des routes écartées où ils se rassemblent et d'où nous viennent la moitié de nos voleurs de première classe et assassins. . . .' (A.N. BB 18 582 (Justice, Nord)).

girls were more likely to stay at home, and, in the very favourable terrain provided by the Département de la Lys and by the equally advantageously placed Département de l'Escaut, we hear of many of them, established in inns off the main roads, as *cabaretières*, and, of course, as receivers.[1]

It was also the presence of large and well-stocked farms round Courtrai, and north of Ghent that would act as a magnet to organised brigandage and *chauffage*. Furthermore, the *Départements Réunis*, in which circulated in abundance both Austrian and Dutch coins, seem to have thus been well provided with the related skills of armies of counterfeiters, dishonest engravers, and goldsmiths: there had already been plenty of trade for them under the Austrians, in the manufacture of *faux assignats*. And, with the French back, there came new and more promising opportunities. The Mons public prosecutor, for instance, complaining to the Minister about the absence of such an official for the *canton* of Fontaine-l'Évêque, in a letter dated 24 Prairial year V [12 June 1797], adds the interesting comment:

. . . Le directeur du jury est tombé malade. . . . il serait pourtant essentiel d'avoir pour cet arrondissement un bon investigateur de police, car cette contrée est la retraite de tous les fabricateurs de gros sous faux, il ne paraît plus dans la circulation que cette monnaie-là. . . . la vente des cloches nous donne ce résultat. . . .[2]

Another gift, in fact, of French liberty to the criminally-inclined!

The minister's correspondents, in the eight Departments we have studied, whether French or Belgian, were very much *au fait* with the

[1] The same official reports again to the Minister on 6 Floréal of the same year [25 April 1797] (ibid.): '. . . Pour ces pays surtout où beaucoup de bois sont encore le refuge indestructible . . . les Brigands ou prétendus marchands de bagatelles et tout à la fois mendians, ce qui y est la même chose, y trouveront toujours une funeste sécurité, des maisons de rendez-vous, des dépôts de vols, des lieux de rassemblement . . . les cabaretiers de cette espèce, à qui ils procurent de l'aisance, et sont receleurs, fauteurs et *capitaines* . . . usant du sifflet [se tiennent] . . . dans un second cabaret à l'écart et auprès d'un bois, ce cabaret [est] tenu par deux filles . . . parmi nos derniers assassins condamnés . . . fut toute une famille occupant un cabaret . . . considérez combien de sécurité un tel hôte et son auberge doivent inspirer aux négotiants voyageurs. . . .'

[2] A.N. BB 18 400 (Jemappes, directeur du jury d'accusation du tribunal de Mons, au Ministre, 24 prairial an V). See also A.N. BB 18 92 (Justice, Aisne, juge de paix du canton de Vervins, au Ministre, 28 pluviôse an IV [17 February 1796]): 'Le 11 de ce mois, Nicolas Martheleuse, du canton de Chimay, pays conquis, a été mis en arrestation en cette commune comme prévenu de distribution de faux louis faits à Larciennes, canton de Florennes près de Charleroi le 15 nivôse dernier, en paiement de trois chevaux mis en fourrière en cette commune. . . .'

criminal and semi-criminal specialities of many of the inhabitants of their areas. Baret, the public prosecutor in Courtrai and Bruges, had had previous experience in such functions for the whole of Belgium in the year III. His comments on the various *bandes* are always interesting, while his handling of Salambier himself, whom he flattered and played up to, is an extremely subtle example of cross-examination. Ranson is an equally perceptive observer; and even Baelde, whom Baret described as quite unfit for his post[1]—his knowledge at least of French was certainly limited—knows his country; his comments on the multiplicity of small cabarets, *à l'écart de la route*, enclosed in woodland and rendered inaccessible by the network of canals, offer a convincing clue to the persistence of banditry in the Lys. Such *cabaretières*, often sisters or whole families of womenfolk, serving beer and *genièvre*, could offer a discreet and almost unassailable retreat to the passing *marchands de bagatelles*.[2] They seem too to have had to hand a plentiful supply of blank papers: *patentes de colporteur*, *extraits de naissance*, and so on. As in any frontier area, papers, genuine or forged, appear to have been readily accessible. Here, for instance, is an eloquent example of such facility, in the region of Leuze, near the French frontier:

... Le 20 ventôse an V [10 March 1797] la brigade de gendarmerie ... de Leuze, fonction faisant dans le hameau de Danmarie, commune de Gradmetz, arrêtèrent chez le nommé Bernard, cabaretier audit lieu, 2 individus qui disoient aller à la foire de Frasnes pour y acheter des jambons, demande leur ayant été faite de leurs passeports, l'un d'eux en présenta un sous le nom de *Jacques-Joseph Minon*, ouvrier journalier demeurant à Leuze ... âgé de 45 ans.... il a été trouvé dans [sa] poche ... un autre passeport sous le nom de *Charles Plamon*, de la commune de Willaupuis, âgé de 24 ans.... Ces deux individus qu'on a su depuis l'un s'appeler *François Daumont*, dit *Proust*, ouvrier de bois demeurant à Flobecq, et l'autre, *Jean-Baptiste Lefebvre*, dit *Sans-Doigts*, de même résidence.... le premier a répondu qu'il y avoit 12 jours qu'en compagnie de Jean-Baptiste Lefebvre, dit *Sans-Doigts*, et de deux marchands de chevaux qu'il ne connoît pas, ils étoient arrivés mercredi 11 ventôse ... chez *Jacques Minon*, près de Leuze, sur la chaussée de Renaix, qu'ils y ont logé le lendemain, surlendemain et en sont

---

[1] '... Il est donc excellent qu'il [Salambier] soit jugé par ce tribunal.... Le C. Baelde ... n'est point en état de remplir ces fonctions, j'en avais souvent écrit au C. Boutteville [commissaire du Directoire exécutif à Bruxelles] ... il est entièrement déplacé à la tête d'un tribunal, sa contenance y est ridicule, ses discours sont ineptes, et le public ne peut cacher le mépris qu'il a pour lui ...' (A.N. BB 18 582, Baret au Ministre, 17 ventôse an V). Anyone who has attempted to read Baelde's rambling letters would agree with the severe judgement stated by Baret.

[2] See note E, p. 253.

partis le dimanche . . . vers 3 heures après-midi. . . . d'où il tenoit les deux passeports? . . . a dit les avoir trouvés dimanche 15 ventôse . . . vers les 4 heures . . . sur la chaussée de Renaix à Leuze, que Jacques-Joseph Minon, vivant dans un état d'oisiveté en un hameau près de Leuze, et d'ailleurs homme suspect . . . avoit enfin avoué qu'il avait vendu ce passeport à Jean-Baptiste Lefebvre pour 12 patars, que sur représentation à lui faite comment il se faisoit que lui qui n'était pas cabaretier logeoit chez lui des individus pendant plusieurs jours et qui plus est ne mettoit pas leur nom à la boîte conformément aux loix de police sur cette partie, il a reconnu son tort et a dit qu'il les avoit pris pour d'honnêtes gens. . . . Minon est prévenu d'être receleur de voleur au point d'aller prendre des passeports sous son nom pour leur en faire la vente. . . .

According to Dinah Jacob, when members of her husband's group were in need of a passport or a certificate, or wanted to change their at best elusive names, as they frequently did, 'sa mère leur fabrique des passeports et certificats, ayant le talent de contrefaire les signatures et les écritures. . . .', a skill as useful as that practised by her father, Moÿse, who, among other things, was an engraver and who could lend his hand in the production of false fiscal stamps. But an even better method, in this area, was to obtain *genuine* travel documents and *patentes*. *La Grande Catherine*, one of Salambier's group, the owner of an inn in one of the faubourgs outside the fortifications of Lille, merely had to walk to Tourcoing, address herself to the *secretaire de la mairie*, who, without demur, provided her with twenty-five blank birth certificates. When called to task by Ranson, this official was to state that he had not thought that he had done anything wrong; had not the Austrians, while in occupation of the town, destroyed all the existing records? There was something to be said, even for the Austrians, even on this side of the border.

There was a great deal more to be said for them on the other side of it. French and Belgian judicial authorities in the *Départements Réunis* are often revealed as being in two minds on the subject of their new or habitual *administrés*. The *substitut* of the *tribunal de la Dyle* (Brussels) reports quite favourably with regard to his flock, in a letter to the Minister dated 2 Pluviôse year IV [22 January 1796]: 'Le patriotisme et l'amour de l'ordre et de la paix dominent ce pays, il auroit toute son énergie, sans cette crainte tacite que les Belges ont des revenans. . . .'[1] But his chief is less enthusiastic: writing a week later, he complains that 'la peur et la menace des revenans autorisent et la lâcheté des uns, et

[1] A.N. BB 18 283 (substitut près le tribunal criminel de la Dyle, au Ministre de la Justice, 2 pluviôse an II).

l'audace des autres.'[1] Neither official was suggesting that the Belgians believed in ghosts, though they may well have done so too. *Les revenans* meant the Austrians. Some might indeed fear their return, but, clearly, many hoped for it, their hopes becoming more insistent with each year of the Directory.[2] The public prosecutor of Brussels was even more pessimistic, on this score, when he wrote to his chief on 26 Nivôse year IV [16 January 1796]:

... Les malveillans dans nos 9 Départements, et surtout dans ceci [la Dyle] prêchent pour la fusillade et s'agitent pour faire proscrire la guillotine. Ils en craignent et redoutent (disent-ils) même l'ombre comme instrument et emblême de la terreur, lorsque, sous des dehors mielleux, ils prêchent l'anarchie, le fanatisme, le pillage l'assassinat. . . .[3]

There was, in any case, at this date, no guillotine in Belgium. The same official was to inform the Minister, in Ventôse year V [March 1797]:

que le citoyen Schmidt [a carpenter from Lille] doit se rendre incessamment à Bruxelles pour y faire construire 9 machines à décapiter. Il a demandé, comme une condition expresse, qu'il lui fût accordé un emplacement national propre à cette construction, et où il soit à l'abri des insultes des malveillans. . . .[4]

The Belgians were clearly not over-enthusiastic on the subject of this particular benefit of the régime of Liberty. Throughout the year IV, every time a capital sentence had to be carried out in one of the Belgian Departments, the judicial authorities had to borrow not only the Lille guillotine, but the Lille executioner and his assistant. These had to be provided, on each occasion, with a military escort, while the instrument of death was packed up in a covered waggon that looked like the type of vehicle in use for Army food supplies;[5] and, indeed, it was mis-

---

[1] A.N. BB 18 283 (président du tribunal de la Dyle, au Ministre, 9 pluviôse an IV).

[2] See note F, p. 253.

[3] A.N. BB 18 283 (président du jury d'accusation du tribunal de la Dyle, au Ministre, 26 nivôse an IV).

[4] A.N. BB 18 283 (Ministre de l'Intérieur, au commissaire pres l'administration de la Dyle, s.d. ventôse an IV): '. . . Il [Schmidt] exige en second lieu la mise en réquisition du nombre de garçons menuisiers qu'il croira nécessaire pour l'aider dans son travail. Il convient de n'employer la voie de réquisition qu'après avoir épuisé toutes autres ressources, et envers les ouvriers qui témoigneroient de la répugnance à travailler sans cette injonction. . . .'

[5] '. . . La peine de mort qui les attend ne peut être exécutée, puisque le Département [de la Dyle] n'a pas les moyens, ni l'instrument nécessaire à la décolla-

taken as such by the members of the Antwerp gang, said to have been commanded by two Flemings, the Boorsbeek brothers, the elder of whom had married one of Dinah's sisters;[1] we are not told, however, what they did with their unexpected catch. Such arrangements must have been extremely inconvenient, especially as the machine was in frequent demand, in the Lys, the Escaut, Jemappes, and the Dyle, during these two years [1796 and 1797]. However, by the year VI, the nine Departments had at last been fully provided for. Already on 14 Frimaire year V [14 December 1796], the *commissaire* attached to the Alost court could write, in a letter to the Minister:

Toutes les villes où siègent les jurys d'accusation ont presque toutes leurs échafauds, quand aux bourreaux, ils sont salariés moyennant une petite somme pour leurs frais de voyage et voiture, on pourroit les obliger de se rendre aux lieux où l'exécution doit se faire. . . .[2]

The executioners were apparently mostly French and were no doubt provided by the endless kinsmen of the Sanson family. The guillotines were of local manufacture; indeed, the best preserved still in working order, dating from this period, so I am informed by my friends in Madame Tussaud's, may be seen in the museum of the city of Bruges.[3]

The rest of what Baret, Baelde, Ranson, Giraud, and others have to say about the particular problems affecting the French border areas and the new Departments, is equally familiar to anyone working on patterns of criminality in the early years of the Directory, and would apply with equal relevance to any Department in northern France at this time, including the Paris area. They refer, for instance, to the

---

tion . . .' (président du jury d'accusation du tribunal de la Dyle, au Ministre, 26 nivôse an IV, A.N. BB 18 283 (Dyle)).

[1] Jean and François Boorsbeek [or Borsbeck], both Flemings, had, according to Dinah, commanded the *bande d'Anvers*. That the elder brother had married one of her sisters is a fact difficult to equate with his declared hostility to Jews and with his unwillingness to admit any into his gang. However, at another stage of her testimony, Dinah states that the brothers had several Jews in a position of power in their organisation. 'Boorsbeek' one suspects, is not a surname, but is probably derived from the village called Borsbeke, just south of Alost. Many bandits were given as *noms de guerre* either their birthplace, or their place of residence.

[2] A.N. BB 18 293 (Escaut, commissaire près le tribunal d'Alost, au Ministre, 14 frimaire an V).

[3] I owe this information to the kindness of Miss Laura Dru, who recently consulted me on the subject of a proposed tableau depicting the execution of Louis XVI.

relative ineffectiveness and incapacity of the *gendarmerie*; and it was hardly likely that Walloon or Flemish *gendarmes* should have displayed a zeal and a willingness to expose themselves to danger, when their French colleagues, during these years, showed every sign of lethargy, though it must be admitted that, in their pursuit of smugglers, the company stationed in Sas van Gent, near the Dutch border—we will return to this peculiar area—seems to have been both extremely courageous and to have succeeded, on a number of occasions, in putting to rout large groups of fully armed and mounted bandits.

Then they complain, as elsewhere, of the passivity, not to say the complicity, of the *juges de paix* and even of the *directeurs des jurys d'accusation* (especially at the level of the *administrations cantonales*, always the weakest link in the chain of command between the government and local authority under the Directory). The public prosecutors attached to Departments display both zeal and honesty in the service of repression, though the judicial officials of Mons were frequently to complain of the delaying tactics employed by their colleagues in Tournai, as when they inquired about the progress of the indictment against Dinah's husband and his alleged accomplices; this may of course have been an example of those inter-communal rivalries so frequent in France, and, in a country like Belgium, in which municipalist sentiments were so very strong, more insistent still.

The prisons of Bruges, Brussels, Tournai, Ghent, Courtrai, and Antwerp were falling down, as they were in most French *chefs-lieux*. One of the gaolers of the Lille prison was an accomplice of the *bande à Salambier*, some of the members of which had escaped a dozen times or more, whether from the *chaîne* or from prison.[1] Dinah's husband, Kotzo-Picard, had, according to her testimony, been in prison, at various times between 1790 and 1796, in Ghent, Lille, Béthune, Antwerp, and Brussels. The mysterious Flemish bandit leader known as 'Swaert Pier' (Black Peter) and of whom we shall hear more had been in prison in Bruges and in Holland, whence he was to be returned to Bruges. The Boorsbeek brothers had served previous sentences in Antwerp and in Ghent. Unlike Salambier himself, most of those who were said to have been members of Picard's organisation were what the French would call *de vieux chevaux de retour*.

In the course of her testimony, Dinah was to tell Giraud:

---

[1] '. . . Je ne saurois trop vous peindre nos affreuses prisons, qui sont de véritables repaires, tant elles sont malsaines et mal-construites . . .' (président du jury d'accusation du tribunal de la Dyle, 9 pluviôse an V) (A.N. BB 18 283, Justice, Dyle).

que son frère Jacob a été deux fois arrêté à Lille pour vol de portefeuille, et
une fois à Abbeville, avec Daniel Jacob, qu'il y a quatre mois son frère,
ledit *Machoker*, et treize autres ont été arrêtés à Béthune, qu'ils restèrent en
prison quinze jours, que *Sara Crack* les a fait sortir pour de l'argent en fab-
riquant et achetant des assignats ... que son mari Picard a été arrêté à
Lille pendant six mois pour vol de portefeuille à la Comédie, qu'il a encore
été arrêté à Bailleul pour vol de portefeuille il y a environ trois mois, et
délivré à Cassel par jugement ... '

It seems clear that no prison could hold such people for long.[1]

Such then was the general situation so gloomily described by
Giraud, the public prosecutor of Jemappes, in a letter to the Minister
dated 24 Prairial year V [12 June 1797]:

... On ne doit pas ... vous laisser ignorer ... que la plupart des grands
criminels échappent aisément aux recherches. Le frétin tombe facilement et
promptement dans les filets; mais pour les grands délits comme assassinats,
sommation de fermes, vols &ca., leurs auteurs disparaissent et se font toujours attendre.

La gendarmerie dont je ne saurois trop louer le choix, la bonne tenue et
le zèle [praise rarely to be heard on the other side of the old border, and,
one suspects, even in this case, purely formal], fait souvent d'inutiles efforts,
les captures sont très rares, parce que personne ne les seconde .... aucune
loi n'établit entre l'accusateur public et les juges de paix une relation déc-
adaire.... J'avois résolu ... de faire un voyage à Tournai pour examiner
par moi-même l'état des détenus ... et surtout cette bande de juifs qui
depuis 13 mois sont à attendre un acte d'accusation, mais j'ai été retenu par
la difficulté de faire payer mon voyage économique.... Ma présence à
Fontaine et à Tournai feroit un grand bien. ...

No money to pay the executioners, who often refuse to carry out
sentences away from their homes in the *chef-lieu* and who, in the
peculiar conditions of the Directory, were desperately anxious to take

---

[1] See also A.N. BB 18 402 (Jemappes, procureur général de Mons, au Grand
Juge, 19 décembre 1809): 'Le magistrat de sûreté de l'arrondissement de Charleroi
ayant eu avis que le nommé Lefebvre, dit *Pellin*, forçat évadé des bagnes de
Lorient, et qui s'était échappé aussi l'été dernier des prisons de Nivelles, se refugiait
à Théméon, chez une tante nommée la veuve Lebouton, dont la maison sans
toiture, à demi détruite, et au voisinage du bois de Viesville, lui facilitait les
moyens de se sauver dans les bois, y envoya le 19 octobre dernier les gendarmes
de la résidence de Fleurus. ... Lefebvre sortit aussitôt de la maison, renversant
un autre gendarme. ...' Here, then, from the Département de Jemappes, thirteen
years after Fleurus, was yet another incidental result of the French victory. Indeed, the whole episode illustrates several themes at once: the proximity to woodlands as a means of escape, the ruined cottage à *l'orée du bois*, the family network,
and the *retour au bercail* of the ex-convict.

on more than one job at once. No money to pay a public prosecutor, anxious to visit all the courts and prisons in the area under his jurisdiction. No money to pay a *gendarmerie* consequently unwilling to display a gratuitous enthusiasm.[1] No money to pay for the return of 'Black Peter' from a Dutch prison to that of Courtrai. No money to pay the troops called in in pursuit of large groups of armed smugglers. All this was bad enough in France proper. But it was much more alarming in a country in which hard currency was circulating in large quantities and in which farmers and livestock dealers, grain merchants, and horse dealers were unwilling to accept the legal tender of the Directory.

Finally, as Giraud concludes: '. . . Beaucoup de choses n'arrivent que par ignorance de ses devoirs et des peines qui sont attachées à leur infraction. . . .' These last were difficulties particular, of course, to Departments in which the lesser judicial officials were still completely unfamiliar with the exact provisions of the French civil and criminal codes. But, in much of this area, especially in the Escaut, the repressive authorities could at least often count on the active co-operation of the well-to-do peasantry. Both Picard and the Boorsbeek brothers are stated to have been put to flight in the course of a number of their marauding expeditions on the roads between Ghent and Antwerp and between the former city and its foreport, Sas van Gent.

What is less familiar, indeed thoroughly surprising, when one takes into account more conventional French *bandes* or *compagnies* operating either in the Paris area or in the south-east, is the enormous extent of the areas in which both Salambier and his friends and the members of the even more elusive *bande juive* are said to have operated, in the latter instance, according to Dinah, over a period of more than ten years, amidst the vicissitudes first of all of a civil war in Holland, then of the so-called *Révolution Brabançonne*, of two French occupations, and of one return of the Austrians. Indeed, these very events no doubt actively contributed to the ubiquity of all these groups: the brothers Boorsbeek, 'Black Peter' and his Flemish band, Salambier, Kotzo-Picard and his men and numerous relatives, and the even more ill-defined *bande* said to have operated in the Pays de Liége, and that may have been connected with Picard's loose command, though this was disputed by the *capitaine* himself.

At one moment, for instance, Salambier and his men are reported in the Rouen area (where they must have come up against a great deal of local competition from other indigenous *bandes*, well settled in the forests of Maromme, La Bouille, and Roumare, bestriding the roads leading to the Norman capital, as well as enclosing the valley of the lower Seine); at the next, they are on the border, operating primarily from Lille and Courtrai, or rather from the faubourgs of both towns, as well as from those of Valenciennes and Béthune:[1] Salambier had been engaged in *chauffage* in the Eure, one of his accomplices, of whom we will hear more later, had carried out thefts in Rouen, Rennes, Meaux, Château-Thierry, Paris, and Valenciennes. The Flemish group is stated to have operated from the forests of Luxembourg and the Pays de Liége, to that of Soignies, often joining up with Salambier's predominantly French group in the Courtrésis, or around Tournai and Mons, or again, in the coastal area between Ostend and Dunkirk. As we shall see, it was purely a matter of administrative and judicial convenience that Salambier and his principal accomplices should have been sent for trial in the Lys (Bruges), as a result of the insistence of the energetic Baret, who seems to have made it his personal ambition to prove the case against the French bandit leader. He and his accomplices might equally well have been tried in the Dyle, in the Escaut, in the Nord, or in Salambier's native Pas-de-Calais.

If we are to believe either the obliging Dinah or what the judicial authorities of Tournai and Ghent were clearly trying to prove—for it would be hard to believe both without reservation—the extent of the activities of the *bande juive* was even greater than those attributed to 'Black Peter' and to Salambier. For what emerges from her testimony and from the indictment, so much of which depends on the evidence of this single witness, would suggest the existence of a highly sophisticated criminal organisation of international proportions; and this is certainly what is implied in a letter written to the Minister by the *commissaire* attached to the Ghent court, an official more familiar with the personnel and the activities of the *bande juive* than his colleague of Tournai, on 2 Nivôse year V [22 December 1796], that is, over nine months after the arrest of Kotzo-Picard and of the other alleged leaders of the group:

Il existe des sociétés d'assurance dans ce département qui peut-être correspondent avec l'étranger, elles garantissent moyennant 10 ou 5 p. % l'arrivée des marchandises étrangères. Ces sociétés donnent de l'audace aux fraudeurs, ce sont elles qui soudoient des brigands pour en assurer l'abord, elles paient donc la rébellion armée contre les loix, elles commandent enfin l'assassinat.[2]

[1] See note H, p. 255.
[2] A.N. BB 18 293 (Escaut, commissaire près le tribunal de Gand au Ministre, 2 nivôse an V). A fortnight earlier, the *commissaire* of the Alost court informed

The official may have been exaggerating, in order to impress the Minister with the gravity of the problems facing the judicial authorities in the northern parts of this water-logged Department.

During these early years of the Directory, the Minister of Justice and his subordinates were to show themselves particularly sensitive to reports of crime and large-scale banditry, both in the old frontier areas of France and in the newly acquired Departments, tending always to give them political implications as examples of activities directed against the French and against the Republic. It is worth noting, in this respect that Sotin, the Minister of Police, faced with mounting evidence of the collusion between the local inhabitants and groups of sea-going smugglers, along the coast of the island of Axel and at the end of inlets like that of the Filipine, should have communicated his fears to his colleague at the Ministry of Justice and should have demanded more energetic measures against convicted smugglers, after they had been released by the local *juges de paix*. There was nothing new about such a situation; but for Sotin it constituted a direct threat to French rule. His solution, and one that was so often proposed, too, as a means of extirpating the murder gangs in the south-east of France, was to demand the setting up of courts-martial and a wider use of the military to supplement the efforts of the hard-pressed *gendarmerie* of Sas van Gent.

He wrote to the Minister of Justice, on 15 Fructidor year V [1 September 1797]:

Déjà j'ai utilement provoqué le zèle de notre collègue le Ministre de la Guerre . . . et les avantages que la force armée nationale a remportés sur les hordes de contrebandiers attestent le déploiement des moyens militaires dans ces contrées, mais . . . il faudra se résoudre à n'attendre de ce brigandage que de la destruction totale des brigands tombés sous le feu des troupes, si d'un côté le Conseil de guerre permanent se déclare incompétent, et que de l'autre les tribunaux ordinaires les acquittent. Je dois à ce sujet vous rappeler le contenu d'une lettre que vous avez dû recevoir du chef d'escadron Target, Commandant la 4me division de gendarmerie dans le département de l'Escaut, il doit vous rendre compte que des contrebandiers qui s'étaient échappés dans l'affaire qui a eu lieu entre eux et la troupe, la nuit du 11 au 12 thermidor [the night of Saturday to Sunday 29–30 July 1797] ont eu l'audace de venir être spectateurs de la vente de leurs chevaux et effects, sans doute dans

the Minister: 'Nous avons tout lieu de croire . . . qu'une foule de brigands mendians étrangers pourvus de passeports et qui s'ensemblent pendant la nuit en sont les auteurs [de ces brigandages]' (A.N. BB 18 293, commissaire près le tribunal d'Alost, au Ministre, 14 frimaire an V).

l'intention d'y apportent le trouble; que reconnus par des chasseurs qui les avaient sabrés, 9 ont été saisis sur la place et conduits au juge de paix avec les témoins, parmi ces brigands, un surtout qui avait ajusté un chasseur d'un pistolet qui rata, fut reconnu à la marque récente d'un coup de sabre que le chasseur lui porta, les témoins déposèrent le fait et ajoutèrent encore à l'opinion publique qui le désigna comme un des plus fameux brigands du pays, le juge de paix le mit en liberté avec ses 8 complices. Enfin, l'impunité enhardit tellement les brigands qu'un d'eux s'est présenté pour réclamer les marchandises saisies. . . . les brigands sont relâchés, la vente des objets saisis est suspendue et la prise presque déclarée nulle: que les tribunaux fâssent encore un pas et ils déclareront coupables les troupes qui ont chargé ces brigands. Cet ordre de choses est intolérable. . . .[1]

As, indeed, it must have been, to the prestige of the new judicial authorities and of the French Army, in the eyes of the inhabitants of the northern section of the Escaut, perhaps rather slow in the uptake, but loyal to the new régime, and in no ways counter-revolutionaries, as some of the French had accused them of being.

Even so, the smugglers, to have dared to appear openly on the main square of Sas van Gent, their faces uncovered, at the time of the sale of the English goods taken off them by the French cavalry, in July 1797, must either have been singularly careless or must have been very sure of the tacit complicity of the Flemish-speaking population and of the local *juges de paix*. Indeed, their immunity makes more understandable the eagerness displayed both by the Ghent and Tournai courts to link up the *bande juive* with a well-organised smuggling enterprise. The smugglers might escape arrest, as they did on this occasion; but at least the judicial authorities had succeeded in holding Picard and a large number of his alleged accomplices. It would be natural for them to attempt to prove a link between the smugglers and the prisoners, even though these last had been detained for the previous seventeen months.

Picard and some of his alleged lieutenants had been arrested at an inn in Ghent, appropriately named *A la Cour Impériale*, on 23 Ventôse year IV [13 March 1796]. They were cross-examined for the first time on 11 Germinal [31 March 1796] by the *juge de paix* of the *tribunal correctionnel of Tournai*. These were not, however, the first arrests, for the brothers Michel and Charles Claes, who were local people, had been examined by the *juge de paix* of Celles, a village near Anseroeul, on 24 Pluviôse year IV [13 February 1796]. Kragine, an Austrian deserter,

---

[1] A.N. BB 18 283 (Justice, Escaut, Sotin, Ministre de la police générale, au Ministre de la Justice, 15 fructidor an V).

whom Dinah had met in the prison of Tournai, and who, at some stage earlier than this, had become his mistress, came forward with vital evidence on the subject of Kotzo-Picard's approaching him in order to obtain chloroform for a gaol-break on 19 Thermidor of the same year [6 August 1796].[1] The other members of Dinah's family and some of their close associates were arrested, just over a month after Kragine's intervention, on 25 Fructidor [11 September 1796], when the *juge de paix* of the *canton du Nord* of Ghent delivered warrants against Moÿse Jacob, his wife Sara, his daughters Rosa and Helena, and various tradesmen and craftsmen said to have been their accomplices. Further arrests were made in the course of 1796; and we learn that the Claes brothers and other local bandits (Daumont and so on) were still in the Tournai prison on 17 Nivôse year V [6 January 1797]. But this group apparently succeeded in escaping later in the same year, probably in March, after the completion of Dinah's testimony. On 24 Ventôse [14 March] the *commissaire près le canton de Celles*, an official who had been responsible for bringing in the Claes brothers, Daumont, Petit, and others, was to write despairingly to the Minister of Justice:

... Le brigandage menace derechef ces contrées. ... de nouvelles bandes de chauffeurs se réorganisent: l'année dernière [1796] elles en étaient encore infectées, et je suis parvenu à les purger de ces êtres dangereux & cruels.
Maintenant que plusieurs de ces scélérats, échappés des maisons d'arrêt ...

[1] Next to Dinah herself, the doubtful Kragine, who as an Austrian and as prisoner-of-war, was a ready pawn in the hands of the police authorities, was certainly the most valuable prosecution witness; the *commissaire* seems to have relied, for instance, on his estimate of Dinah's reliability as a witness. We read in the indictment: '... Que depuis 15 jours la femme Picard n'a cessé de répéter audit Kragine ces différens aveux, qu'il a regardé qu'ils étaient dits avec sincérité, qu'elle lui a déclaré en outre que led. Picard étoit chef de la brigade dont faisoient partie les détenus en cet arrondissement ...' (A.N. BB 18 400).
'Tandis que Picard et ses complices ... se trouvoient détenus ... un nommé *Jean Kragine*, chirurgien au service d'Autriche et prisonnier de guerre s'y trouvoit aussi. Cette circonstance lui fournit l'occasion de lier connaissance avec Dina Jacob, âgée de 24 ans, qui se rendoit journellement dans ces prisons pour porter à Picard, son mari. ... Kragine, ayant été mis en liberté, vint le 19 thermidor an IV faire la déposition suivante: ... led. Picard lui a demandé si d'après la connaissance de son art il ne pouvait pas donner un somnifère au géôlier au moyen duquel ils pouvoient s'évader ...' (*Acte d'accusation*). Judging from the facility with which this group, mostly local people, it is true, seem to have escaped from the various prisons of Tournai, it would seem that Kotzo-Picard need not have bothered with anything so elaborate as chloroform. It is true that, as a stranger to the region, he may not have had help from outside.

reparaissent. . . . il est impossible de les atteindre sans le secours d'une brigade de gendarmerie. . . .[1]

In this area at least, it is clear that banditry could survive quite well in the absence of Kotzo-Picard. Clearly, the Claes brothers must have commanded a certain amount of local support, in order thus to be able to resume their activities in an area that they had devastated in the course of 1795 and the early months of 1796. They seem, however, eventually to have been recaptured, to be included in the mammoth trial that the Tournai prosecutor was preparing for Picard and many others.

The reason for the transfer from Ghent to Tournai of Picard himself and of some of his Jewish companions, seems to have been that, in the course of the last four months of 1795, a winter apparently less severe than that of the previous year, and of the first three months of 1796, he and his brother 'Fromme', along with the Claes brothers, Daumont, and others, had been accused by a number of eye-witnesses of having participated in the same series of attacks on farms and lonely houses, in the region north of Ath and Leuze, just south of the linguistic border of the two Flanders, in the quadrilateral contained by the roads from Tournai to Courtrai, from Tournai to Ath, from Ath to Lessines, and from Lessines to Renaix: an area a little to the east of the region, on both sides of the Franco-Belgian border, in which Salambier and his men were said to have operated from the end of 1795.

The first of these attacks took place at Oudecq during the night of 23–4 September 1795, that is if we are to believe the indictment, for, according to Dinah, who is by no means consistent in her testimony in this respect, her husband had spent that night engaged on an operation near Sas van Gent. The next was at a village called Saradaie on the night of 4–5 November: the third was at Ellezelles, between Flobcecq and Renaix, again in the *canton* of Celles, on the night of 14–15 December. A week later, they attacked a farm near Flobecq (20–1 December, a night during which Dinah, as we shall see later, would have her husband once more tied down in a similar operation near Sas). On the twenty-third of the same month, they carried out a fruitful operation near Anseroeul. They were next seen in Frasnes, on the night of 3–4 February 1796; and the last operation to be attributed to them took place near Bouvignies, on the outskirts of Ath, on 1–2 March 1796. There are also reports of their activities in Everbeek, Wannebecq, and Chièvres.

[1] A.N. BB 18 401 (Justice, Jemappes, commissaire près le canton de Celles, au Ministre, 24 ventôse an V). See also note I, p. 255.

But according to Dinah, who seems to want to have it both ways, this had been only one of six or seven areas in which the members of her husband's *bande* had, at one time or another, been engaged in *chauffage*. To the north in the second half of 1795 and the spring of 1796, that is at the very time when the series of attacks just listed had been taking place, she would have them concentrated primarily in the region between Ghent and the old border with Dutch Flanders, beyond Sas van Gent.

The border itself had gone, in accordance with the provisions of the Treaty of the Hague, which provided for the incorporation of the whole of the Dutch enclave on the left bank of the Schelde, in the new Département de l'Escaut, making of the island of Axel, with the port of Ter Neuzen on its northern coast, and those of Axel and Sluis to the south, facing one of the many wide inlets of the great river, as well as Breskens, opposite Flushing, and the town of Hulst, French territory. Much of it was subjected to the surveillance of the *gendarmerie* of Sas van Gent, and of the cavalry stationed at Fort Sainte-Marguérite, under the command of the *adjudant-général* Target, no newcomer to repression, for he had served with zeal in the Revolutionary Army of Lille, in the winter of 1793. He was too no stranger to the Belgian Provinces, for he had been the founder of the Brussels club set up by the French in December 1792.[1]

The frontier between the *Départements Réunis* and the Netherlands, in this much-disputed area, was the main estuary of the West Schelde that separated what had been Dutch Flanders from the island of Walcheren. Before the Treaty, this had already been an area much favoured by smugglers, possibly Flemish, possibly Dutch, most of them no doubt both (some of them are said to have come from Zelzate, on the Belgian side of the former border) who had specialised, from the outbreak of war between the Republic and England, in bringing in English goods by sea, via the inlets dividing the strange island of Axel from the mainland, and the tidal rivers running up to the mudflats of Sas van Gent and Filippine, the latter place connected to the southern inlets of the estuary by the river of the same name. Filippine and Sas van Gent, thus favourably placed at the end of deep sea channels, at high tide could offer smugglers a far more attractive point of unloading than the traditional ports of Ter Neuzen, Sluis, and Axel. The removal of the frontier, far from bringing to a halt the activities of smugglers in an area where it was always difficult to distinguish between sea and land,

---

[1] *Les Armées révolutionnaires*, pp. 244, 333 (107), 673, 768.

seems rather to have stimulated them, by extending their bases to Flushing and Middelburg, as well as to Ghent.[1]

It is in this rather improbable area that the always imaginative Dinah was to locate some of the principal operations of her husband's 'gang'. She reports them as having set out from Ghent at nightfall, to attack isolated houses and farms situated between Sas and Sluis, and Sas and Axel—one such house, she says, as if she herself had been there, was situated on a dike—and she goes on to say that these operations had been particularly fruitful, one of them bringing in a haul of 12,000 Dutch florins.

The great difficulty with Dinah's testimony is that it always contains areas at least of likelihood: for instance, isolated farms and houses in this coastal area very probably would contain large sums of money, as well as valuables and English textiles. There would be plenty to tempt a group of enterprising, well-armed, and well-informed brigands: and Kotzo-Picard was clearly all three. But, cross-examined by Giraud, he was vigorously to deny ever having been engaged in *brigandage* in and around Sas van Gent, during the period mentioned by his wife:

... a répondu qu'il ne pouvoit absolument déterminer où il se trouvoit le 21 & 22 frimaire derniers (an IV) [the night of Saturday to Sunday 12–13 December 1795, a date mentioned by Dinah as that of an attack on a watchmaker near Sas: once more, it is a *likely* enough date for an attack on a shop as it was at the week-end, a time when, for instance, the *bande d'Orgères* favoured breakings-in in village shops] qu'il croit cependant qu'il était à Gand, d'autant qu'il a essuyé une maladie dans le courant de décembre; que le 1er et 2 vendémiaire derniers [the night of 23–4 September 1795, when, according to Dinah, he is supposed to have attacked an isolated farm north of Sas, killing several members of the farmer's family, and getting away with the Dutch florins] il étoit à la foire de Sas-de-Gand [so he admits to having been in the area], qu'il ne peut se rappeler où il étoit le 9 et 10 novembre, non plus que le 22 ou 23 d'octobre [more dates mentioned by the ever-precise Dinah] ... qu'il n'étoit point sorti de Gand pendant tout ce temps-là, qu'il avoit été seulement à la foire de Sas-de-Gand à la fin de septembre dernier, qu'il avoit été plusieurs fois de Gand à Renaix pour y vendre des marchandises, mais qu'il n'a jamais été à Flobecq. ...

Yet Dinah gives not only dates, but details:

... Que vers le mois de décembre & janvier derniers, son mari, accompagné de son frère, commandoit 20 hommes, et les 2 frères Boorsbeek, 30, que son

[1] See note J, p. 256.

mari fut porté à 6 lieues de Gand sur la route de la Hollande, qu'il y vola un horloger en prenant une grande quantité de montres et d'argenteries . . . que son mari a eu pour sa part 21 pièces d'or étrangères de 3 espèces de 6 couronnes, de 8 et de 12 . . . qu'au mois de décembre dernier son mari a commandé une bande de brigands de se porter dans une grande maison qui est seule sur la route de Sas-de-Gand à Middelburg. . . .

Whom is one to believe? The husband is not particularly convincing in his denials. He had, after all, on his own admission, been to the fair at Sas, had also been to Renaix, if not to Flobecq, only three miles away, on the road to Lessines, that is uncomfortably near both that village, and the even nearer Ellezelles. Whatever we may make of his movements during the winter and the spring, one thing at least is clear: even Picard could not have been in two places on the same night, whatever gifts he may have possessed: he cannot have been both in Sas *and* in Flobecq, both in Sas *and* in Oudecq. Dinah was either overdoing it, or had managed to get confused in the intricate details of her own testimony. But, as an itinerant pedlar, which appears to have been his official trade—he was to describe himself as a *marchand*—he could readily explain his presence either in Sas or in Renaix; and he was being asked to prove where he had been at precise dates: the night of this, or the night of that—never an easy exercise in memory, especially for a man often travelling for his business. He could reasonably reply that he could not remember. Why should he if, during these months, he had been in Ghent most of the time? Furthermore, Dinah is difficult to pin down, for her testimony does not indicate clearly whether her husband had actually been on these expeditions or had merely master-minded them from afar, sending the Boorsbeek brothers and others off on their operations, while he himself remained in Ghent.

What would make Dinah so convincing was the fantastic knowledge that she displayed of the geography of crime and *brigandage*, not only in East Flanders, but on the edge of such places as Lille, Courtrai, Brussels, Amiens, Saint-Omer, Ath, and Tournai. She may have been making up the names of the members of the so-called *bande juive*—she had enough relatives to form several armies of such people—but the addresses that she provided were genuine enough, were verifiable, many of them had come to the notice of the police authorities many times before. Kotzo-Picard and her other relations may have been in the habit of moving, of changing addresses as often as she stated, for entirely innocent reasons—they were, if we are to believe them, pedlars and itinerants. Yet so many moves, so clearly recalled, and so closely related, as it would seem, to the flux and reflux of outside events,

to the fortunes and reverses of the French and Austrian armies, must
have appeared as indisputable proof of both the political unreliability
and the criminal intentions of Picard and of his friends and relatives.
Once this was established in the minds of Dinah's interrogators, it
would follow as a matter of course that anyone who could be connected with Dinah and her husband would earn membership in the
famous *bande juive*.

Exactly what may have been the relations between the Ghent Jews
and the smugglers north of the city can only be a matter for conjecture.
The likeliest explanation would be that the smugglers had recourse to
the Jews when they were seeking to dispose of smuggled goods. For it
is difficult to see how Picard could have been a more active help in
their actual operations. The smugglers had all the advantages of local
knowledge; they knew the coast, with its deep indentations, frequent
mudflats, and tidal inlets, its isolated squat white farms situated on
dikes within walking distance of the Filippine. They were expert in the
many whirling currents of the river world of the estuary, and they
seem to have possessed a sizeable sea-going fleet and plenty of shallow
boats and barges useful for unloading goods on the flats. In such an
area, there must always have existed a wide community of crime, to
include privateers, smugglers, wreckers, river-workers, bargees,
beachcombers, those who lived off the scornfully rejected débris of a
proud sea, a dirty froth left on the shore by the receding tide: drift-
wood, cork, the clothing of the drowned, the bloated body of a dead
sheep, perhaps even the purses of gold pieces green with salt, seaweed,
those who preyed on sea birds and canal fowl. Boorsbeek and his
brother were stated normally to be mounted, on occasion using their
horses to swim across the inlets of this muddy shore, not unlike the
estuaries of the Colne, the Stour, and the Orwell, a coast well known
also to the Dutch.

The smugglers were certainly far more at home in this watery jungle
than the *gendarmes* based on Sas. But they no doubt needed support,
allies, rendez-vous, and safe hiding-places further inland. And these,
along with skills in receiving, in the provision of false papers, the Jews
and some of their Christian contacts could certainly have provided, if
required, thanks to their knowledge of safe inns, kept by Christians—
one would not be likely to find Jewish *cabaretiers* in this part of Europe
—on both sides of the estuary, as well as further afield.

Dinah also reports members of the *bande* as having attacked farms
on the road from Antwerp to Ghent, in the neighbourhood of Saint-
Nicolas, Lochristi, and Lokeren. Another group is said to have oper-

ated near Alost,[1] and on the road from Brussels, via Malines, to Antwerp.

The *bande* is also stated to have used a number of alternative bases
just outside the walls of Ghent, at the northern exit, beyond the
Dammepoorte (La Porte aux Dames, a familiar landmark in most
Flemish towns, and a monument that recurs as insistently, in the
testimony of Dinah, as the Porte d'Anvers, also in Ghent, and the
Porte de Laeken, outside Brussels: Dinah seems obsessed with this
Gate or that Gate, so much of her testimony reads like an incantation,
or as one historian[2] familiar with popular religion in the eighteenth
century has suggested, like a *procès en sorcellerie*). The Dammepoorte
seems to have been a peripheral quarter frequented by watermen,
sailors, prostitutes—Dirks, whom Dinah describes as a Flemish friend
of her father's, at one time ran a brothel there;[3] and his inn was
apparently used as a rendez-vous for Kotzo and his friends.

The Jews were said to have had agents, receivers, and various
specialists, such as engravers and goldsmiths, within Brussels itself, or
just outside, beyond the Porte de Hal. Members of the gang are stated
to have been arrested in Bruges.

In the vicinity of Lille, she continues, they had attacked farms and
isolated houses in a number of *communes*, mostly within walking distance of Wazemmes and the other faubourgs of the city, in which the
bande à Salambier was also reported to have operated. The two groups
may well have had many friendly inns in common. But a more innocent

---

[1] On 24 Prairial year V [12 June 1797] the *commissaire près le tribunal de Gand*
reports to the Minister: 'J'ai pris des renseignemens concernant l'assassinat . . .
commis dans la commune de Bavegem, canton de Lede. . . . le prévenu est
actuellement en la maison d'arrêt de l'arrondissement d'Alost . . .' (A.N. BB 18
293, Justice, Escaut). Bavegem is a village a little to the south of the highroad
from Alost to Ghent, that is in an area in which the Boorsbeek brothers are said
to have been active in the course of the previous year. Of course, this particular
murder may have been a private affair, the result of a family dispute or a quarrel
between neighbours.

[2] This point of view was expressed by Mr. Robin Briggs, of All Souls College,
in the course of a paper that I read, on the subject of the 'Jewish organisation', to
my seminar. See also note K, p. 257.

[3] '. . . La première expédition qui a été faite à Gand par son père . . . et Dirks,
actuellement arrêté à Anvers, fut hors *la Dampoorte*, chez un individu qui
occupoit seul une maison. . . . Dirks dans ce tems-là tenoit bordel hors lad.
Dampoorte où se sont commis une infinité de crimes . . . son père . . . a été de
l'expédition de Vollezelle la nuit du 4 au 5 messidor . . . dans cette année qui
correspond à l'an 1790 v.s. a été fait un vol à Koekelleberg [*sic*] près de Bruxelles. . . .'

explanation of this apparent predilection on the part of Dinah's family
for localities in the faubourgs, outside the walls of cities, is that it may
have been imposed upon them by the experience of a Jewish past, both
in France and, possibly, in parts of the Austrian Netherlands, where the
old municipal ordinances would have forbidden Jews residence, or
even an overnight stay, within the walls. Certainly, in eighteenth-
century conditions, Jews, as much as horse dealers and carters, would
be especially familiar with the colourful world of the faubourg, with its
rapid turn-over of new faces. It was no doubt yet another case of the
repressive authorities themselves creating the conditions most favourable to criminal activities and to the difficulty of their detection, by
assigning to such people an enforced location that was well out of reach
of the *commissaires de police* and of the armies of informers that the
police could control *intra-muros*, through the six-monthly renewal of
patentes.

Two members of the group are stated, by Dinah, to have been sent
to prison in Ghent, at some unspecified date, for having co-operated
with two Austrian recruiting agents in the theft of a child named Louis
Martin, in the neighbourhood of 'Thilt', a locality we have been unable
to identify (Giraud is not good on Flemish names.). Dinah, that
indefatigable travel agent, then goes on to claim that another section of
her husband's group had attacked farms, this time in the neighbourhood of Arras and Béthune. One of these operations is said to have
taken place in a village that she names as 'Curée' a quarter of a league
from Arras, on the road to Douai. These attacks she attributes to the
bande de Lille, which she claims was at one time commanded by one of
her brothers, Abraham or Daniel.[1]

It is hardly surprising that travelling Jewish tradesmen should have
had a number of contacts and habitual addresses (Dinah would
describe them as 'safe' addresses) in Paris, and, at the time of Kotzo-

---

[1] '. . . Que son frère Abraham Jacob est chef de la bande de Lille, composée de
20 à 30 individus . . . [elle] . . . a répondu qu'il s'est commis un vol dans la
commune d'Ecurie près d'Arras, sur la route de Douai chez le C. Lefebvre,
fermier aud. lieu, un autre à Bornes, à 2 lieues d'Arras sur la route de Bapaume,
que ces deux vols ont été commis il y a deux mois environ, enfin qu'il s'en est
commis plusieurs autres dans les environs d'Arras et d'Amiens . . . que le nommé
David, juif, est le chef de la brigade qui les a commis, qu'il demeure ordinairement à Amiens, que sa brigade est composée ordinairement de 20 à 30 personnes,
savoir: 1. Carlles Rous ou Lion Lévi, demeurant à Saint-Omer; 2. Jonas Homkain,
se prononce en allemand Konikhem; 3. Lichtem, domicilié ordinairement à Lille;
4. Isaac Cracq, domicilié ordinairement à Lille; 5. Chmousse, juif, tambour ci-
devant à Bruxelles; 6. Abraham Jacob Lévi, actuellement à Paris. . . .'

Picard's arrest in Ghent, in March 1796, she would have us believe that there was something like a *sauve-qui-peut* among the Jewish communities in Brussels, Ghent, Lille, Courtrai, and Amiens, in the direction of the French capital. If such a move had in fact ever taken place, it would, according to Dinah's own testimony, have been a highly unwise one, for she adds that there was a rumour reaching Brussels in the spring of 1796, and accredited by her brother Abraham, then living in Paris, that the Minister of Police had ordered a general round-up of Jews, especially *juifs allemands*, in the city, though I have found absolutely no evidence of such instructions in the papers of the *commissaires de police* of the various Divisions, officials not generally noted for their sympathy towards those *de la nation juive*, and who would certainly have obeyed such orders, had they ever been given, with the same zeal that they displayed in bringing in Piedmontese and other Italians, southerners, and Lyonnais, at every moment of crisis. Jews from the *Départements Réunis* or from the Batavian Republic and the Rhineland, had no doubt as legitimate reasons for going to Paris as any other traveller about his business. Certainly there is no hint, even in Dinah's evidence, that her relatives were ever involved in active criminal operations within Paris itself. She merely states that the *bande de Paris* was the biggest of them all, and that is the first and last we hear of it.

Of course, any Jewish merchant from the north of France or from Belgium would know where to stay when in the capital. As we shall see, when dealing with Salambier, the wife of a Jewish tradesman from Dunkirk had the address of a lodging-house to which to report, 112, rue Notre-Dame-de-Nazareth, when she wished to escape from her husband, his German mistress, and his Jewish accomplices (She herself was a Christian). She was, however, followed, and contacted there by associates of her husband, who demanded money of her. Dinah would no doubt have put a criminal interpretation on such a move. But, in all probability, the woman went to this address because it was that of a lodging-house well known to members of the Jewish community. It is only too easy to suggest that, because Jews frequented such and such an address, they did so for some occult purpose. They could equally have gone there because they had been there before, and knew nowhere else to go. The same address turns up several times in Dinah's evidence, a detail that might tempt the unwary historian to jump to conclusions and to argue that the *bande juive* and the *bande à Salambier* were indeed interconnected, sharing a *réseau* and a base in Paris.

Perhaps the sheer extent of the combined areas of alleged *brigandage*, apart from forming a monument to Dinah's retentive memory or fertile imagination, is a sort of left-handed compliment to the growth of *la Grande Nation*. It is also an eloquent reminder of the degree to which *le pourtoir de Paris* had been stretched, to accommodate both conquest and crime, two swift horses, like those of the Boorsbeek brothers as they galloped over the sand dunes and polders of East Flanders, like those of the *gendarmes* of Sas van Gent, as they rode down the armed smugglers—several hundred of them—who, after abandoning some sixty carts, brought to the inlet to unload goods shipped in from England (two ships rapidly put out to sea as soon as the *gendarmes* had been sighted), were seen, running, heads down, dropping their muskets and their pistols in the long corn, below the level of the jetty, at the Fort Saint-Marguérite, near Axel, in June 1797—[1] two horses that might be described, during these years, as running neck and neck. Indeed, we hear too that 'Black Peter' had been taken in Holland, in the year V, and that the Dutch authorities—with characteristic meanness, complained Baret—[2] had refused to pay the cost of his transport to Bruges. Baret had to send an escort, out of Lys public funds, to go and fetch him. Even though the murders attributed to Salambier and his alleged accomplices are much more localised: twenty or thirty kilometres in a band down both sides of the old Franco-Belgian border, from the Channel coast, to the level of Valenciennes, Béthune, Mons, and Leuze, the total extent of their operations and the extreme mobility of their attacks testify to the 'europeanisation' of armed banditry in these early years of the Directory. Now crime, like the armies of the Republic, like the military bigamist, had crossed the old frontiers, as it headed from Paris to Brussels, Ghent, Malines, and Antwerp, and, in the case of Dinah's family, as it moved often in just the opposite

[1] See note L, p. 258.

[2] '. . . J'attends l'exécution de la promesse que m'a faite un honnête citoyen de ce pays qui, devant aller en Hollande, pour ses affaires, s'est engagé à ramasser mon homme à ses frais, tant est grande la frayeur que ce *Swaert Pier* avait inspirée dans ce pays et le désir qu'on a de le voir puni, Salambier et ses complices connaissant tous ce *noir Pierre*, qu'ils appellent un *bon garçon* . . .' (A.N. BB 18 8 582, Baret au Ministre, s.d. an V).

See also A.N. BB 18 582 (Baret au Ministre, 13 nivôse an V): '. . . Je l'avais [*le noir Pierre*] enfin fait saisir à Bruxelles, il y a quelques mois, mais, malgré mes instructions, . . . le défaut de gendarmerie nationale ayant forcé de le mettre sous l'escorte de deux cavaliers, il échappa à 2 lieues de Gand. Depuis il a été arrêté de nouveau en Hollande. Les Hollandais ont réclamé le paiement d'une prison qui avait été promise par l'ancien Magistrat de Bruges. Je me serais fort bien arrangé avec eux pour la prime. . . .'

direction, from Gröningen to Sas van Gent, from there to Ghent, Courtrai, Tournai, Lille, Saint-Omer, Amiens, and Paris.

In view of all this, it is not, therefore, stretching the bounds of fancy too far to pull the map north-eastwards, so as to take in the nine *Départements Réunis*, and, indeed, after May 1795, what had been Dutch Flanders, as well as the still Dutch island of Walcheren. As far as the so-called 'Jewish organisation' is concerned, we have assembled only some of the central pieces of a vast jigsaw that seems to have stretched from Frankfurt, Cologne, and Groningen, down to the Pays de Liége and as far west as Paris. For a complete reconstruction of this immense network—a network that may in fact have been that of perfectly innocent and normal trading activities—it would be necessary to pursue one's investigations in the records of The Hague and of the Provinces of Gröningen. We are moving in fact in an area in which there are no fixed frontiers, neither in terms of states nor in those of crime.

The *route du Nord* had possibly never been so busy as during the first three years of the Directory, just as, as Vidocq was to observe, the gold braid, the épaulettes, the gold, silver, and brass buttons and badges of rank never flourished so baroquely, in the faubourgs of Lille, among the self-appointed officers of the *armée ambulante* (and this it certainly was, another name indeed for *la caravane*), as during a period in which Lille, from having been in the war zone, now offered a natural, and readily accessible, haven to deserters from three or four armies. Here was a retreat for adventurers, Belgian speculators, war contractors, food commissioners, false *commissaires des guerres*, self-appointed military transport officers, those who could provide, for a sum down, genuine-looking *congés de maladie*, and piles of blank forms, enabling soldiers, themselves real or imaginary, to draw rations for themselves, and fodder for their horses,[1] at each *étape*. Here too could be found the genuine, but complaisant *officier de santé*, willing, at a price, or out of counter-revolutionary commitment, to hasten the exit

---

[1] And these would probably be stolen, for the army would put a premium on horse-thieving. On 23 Germinal year IV [12 April 1796] the *directeur du jury d'accusation* of the Alost court consults the Minister on the subject of four employees of the *charrois militaires* who had deserted from the Antwerp garrison, taking with them twelve horses and their harness. 'De ces chevaux, 2 ont été vendus à Anvers même, 4 l'ont été à Wise; mais l'activité de la force armée d'Alost a rendu à la République 9 desd. chevaux. . . . le délit est commencé à Anvers, hors du ressort d'Alost, il a été commis par des employés aux charrois qui peuvent être considérés comme militaires, il a été continué sur le territoire d'Alost . . .' (A.N. BB 18 293, Justice, Escaut).

from the armed service in the name of the Republic of some sturdy peasant; the female camp followers; and the military prostitutes, the whole colourful riffraff that thrived on the fringes of eighteenth-century armies and that could, in a matter of seconds, provide the traveller either with the uniform of an officer in the Hungarian hussars,[1] or a civilian outfit for anyone anxious to move fast in the other direction, and resume the relative anonymity of *l'habit du citoyen*. The rue de l'ABC and the rue Esquermoise already housed many comforts and many skills, from the readily available *montante*, to the reader in cards and those who, with a sharp pin and coloured inks, could consecrate military, naval, criminal, artisanal, or lustful vocations, in the blue and red flames of the dragon's breath, in the intertwined snakes and undulating nudities of flaming-haired girls, the exotic and eastern magic of the tattoo artist.

Nor was *la caravane* the only name for the variegated members of an army about as military as the braided, uniformed participants in the circus of the late Lord George Sanger. For, in undated notes drawn up by Giraud, for the guidance of his Minister, we read too: 'ils sont connus sous la dénomination de Brigands de *la Forêt Noire*, puisqu'ils avoient un chef appellé Chef de la Forêt Noire' and, in another letter, probably earlier—it is dated 24 Pluviôse year IV [13 February 1796]—the same official writes to his chief:

. . . Ces prévenus [it could have been Picard and his accomplices, though Picard was not actually arrested till the following month, so it is more likely to refer to the Claes brothers, already held] sont simplement des attroupés en armes contre la propriété des particuliers, ils avoient véritablement un chef, mais c'étoit *le chef de la forêt noire* qui pille, incendie et tue sans étendard, sans aucun signe de révolte militaire . . .

adding that they had been particularly active in the region of Havré, a locality that I have been unable to identify, but that was presumably in Jemappes.

Who then was this mysterious commander-in-chief of the black and bannerless army? 'Black Peter'? Kotzo-Picard? François Boorsbeek?

---

[1] One of those condemned in the Salambier trial, François Dubreuil, 'avoit l'uniforme des chasseurs d'artillerie. . . . Cet homme me dit qu'il est déserteur du parc d'artillerie de Malines, qu'à Bruges il avoit rencontré Sauvage qui lui avoit avancé de l'argent et l'avait vêtu en lui promettant de le faire engager dans une bande près de Courtrai. . . .' (A.N. BB 18 582). The interesting piece of information contained in this report is the facility with which members of the *bandes*, in this frontier area, were able to obtain military uniforms which would give the wearers the most perfect cover.

Or the improbable Salambier? Or was there indeed such a person at all? Might he not be a creature of the imagination of a hard-pressed public prosecutor? Or might he not have arisen, fully formed and of terrible countenance, from the panic fears of the local population, ever prone to endow bandits and brigands with super-human powers, mysterious attributes and enormous physical strength? What seems likely is that the title, from whatever dark recesses it may have come originally, had been designed to terrorise, rather than to reflect any particular geographical origin, for we are far from Alsace, and the Black Forest, *outre-Rhin*, also during this period the theatre of endemic banditry, would be quite unfamiliar to the inhabitants of these flat lands. Forests were bad enough at best, black forests could only be fearsome, like 'Black Peter himself, no doubt a denizen of such evil-sounding places. For in these lands, Breughel's black trees cloud the winter sky, the stark bare branches of the impending Apocalypse, heralded by the red and black horseman as he spurs his rearing, masked steed, its eye like that of death encased in the madness of a circle.

Or, more banally, *la forêt noire* may have had quite another significance, for, in the Pays de Caux, in the year III, the expression is used to describe the black market operated with immense profit by the local farmers.[1] Salambier, at least, with his experience of Rouen, would have been aware of this current usage. But it seems more likely simply to indicate a semi-military organisation engaged in crime and *chauffage*; and, by the accounts of the victims themselves, both Salambier's men and those said to have been commanded by Kotzo-Picard can be accurately described as *chauffeurs*, as they regularly employed this and other forms of torture, when attacking farms and isolated houses:

Ils ont poussé la scélératesse au point de vouloir lui couper les oreilles pour prendre plus vite ses pendans d'or . . . . après avoir tout pris, ils l'ont jettée de la cuisine en sa chambre sur son lit, pieds et mains liés derrière le dos, qu'ils en ont usé de même à l'égard d'Amélie Delcroix, sa servante . . . qu'Emmanuel Coppenhal, son domestique, qui étoit couché dans l'écurie, fut par eux saisi, le pistolet à la main, le menaçant que s'il parloit, sa vie étoit nulle et l'ont ainsi lié dans lad. écurie. . . .

This of the attack on the farm of the widow Dubiez, near Anseroeul, on the night of 23 December 1795. And this of a similar operation near Frasnes, on the night of 3–4 February 1796:

Michael Claes entra le premier, les deux pistolets à la main, criant *à moi*

---

[1] 'Politique et subsistances en l'an III: l'exemple du Havre', reprinted in *Terreur et subsistances*.

hussards et dragons, et passant dans les appartemens . . . il dit au maître *arrête, coquin, ou je te brûle l'âme, il faut le lier*. . . . l'un d'eux nommé *Sans Doigts* lui déchargea sur la tête un coup de crosse de fusil. . . . la femme du blessé leur dit de suite *ne tuez pas mon mari, je vais vous donner les clefs*, alors ils ouvrirent un coffre où ils ont pris une quantité d'argent blanc et monnoie de cuivre, des cuilliers d'étain, des balles, de la poudre à tirer et des pierres de fusil, 5 chemises, dont 3 de femmes et 2 d'hommes, une culotte de panne verte . . . une veste et une culotte de toile de coton blanc, une veste de velours noir, un chapeau rond fin, une canne de bois de cérisier, 2 sacs remplis de bas neufs de couleur différente, une autre paire de bas prêts à emballer, le nombre portant 250 paires. . . .

a mediocre haul perhaps, for such an organised group of bandits, pretending to be soldiers. But the farmer, as well as being hit over the head with a rifle butt, had received two bullets in the stomach. He died two days later from his wounds. It was, too, an unusual haul; for what would a Walloon farmer be doing with 250 new pairs of stockings? One suspects that, as in Upper Normandy, farmers were profiting from a period of near-famine to get themselves paid in kind, and this may account for the persistence of banditry in a part of Jemappes not known to have been particularly rich, at least as far as agriculture was concerned. Both these accounts come to us from survivors.

Dinah describes another operation in the following words:

Que les particuliers qu'elle peut avoir omis relativement à la bande d'Amiens sont [allés] dans un village appellé Curée à un quart de lieu d'Arras sur la route de Douai, chez Lefebvre, fermier aud. lieu, il a été volé et massacré plusieurs personnes, que la servante a été accrochée et pendue à la cheminée, que *David Lion Lévi* et toute la bande d'Amiens avoient commis ces vols et massacres il y a deux mois et demi. . . .

The methods and the language used, the threats, the gratuitous violence, as well as the articles stolen, mostly clothing, are entirely reminiscent of the outings of the *bande d'Orgères*. Whether or not, apart from Picard himself, there were Jews in these groups, there is no doubt whatever that we are dealing with *brigandage* in its most characteristic, quasi-military form: 'que ledit Bréda [a farmer at Hubernez, near Flobecq] étant monté au grenier pour crier au secours, il avait entendu une quantité de coups de fusil qui lui avaient fracassé les vitres. . . .'

Picard's Jewish accomplices seem to have been both quite as drunken and quite as cruel as members of more conventionally composed Christian bands: Dinah recalls, at one stage:

... Ledit Lion ... après avoir un jour exercé ses brigandages ... revint à la *Maison Blanche* en la ville de Gand, où étoit leur rendez-vous ordinaire avec leurs compagnons, que là ils se battèrent [*sic*] à coups de couteau à cause que l'un des compagnons voleurs avoit plus une plus grosse part que les autres. . . .

and at another that Sisken Vandamme 'a reçu un coup de couteau à la gorge, et qu'elle l'a vu entrer chez Teÿers, cabaretier chez le Dampoorte ... avec ses blessures ... et que Teÿers s'est moqué encore de lui. . . .' We learn, too, from her testimony, of the quarrels between rival groups: 'que ces deux bandes se sont rencontrées sur le même chemin et ont eu des rixes sanglantes entre eux, que peu de jours après les deux partis se sont réconciliés. . . .'

Judging by the very rare descriptions given by Dinah of the appearance of her husband and his accomplices, it would seem that they were less ostentatious and less attached to badges of rank than the rather childish Salambier, whose greatest ambition would have been to have become captain of a privateer in service against England. It is true that, in the attack on the farm near Frasnes, Lefebvre, nicknamed *Sans-Doigts*, is described as wearing a *bonnet de police*; another participant, Pierre Moreau, was to state that in the course of a night attack in the same area: 'J'étois alors déguisé avec de la terre grasse sur la figure. . . .' 'Fromme', the rather improbable name of Kotzo-Picard's brother (but what *are* we to make of people said to be related who either have no surnames or have different ones?) refers, with a note of pride, to his brother's long experience in crime:

Je déclare que le Capitain Picard, Juif, paroisse Saint-Pierre à Gand près la place d'Armes ... m'a dit qu'il y a 12 ans qu'il faisoit le métier de voleur, et que pour faire mes [*sic*] expéditions le nommé Hubert Lebrun, de Gand, paroisse Saint-Pierre, près du cabaret ayant pour enseigne *Saint-Hubert* [a strangely suitable emblem for an organisation going under the name of *la forêt noire*! Everything is right in the imagery of this group] était celui qui lui mettait les hommes en main. . . .

Certainly Picard and his accomplices, a number of them deserters from both the French and Austrian armies (they had other wars to fight than those of the Republic or of the Emperor) showed an intelligent concern for security indicative of either a military past or of long experience of armed banditry, or of both; Dinah reports, for instance:

... il s'est ensuite écoulé un certain temps avant que les vols ont commencé parce que l'hiver étoit trop rude à la fin de 1794 et le commencement de l'année suivante (v.s.) et qu'ils ne font pas d'expédition quand il y a de la neige crainte d'être poursuivi à la piste. . . .

And she adds a further detail: '. . . que depuis cette époque jusqu'au commencement de l'an 1796 (v.s.), cette même bande commettoit des vols tous les 15 jours et toujours au déclin de la lune. . . .'

They showed a similar professionalism in their concern to keep on the move and never to stay in a locality long enough to become known in their habits, in their comings and goings, by day or by night, never to become easily recognisable to the police, the repressive authorities, and the many informers who would be in their service in any large city:

. . . ils ont allé demeurer à Gand dans un cabaret, marché aux bêtes, nommé *Saint-Antoine*, où ils ont resté 5 ans. . . . à la fin de l'année 1790 (v.s.) elle est partie de Bruxelles pour Lille avec son mari où elle a pris quartier dans la rue dite Marché au Verjus, chez le C. Gobert, fabricant d'étoffes de coton. . . . son père avec sa famille est parti pour Courtrai où il s'est établi rue de la Lys, au coin du pont, chez la nommée *Grosse Jeanne* [no doubt either a prostitute or a former one]. . . . à l'arrivée des Français . . . son père avec sa famille est retourné à Gand. . . . elle demeuroit à Gand avec son mari chez Verbeken, vis-à-vis la petite boucherie. . . . à la fin de cet hiver la déclarante avec son mari sont changés de domicile et pris un quartier vis-à-vis la maison dud. Verbeken [they had merely crossed the road]. . . . un mois après cet événement elle est changée de domicile et a pris quartier, avec son mari chez le nommé Ducarme, éperonnier, rue des Vaches, à Gand. . . . qu'au mois de nivôse dernier correspondant au commencement de l'année 1796 v.s. la déclarante a pris sa demeure chez Lefebvre, au cabaret nommé *A la Cour Impériale*, situé sur la Place d'Armes à Gand . . . [her last address and one at which her husband was arrested: a total of seven changes of address, four of them in Ghent, during a period of only six years].

They always took the additional precaution of never staying as a group in the same house: '. . . ils se sont partagés en ces deux maisons pour tromper les voisins et écarter tout soupçon qui auroit pu naître par un trop grand concours des individus. . . .' though Dinah, however unfaithful she may have been to her remarkable husband—and she is very insistent in her testimony that Picard, and Picard alone, was in command of *la bande*—seems to have been prepared always to follow him around, while her parents were never very far away: sometimes in the same inn, sometimes just the other side of the street, occasionally, a couple of streets away, on the other side of the cattle market or the *marché aux herbes*. In this respect, at least, the unity of this extensive Jewish family must have jeopardised security, that is if its many members were engaged in all the criminal activities described by Dinah. One would be tempted to think that such a touching family solidarity would, on the contrary, have witnessed in favour of the innocence of most at least of Dinah's relatives. It could, conceivably, be argued that this very unity made the *bande* much more impenetrable to outside interference, especially to informers, amateurs, dangerous newcomers, and physical cowards. Like so much else about this group, there is no means of deciding in favour of one interpretation or another.

But there are plenty of other examples of this constant concern for security. They were, for instance, in the habit of leaving in several groups, rather than as a single body, and at different hours of the night, when they set off on an armed expedition. When, for instance, Picard and his alleged Jewish accomplices—a dozen or more according both to Dinah and to some of the French and Walloon witnesses—left Ghent for Mons, before picking up the Claes brothers, who had the advantage of knowing the terrain, one group went ahead on horseback, while Picard, possibly to emphasise his status, travelled behind in a hired carriage, which he dismissed before reaching one of the rendez-vous just outside Leuze, on the road to Renaix. Salambier, too, liked his comforts; but, unlike Picard, he was to continue to travel in a stolen cabriolet, whose owner he had certainly murdered; he had only taken the elementary precaution of having the stolen vehicle re-painted, a few days after its theft.

On their return from an expedition, Picard and his men would meet in more than one inn to carry out the division of the booty. In the attacks on farms in the Ath region, they always took the precaution of placing scouts both on the highroad and at the back entrances of farms. Speaking Yiddish among themselves, they were perhaps less likely to give themselves away, even when boasting in their cups. But the possession of what was in effect a secret language could also have grave disadvantages, for it picked the Jews out to the many observers and informers to be found in inns, from the general mass of Walloons and Flemings; and, in the countryside at least, *les gens de la nation juive* must have been something of a rarity, and, therefore, easily recalled; and, even in a town like Tournai, they would stand out. One could well understand the feeling of indignation given free rein by one of the Jewish merchants accused in Dinah's mammoth statement, Gabriel Haÿman, and of his travelling companions, in a petition drawn up in Yiddish and addressed to the Minister of Justice, on 12 Vendémiaire year VI [3 October 1797]:

Une femme se faisant appeller Dimant [*sic*] Jacob . . . est la cause de nos mal-heurs . . . elle s'abandonne aux plus affreux désordres, elle a un enfant avec un autre que lui [Picard]. . . . c'est ainsi que cette femme est devenue à Tournai le fléau des étrangers, c'est-à-dire de tous les gens qui ne sont pas du pays, que tous les jours . . . elle ne cesse de dénoncer et faire arrêter toutes sortes de personnes, sans les avoir jamais ni vues ni connues. . . . En nivôse an V [January 1797], nous 3 pères de famille, chargés de 14 enfans, étant en route pour objet de commerce, nous allons à Tournai où nous ne devions que passer, nous nous arrêtons dans une auberge, pour nous rafraîchir avec une bouteille de bière. Là se trouvent 2 gendarmes appostés exprès par la femme Jacob, nous parlions hébreu. . . . on se contente de dire vaguement (et c'est toujours la femme Jacob qui parle) que nous avons volé du côté de Paris, du côté de Lille et du côté de Bruxelles. . . .

There is no reason why we should disbelieve them. Their rôle, clearly, in Dinah's scheme of things, was to give body to one of her two principal theses: the existence of *three bandes* (Paris, Lille, and Brussels, as in this instance) or the even more ambitious theme of the existence of *seven*. Clearly, by this time, thanks to Dinah, Tournai, an important road and communication centre from east to west, had become something of a trap to any obvious Jew, passing on his way, on his legitimate business, to or from Brussels or Lille. This would be the sense of the advice given to Dinah by an emissary of her brother, who had sent him from Paris to warn her 'que ce *Francfort* lui a dit qu'il y a une grande trahison, qu'on arrête partout indistinctement les juifs, prévenus ou non, qu'il en est d'arrêtés à Paris, dans les campagnes, jusqu'à Lille. . . .'[1]

We hear a similar complaint, nine months before Hayman's petition, on 16 Pluviôse year V [4 February 1791], when Israël Lyon, described as *marchand, domicilié à Ysdem* (Meuse-Inférieure, a Department which combined Dutch and Belgian Limburg, with its *chef-lieu* in Maastricht), aged sixty-one, was interrogated by the *juge de paix* Hoverlant. Lyon stated:

[1] Dinah goes on: '. . . Que dans le tems un nommé *Ian*, le plus scélérat de toutes ces bandes, étoit sauvé de Bruges, que les chefs des bandes de Paris sont:
   Abraham Jacob Lévi, son frère;
   François Boorsbeek (a man apparently gifted with the capacity to be in half-a-dozen places at once);
   Isaac Cracq (previously stated to have belonged to the *bande de Lille*);
   Aaron Lévi, simple voleur;
   Daniel Jacob;
Que le nombre de ces brigands peut monter à 80 voleurs dont les noms ne lui sont pas présents, mais que si on lui permettoit de se rendre avec le C. Kragine et une escorte à Paris ou ailleurs, elle sauroit les reconnaître et les faire arrêter.
   Qu'il est un jeune homme natif de Paris âgé de 19 ans nommé *Fardelle* qui a servi son mari pendant 6 mois ainsi que son frère Abraham Jacob dit Lévi, qui pourroit donner de grands renseignements sur tous les faits des individus de la bande de Paris, même de tous les autres. . . .'

... qu'il étoit sortie d'Ysdem quelques jours après le 27 vendémiaire an V [18 October 1796] et s'étoit rendu à Arras, Amiens et Saint-Omer, et que de la ville d'Arras il avoit envoyé par la poste un louis d'or à sa femme qui demeure aud. Ysdem ... qu'il avait effectivement eu aujourd'hui une entrevue avec la nommée Dinah Jacob dans un cabaret et qu'il l'a connue à La Haye il y a un assez grand nombre d'années, qu'alors elle étoit toute petite, qu'il étoit arrivé hier au soir venant de Lille, qu'il étoit logé au cabaret occupé par la femme Midavaine au coin du pont Notre-Dame. ...

Dinah, of course, has no hesitation in identifying this old friend of her family:

a déclaré bien connaître led. Lion sous le nom d'Hettenbaeker, dont elle a reconnu l'identité ... qu'elle le connoît très bien pour un voleur et un brigand faisant partie d'une bande de voleurs dont les nommés Jean et François Boorsbeek frères étoient chefs ... qu'il y a environ 6 à 7 mois environs led. Lion a été arrêté en la ville d'Oudenarde pour avoir pris une bourse. ...

Gabriel Haÿman, the author of the petition already quoted, adds: 'qu'il avoit quitté ce jour lad. ville [de Lille] pour aller voir sa fille, Victoire, âgée de 16 ans, mariée à Cisquin, juif de nation, marchand rouleur demeurant à Trèves ... qu'il connoissoit led. Picard depuis 5 à 6 ans comme marchand. ...' And, in order further to discredit Dinah, he recounted a story about finding her copulating with an artilleryman, four years previously, on entering an inn in Lille.

Dinah, ever ready to oblige, went on:

Que si elle se trouvoit quelque part où il se trouveroit de ces brigands, elle les reconnaîtrait au geste, à la manière de s'asseoir, de saluer, de mettre leur chapeau, que lorsqu'ils se rencontrent, ils disent par des signes de reconnoissance *hé bien Masemack*, c'est-à-dire, *avez-vous fait bonne capture? Avez-vous bien volé?* Qu'ils appellent l'instrument avec lequel ils foncent les portes *Schokeres*, &ca. ... Sur demande à elle faite des particularités de Paris et autres lieux, a répondu que si elle s'y rendoit, elle auroit bientôt appris tout ce qui s'y commet mais qu'elle a entendu lire à sa mère une lettre de Paris de son frère Jacob que les *Masemakers* ou vols et brigandages alloient bien, que la saison devenait favorable, qu'ils sauroient en tirer avantage ... qu'elle connaît la plupart de ses complices et qu'elle pourroit contribuer beaucoup à les faire arrêter si l'on permettoit qu'elle se rendît sous bonne escorte là où elle sait qu'ils se rassemblent, soit à Paris, Bruxelles ou ailleurs. ...

Her co-operation must have seemed an inestimable break-through to the judicial authorities, who would otherwise have been completely at sea with the numerous personnel of what would normally be a largely autonomous community, enjoying its own chain of refuge, and defying the skills of the most experienced informers. And it was in fact likely that Dinah was used just in the way that she had proposed, in the course of her testimony, being taken from place to place, from Ghent to Lille, from there to Amiens and Paris, presumably accompanied by a numerous escort—her sudden appearances cannot have been particularly welcome to her extensive family—literally putting the finger on her relatives and on her husband's alleged accomplices. Dinah, and often Dinah alone, afforded them the clues, gave names to people who had none, and furnished them with an apparently coherent narrative that had the great merit of appearing to fit together, as if it corresponded to some master plan. To each, she was careful to assign a precise rôle. She never hesitated, she was never at a loss for a detail. Here, for instance, she is talking on the subject of her father, Moÿse, of her sisters, and their assistants:

que le nommé *Jacob*, son père, graveur à Gand, reçoit chez lui les vols faits par divers brigands, qu'il cherche à en opérer . . . (?) et de faire fondre les argenteries volées . . . qu'*Hélèna*, sa soeur germaine, vend les vols et distribuoit ci-devant les faux assignats fabriqués par son père . . . que le nommé *Sander*, fripier, demeurant à Gand, achetoit les vols et désignoit les maisons pour commetre les vols, que *Noyelle*, orfèvre, avoit fondu les argenteries des églises et autres, que le nommé *Larue* fournissoit les armes aux brigands, que l'on achetoit ou prêtoit en un jour 40 pistolets qu'il demeure près de Saint-Bavon, dans la rue de la Croix . . . que *Picard* a vendu de ces pièces d'or [stolen from a house on the road to Holland] à une veuve d'orfèvre demeurante sur le marché aux herbes à l'enseigne d'une demi-lune [a half-moon always carries the suggestion of clandestine dealings and crime], que cette femme achète tous les vols en secret, qu'elle soutient ainsi les voleurs depuis 10 ans qu'elle achète tout ce qui est bijouterie, perles, diamans, &ca. . . .

She was then asked if she knew of any people engaged in distributing counterfeit coins. Back came the answer:

a répondu que dans les environs de Bruxelles, le nommé *Sélech*, juif allemand, et une vingtaine d'autres parmi les quels se trouvent *Sisskinde* et *Sauvi*, juifs, fabriquent & distribuent de la fausse monnaie, que *Sauvi* est en quelque sorte le chef des fabricateurs . . . qu'elle connaît à Bruxelles le nommé *Pierrart*, orfèvre, demeurant près de la porte du Lach [*sic*], qu'il achète les vols, et soutient les voleurs & répand la fausse monnaie, que sa fille est mariée avec l'un des chefs des brigands nommés *Machoker*, et parfois *Charles Cranitz* . . . on a partagé les effets volés chez *Antoine*, hors la Dammepoorte, un des voleurs, et dont la femme vend du lard. . . .

And so on and so on. One wishes that, once at least, she were to say

'I do not know' or were to express some doubt. The girl's memory is prodigious. We move rapidly through a hidden and mysterious itinerary, the geography of which is marked out, in the prevailing darkness, by inn-signs: *A la Cour Impériale, Au Saint-Hubert, A la Demie-Lune, Au Hocheport, Au Saint-Antoine,* by proximity to bridges, markets, gates, and cathedrals (*près de Saint-Bavon*), as well as by the physical deformities of some of the innkeepers and their wives ('chez un tourneur de bois qui avoit une grande tâche sur un oeil . . .'). She and she alone can find her way in this tribal community of in-laws, first and second cousins, lovers, and mistresses. Certainly, at twenty-four, she had had plenty of time to familiarise herself with pretty well every face that had passed through the many inns in which her parents had lived, ever since their departure from Holland. She can recall the arrival of a man who whispers in her brother's ear in an inn, and concludes that he must have been an emissary of one of the *bandes*. She can remember what one of the Haÿman had said to her father, years before, when she was only eleven or twelve, in the course of a visit to Brussels.

Yet her testimony is shot through with glaring contradictions; as we have gathered from the quotes at the beginning of this chapter, her estimates of the number of *bandes* in existence vary from seven to three, and she is equally wild in her calculations as to the number of men and women actively involved in their operations; sometimes it is eighty, most of them apparently Jews, at other times, it is six or seven hundred, both Jews and Christians. She does not explain why her husband, who was living in Ghent, an area that he presumably knew well, should have agreed to take command of a series of operations around Ath and Leuze, in a region with which he does not seem to have been familiar.

There are many other obscurities, even concerning the girl herself. There are suggestions, for instance, that she was no newcomer to the courts and that she had been cross-examined by the redoubtable Baret in the course of the year III, when he was public prosecutor for the whole of Belgium. Again, it is not clear why the judicial authorities of Tournai should have been so concerned to prove the existence of a *bande juive*, if no such body had ever existed. We are a long way from the *affaire Calas*; Baret, Giraud, and the other prosecutors were neither fabulists nor anti-semites: people had been killed, farms had been attacked, there had indeed been *bandes* in the *Départements Réunis*, some were still in activity at the time of the immensely protracted *instruction*. Why then blame the Jews, when there were plenty of more obvious candidates: deserters from the Austrian, French, and Dutch armies, Flemish and Dutch smugglers and *passeurs*, Belgian privateers from Sas van Gent, Sluis, and Ostend, Salambier's people, about many of whom we have plenty of information? For the Jews do not appear very likely candidates of rural brigandage; they were mostly townsmen, though those from Alsace would also have plenty of experience of rural life, of horse dealing, of the cattle trade, and of the butcher's profession. There were, it seems, very few Jews ever in the Austrian Netherlands; and Dinah's hundreds come as a surprise. (There was, however, a sizeable Jewish population in the *Départements Réunis* by the time of the Concordat.) They may, as she often suggests, have been recent arrivals, having come in from Holland and the Rhineland at the time of the annexation.

There is, however, independent testimony as to Picard's rôle as *capitaine*: for the French and Walloon members of the group active around Ath describe, in detail, his presence, and recognise his leadership; of course, they too may have had an axe to grind, for, on several occasions they were to complain that they had been done out of their share of the spoils by Picard and a dozen or so other Jews.[1] *Les juifs ont bon dos*; and popular mythology, at the end of the eighteenth century, was ever ready to accredit them with any number of ritualistic crimes, from the poisoning of wells to the murder of small children. It is then just possible that the whole affair of the *bande juive* is an exercise in familiar mythology, a sort of rural and urban *Grande Peur*, in sensitive frontier regions, on the subject of dark and mysterious strangers (and strangers, in northern Europe, are always dark). Yet the judicial authorities would hardly be likely to fall for this sort of thing, and, faced with the reality of continuous banditry in the areas under their jurisdiction, it is difficult to see why they should have galloped after non-existent bandits when there were plenty of very real ones in the offing. Giraud, in particular, frequently refers to the presence of *local* brigands. There is no reason to think that, by choosing the Jews, he was attempting to place suspicion away from his own people, for, like most of the judicial officials, he was presumably a Belgian. Finally, there is nothing basically improbable about the presence of a Jew at the

---

[1] One of the Claes brothers was to complain that the Jewish members of the group went off with most of the loot: 'nous n'avons rien eu pour notre part, ce sont les juifs désignés dans l'affaire de La Louchère qui ont tout tenu . . . je déclare que l'argent que j'ai reçu dans toutes ces expéditions consiste dans 40 couronnes cachées chez moi dans la terre près du lit des enfants et que les bas volés sont cachés près d'un parc où il y a de la chicorée, plus une paire de boucles d'argent que j'ai cachée dans la paille au grenier du côté de la cour et un pistolet sur le même grenier sous la paille. . . .'

head of a bandit group. The Jews, after all, practised most of the skills exercised by Christians; there were outdoor, as well as indoor, Jews, courageous ones as well as prudent ones, violent Jews as well as gentle ones. Apparently, in this part of the world, there were even Jewish sailors and watermen.

It is, nevertheless, clear that the authorities are not quite sure of what to make of such a mass of detailed information, of a story that comes out so pat, and that they are not entirely convinced about Dinah's reliability as a witness ('Tel que soit le dégré de crédulité que puissent mériter les dépositions faites par lad. Dinah Jacob. ...') or by her profession of attachment to the public weal:

... qu'elle étoit peiné d'avoir lié son sort à un homme qui s'est rendu indigne de sa confiance qu'elle avoit eue en lui par la conduite infâme qu'il a tenue en s'associant à une bande de brigands dont il étoit même le chef, que quoique ses proches parens même fûssent complices dud. Picard dans ses brigand-ages, et quoiqu'il eût coûté à son coeur pour dénoncer leurs forfaits, elle croit devoir à la sûreté générale et pour le bien de la chose publique de dévoîler leurs crimes. ...

So much public spiritedness does not somehow ring true. Of course, it was easy too for Picard and for her relatives to attempt to discredit Dinah as a witness by enlarging on her dissolute behaviour: the fact that she had one or more illegitimate children, the suggestion that she was Kragine's mistress; and Kragine was a Christian. Anyhow, the authorities were not taking any chances. Pretty well everyone named by Dinah who could be arrested was arrested; though one of them, François Boorsbeek (*le batelier*), apparently got away to Cologne, and a number, including: '*Jacob Moÿse*, père delad. Dinah; *Sara*, sa mère; *Hélèna*, sa soeur; *Rosa*, sa soeur; *Mathieu Stevens*; *Larue*, armurier; *Smitz*, ex-procureur [always a bad sign]; *Noyelle*, orfèvre; La femme *Ducarme*; *Alexandre Faÿes* et *Pierre Etauvan*' all picked up in Ghent, at addresses given by Dinah, nearly six months after Picard's arrest, as the result of her accusations, had subsequently to be released, after appearing before the *juge de paix*, in the absence of any incriminating proof against them. This is certainly a serious blow to the credibility of much of Dinah's story, for she had given her parents and her sisters leading rôles in the organisation, as well as attributing to Larue the job of keeping the groups supplied with weapons, and to Noyelle, that of melting down stolen jewellery and plate. She was even to add the detail that her father had actually been wounded in the leg, in the course of an encounter with the *gendarmerie*.

Certainly there are some very odd gaps in her relentlessly picaresque account of her husband's doings. If he were *all* the things that she claims he had been, and if the two had been married for a number of years—and, from her account, it is clear that they were already married in 1790, when she was seventeen or eighteen—she must have been aware for a very long time of what he was up to. What, then, induced her to come forward when she did? The promise of a substantial reward? Or because she realised that the game was up for her husband and her family? (This seems unlikely, as, without her testimony, the authorities would not have known about Moÿse and the rest of them; even with her testimony, they had to release them, because of insufficient evidence.) Or she may merely have used these frightful means to gain the freedom for Kragine and for herself to live out their own lives without fear of molestation on the part of her husband and her relatives.

There is little to hold on to on such a slippery terrain. Unfortunately, in the absence of information about the actual outcome of the trial in Tournai—we do know, however, that some thirteen members of what is claimed to have been Picard's gang were later executed in Ghent, and that others were being held in Tournai as accomplices of Salambier—it is difficult to know how much to believe in her long account. The Minister himself was clearly worried about certain aspects of the case, and must have been harrying Giraud to get on with the trial—Merlin had been lobbied by some of the relatives of the Jacob and Haÿman families, claiming that the prisoners were innocent and that their long detention (over eighteen months) without trial represented a blot on French justice and was reminiscent of the practices of the Austrians—for the unfortunate Giraud is constantly at pains, in his letters to his chief, to emphasise the immense difficulties of the *procédure*, with so many witnesses, over such a vast area, to be heard. There were also the usual quarrels between the judicial authorities of Mons and Tournai.

Dinah was at least successful in one respect; for in her insistence on her husband's paramount rôle in all these great enterprises, there is an element of admiration. Was she not married to the greatest brigand of them all? Time and time again, she returns lovingly to the theme that he was in fact the head of *all* the *bandes*, that they *all* recognised his command. For, in the indictment, we read: '*Récapitulation.* De tout ce qui précède il résulte que le nommé *Gaudechaux* [sic] *Picard* est prévenu 1. d'avoir été chef de plusieurs bandes de brigands qui ont désolé le pays. . . .' He seems indeed to have been recognised as such by those who, like the Claes brothers, are described as his principal lieutenants. On one occasion, wounded in the hand by the fire of a group of peasants, north of Ghent, he is said to have started back to the city. 'Picard étoit alors accompagné de *David Paul*, juif natif d'Amsterdam, lequel protestoit qu'il mourroit avec lui s'il étoit en danger. . . .' (He was in fact to be killed, subsequently, by one of the Boorsbeek brothers.)

Dinah at least seems to have subscribed to a similar code of honour, for there is a decidedly sneering note in what she has to say about a minor member of the gang, Louis Salomon, described as a forty-five-year-old *marchand à Lille:*

qu'elle le connoissoit pour être juif de nation, connu en hébreu sous le nom de *Wolf Burshteede* . . . que cependant il n'est pas aussi déterminé voleur de nuit que les autres quand il a de l'argent, mais que quand il n'en a pas, il vole alors comme les autres, principalement le jour, en escamotant de l'argent, des portefeuilles et d'autres choses. . . .

For Dinah, the real test is an expedition by night. Pickpocketing was really unworthy of a man like her husband. But it was good enough for a Salomon, who was not even a real bandit; he only became one when he was out of cash. Similarly, the contempt displayed by the Claes brothers for Jean Frénay, the French deserter, who, so they said, could not be trusted to 'go in,' is equally evocative of this idealisation of physical prowess. And, in this part of the world, unlike the Beauce, courage was not just a mark of personal honourability among bandits; it was often, too, a guarantee of survival. For in the two Flanders as well as in the Tournésis, the local peasants did not sit down submissively while the bandits roamed the countryside and pillaged their farms, insulting and brutalising their women. There are plenty of accounts of pitched battles between Picard's mounted men and countrymen on foot, often unsupported by the *gendarmerie*:

. . . que vers le mois de décembre & janvier dr. son mari, accompagné de son frère, commandoit 20 hommes . . . que son mari fut porté à 6 lieues de Gand sur la route de la Hollande . . . que la bande Picard avait été chassée par les paysans au bruit du tocsin, qu'ils en imposoient en lâchant des coups de pistolet. . . . qu'il fut blessé l'hiver dernier . . . dans une affaire au-delà de Bruxelles sur la direction de Gand à la distance de 13 lieues de cette dernière commune, étant chassé par les villageois des environs, qu'il fut abattu avec son cheval. . . . *Lion Lévi* étoit d'un vol tenté environ dans le tems près de Bruxelles où les voleurs étoient attendus par des volontaires qui s'étoient placés en embuscade . . . que plusieurs furent arrêtés, que 2 juifs de cette bande restèrent sur le carreau. . . . à la fin de l'été de la même année [1795] les mêmes brigands ont volé dans une commune au Pays de Waes entre Gand et Anvers où ils ont tenu tête à coups de sabre et de pistolet aux paysans . . . on a même sonné le tocsin et les voleurs ont été poursuivis jusqu'à la tête de Flandres où François Boorsbeek, surnommé *le batelier*, a coupé le cable d'une chaloupe et les a ainsi faits passer l'Escaut vis-à-vis d'Anvers. . . .

In the Ath-Leuze region, most of the people arrested and sent to the prison of Tournai were in fact either local people, with local knowledge as to the contents of the farms selected for attack, the location of servants (whether they slept in the house or in the stables), and of dogs, or French deserters.[1] Some of the members of this particular group are stated to have been inhabitants of Ghlin, near Mons. The servant of one of the farmers robbed, Amélie Delcroix—a Walloon name if ever there was one—'a cru reconnaître parmi eux [her aggressors] le nommé Auguste Desfontaines. . . .'

One of the accused states:

que le rendez-vous fut par eux fixé chez la soeur dud Mit [Demit] au faubourg d'Ath où se rendirent un jeudi soir tous les complices, que vers onze heures de la nuit ils sont partis bien armés pour lad. ferme d'Aubois [*sic*] . . . se sont rendus dans la maison de la soeur . . . qu'à leur arrivée, ils cachèrent leurs effets dans un four qui se trouve à côté de la maison, faubourg d'Ath, porte de Tournai. . . .

Two of the farmers were able to recognise most of the shirts and articles of clothing taken from their homes, and that were discovered in the oven of the house in a suburb of Ath. One of the gold rings found in this hide-out was marked with the initials M.I.F.[2]

Another witness, also a victim of their operations, and a neighbour, shows a similar acquaintance with alleged members of the group:

que Michel Claes lui a dit qu'il avait volé une montre d'or à Mons, qu'il a vu fort souvent chez ce Claes de grandes boucles d'argent de souliers, de l'argent blanc en quantité, même un louis d'or . . . que ce Michel Claes, avec son frère, faisoient beaucoup de dépenses de bouche, et souvent qu'il les a vus

---

[1] Dinah's list of some eighty names included such people as: 'Aaron Lévi, Steyck, *receleur*; Simon Heigs (ou Heix), Pacher, Daniel, Michel & Abraham Sangais, Schlaume Nakmous, Jonas Homkain, David Lion, Carles Trout, Toron, Moïse Hooker, Hux, Marchus, David Lichtem, Carles Rous ou Lion Lévi, Isaac Cracq, Chmousse, Sisken Vandamme, Jacob Quescelle, Abraham Langmise, Fagimine, Marens, Pacq, Chlomère Narmon, Chemkeisen, Daniel, Moïse Mink, Moïse Meintzère, Selech, *juif allemand*, Sisskine, Sauvi, Chtaiffe Wolf, *parisien*, Baldovers, Pierrart, *orfèvre*, Berr, Isaac Melech, Israël Lion, Marousse Keuppen, Louis Salomon dit *Wolf Bursteede*. . . .'

[2] See note M, p. 258.

partir de chez eux quantité de fois ne pouvant savoir s'ils étoient armés ou
non à cause de la nuit, qu'il les a vus souvent revenir le matin chargés de
besaces pleines . . . que toute la commune de Wannebecq a toujours regardé
lesd. Claes pous des voleurs. . . .

Two members of the group were French deserters, and only Picard,
his brother 'Fromme', Jacobus, and Vandamme, were Jews from
Ghent. It is true that one of the accused also referred to 'seize autres
dont les noms lui sont inconnus'. But it would take a considerable
stretch of imagination to assert that this was a Jewish group, even if
most of the locals involved were anxious to prove that Picard and his
brother were the real leaders.[1]

To conclude, whatever we may make of Dinah, she was certainly a
very dangerous person to have been at large, with so much detailed
knowledge; and she was a very dangerous person, too, to have been
held in prison, with her facility for recognising people as she was taken
from cell to cell. Of course Picard may have loved her; it is the occupational risk of even the most experienced bandit. Certainly he seems
to have been deeply enmeshed in her extensive family.

There are indications too that he was something of a fool: once in
prison, he had readily confided in the dangerous Kragine, boasting to
him of the number of years that he had been in banditry and of the
huge bodies of men that he had had under his command. There is a
genuine note of simplicity, as well as of searing rage, in the petition
that he addresses from his prison to the Minister, on 16 Fructidor year
V [2 September 1797]:

. . . On dit qu'il faut avoir étudié pour écrire au Ministre, moi, je dirais le
contraire parce que je suis un ignorant, les savans mettent un voile devant
leurs pensées et moi je mets ma pensée devant le voile, mais malgré mon savoir, je ne sens pas moins le mal qu'on me fait.

Je suis détenu depuis 18 mois dans un affreux cachot comme un vil criminel au gré de quelque domination hypocrite, tel que le commissaire près du
Directoire du jury d'accusation à Tournai et ses frères qui cherchent à s'ab-
reuver du sang de leurs semblables. . . . j'ai reçu vos réponses C. Ministre,
que vous avez daigné de faire à Sara Jacob, mère malheureuse de ma perfide
femme. Son successeur, Ghlinghin, associe mon épouse avec un nommé
Gragine [*sic*] autrichien, déserteur ou prisonnier de guerre, qui pour avoir un
asile et de la subsistance, aurait sans doute signé la mort de tous les vrais
Français. . . . Le C. Plapier, successeur du C. Ghlinghin, a arboré le pavillon
neutre à mon égard, il aime mieux un verre de gassine (?) ou de curaçao,

---

[1] See note N, p. 259, for a detailed list of those accused of having belonged to
the gang.

que de se mêler de ses affaires . . . Picard, arrêté à Gand le 21 ventôse an IV . . .

Despite his apparently cosmopolitan associations he was in fact French, either by birth or by naturalisation for he was born in Habsheim, in the Haut-Rhin. He may have been proud of the fact, though it is more likely that he was trying to engage the sympathy of the Minister by depicting himself as the victim of perfidious Walloons, of an alcoholic official from Tournai, and of an Austrian deserter. Unfortunately, apart from this letter, this is about all that we know about him. Unlike Salambier, he did not oblige the historian with a long *curriculum vitae*.

There is always a danger, when a historian concerns himself with bandit groups, that he may take the leaders at their own estimation of themselves, may glamourise them, endowing their essentially horrible activities with an aura of adventure, mystery, and daring-do. Picard and his accomplices were certainly not nearly as omniscient as Dinah would try to make them out to have been. They were not the prestigious manipulators of a vast international criminal organisation, a sort of eighteenth century *cosa nostra*. And if Picard was undoubtedly a brave man, he was, when all is said and done, only a cheap thief and robber, not above picking pockets, when there was nothing else going. He might call himself *capitaine*, but he was only the self-styled officer of rather a seedy army of occasional thieves and shabby middlemen. Many of the crimes that were attributed to him and his accomplices constituted the characteristic activities of the very poor, of the totally indigent, for whom the theft of clothing and linen might make the vital difference between starvation and temporary affluence, especially in famine years like 1794, 1795, and 1796.[1] The Claes brothers, after their nocturnal sorties, returning, in daylight, to their two homes, laden with sacks bulging with loot, were to give themselves away by their unwonted spending on food and drink, no doubt at their local inn. Such things would not go unnoticed in a vigilant, all-knowing countryside.

We have felt the need thus to enumerate in detail the objects that

[1] A.N. DD III 86 d 17 (Comité de Législation, Gard, municipalité de La Salle, Gard, à la Convention, 20 ventôse an III [10 March 1795]): '. . . Il arrive de là que certaines classes se ruinent & que beaucoup d'autres meurent de faim. Il arrive encore que dans un pays on est dans la plus extrême misère & que dans l'autre on vit plus au large & avec beaucoup plus d'agrément qu'on eût jamais fait. Si ce désordre n'est pas incessamment réprimé, il en résultera deux maux inévitables, ou la famine pour certains pays, ou la guerre civile & l'établissement du brigandage. . . .'

they were accused of having stolen from farms in villages like Bouvignies or Flobecq in order to bring Kotzo-Picard and his so-called
bande down to size: there is nothing romantic about banditry on this
scale. These people were prepared to kill for a pair of ear-rings (taking,
in their febrile haste, the ears with them too); and they were prepared
to kill one another, later, for a gold watch or a clock. Salambier, too,
had pretensions, a certain *manie de grandeur*, exploited to great effect by
the observant Baret; but it is likely that, in his case too, poverty, need,
and hunger had been the three sad muses that had set him off on the
dangerous road to *brigandage*. Kotzo-Picard was a run-of-the-mill
pickpocket, who, so we are told, got caught in the act, in Béthune;
his wife's relatives could, at a pinch, melt down a piece of stolen church
plate, provide a paper that might pass as a passport, or turn out easily
forged *assignats*, all useful skills, but by no means rare. We must not
be dazzled by Dinah's perhaps rather pathetic efforts to make of her
husband a figure of international proportions, a man at home in a dozen
capitals. When raising a force to carry out an attack on a farm, he often
had to make do with some poor wretched deserter, driven to banditry
in order to keep himself in food, and such a poor trembling bandit that
he had to be pushed by the shoulders, from behind, into closed pre-
mises, or even had to be left outside, covered by a pistol. Or he had to
take in some poor woodsman, made desperate by two bitter winters,
precipitated into armed robbery at night by the intensity of the cold, by
the need to cover his own nakedness and that of his family: a woman's
stolen skirt might clothe several children, a good coat could warm a
whole family sleeping on the floor.

Kotzo-Picard and his wife's relatives were no doubt well-travelled
people: some had been to Alsace, some to Holland and the Rhineland,
some to Paris. But they were travellers of the fairground variety; and it
was to the fair, as well as to the seedy carters' inns of the faubourgs,
that such people belonged. The *tigre marin* might also be part of the
troupe, while many of Salambier's people had been conjurors and fairground entertainers. Picard himself is reported as paying frequent
visits to the fair at Sas van Gent, in search no doubt of thefts to commit,
but also possibly for his own entertainment.

And there we must leave these poor wretches, divested at least of
some of their lustre. The indictment against Picard and his accomplices
was completed in Germinal year V [April 1797]. But the trial was to
take nearly two years to get under way.[1]

---

[1] A.N. BB 18 400 (directeur du jury d'accusation du tribunal de Tournai, au
Ministre, 13 vendémiaire an VI): '. . . une partie de cette bande est ici . . . une

ii   The *Bande à Salambier*

November 1795–June 1797

François-Marie Salambier, stated at the time of his trial to be about thirty-two and 'assez robuste de corps' was a native of Isbergues, near Béthune, in the Pas-de-Calais. Married, with several children, before taking to the roads, he had lived in Aire, in the same neighbourhood. His wife and family were stated to have still been residing there at the time of his arrest. He had an elder brother, Placide-François Salambier, aged thirty-six and calling himself *laboureur et tisserand, demeurant au Mont-Bernarchon.* The younger man is described, not very helpfully, as *marchand colporteur.* Both stated that they could not read or write, signing their cross-examination with a cross. We know nothing of Salambier's antecedents before, at twenty-nine or so, he took to banditry.

As an active bandit Salambier first appears on the scene in November 1795, though he is said to have been engaged in *chauffage* in and around Rouen and in the Eure earlier than that. His activities as a highwayman and a brigand lasted just over a year, to the end of 1796, when he was caught. He was condemned to death and executed in Bruges, with twenty-one of his accomplices, on 30 September 1798, at the end of a very long trial before the criminal court of the Département de la Lys. Three others of his associates were sentenced to long periods in the galleys.[1]

This was not, however, the end of his gang. For there were a number of other trials, both in Lille, and in Courtrai, in 1799, 1800, and 1801, when six *chauffeurs*, said to have been survivors of the original group,

---

autre partie est à Bruges, Gand, Bruxelles &ca . . . il faut ouvrir une correspond- ance avec Renaix, Bruxelles, Gand, Bruges, Cambrai &ca . . . lancer de nouveaux mandats d'amener, d'arrêt, peut-être jusques du côté de Maestricht, entendre une nouvelle foule de témoins.' Further accomplices had been condemned to death by the Ghent court in Ventôse year VI [March 1798] '. . . Les trois individus pour lesquels on réclame sont prévenus faire partie de plusieurs bandes de chauffeurs inculpés d'assassinats et d'une multiplicité de vols commis à force ouverte dans une étendue de 40 lieues environ . . . 13 de ces brigands viennent d'être con- damnés à mort au tribunal criminel du département.'

[1] A complete list of the 26 tried on this occasion, together with their ages, places of birth, physical appearance, and remarks about their personalities can be found in the Appendix at the end of this chapter.

were executed, on Saturday 24 January. At that date, five others were in Lille prison, awaiting trial by the Douai court.[1]

We first hear of Salambier and his friends as the result of a murder committed at Fresnes, near Condé, just on the French side of the border, on 10 November 1795. On this occasion, a woman had been murdered in her farm, at eight-thirty in the evening. Almost a fortnight later, on the night of 22–3 November [Sunday to Monday], they are reported at La Houlette, in the *canton* of Le Quesnoy, where a doctor, his in-laws, and his six children were found by neighbours, cut to pieces with sword, bayonnette, and sabre thrusts. At least eleven people had taken part in this sanguinary operation, judging from the number of dirty plates and glasses left round the table and found on the Monday morning. From the weapons used, Ranson, the public prosecutor of the Douai court, guessed, rightly as it turned out, that in the group there must have been some deserters, probably officers.[2] On the night of Monday to Tuesday 14–15 December, other members of the group—and on this occasion some of them were identified as residents —are reported to have broken into the house of a well-to-do merchant in the *commune* of Lomme, just outside Lille, on the road to Armentières. Some of the accomplices of the *bande* had taken up residence previously, in this conveniently-placed village, at an important road junction, and within easy walking distance of Lambersart and the other north-western faubourgs of the city.

Nearly a month later, once more on a Sunday, 10 January 1796, a farmer from the outskirts of Nord-Libre (the revolutionary name of Condé!) was found strangled by his handkerchief, early on the Monday morning, by a group of revellers, his body lying beside the highroad from Tournai to Mons, near the village of Basècles, just over the border, close to the *bourg* of Péruwelz. The group then must have moved further up the highroad, in the direction of Barry, for on the Monday [11 January] they broke into a farm in the isolated village of Willaupuis, *canton* of Leuze: having ransacked the place and made off with a large sum in Austrian currency, they left the farmer lying dead in his yard. Again, the victim had been killed *à coups de sabre*.[3] This is

---

[1] A.N. BB 18 582 (Justice, Nord, commissaire près le tribunal de Douai, au Ministre, 4 pluviôse an IX): '. . . 5 de ces misérables sont ici en maison de justice, ils attendent leur mise-en-jugement . . . le directeur du jury de Valenciennes instruit une affaire qui doit conduire ici un nombre considérable de brigands de cette espèce; à Lille, d'autres prévenus sont arrêtés; il y en a à Cambray. . . .'

[2] See note O, p. 260.

[3] A.N. BB 18 579 (Ministre de la Police générale, à l'administration municipale du canton de Nord-Libre, le 25 nivôse an IV): '. . . Un fermier de la banlieue de

the nearest that Salambier's men ever got to the Picard group, that was
operating in the same canton, but a little further to the north, at the
same time.

After a pause of about five weeks, we hear of them once more, again
on the Belgian side of the former border, when they broke into a farm
near Poperinge, on the main road from Menin to Bergues and Dunkirk.
The same day, there is the report of a murder committed outside Aire,
where Salambier's family was living; we do not know, however,
whether it can be attributed with any certainty to the *bande*.

At this stage, we lose sight of them. Some of the accomplices,
including innkeepers living in the faubourgs of Lille, had been
arrested; others had turned informers. Salambier himself may have
gone on one of his Norman trips. The group is credited with a single
murder, in June 1796, in the *commune* of Longprez, a locality that we
have been unable to identify but that, according to Ranson's indictment, was within an hour's walking distance of Lille.

After that, there is no sign of them till the night of Monday to
Tuesday 7–8 October 1796, when their presence is reported once more
in the immediate neighbourhood of Lille, near the village of Houplines,
on the outskirts of Armentières, where they are said to have committed
a couple of murders; one of the victims was a travelling salesman, on
his way back from a Monday market.

The next affair, which was to prove the undoing of Salambier himself, though he was steadfastly to deny actually having committed the
murder, and of his principal accomplice, Heller, *dit Bonaventure Berry*
(He was in fact from Burgundy, having been born in a village in the
Yonne.) was situated well beyond the usual area of operations of a
group that seems to have clung closely to its bases in inns and lodging-
houses in the suburbs of Lille, Valenciennes, Courtrai, and Dunkirk, a
fact which suggests that the crime may have been committed, without
previous planning, on the spur of the moment. The two men had been
staying at an inn, *Le Duc* (de Brabant?), in the Flemish village of
Kontich, on the road from Malines to Antwerp. There they had struck

cette commune s'étant transporté à Basècles, département de Jemappes, à 2
lieues de son domicile, y a été étranglé avec son mouchoir; et on assigne pour
cause à cet assassinat que le patriotisme de cet infortuné père qui laisse une veuve
et 8 enfans, que cet événement plonge dans la misère, et qui a eu lieu le 20 de ce
mois. Un autre attentat a été encore commis à 2 lieues de cette commune, 15 à 20
hommes ont forcé la porte d'un fermier de la commune de Willaupuis, canton de
Leuze. . . .' The political nature of the first crime does not seem at all established,
even if the farmer had been a well-known republican.

up an acquaintanceship with a local innkeeper, Paul van der Auwera, who, no doubt in his cups, had been unwise enough to reveal to his two companions that, on the following morning, 21 November 1796, he would be driving to Brussels, in order to settle some debts and that if they were travelling in that direction, he would be happy to take them with him, in his visibly smart cabriolet. They accepted, presumably with alacrity, and early the next morning the three set off on the road to Brussels. Exactly what happened after that is not clear.[1] What is certain is that van der Auwera never reached Brussels and was never seen alive again. On the other hand, his gig and horses were to turn up, a few days later, with Salambier and Heller, at a village not far from Dunkirk. The gig, which had been repainted, was recognised by van der Auwera's wife. The two men had in the meantime moved on; and it was on the basis of the poor woman's evidence that they were subsequently arrested in a village near Ostend, about a week after the alleged murder. In the indictment drawn up against Salambier and his accomplices, in September 1798, it was stated, on the basis of evidence supplied by Salambier himself, who put all the blame on Heller, that the man had been murdered on the road between Laeken and Brussels in broad daylight and that his body had been tipped into a ditch:

Salambier et Heller, après l'assassinat commis à Bruxelles [*sic*] sont venus d'une traite se refugier à Ghistelles, ont passé deux jours avec Lachaise pour faire défigurer la voiture qu'ils avoient volée et sous la protection de Lachaise sont allés à Ostende prendre un reçu de patente de colporteur . . . le commissaire du Directoire Exécutif près ce canton, incapable d'une pareille place, quoique tout français aimant la République, me disoit, sur les reproches que je lui faisois d'avoir accueilli ces sortes de gens: *ce sont de bons bougres, ils parloient de tuer, de massacrer, c'est mon genre, je les ai pris pour de bons patriotes comme moi.* . . .

During the night of 10–11 March 1797, an innkeeper, his wife, and her parents were slaughtered in their inn, in the village of Beaudignies, on the road from Le Quesnoy to Valenciennes. This particular crime bears all the marks of the gang's usual forms of attack, as well as witnessing for the predilection of its members to masquerade as travelling salesmen. In a letter dated 13 March, two days after the murders, the *commissaire* attached to the *administration municipale* of the *canton* of Le Quesnoy, gives the Minister the following details:

. . . Un assassinat effrayant a été commis la nuit du 20 au 21 [ventôse] . . . dans la commune de Beaudégnies sur le C. Etienne Frappart et sa femme,

---

[1] See note P, p. 260.

aubergistes, . . . et N. Rappe leur père. . . . un enfant de 10 mois en est le seul qui aît échappé à la fureur des assassins. . . . Je vous adresse une liste de 6 individus sur qui les soupçons des habitans de la commune de Beaudégnies se portent et qui paraissent fondés d'après les dires de différentes personnes qui ont vu ces individus, tantôt à 4, tantôt à 2, vendant des cartes ou d'autres futiles marchandises de cette espèce qui ne peuvent par leur produit subvenir aux dépenses que font ces individus. . . .

And he adds a comment indicative at least of the assumptions of the judicial authorities on the subject of the origins of suspects:

. . . On les regarde pour être Auvergnats, Lillois ou Liégeois d'après leur accent, et ils disent qu'ils vont acheter leurs cartes à Dinant, il est à croire que lorsqu'ils ont commis quelque crime, ils se refugient dans ce pays, et je crois que c'est vers le Pays de Liége qu'une surveillance stricte pourrait les atteindre. . . .[1]

Auvergnats and Liégeois at least had the merit, in this part of France, of making first-rate suspects. But the *commissaire* is stretching credulity rather far when he suggests that there may have been any connection between the accent of the Massif Central and those, equally distinctive and themselves totally different, of Lille and Liége.

Although most of the crimes attributed to the group had thus been committed in the Nord, the Dyle, Jemappes, and the Pas-de-Calais, Salambier and twenty-four of his accomplices were tried in Bruges, at the insistence of the public prosecutor of the Dyle, Baret, who, as we shall see, had done a deal with Salambier in order to obtain this result.

As might be expected, the principal element of the *bande* comes from the Pas-de-Calais, the place of origin of five members, including Salambier himself. There are five men from the Nord, most of them inhabitants of the suburbs of Lille. There are two Belgians; a third man is described as from both Lille and Ostend. Thus fourteen of those tried in September 1798 came from the border area.

The presence of three Normans can perhaps be explained by the fact that, according to the indictment, the gang had operated at various times in the Seine-Inférieure and the Eure. It does not seem to have had any connections with Paris, though one of the Normans had been arrested there while staying with his father. There are two men from the east, one from the Vosges, the other, from the Haute-Marne.

The presence of a few southerners is more difficult to account for. Péage de Roussillon, the birthplace of one of those condemned to

[1] A.N. BB 18 581 (B. Cappen, commissaire près l'administration municipale du Quesnoy, au Ministre, 23 ventôse an V). The Minister forwarded this letter to his colleague at the *Police générale*.

death, was an old border town on the Rhône. Another southerner, who came from Figeac, and who is said to have lived in Valenciennes, was presumably an itinerant pedlar.

When we move down to the level of the accomplices, and of those still in flight at the time of the trial, the local, not to say the family, character of the *bande* becomes much more apparent. For instance, among the receivers believed to have been operating for the gang, faubourg Notre-Dame, there is an extended family group, composed of Legros, one of those condemned to death, *cabaretier*; Rosalie Deloutre, his wife; Berton, likewise condemned to death; Charlotte Deloutre, Berton's wife; Marie-Henriette Verdière, widow of Olivier Deloutre; Marie-Anne Deloutre, *tricoteuse*; Ludovine Deloutre, *ouvrière*; and Constance Deloutre, *ouvrière*, 'demeurant toutes les trois audit Faubourg' and presumably sisters. In any case, they were all stated, in April 1797, to have been living in the *cabaret* kept by Legros, 'lors de son arrestation cabaretier et demeurant à Wazemmes'. With a surname such as Deloutre, there can be little doubt about their Lillois origins.

On 6 February 1798, in the course of his investigations, Baret identifies further accomplices, most of them stated to be in flight or in hiding.[1] There is the wife of Lamblin or Lammelin, whose maiden name is Lemaire, stated to have been one of her husband's aliases. She too kept a *cabaret* in one of the faubourgs of Lille. Questioned by Baret, the ever-obliging Salambier was to provide the following information:

... Il m'ajoute que la femme de ce Lammelin ayant été femme de chambre chez Mr de la Granville, près de Lille, a donné des éclaircissements à son mari pour aller piller ladite maison de Granville [an operation that brought in a considerable haul of Austrian currency]. ... elle a chez elle la femme du nommé Bouton, dite *la Grande Catherine* ... son principal rôle était d'aller à Tourcoing chercher des passeports qui s'y vendaient 12 à 15 francs. ... un agent municipal en fabriquait [des extraits de naissance] s'appuyant sur le prétexte que les Autrichiens avaient pillé les anciens registres ... [In this frontier area, the Austrians, apart from weighing so heavily on the hopes and fears of the Belgians, appear as providential allies of those in need of a respectable identity and the means to travel].

[1] 'Le trop fameux *Théodore Leroi*, dit *Berger*, se tient ordinairement entre Saint-Amand et Valenciennes, il couche très-souvent dans un des faubourgs de Valenciennes, en partant de Saint-Amand il doit passer une petite rivière, pour arriver à ce faubourg. Ces données sont bien vagues; mais j'espère qu'elles seront plus claires pour ceux qui connaissent les lieux' (A.N. BB 18 582, Baret à Ranson, 1er pluviôse an V). Salambier was as usual doing his best, by offering as accurate a description of the place as he could call to mind from his prison in Bruges.

And in another list of names supplied to the Minister, we read: '22. *La Grande Catherine*; sa destination était d'aller acheter à Tourcoing de faux passeports et extraits de naissance. . . . 29. *Le petit Matelot*, non arrêté, il est remarquable en ce qu'il s'est encrusté sur la main une croix et une chaîne.' As he had had himself tatooed, there is in fact every likelihood that he had at one time served in the Navy. Unfortunately, this is the only time we hear of this picturesque character.

Then there is the almost inevitable group of Jewish old-clothes' merchants that includes the following:

. . . *Bernard Lion*, juif, demeurant ordinairement à Amiens, il doît avoir sa femme à Pontoise, non-arrêté.

. . . *Mayer*, juif, résidant à Amiens, non-arrêté.

. . . *Simon*, juif résident à Lille, non-arrêté.

. . . *Lévy*, aussi juif à Lille, non-arrêté. . . .

And in notes prepared by Baret for the information of Ranson, there is a further reference to this Lévy:

. . . Un des chefs de voleurs à Lille est un certain Lévy, qui loge au marché au fil, chez une marchande de poteries; il est souvent accompagné d'un autre juif à . . . ? bruns, ce Lévy étoit il y a quelque tems à Gand, où il avoit réuni une bande pour faire un vol considérable, entre Gand et Bruges, leur projet n'a pas réussi. . . . les nommés Lévy de Lille et tous ceux qui les fréquentent sont de la grande bande de voleurs. . . . Tels sont les détails que m'a donnés le nommé Mancheron, autrement dit Félix Mongé. . . .[1]

Possibly associated with this trade network of Jewish *fripiers* extending from Lille to Amiens, is another similar group based on Dunkirk, the object of a denunciation made by the wife of one of them, in a statement to the *greffier* of the *canton du Midi* of that port, in November 1797:

. . . que son mari était en société avec le juif *Jacob Aron*, qui le trompait. . . . elle éprouva de la part de Jacob et des autres juifs qui habitaient la même maison qu'elle et son mari, et de tous ceux qui y fréquentaient journellement

---

[1] Baret's informant went on: '. . . Le receleur de leurs vols à Valenciennes est un certain *Méhé*, on me dit homme de grande taille, à côté du quartier des canon-niers, dit Saint Jean, au cabaret chez lequel se retirent les Juifs. . . . [Dinah, so generous in her distribution of leaders and agents from Amsterdam to Paris, rather surprisingly makes no mention of Valenciennes, though she names some in Saint-Omer.] Trois Lillois frères, tous 3 blonds, sont aussi des voleurs et se tiennent ordinairement à Saint-Saules, près Valenciennes. On doit y trouver aussi 2 racommodeurs de fayänce, un certain *Prudhomme* et sa femme, qui est une petite bossue, tous de la même trempe. . . .' (A.N. BB 18 582, Baret à Ranson, ˙er pluviôse an V).

toutes sortes de tracasseries et d'injures, qu'une fille allemande nommé Catherine [another one!] qui demeure actuellement avec son mari, l'a prévenue que si elle ne prenait pas le parti de s'en aller [de chez elle] son mari lui donnerait un coup de couteau pendant qu'elle dormirait, que son mari étant arrivé de Paris . . . elle lui fit ses plaintes de ce qu'à son arrivée, d'une absence de trois mois, il avait préféré d'aller souper avec les autres juifs plutôt qu'avec elle. . . . qu'arrivée à Paris, elle fut loger dans la rue Nazareth, dans un hôtel garni, no 112, tenu par le citoyen Duval, où elle prit une chambre. . . .

The woman, Augustine Sergent, went on to complain that, while in Paris, she had been threatened by some of her husband's Jewish associates, who had accused her of having made off with linen, clothing, and cutlery belonging to a woman called Wall and that had been stolen by Salambier and his friends, in one of their operations in the neighbourhood of Ostend. Whatever we are to make of this affair, her statement seems to link *la bande à Salambier* with a group of receivers spreading as far as Paris.

No doubt there were many other accomplices of a group both loose and extensive. Ranson refers, in a letter dated 10 December 1796 to 'Rohart et Guerva, habitants de la commune de Longprez, près Lille, le premier ci-devant cordonnier . . . le second, manouvrier, chefs d'une bande de chauffeurs. . . .'[1]

The Haÿman daughters, too, had gone up to Paris in order to lobby the Minister in favour of their father. Dorez, an official of the Tournai court, writes, to his chief, on 28 April 1798: '. . . Quant à *Gabriel Haÿman*, je vous observe qu'il a été reconnu pour être aussi de la bande de Salambier, qu'il a été conduit à Courtrai, et l'on dit qu'il y a été en arrestation. . . .'[2]

A word now about the composition of the *bande à Salambier* in terms of occupational categories. There are as usual a number of pedlars, or people describing themselves as such. Berger, for instance, 'marchand colporteur au moment de son arrestation, auparavant fabricant de gommelat pour raccommoder de la faïance', is a good case in point; for his previous occupation would have taken him above all to fairs. Peasant women, with broken plates or jugs, would need his services, as much as they would need those of *Romary*, originally from the Vosges, 'fabricant de pommades d'odeurs et de crayons', who, on similar occasions, might administer to the needs of their coarse-grained faces and bodies. *Romary* no doubt plied all over northern France, from Épinal to Lille. *Heller* again seems to have

[1] See note Q, p. 261.   [2] See note R, p. 262.

belonged to the violent, yet joyful world of fairs and *kermesses*, for Baret writes of him: 'c'est une espèce de comédien de campagne'. He must have been either a wandering conjuror or he played a musical instrument. Cambon, who is described as a *calendreur et marchand de lacets*, may indeed have been an inhabitant of Lille, but his second trade would have taken him too to every fair that was going.

The presence of a number of deserters from French and Belgian corps gave to the whole group, as it did to that of Kotzo-Picard, something of a military mentality, several of the members are punctilious on points of honour and we gather, from a letter addressed by one of Baret's colleagues to the Minister, on 9 November 1798, that:

le nommé Lamblin . . . l'un des condamnés à mort dans la procédure Salambier, avait envoyé quelques heures avant l'exécution du jugement du tribunal au tribunal criminel . . . une espèce de testament par lequel il disposait d'une somme de 480 l. en faveur de la compagnie de grenadiers du 3me bataillon de la 51me demie-brigade. Il demandait que cette somme fût prise sur le prix des effets qui avaient été trouvés sur lui au moment de son arrestation. . . . La compagnie des grenadiers n'a pas eu plutôt connaissance de la disposition de Lamblin qu'elle a invité son capitaine, le Citoyen Grognet, à se transporter au tribunal criminel pour y déclarer qu'ils répudiaient la libéralité qui leur était faite d'une main aussi impure. . . .[1]

Unusual rectitude for soldiers. One would have thought that the poor man's dying gesture might have been accepted. One member of the group, Daniel Sauvage, is described by Baret as 'toujours froid, ne s'inquiétant de rien, riant de tout ce qu'on peut lui dire, couvert d'honorables blessures reçues à l'armée. . . .'[2] Bertoux, too, an older man, had been honourably discharged from the old royal army and was in receipt of a pension as an *invalide*.[3] Derenaud, who had no military experience—he was thirty-four at the time of his condemnation—seems at least to have given proof of military boastfulness and violence, while in prison. Ranson reports, in a letter dated 8 December 1796: 'Le directeur du jury m'a dit que Derenaud, accablé du poids d'une déposition, a menacé le témoin de le faire assassiner par un des 1,500 de sa bande. . . .'[4] Nearly three years after the execution of Salambier and his accomplices, Ranson reports on 24 January 1801:

[1] A.N. BB 18 582 (commissaire près le tribunal de la Lys, au Ministre, 19 brumaire an VII).

[2] A.N. BB 18 582 (Baret au Ministre, 13 nivôse an V).

[3] A.N. BB 18 582 (jugement rendu par le tribunal criminel du departement de la Lys, le 9 vendémiaire an VII).

[4] A.N. BB 18 582 (Ranson, au Ministre, 18 frimaire an V).

6 chauffeurs de la bande trop fameuse de Zenon Duhem [who seems at one time to have served under Salambier], condamné en l'an V, ainsi que 7 de ses complices en l'an VII, ont été exécutés ici [Douai] à mort; ils sont morts comme ils ont vécu. Puisse un aussi terrible exemple arrêter le cours des crimes trop nombreux de ces bandes de voleurs assassins; il y en a dans tous les arrondissements de ce Département. . . .

Whatever the limited proportions of such *bandes* and the short periods of their active existence, clearly they were a great source of concern to the judicial authorities. Banditry in the plains of the Beauce was a great nuisance. But what happened on the frontier was a matter of national interest.[1] Indeed, it is likely that Baret's insistence that the main group should be tried in Bruges, rather than in one of the French Departments, may have been dictated as much by the desire to impress local Flemish opinion with the effectiveness of French justice as to get as much as he could out of the loquacious Salambier.[2] Local prosecutors may also have feared that the development of endemic banditry on the border and in the Lys might eventually polarise popular opposition to the French. Speaking of the *marchands de vétilles* and the numerous little inns in which they could find refuge, off the highroads, Baelde refers to an army

d'où nous viennent la moitié de nos voleurs et assassins de première classe. Si jamais il se fournit une coalition anti-française, ne trouveroit-elle pas cette armée toute propice à ravager le pays et ses habitans surtout dévoués à la république. . . .[3]

While one of the leaders, Séraphin Dubuc, took visible pleasure in giving impudent answers to his cross-examiner in Saint-Quentin, at the end of the year IV, Baret conducted with his prisoner a series of

[1] See note S, p. 262.

[2] Baret was in a position to exercise over Salambier an extremely insidious form of blackmail, for the so-called *chef des brigands* seems to have been anxious above all not to have his case transferred from Bruges to the *tribunal criminel du Pas-de-Calais* where his family would be known. His concern in this respect is revealing of his pride as a father and his desire that his name should not be besmirched in his own part of the world. This obsession thus became the basis for a sort of unwritten contract between Salambier and his principal cross-examiner. 'Une autre considération,' states the Minister of Justice in a letter addressed to the *tribunal de cassation*, in support of Baret's demand that the trial should take place in Bruges, 'non moins intéressante est qu'il [Salambier] parait disposé à tout révéler si on le juge hors du département du Pas-de-Calais dans lequel il est né et où il a son domicile . . .' (A.N. BB 18 582, Ministre au tribunal de cassation, s.d. pluviôse an V).

[3] A.N. BB 18 582 (Baelde au Ministre, 22 ventôse an V).

conversations that were not lacking in affability and that might, in other circumstances, have been described as intimate. Writing early on in his investigations, on 2 January 1797, he informs his chief:

. . .1. François Salambier, autrement connu sous le nom de *Guéry* ou *Carpentier*, exerçoit ses ravages depuis Rouen jusqu'à Anvers. . . . Cet homme, âgé d'environ 30 ans, taille petite, mais corps robuste, belle tête, annonce le plus grand caractère, il veut, dit-il, mourir en républicain . . . qu'il se défendra au tribunal parce qu'il ne veut pas passer pour un imbécile . . . et qu'après son jugement il donnera tous les renseignements qu'on exigera de lui, qu'il y attache toutefois une condition, c'est de ne pas aller au supplice avec la chemise rouge. . . . il fait des chansons sur tous les bandits de la troupe et ne s'épargne pas lui-même. . . .

At this stage, it is true, he had nothing to lose. Later in the same month, Baret has this to say:

. . . Son caractère altier ne veut pas recevoir d'affront . . . il . . . s'est fort attendri sur le sort de sa femme et de ses enfans et prétend que par les services qu'il veut rendre, il leur évitera de rougir de sa mémoire. . . . Pour l'animer, je lui dis quelques fois que j'aimerais mieux le voir commandant un corsaire pour le service de la République que dans les fers, je vois ses yeux s'animer, il me répond: *il n'y a pas plus d'un an que je suis un scélérat.* . . .[1]

Two months later, he reports once more:

. . . une âme atroce, profondément réfléchi pour un homme sans éducation, il croit qu'il parviendra à captiver la confiance du tribunal pour en obtenir certaine douceur. . . . il affecte le sentiment, on lui parle lentement, il dit qu'il n'est pas assassin . . . il jure qu'il n'a jamais porté le coup. . . . Je vais le consoler dans son cachot, je cause avec lui, il se développe. . . .[2]

Baret did indeed know his man, for, by this mixture of flattery, patience, and vague promises, he induced Salambier to give all the names of his colleagues and accomplices.[3] Like so many bandits, he was probably a victim of his own conceit. He was extremely sensitive about being illiterate and liked to impress Baret with his wisdom and popular lore.

Séraphin Dubuc belongs to a more familiar category: the cheeky, impudent, thief, a man that the French would describe as *crâneur*. He clearly much enjoyed his own jokes, especially when he thought that they were at the expense of the man who was questioning him. This is how this rather one-sided conversation was to go, in Saint-Quentin, on 3 Fructidor year IV [20 August 1796]:

[1] A.N. BB 18 582 (Ministère de la Justice, Nord).
[2] A.N. BB 18 582 (ibid.).   [3] See note T, p. 262.

. . . a répondu s'appeller *Séraphin Dubuc*, âgé de 30 ans, voleur de profession, sans azile. . . . [dit] avoir été arrêté à Pont-à-Marc, mais il ignore pourquoi il a été arrêté, et qu'il a été arrêté, parce qu'il était sûrement un coquin. . . . d'où il vient? . . . qu'il venoit de Cambrai en se sauvant de Rouen, parce qu'on était à sa poursuite . . . a été repris de justice au moins 20 fois . . . aux fers, 7 à 8 fois . . . qu'il n'a jamais passé la ville de Rouen, attendu qu'il y a trop loin pour aller jusqu'à Brest ou à Toulon . . . il a été à Paris trouver des horlogers, pour voler leurs marchandises . . . qu'il a souvent frappé des individus qu'il dépouillait, mais qu'il n'attendait pas pour savoir s'ils étaient morts, attendu qu'il s'en allait de suite, qu'il désire que ceux qu'il a assommés soient morts, parce qu'on le guillotinerait de suite [and, throughout his cross-examination, he returns lovingly to this death-wish, he seems to court the guillotine as others might a beautiful girl—[1] and, of course, *la Veuve was* a girl—and with such insistence that the examining magistrate is clearly puzzled, and tries to point out to him that as he has not been accused of a capital crime, he will probably get away with a sentence in the galleys. This will not do for the irrepressible Norman, who returns again and again to the fact that he has *earned* the guillotine. Meanwhile, he outlines his recent movements]. . . . qu'en partant de Reims,[2] il est venu à Saint-Quentin où [il] a volé un marchand de cette commune 80 pièces de mousseline, et qu'il en a pris pour sa part 30 pièces, qu'il a envoyées à une de ses femmes [note the sexual boastfulness] . . . que c'étaient deux Juifs munis de patentes et qu'ils vendaient ces sortes de marchandises dans les villages. . . .

Questioned further, he added that he had escaped from the *chaîne* nearly two years previously and that he had then taken part in a *chauffage* in a farm near Évreux, had then gone to Lille and had participated in a number of *caravanes* in the region of Courtrai. He claims to be a *garçon de campagne*, a member of the *Pègres* and well up in the vocabulary of *l'ergot* [sic]. While in Rennes, 'il logeait tantôt à l'auberge, tantôt en chambre garnie. Il a travaillé chez un menuisier de Château-Thierry. A Meaux, il a volé 28 montres chez un horloger, 80 autres à Paris, sur les quais. . . .' On arriving in Lille, he is said to have thrown a handful of coins down in the street. Why did he do this? 'que c'était pour faire la charité aux indigents. . . .' And he concludes his statement on a suitably defiant and insolent note: 'a déclaré savoir

[1] '. . . il espère que son cou est [sic] sous le couteau de la guillotine, mais que s'il sort encore, celui qu'il rencontrera pourra s'en repentir . . . qu'il préféreroit être guillotiné que de déclarer la femme à qui il a envoyé la . . . mousseline. . . .'
[2] '. . . à lui demandé s'il est muni d'un passeport? A répondu qu'il avoit un passeport sous un autre nom que le sien, avec lequel il voyageait, mais qu'il l'a laissé à Reims, attendu qu'il a été obligé de s'enfuir en chemise, attendu qu'il avait quelqu'-affaire de boutique, qu'il avait volé quelques couverts d'argent, mais toutes bêtises, qui n'en valaient pas la peine. . . .'

écrire, mais ne pas vouloir signer'. And that indeed is the last we hear of this *gai luron* who had been on so many *caravanes*, far beyond the geographical limits credited to his friend Salambier and his *bande*.

The group attributed to the leadership of Kotzo-Picard and the *bande à Salambier*, though operating in neighbouring areas and no doubt sharing a certain number of receivers as well as a chain of comparatively reliable inns and *cabarets*, pose to the historian problems that have little in common. Dinah's story is above all a challenge to historical interpretation, as it must have been a challenge to Giraud and the other officials who had to wrestle, month after month, with this enormous flow of evidence, much of it unsubstantiated from other sources. How far are we to go with Dinah? What was Kragine up to? What was the extent of the control exercised by Kotzo over the other malefactors identified in the raids on farms in the Leuze area? How likely was it that, in the late eighteenth century, Jews might have become active bandits? There can be no firm answer to any of these questions. Yet the *affaire Kotzo-Picard*—or perhaps it should be called *l'affaire Dinah Jacob*—throws interesting light on such matters as the relations between Jews and Christians, French prejudices on the subject of the population of the *Départements Réunis*, and the alarms and preoccupations of the judicial authorities in a sensitive border area.

Salambier's group presents other points of interest. In composition, it is very much what one would expect of any bandit group, at this time and in northern France. In its operations, it was normally brutal and cruel, not especially successful, and often exceedingly careless. Its leader seems to have been exceptionally so. The group did not last very long as such; and it is clear, from what happened during the period 1797 to 1800 or so, that banditry could go on in its absence. Salambier was no monopolist. But while, even as seen through his wife's voluminous testimony, Kotzo-Picard remains a figure mysterious, faceless, without a past, and, indeed, without a future—for we do not know his ultimate fate: execution is, after all, the most satisfactory and exemplary end to the life of a bandit—both Salambier and the impudent Dubuc, in their exchanges with their interrogators, acquire human proportions and develop personalities of their own. And Salambier at least obtained for himself the traditional last act of anyone walking in the traces of Cartouche and Mandrin.

The history of both groups brings out certain aspects of criminality that were perhaps peculiar to the *Départements Réunis*. There was, first of all, the availability of a great deal of hard currency, and this would put a premium on banditry. Then there are the geographical imperatives of a coastal area and of a land cut by many canals and waterways. From every account, it is apparent that the Lys and the Escaut especially constituted very good bandit country. And here banditry would have a past, the advantage of long experience and of the presence of populations of smugglers. As the Belgian church had been extremely rich, and as root-and-branch dechristianisation and icono-clasm had left the nine Departments undisturbed, the theft of church plate would be a profitable addition to the normal activities of *chauffeurs* and brigands. And as these were frontier areas, deserters would always be in ready supply as recruits, while the obtaining of papers—true or false—would be rendered easier than elsewhere. And, again, as we are dealing with a moving, itinerant, and cosmopolitan population, detection and identification would be that much more difficult than in areas further inland.

Of course, there is a great deal that we do not know. *Frontaliers* will naturally have foisted upon them certain forms of crime, as well as the habit of secrecy, made more secure, in these areas, by the impene-trability of local dialects. It is their compensation for the dangers in which geography has placed them, over the centuries. Habit can accustom people to almost anything, even to the semi-permanence of war and to the clattering passage of men-at-arms. One had to live with this sort of thing.

Yet, however impenetrable the area may have seemed to French observers, it was now on the very doorstep of Paris as a result both of recent conquest and ancient habits of movement and migration. It has been suggested, in a recent study of the future development of Paris over the rest of the present century, that the French capital would expand more and more in the direction of Brussels, the capital of a sort of Europe. But it has been our purpose, at least in the present chapter, to argue that, in terms both of people and of movement, after 1795, Paris was not only *Paris-près-Pontoise* it might also have been described as *Paris-lès-Lille* and *Paris-lès-Bruxelles*. A marriage, for better or for worse, but a marriage none the less.

Appendix

List of the Condemned in the Salambier Trial
of September 1798

'1. *François-Marie Salambier*, marié, 32 ans, natif d'Isbergues (arrondissement de Béthune) marchand colporteur demeurant à Aire, assez robuste de corps . . . à mort.'

'2. *Narcisse Duhamel*, 24 ans, menuisier, natif de Lille, y demeurant, à mort . . . .'

'3. *Jean Derenaud*, dit *Chopine*, environ 34 ans, natif de Vielville (?), marchand colporteur, demeurant lors de son arrestation à Lille, à mort.' He is described elsewhere, in notes drawn up by Baret, as 'tenant cabaret à Lille', hence his nickname.

'4. *Joseph Lamblin*, ou *Lammelin*, dit *Lemaire*, jeune homme, natif d'Auxerre, marchand forain, à mort.' But elsewhere it is stated that he was married and that he had adopted his wife's name of Lemaire.

'5. *Auguste-Joseph Gallois*, 30 ans, maréchal, natif de Fives, demeurant lors de son arrestation au faubourg Notre-Dame de Lille, à mort.'

'6. *François Ponto*, dit *Auguste Martel*, environ 29 ans, natif de Rouen, demeurant lors de son arrestation à Valenciennes, marchand, à mort. . . .' There is a further description of *Ponto* or *Martel* in the notes that Baret had sent to the Minister during the early stages of the investigation, in Nivôse year V [January 1797]: '*Auguste Martelle*, fils d'un négotiant de Rouen, ami intime de *Labbé*, [a été] arrêté il y a 15 mois porteur d'un sac rempli de rossignols, déjà condamné à mort par le tribunal de Rouen.'

'7. *Antoine Guillon*, dit *Dauphiné*, 50 ans, marié, natif du Péage de Roussillon, journalier, demeurant dernièrement à Dunkerque, assez robuste de corps, à mort. . . .'

'8. *Louis Dubreucq*, 23 ans, jeune homme, marchand fripier, natif d'Aire et demeurant dernièrement à Lannoy,' a village on the outskirts of Roubaix and on the border, 'à mort'.

'9. *Louis Bertoux*, 32 ans, marié, portefaix, ex-pensionné de la République, comme invalide, natif d'Aire, y demeurant, à mort. . . .'

'10. *François Moutier*, dit *Cadet*, environ 30 ans, marchand brocanteur et fripier de profession, natif de Livette [*sic*] dans la ci-devant Normandie, et lors de son arrestation, chez son père à Paris, corps robuste . . . à mort.'

'11. *Pierre-Jean Villedieu*, environ 26 ans, sous-lieutenant au 13me régiment de chasseurs à cheval, natif de Mortagne, aux Perches [*sic*] . . . maigre de corps . . . à mort.'

'12. *Théodore Leroy*, dit *Berger*, veuf, 44 ans, natif de Ferlinghem, marchand colporteur au moment de son arrestation, auparavant fabricant de gommelat pour raccommoder de la faïance, sans domicile fixe . . . ayant deux dents qui lui sortent du devant de sa bouche . . . à mort.'

'13. *Casimir Noë*, marié, 39 ans, marchand fripier, natif de Figeac, demeurant dernièrement à Valenciennes, à mort.'

'14. *Louis Joseph-Cambon*, 38 ans, natif de Lille, calendreur et marchand de lacets, demeurant à Lille, mince de corps, 24 ans de fers. . . .'

'15. *Esprit-Louis Meunier*, dit *Saint-Amand*, 65 ans, marié, natif de Visannes dans le ci-devant Comtat d'Avignon, et demeurant au moment de son arrestation à Wazemmes, faubourg de Béthune à Lille, assez robuste de corps, 24 ans de fers. . . .'

'16. *Jean-Baptiste Quesnoy*, dit *Blondin* ou *l'Horloger de Camphin*, environ 34 ans, horloger de profession, natif de Hesdel (Pas-de-Calais) et demeurant à Camphin, 24 ans de fers. . . .'

'17. *Daniel Sauvage*, dit *Aimable Pouillet*, environ 23 ans, jeune homme, natif de Bourthe en Boulonnais (Pas-de-Calais) au moment de son arrestation marchand de chevaux et sans domicile fixe . . . le corps robuste et les cheveux très fournis . . . à mort.' In a more detailed report that Baret had sent to the Minister in January 1797, we learn that he had been arrested by countrymen from the Lys 'comme vagabond insolent et porteur d'armes à feu'. He was also accused of having committed a theft from the church of Surezeele, near Ostend, and was said previously to have escaped from the prison of Saint-Omer.

'18. *Jean-Baptiste Legros*, 36 ans, marié, ci-devant capitaine des Belges, lors de son arrestation, cabaretier, natif de Vauréal (district de Pontoise, Seine-et-Oise) et demeurant à Wazemmes . . . à mort. . . .'

'19. *Pierre-François-Jean Berton*, marié, 31 ans, natif de Francpas (Haute-Marne), officier belge, demeurant faubourg de Béthune à Lille . . . à mort.'

'20. *Joseph Wilminot*, dit *Jean-François Romary*, 31 ans, marié, fabricant de pommades d'odeur et de crayons, natif d'Etignies (Vosges), sans domicile fixe, mince de corps, à mort.'

'21. *Jean-Baptiste Dufour*, environ 31 ans, poissonnier, natif de Gonnehem et demeurant à Busne, canton de Saint-Venant, Pas-de-Calais . . . à mort. . . .'

'22. *Jean-Charles Genyn*, dit *Bruxeller*, dit *Charles Lefranc*, 25 ans et $\frac{1}{2}$, marié, marchand colporteur, natif de Gand, sans domicile fixe . . . ayant le bras droit coupé . . . à mort.'

23. *Bonaventure Berry*, dit *Heller*, environ 24 ans, jeune homme, brocanteur, natif de Saint-Aubin-Châteauneuf (Yonne), sans domicile fixe, sortant de la 11me compagnie des Fédérés de Paris, à mort.' In an earlier report, Baret

describes him thus: '*Joseph Heller*, se dit natif de Bourgogne, autrement
nommé *Bonaventure Berry*, a été arrêté avec Salambier. . . . c'est une espèce
de comédien de campagne. . . . Salambier voudrait le sauver tandis qu ['il]
charge Salambier pour assassinat commis près de Bruxelles. . . .'[1]

'24. *Albert-Guillaume-Joseph Labre*, dit *Labbé*, 35 ans, marié, marchand, sortant du 5me bataillon des tirailleurs belges, natif de Lille, demeurant à Ostende
. . . .' He is described in another report as '*Albert-Guillaume Labbé*, fils d'un
boucher de Lille, ci-devant capitaine des chasseurs belges, aide-de-camp du
général Compère et en dernier lieu négotiant à Ostende.' It was in his house
there that Salambier had taken refuge, after the Laeken affair. *Labbé* is also
said to have taken part in the theft of a sum of 24,000 piastres stolen from a
merchant in Ghent. Baret was to write on this subject: '. . . Il [Salambier]
m'avait parlé d'une théière d'étain volée par Labbé et lui dans l'église d'Ostende, ils l'avaient prise pour de l'argent et s'apercevant de leur erreur,
Labbé l'avait jettée dans la citerne. . . .' Labbé must have been a beginner; an
experienced robber of churches would have known the difference between
tin and silver.[2]

'25. *Louis Masquelier*, environ 64 ans, marié, voiturier et laboureur, natif
d'Orcq près Tournai (Jemappes) . . . à mort. . . .'

---

[1] A.N. BB 18 582 (Baret au Ministre, 13 nivôse an V).
[2] A.N. BB 18 582 (Baret au Ministre, 26 nivôse an V).

Conclusion

'. . . Au cours de la matinée, il se produisait comme une rotation dans cet immense afflux de la périphérie vers le centre. Dès huit heures du matin, le gros de la multitude venait non plus de l'est, mais du nord-est de la ville, puis franchement du nord. Cependant que l'afflux du sud, faible aux premières heures, commençait à s'épaissir. Puis la rotation se poursuivait du nord vers le nord-ouest et vers l'ouest. L'origine des mouvements semblait se déplacer, comme un nimbus poussé par le vent, de Montmartre vers Batignolles, de Batignolles vers les Ternes. Il en allait de même symétriquement au sud, où l'afflux principal, venu d'abord de Javel et de Vaugirard, cherchait ensuite à descendre par la rue de Rennes et le boulevard Saint-Michel. . . .'

Jules Romains, *Le 6 octobre:*
'Par un joli matin Paris descend au travail.'

'. . . Prenons la rue Gambetta et marchons dans cette ville, et si vous pouvez être sûr d'une chose et c'est bien d'être à Nanterre, cet ancien village qui vit naître vers 420 ou 421 sainte Geneviève, patronne de Paris, et qui est devenue cette ville industrielle dépassant cinquante mille habitants.

Depuis 1818, à la Pentecôte, chaque année, on couronne une rosière. Prétexte, bien entendu, à de très nombreuses libations, dont la population m'a l'air assez friand.

Dans le vieux Nanterre, au bout de la rue Gambetta, il y a l'église Sainte-Geneviève. En avant de la façade, au coin de la rue Maurice-Thorez, dans un jardinet, et si vous avez un peu de temps à perdre, vous pourrez toujours voir le puits d'où sainte Geneviève tirait l'eau qui rendit la vue à sa vieille maman. Une petite chapelle marque l'emplacement de la maison de la sainte et si cette promenade en plein soleil vous a donné soif, ce n'est pas les cafés qui manquent. . . .'

Claude Néron, *Max et les ferrailleurs.*

So much for continuity. But most of what I have tried to say can only be of purely historical and retrospective interest. It is not, indeed, the vision of a sylvan, riverside paradise lost, although the *partie de campagne* still had something to offer the Parisian in the nineteenth century—the Impressionists could not have done without Bougival, Chatou, Vaucresson, and Le Pecq—although the valley of the Marne could still attract the modest heroes of Simenon's novels about week-enders, although Albertine Sarrazin, having escaped from prison, and having broken her leg in the course of the operation, was able to hide out for some weeks, while her leg set, in a discreet, shuttered *bicoque* on the borders of the Brie, although, finally, Ben Barka, was disposed of, by the late Minister of the Interior of the kingdom of Morocco, in a villa in the valley of the Bièvre. Let us not be deceived by these modest achievements, by those of Landru, in his villa in Gambais (provided with a widow-driven heating system) and of Weidmann, in his rented *faux-manoir normand* in La Celle-Saint-Cloud. These are flashes in the pan, a last assertion of an anarchical identity so long the mark of the *communes* of the *pourtoir de Paris*. The Simenon fan will find little to please him now in the valley of the Marne, and in Arceuil, Alfortville, Maisons-Alfort, Antony, Robinson, Villeneuve-Saint-Georges, and Saclay, his horizon will be confined to the Buffet-like tower blocks of totally insensitive architects, the inhuman, centreless, cultureless abodes of *Le Déménagement*, the social wilderness of La Courneuve where teenagers murder publicans, in order to combat boredom, the total void of Nanterre with its half a million unhappy inhabitants, and only a very distant reminder, in the *fête de la rosière*, that this too was once, a very long time ago, a village of the Île de France. No, it is not the sort of nostalgic tourism I recommend, no place here for the *promeneur solitaire* of the next decade, no place even for the *promeneur tout court*, for where is there to walk in this concrete jungle, mined, not by quarries, but by underground *parkings* for the cars of the hurried, unseeing, brutalised commuters, *parkings* housing an army of the night far more sinister than the denizens of the old quarries or the mythical soldiers in white uniforms? Where is there to walk in Ris-Orangis, in Rungis, in Chilly-Mazarin (*sa Résidence, son tennis, son équitation, sa piscine, son parc, ses crêches, son standing*), in Savigny, in Châtenay, in the old bandit country of the late eighteenth century, at the edge of the *auto-route* and under the direct path of the take-off and the landing of the jets, Orly-based? Where is there to walk in the Pays de France, in the once wide cornfields of the District de Gonesse, in the lost village of Roissy-en-France, the terrain of bulldozers and soon to be operating as Paris' third airport?[1] Where now is the romance of Paris-près-Pontoise, when it is *Pontoise* that is getting nearer and nearer to Paris, and not the other way round, soon to be connected directly to Paris by the *métro-express*, as *le Grand-Paris* heads westwards, towards the petrol refineries of Port-Jérôme and the new industries of the Seine estuary—Paris has never been more closely tied, than now, to its foreport, le Havre—and northwards, no longer by the old *route du Nord* of the *chaîne* and of the *Semaine Sainte*, but by a brand new motor-road that avoids the old road of bandits, brigands, bigamists, young officers, and resourceful Belgians and Lillois, towards Brussels, the capital of a sort of Europe. I would not like to predict where it will stop, but it is already in the process of engulfing most of the rural *communes* that have been the subject of this study. There is no victor in this: neither Paris, nor the lost villages of its *ceinture*, nor indeed the now extinct Seine-et-Oise. Only a uniform drabness, a common, all-enveloping ugliness.

[1] It has been operating since 1973.

Notes

Chapter 1

(A) Successive French régimes were to use the threat of expulsion from Paris or actual expulsion as the supreme deterrent, especially in cases in which no strictly legal condemnation could be applied to the victim. The Empire especially favoured this form of punishment, notably in defence of moral orthodoxy. There is a police report dated 17 March 1809, submitted to the Minister: 'Le nommé Léonard Cabris, coutelier à Angoulême, a quitté cette ville après y avoir abandonné. . . ses enfans dans un état voisin de l'indigence, pour venir à Paris où il a toujours mené une conduite déréglée. La Demoiselle Cabris (Marie Madeleine Julie) l'un de ses filles, âgée de 18 ans, vint également à Paris chercher un azile chez une parente, la dame Gayet, cordonnière, rue Bondy. L'inconduite & l'immoralité poussèrent bientôt le Sr Cabris à fonder des ressources criminelles sur le parti qu'il pourrait tirer de la jeunesse de sa fille et, en abusant de l'autorité paternelle, la força de venir demeurer avec lui dans une maison peu convenable à des personnes de bonnes moeurs. . . . La Dlle Cabris se mit sous la protection des autorités. . . . Mais la raison de cet enfant ne put résister à de pareilles secousses, elle fut bientôt reconnue en démence. . . .' At the time of writing she had been cured and was about to leave Charenton. The police, therefore, advised the *Ministre de la Police générale* that her father be given a passport and ordered to return to Angoulême, where he would have to live under the surveillance of the local *gendarmerie* (A.N. F7 7010).

During the crisis of the years III and IV, there was a concentrated effort on the part of the authorities to expel from Paris those who could not prove more than a year's residence in the city. That these measures of expulsion were directed primarily against those living in lodging-houses is clear from a report concerning the 12ᵉ *arrondissement* and dated 19 Ventôse year IV [9 March 1796]: '. . . Elle va frapper une class très utile d'ouvriers qui habitent en grand nombre sur notre arrondissement' (A.N. F11 1178). But it is unlikely that the order was carried out systematically, for another report, dated 3 Germinal year IV [23 March 1796] states: '. . . Le nombre de cartes retirées aux personnes non-domiciliées depuis un an ne monte encore qu'à 2,403, donnant 12,323 bouches pour dernier résultat . . .' (A.N. F11 1183). See, on this whole question of expulsion from Paris, my *The Police and the People: French Popular Protest*, 1789–1820, Oxford, 1970.

Such measures were far more likely to be directed against women than against men and they reflect, like so much of the legislation of the revolutionary period, the prevailing climate of anti-feminism. A circular put out by the Minister of the Interior, dated 8 Germinal year IV [28 March 1796] pointed out: '. . . Relativement aux femmes des militaires invalides leur domicile de droit est toujours le domicile de leurs maris; ainsi, à quelqu'époque qu'elles soient venues à Paris, elles suivent la condition de leurs époux et n'ont point d'autre domicile que leurs époux . . .' (A.N. F11 1183). In other words, if they were divorced or were abandoned by their husbands, they would lose the right to stay in Paris.

(B) A.N. BB 18 832 (juge de paix du canton de Luzarches au Ministre, 1er floréal an V): '. . . Une fille d'ici vient d'avoir la certitude que l'homme auquel elle s'est unie par le mariage et qui s'était toujours dit garçon, était marié, qu'il a femme et enfant. Cet homme n'avait tout au plus que 2 mois de domicile dans la même commune que la fille. . . .' Luzarches seems also to have been placed on that other highroad, that of madness. We hear of a *dame* Boucher, the wife of a professor at the *Conservatoire*, who, during her frequent outbreaks of alcoholism, was liable to run away. A police report dated 17 March 1809, states: '. . . Elle a repris sa vie vagabonde, et la gendarmerie impériale vient de l'arrêter depuis peu dans les environs de Luzarches . . .' (A.N. F7 7010).

On the subject of bigamy, see also my *Reactions to the French Revolution*, London, 1972, pp. 266–7.

It was not merely the increased mobility caused by war that provided the military bigamist with so many opportunities to reach the figure proposed by Somerset Maugham, in his story, *The Round Dozen*. Even in a Department *de grande circulation* like the Somme, the registers of births, deaths, and marriages were frequently falsified, especially in rural areas. On 25 Prairial year VII [15 June 1799] the *accusateur public* of the Amiens court was to write to the Minister: 'Je crois devoir vous prévenir que le plus grand désordre règne dans la tenue des registres aux actes civils et singulièrement dans ceux concernant les mariages. J'ai entr'autres, l'exemple que dans une seule commune 12 actes de mariage presqu'à la suite l'un de l'autre ont été antidatés de deux ans. Encore plusieurs de ces mariages sont-ils feints & supposés et d'hommes de 20 à 21 ans ou environ avec des femmes plus que septuagénaires. . . . On enlève et on remet à volonté des feuillets dans les registres, on surcharge le chiffre des pages, on contrefait des signatures et souvent on écarte des actes valables et en bonne forme sur lesquels reposent la tranquillité des familles et l'ordre des successions pour en introduire d'autres étrangers aux premiers et qui ne seront par la suite que des sources de confusion . . .' (A.N. BB 18 848, Somme). Such things were to be expected in somewhere right off the beaten track like the Ardèche (see *Reactions to the French Revolution*, pp. 75, 261); but they are far more dangerous when committed in an area like the Somme.

(C) A.N. BB 18 846 (Ministère de la Justice, Somme) (commissaire près le tribunal des Deux-Nèthes [Anvers], au Ministre, 27 fructidor an IV): 'Lorsque j'ai reçu votre lettre du 19 . . . sur l'évasion des nommés Vanhemelen et Melchior Geens, il y avait 2 jours que le premier était repris . . . un cri général s'élève contre ces évasions multipliées, qui font ressembler le départ des condamnés pour le lieu de leur peine à des mises-en-liberté. . . . il serait à désirer qu'il y eût pour ce pays une chaîne plus rapprochée que le dépôt de Bicêtre. . . .' Three Belgian convicts, Melchior Geens, 25½, of Lierre, Jean-Baptiste Vanhemelen, aged 29, also from Lierre, *batelier de profession*, and a certain Mast, from Ghent, had escaped from the *chaîne* just outside Péronne, in Thermidor year IV [August 1796], owing, it seems, to the carelessness of the *gendarmes* escorting them. They took cover in thick woodland just off the road. Vanhemelen, nicknamed *le pontassier*, had been the leader of a gang of robbers who had attacked farms in the Malines area in the course of the bitter winter of 1795.

(D) There were, too, very good legal reasons why the horse market, in the Faubourg Saint-Marceau, as well as those in other cities, should have been such a natural magnet to crime, if only because it was extremely easy to dispose of a stolen horse at a fair or market. There are some revealing remarks on the subject in a letter addressed by Fouché who clearly attached a great deal of importance to the matter, to the *Grand Juge*, on 23 November 1810 (A.N. BB 18 578, Nièvre): '. . . les vols de chevaux, et même de boeufs de labour se multiplient notamment dans le département de la Nièvre. L'effronterie de cette classe de voleurs est telle que l'un d'eux, traduit dernièrement à la cour de justice criminelle de la Nièvre, répondit au Président qui lui disait qu'il était accusé d'avoir volé un cheval: *vous vous trompez, car j'en ai volé deux*. Le nouveau code pénal détermine des peines plus fortes que le précédent contre ce genre de délit. Mais on demande s'il abroge les anciennes loix qui légitiment l'achat fait en foire d'un cheval volé. On represente que, dans le cas contraire, la difficulté d'atteindre le coupable sera la même qu'auparavant. Celui qui aura volé un cheval, le conduira à une foire convenue, il y trouvera ses complices qui achèteront le cheval et iront le revendre ailleurs.' The *Grand Juge* commented: '. . . On ne saurait exiger que les individus qui s'y rencontrent se connaissent ou que ceux qui achètent prennent des informations sur ceux qui vendent. Ce serait apporter aux affaires des entraves que des marchés multipliés et consommés rapidement, souvent loin du domicile de ceux qui y prennent part, ne comportent pas. Il est donc impossible d'assujetir ici les acheteurs aux règlements de police du commerce ordinaire. Il s'ensuît que des achats exempts de toute formalité sont reputés par là même de bonne foi, ils ne peuvent en conséquence entraîner ordinairement de responsabilité pénale, ni exposer aux effets de la revendication. Mais nul doute d'ailleurs que l'individu convaincu de connivance avec les auteurs d'un vol auxquels il aurait paru acheter en foire les objets volés ne fut dans le cas d' être poursuivi criminellement . . . ': hardly a helpful suggestion! On the subject of the circulation of horses within Paris, see below, chapter 3.

The habitual military areas of north-eastern France naturally offered conditions that were particularly favourable, especially in time of war, to the activities of horse thieves and *maquignons*. There is an informative letter on the subject from the *commissaire* attached to the Laon court, to the Minister, and dated 12 Nivôse year V [Sunday 1 January 1797]: 'Un délit qui se répète journellement et surtout dans le département de l'Aisne est le vol de chevaux. Des individus se disant marchands de chevaux paraissent être les auteurs du vol, ils ont des affidés dans beaucoup de communes et dans plusieurs Départements, à leur aide ils se procurent les plus beaux chevaux, sans bourse délier, ceux volés circulent, aussitôt le vol, de manière qu'en 24 heures ils ont eu quelquefois 10 maîtres, et que la trace en est perdue, les foires ne sont plus même à l'abri des coups de main, les vols y sont fréquens. . . . il est commun maintenant, lorsqu'on leur demande quelle est la profession qu'ils exercent, de les entendre répondre: *voleur* . . . ' (A.N. BB 18 92, Aisne, commissaire près le tribunal de Laon, au Ministre, 12 nivôse an V).

(E) Fontainebleau was singled out by successive Parisian authorities both as a centre of Counter-Revolution and of royalists during the Terror and of neo-terrorists and *babouvistes* under the Directory. One way or another, it would seem that the place could never acquire any merit in Parisian eyes. A report of 6 Messidor year IV states: '. . . le nombre de ces anarchistes [refugees from Paris] s'est accru sous nos yeux par une conséquence nécessaire de la loi du 21 floréal [an IV] qui a éloigné de Paris les partisans de l'anarchie . . . ' (A.N. F1b II Seine-et-Marne). The town furthermore was reregarded as a centre of crime by the suspicious and vigilant police and judicial authorities of the capital. In the year VII, we hear of a young man, Prévost, whose father ran a gaming house in the Palais-Royal and who, having killed a player, a Belgian soldier, in the course of a dispute over gambling debts, fled to Fontainebleau, hiding out at his grandmother's place, to the full knowledge of the local *juge de paix* (A.N. BB 18 762). Hubert, a member of a gang of professional burglars, accused of a robbery in the rue des Deux Écus, in Paris, has the evocative nickname of *Fontainebleau*. One could ask for no better consecration of a criminal vocation (A.N. BB 18 B744, 20 pluviôse an IV). See also my *Police and the People*, p. 163 (3), on the subject of the neo-terrorists grouped there around the Loys couple, in the year IV, and p. 236 (3) on that of Paris prostitutes who had come from that *commune*.

(F) '. . . Trois des boulangers de cette ville [Rouen] m'ont assuré que des farines achetées par eux sur la halle de Paris ne pouvaient leur parvenir, parce que l'ordre de les empêcher de sortir avait été donné par M. le Préfet de Police. Cet ordre, comme je viens de l'apprendre, à l'instant, s'est étendu au-delà des murs de la capitale et il a été également signifié aux marchands de grains de Saint-Denis . . .' (Girardin, Préfet de la Seine-Inférieure, au Ministre de l'Intérieur, 22 avril 1812). Girardin, in a second letter, dated 31 July 1812, places the blame for the crisis on the exigencies of the Paris authorities: '. . . Que l'on ne cherche pas ailleurs la véritable cause de la disette . . . elle a été celle de beaucoup d'autres disettes et . . . elle en produirait encore par la suite, si la leçon que l'on vient de recevoir ne suffisait pas pour persuader qu'il faut que Paris paye toujours le pain sa véritable valeur et qu'il doit renoncer désormais à un privilège dont les conséquences sont aussi fâcheuses pour le reste de l'Empire. . . . Les décrets des 4 et 8 mai ayant été fait uniquement pour lui [Paris] j'ignore s'il en a recueilli de grands avantages; mais ce que je sais, c'est qu'ils ont produit beaucoup de mal dans ce Département . . .' (A.N. F11 718, crise de 1812, Seine-Inférieure). 'La mère voyageait pour trouver du pain, elle vendait jusqu'à son dernier chiffon, les boulangers de la campagne ne pouvant lui en fournir, elle allait donc à la ville [Rouen] et, après bien des peines, si elle parvenait à obtenir un pain, elle le cachait de son mieux pour le porter à ses enfants. . . . Vaine espérance, arrivée à la barrière, elle était fouillée impitoyablement, on lui enlevait le pain qu'elle avait payé . . .' (Petition of an inhabitant of a rural *commune* in the Eure, dated 22 December 1812, A.N. F11 709).

'. . . Ce qui nous reste de la plupart de ces objets [candles, soap, material, coffee], concentrés le plus ordinairement dans les grandes communes, ne peut en sortir pour la consommation des habitants des campagnes, puisque ces habitans au sortir de ces villes, sont fouillés pour abandonner les objets qu'ils employent, comme ils l'étaient avant la Révolution sous le régime odieux des gabelles et des aides . . .' (the club of Bacqueville-en-Caux to the Convention, 16 Pluviôse year II [4 February 1794], A.N. F11 205).

See also A.P.P. A/A 187 (commissaire de police de la Section du Muséum, à la Commission, 5 fructidor an II): '. . . Marie-Denis Guenot, femme Duvent, marchande de savon depuis 8 jours, et avant ouvrière, demeurant rue de Viarmes en garnie . . . combien elle vend son savon? Répond qu'elle le vend 32 s., et qu'elle le paye 28 s. . . . elle l'achète à la Chapelle près Paris, chez une bourrelière, en face de la ci-devant église, et qu'à la Chapelle il y a dans ce moment 5 fabriques en train, qui en font beaucoup . . .'

This was a case of bringing an article into Paris. And see also Ibid. (15 fructidor an II): '. . . Marguerite Thièry, fille majeure, demeurant à Sucy-en-Brie . . . où elle alloit avec la viande qui est dans sa charette? Répond qu'elle allait la porter chez le C. Turbert, traiteur, rue du Harlay, au palais de justice. . . . lui avons demandé si elle a connoissance de l'arrêté du Comité de salut public qui défend aux traiteurs et aubergistes d'acheter ailleurs qu'aux bouchers à Paris . . . répond que non.'

(G) In a report on an epidemic in the village of Ury (Seine-et-Marne), dated 7 January 1815, a doctor suggests that one form of relief would be to distribute hemp to the women of the village and 'de les laisser filer chez elles. . . . je dis qu'il faudrait qu'elles travaillent chez elles, car il n'est pas sans danger pour les moeurs de réunir dans un lieu clos un grand nombre de personnes, bien qu'elles soient du même sexe . . .' (A.N. F8 79). Although reporting on an epidemic, the doctor does not seem to have been concerned so much with the danger of infection presented by a crowd of women gathered together in a closed place. He was not thinking in terms of public health; what he had in mind was public morality. Never, he seems to sugest, should one ever bring people together. They would be up to no good. This obsession with the dangers presented by any form of assembly was shared by most late eighteenth-century authorities. Fairs, they would argue, could only be a magnet to crime; any large gathering of people would be likely to lead to trouble. It therefore followed that opportunities for such gatherings should be reduced to a minimum and that when there was no way of avoiding them, they should be strictly controlled. A printed report published by the Rouen authorities, in the course of the famine of 1796, stresses these dangers: '. . . S'il y a 36 marchés dans le cours de l'année, ils y occasionnent réellement une perte de 36 jours. . . . D'ailleurs, on n'a pas assez remarqué combien la trop grande fréquentation des Marchés préjudicie à la pureté des moeurs: c'est là que l'homme des champs contracte le goût et la funeste habitude de l'ivresse et de la négligence, qui occasionnent souvent la perte de ses moissons et la ruine de sa famille . . .' (A.N. BB 18 297, 5 thermidor an IV). The connection between market days and rumours is well illustrated in an interesting report from Versailles, dated 11 Floréal year VII [30 April 1799] and addressed by the *accusateur public* to the Minister (A.N. BB 18 834): '. . . Le bruit s'est répandu dans la commune de Versailles, les 8 et 9 du courant, que l'on devait fusiller, près de la pièce d'eau dite des Suisses, 2 gendarmes, convaincus, à ce qu'on assurait, d'avoir assassiné 2 conscrits.

Ce bruit s'est tellement accrédité dans l'esprit du peuple qu'une grande foule s'est portée au lieu désigné . . . dans l'intention d'assister à cette espèce de spectacle. . . . le même bruit s'est soutenu le lendemain. . . . il est à remarquer qu'on parait avoir choisi, pour répandre et accréditer le bruit calomnieux dont j'ai parlé, l'un des jours ou le marché de Versailles attire dans cette ville un assez grand nombre d'habitants des campagnes. . . .'

What appeared to offer threats to public order would present the pickpocket with his opportunity. '. . . Le nommé Joseph Compère, juif, natif de Paris, âgé d'environ 30 ans . . . se disant commis marchand . . . n'exerce véritablement d'autre profession que celle de filou, et n'a d'autre asile que celui que lui donnent des femmes publiques qu'il met souvent à contribution. C'est un filou extrêmement adroit qui a été déjà arrêté nombre de fois pour vol dans les foules pour y voler des montres surtout aux portes des spectacles, dans les églises et aux revues de S.M. l'Empereur . . .' (A.N. F7 7010, rapport du 9 thermidor an XII). In other words, public worship and military display, in the service of crime—a pleasing combination.

(H) The Prefect of the Calvados reports, on 21 April 1812: '. . . On fait circuler sur les bords de la mer les bruits les plus absurdes & les plus fâcheux. Des étrangers bien vêtus ont été remarqués parcourant la côte et se plaisant à donner les nouvelles les plus alarmantes . . .' (A.N. F11 707).

Similar rumours are reported, from the Atlantic coast, by the Prefect of the Deux-Sèvres, on 25 July of the same year: '. . . il n'est qu'un cri dans ce dé-partement contre les négotians de Marans et de la Rochelle. La clameur pub-lique les accuse sans ménagement d'avoir vendu nos grains aux Anglais. Il est de fait que d'immenses quantités de grains sont passées depuis un an dans le département de la Charente-inférieure. On se demande ce qu'ils sont devenus. . . .' (A.N. F11 718).

The Mediterranean region was not immune. A report from the Drôme, dated 3 September, states: '. . . une compagnie composée de 7 à 8 individus parcourt depuis une quinzaine . . . toutes les campagnes de la Valloire et s'achète à tout prix tous les bleds . . . et les embarque sur le Rhône. . . . On craint que cette compagnie . . . ne fasse cette spéculation qu'avec des inten-tions perfides, qu'ils ne les conduisent sur quelques ports de la Méditerranée pour les y embarquer afin d'y être pris par les bâtiments anglais qui circulent le long de nos côtes, et avec lesquels ils sont peut-être d'accord de leur vendre sans doute à des prix beaucoup plus hauts qu'en France; car s'il est vrai que le Midi ne manque pas de bled . . . comment ils y vendent celui qu'ils y con-duisent . . .?' (A.N. F11 709).

Rumours of this kind during the 1812 crisis may have found readier cre-dence on the Channel coast, and especially on both sides of the Seine estuary, than elsewhere owing to the fact that all the coastal region had been particu-larly affected by the harvest failure. 'Cet accident fâcheux,' writes the Prefect of the Eure on 22 December, 'a été commun à presque toute la ci-devant Normandie et surtout a frappé davantage les bords de la mer, le Pays de Caux, qui avoisine l'embouchure de la Seine, et l'entrée de la Manche a beaucoup souffert, dans un rayon d'environ 2 lieues de largeur . . .' (A.N. F11 709).

(I) On 4 August 1812, the Sous-Préfet of Pithiviers was to report to the Minister of the Interior, on the subject of the conduct of the *maire* of Andon-ville: '. . . J'ai requis Mr l'Officier de Gendarmerie . . . d'y envoyer des gen-darmes pour y rester en garnison aux frais des récalcitrants jusqu'à ce que mes réquisitions fussent entièrement remplies. Un Gendarme s'étant présenté à Andonville, chez le Sr Marchon, maire de cette commune, ce fonctionnaire n'a point voulu le recevoir, il a refusé de le placer chez les habitants et de faire connaître les particuliers qui n'avaient point fourni le bled demandé. . . . Il s'est contenté . . . d'écrire . . . qu'il n'y avait plus de bled dans sa commune . . . que pour lui il ne devait agir que d'après les déclarations qui lui avaient été faites par les habitants, et il a renvoyé le gendarme. . . .' Such impudent defiance of higher authority on the part of a rural *maire* is all the more surprising in this context because Andonville, far from being isolated, was situated on the busy road from Pithiviers to Angerville, one of the main links between the Gâtinais and the Beauce (A.N. F11 712, crise de 1812, Loiret).

Much the same point is made, at an earlier date—at the height of the Terror of the year II—by the Committee of Nanterre, in a letter to the Committee of General Security dated 22 Nivôse; and Nanterre, it should be emphasised, was within easy walking distance of Paris: '. . . La loi reste sans force dans un pays où la force armée est dans les mains des gens qui ne se soumettent point à la loi et qui se tiennent tellement tous qu'il est impossible d'acquérir aucune preuve de leurs prévarications . . .' (A.N. F7 4783). This would apply to the *garde nationale* of absolutely *any* rural *commune* on the perimeter of Paris.

(J) In the Seine-et-Oise, *sociétés populaires* are stated to have been in existence, at the beginning of the year III, in:

canton Versailles: Versailles, Le Chesnay, Rocquencourt, Guyancourt, Bois-d'Arcy, Buc, Saint-Cyr.

canton de Jouy: Jouy, Verrières, Bièvres, Igny.

canton de Longjumeau: Longjumeau, Champlan, Wissous, Chilly, Massy, Saulx (A.D. Seine-et-Oise L 11m Versailles 54).

District de Gonesse: Gonesse, Montmorency, Écouen, Luzarches, Achères, Livry, Louvres, Viarmes. The *société* of Gonesse was affiliated to the Cordeliers Club (ibid. L 11m Gonesse 23).

District de Dourdan: Ablis, Auffargis, Authon, Bonnelles, Bullion, Clairefontaine, Dourdan, La Celle, Les Essarts, Rambouillet, Rochefort, Saint-Germain, Saint-Chéron, Cernay.

District d'Étampes: Boissy, Lardy, Chamarande, La-Ferté-Alais, Milly, Étampes (ibid. L 11m Étampes 48).

District de Montfort: Neauphle-le-Château, Houdan, Septeuil, Garancières, Montfort (ibid. L 11m Montfort 31).

District de Pontoise: Pontoise, Chars, Franconville, Beaumont, Ile-Adam, Taverny (ibid. L 11m Pontoise 133).

District de Versailles: Limours, Brüs, la Celle-Saint-Cloud, Chévreuse, Massy, Meudon, Palaiseau, Saint-Cloud, Vaucresson (ibid. L 11m Versailles 70). There was also a very active club in Sèvres. I do not possess the list of clubs for the Districts of Mantes and Corbeil, but, clearly, in this Department, they were thin on the ground and were confined mainly to *lieux de passage*. The rural clubs in any case only enjoyed an ephemeral existence of a few weeks or two months at the most. Most had disappeared at the time of the harvest of 1794, in Messidor year II.

The figures for the Seine-et-Marne are even less impressive; the ten places in the District de Melun with clubs were: Melun, Brie-Comte-Robert,

Boisserie-le-Bertrand, Chaumes, Avon, Samois, Thomery, Mornant, Perthes, Tournan (A.D. Seine-et-Marne L 566). We know also there were clubs in Nemours, Moret, Montereau, Rozoy, Coulommiers, Fontainebleau, Mauperthuis, La Ferté-Gaucher, Signy, Guignes, Saint-Méry, Ozoir-la-Ferrière, Provins, Meaux, Saacy, Lagny.

In the Département de Paris, there were clubs in Franciade (Saint-Denis), Belleville, Nanterre, Passy, Bagnolet, Neuilly, Gennevilliers, Mont-Marat (Montmartre), and Courbevoie, all in the District de Franciade; in that of Bourg-l'Égalité, there were clubs in the *chef-lieu*, as well as in Vitry, Villejuif, Montreuil, Vaugirard, Sceaux, Charenton, Champigny, Gentilly, and Thiais. There was presumably a club at one time in Vincennes, though it does not appear on the list drawn up in Vendémiaire year III (A.N. F1a 548).

(K) A.N. BB 18 832 (Justice, Seine-et-Oise, juge de paix au Ministre, 26 ventôse an V). A hussar had been killed in a rural *cabaret* on Saturday 21 January 1796—that is, as in the incident related in n. L below, on the anniversary of the death of Louis XVI—and anniversaries of celebrated deaths are constant invitations to more obscure deaths; he had wanted to take part in a *noce*—a wedding or a christening—but the participants had told him to go away. Beside himself with rage, he had come back armed, threatening the villagers with his pistol and his sabre. He was then set upon and stoned to death by about a dozen countrymen. Apart from illustrating the importance of historical anniversaries in the politics of vengeance, the murder of the hussar also brings out the reinforcement of rural solidarity on the occasion of a wedding or of some other family event, in the face of urban interference, more especially when the stranger was a soldier.

There was, of course, another side to this conventional view of rural or provincial 'tribalism'. Soldiers, too, could often be at fault. We hear, for instance, of another hussar who killed a livestock merchant in a *cabaret* at Cléry, near Marines, in the same Department (A.N. BB 18 830, juge de paix de Marines, au Ministre, s.d. brumaire an IV). Another case of military brutality concerns events at the time of Carnaval, in the Belgian town of Soignies, near Brussels, in February 1807. The *directeur du jury* of the Mons court wrote to the *Grand Juge* on 7 April: 'Un viol s'étant commis en la ville de Soignies, j'ai fait contre les prévenus . . . les poursuites . . . mais ayant appris que les prévenus avaient pris la fuite, et la rumeur publique m'ayant instruit qu'ils s'étaient enrôlés dans le régiment des Chevaux-légers belges qui se formait à Liége, je me suis adressé à mon collègue servant en cette ville. . . .' In an earlier letter, dated 11 March, he gave the following details: 'Il s'est commis un viol la nuit du 8 au 9 février dernier en la ville de Soignies sur une jeune fille honnête qui se trouvait dans une auberge où on donnait bal à cause de carnaval et qui est devenue la victime de la brutalité de plusieurs libertins. Il importe à la société que les coupables soient punis; un exemple devient d'autant plus nécessaire que déjà une jeune fille a été horriblement maltraitée en la même ville. . . .' Many military vocations in the eighteenth century no doubt had similar origins (A.N. BB 18 402, Justice, Jemappes).

There is a further example of the gratuitous violence of the military from the same Department. On 8 Messidor year XII [27 June 1804] the Prefect of Jemappes writes to the *Grand Juge*: '. . . Un assassinat a été commis dans la commune de Harchies, arrondissement de Tournai, pendant la journée du 28 prairial dernier [Sunday 17 June 1804]: un nommé Tocquet, conduisant une voiture de trèfle pour les chevaux du 2me régiment de chasseurs dans diverses écuries de cette commune, arrivé au point du déchargement de la quantité requise de rations et après l'avoir effectué, le nommé Siegentèle, chasseur, lui demanda une ration de plus et voulut la prendre de vive force sur la voiture, Tocquet s'y étant opposé et ayant absolument refusé de la lui donner, ce militaire alla chercher un bâton de fagot: revenant et s'avançant ensuite sur le conducteur, qui pendant ce tems avait fait partir ses chevaux, il lui jetta le bâton qui l'atteignit à la tête et le renversa aussitôt; Tocquet mourut un instant après. Le commandant du corps a fait arrêter sur le champ Siegentèle . . .' (ibid. BB 18 402).

(L) A.N. BB 18 834 (Andrieu, de Mantes, au Ministre de la Justice, 9 pluviôse an VII [Monday 28 January 1799]). The events described occurred in the village of Fontenay-le-Saint-Père, in the Vexin français, over the river from Mantes. Andrieu, and some friends, arrived at the local inn. The *juge de paix* and other inhabitants had been drinking since midday, celebrating the anniversary of the execution of Louis XVI, on the previous Monday. The *juge de paix* was also the owner of the inn and wine-shop. On his arrival in the room on the ground floor, says Andrieu, 'de jeunes citoyens et citoyennes m'engagèrent à danser avec eux; mais leur ayant observé que, censé étranger [and, in this rural world, he would not only be a stranger, but almost a foreigner, as he came from the town, Mantes] je ne le pouvais . . . Jean-François Thomas, agent de la commune de Jambville . . . m'invita à accepter un verre de vin (*dans son verre, c'est l'usage de la campagne*), je le remerciai en lui observant que j'étais avec un de mes amis dans l'appartement au-dessous. . . . il réitéra son invitation, alors j'acceptai et bus son verre. . . .' What followed has all the lack of logic of a drunken brawl between countrymen and townsmen. Some of the villagers accused Andrieu of being a spy, set upon him and finally took him in charge, shutting him up in the *corps de garde*. The incident might well illustrate the theme of dangerous invitations.

(M) A.D. Oise Grand Registre du comité de surveillance de Précy-sur-Oise [non-inventorié] (séance du 9 pluviôse an II): '. . . la citoyenne Cothereau . . . nous a déclaré qu'en arrivant de Senlis, sa domestique lui a déclaré que le 6 de ce mois [25 January 1794] sur les 11 heures et ½ du soir, étant seule dans la maison avec la fille de la veuve Pilorget, cette jeune personne demanda à aller faire un besoin, la bonne lui dit d'aller dans le jardin, cette jeune fille

revint toute effrayée et dit à la bonne après avoir eu la présence d'esprit de
mettre les verroux à la porte, qu'elle avait vu dans le jardin un grand homme
habillé de bleu et en bonnet de laine, que sûrement c'était un revenant, la
bonne la rassura, mais quelques instants après elle entendit du bruit à la
porte et après s'être assurée qu'on avait l'intention de l'ouvrir, elle fit beaucoup de bruit et appella le C. Cothereau, son maître, pour faire croire qu'il
était à la maison et entendit quelqu'un se sauver en courant. . . .' The ghost
was probably a live soldier. On the subject of feminine fright, see also BB 18
299 (Justice, Eure, assesseur du juge de paix du canton de Pont-Audemer, au
Ministre, 29 floréal an VII): '. . . Jean-Jacques Guenet, ex-noble et frère
d'émigré . . . a promené lui-même dans la commune [de la Haye-Malesherbes]
un mannequin, tantôt sur son cheval, tantôt sur une bourrique . . . et la face
tournée vers la queue, ce mannequin était couvert de sang, masqué et tellement effroyable que plusieurs citoyennes enceintes en eurent tellement frayeur que quelques-unes en gardèrent le lit pendant plusieurs jours, ce mannequin était rempli d'écriteaux sur lesquels on lisait: *Plumet, buveur de sang,
Jacobin, terroriste, Septembriseur*, &ca. . . . Le C. Guenet s'est permis de sonner du cor à heure indue, s'arrêtant aux carrefours . . . il se faisait éclairer par
un de ses gens qui portait devant lui une torche allumée . . . il passait par des
rues fort étroites dans une campagne où toutes les maisons sont couvertes
en chaume. . . .'

(N) A.N. W1a 94 (tribunaux révolutionnaires, Descombes, Antoine Descombes à l'administration des subsistances de Paris, 16 août 1793): '. . . Un
Municipal [de Provins] disoit hautement ce matin devant plus de 30 femmes,
que le bled regorgeoit à Paris, et cela pendant que mon collègue demandoit
quelques gendarmes pour une opération. . . .' Descombes wrote again to the
same body, on 12 September 1793: '. . . La calomnie crie partout, dans cette
ville et dans les campagnes, que j'envoie la farine à l'ennemi; ce ne sont pas
mes propres dangers que j'envisage, mais les intérêts seuls des habitans de
Paris. . . .'

See also A.N. BB 18 822 (s.d. prairial an IV) on the subject of a complicated affair concerning a false *acquît à caution* for the delivery of a consign-
ment of wine at Champigny-sur-Seine to be addressed to Morel, a wine-
merchant established at 1746, rue Caumartin. Morel, who claimed to be
illiterate, had brought to Bray-sur-Seine a quantity of lace, travelling with
another wine-merchant from rue Neuve-des-Petits-Champs, whom he
claimed not to know, though in fact they were neighbours. So Morel appears
to be rather a suspect witness. But he sought to discredit the Fontainebleau
court, who had given the case against him, in the eyes of the Minister of
Justice, by claiming that his judges had not been unbiased: 'l'imputation
faite aux juges d'avoir été influencés par leur prévention contre tout acheteur
pour Paris. . . .' Morel at least knew the sort of reputation enjoyed by all the
inhabitants of the Brie amongst resident Parisians.

(O) A.N. BB 18 745 (Ministère de la Justice, Seine, Marie-Claude Bourdon, 48 ans, native de Coucy-le-Château, demeurante à Paris depuis environ 6 ans, rue Vieille du Temple, près l'égout No 158, division de l'Homme-Armé, sans état, au Ministre): '. . . Vous expose que le 20 juillet 1795 (v.s.), Pierre Levasseur, son mari, auroit été . . . vers les 7 heures du matin, accompagné d'une de ses filles malade depuis longtems, se promener sur le canton de Belleville, afin d'y prendre un peu d'air frais, pour aider au rétablissement de sa santé, et se promenant le long des jardins, sa fille auroit eu la foiblesse de s'asseoir au pied d'un groseillier, nommé cassis, et en mangea, et une branche se fut trouvée cassée, et elle la prit pour la rapporter à une de ses soeurs, âgée de 9 mois, qui étoit aussi malade depuis sa naissance, alors le père et la fille, après avoir mangé ce que leurs idées les avoient forcés de faire, rentrèrent sur le chemin de Belleville pour revenir chez eux, avec cette branche de groseille cassis, 5 gardes-champêtres, les voyant avec cette branche, l'un d'eux, nommé Robinat, cria *arrête, arrête*, et ayant son fusil, coucha la fille en joue, le père, voyant cet homme dans une furie horrible, dit *ne tirez pas sur ma fille, je payerai le dommage que ma fille a causé*, ce Robinat répondit *ce n'est pas après la fille que je veux tirer, c'est toi qu'il faut que je tue*, Levasseur lui répondit que l'on ne tuoit pas comme ça un homme pour un objet semblable et l'en défiait, Robinat ne perdit pas de tems, lâcha son coup de fusil à Levasseur qui le reçut dans le bas ventre, en voyant qu'il n'étoit pas dangereusement blessé, rechargea son fusil et tira sur lui à bout portant et ne s'est pas encore contenté de cela, racheva de l'assassiner à coup de crosse de fusil et pour terminer sa vaillantise, chargea le cadavre sur les épaules et le porta chez le juge de paix de Belleville, dit en entrant *en voilà encore un de mort*! Le juge de paix, pour remercier Robinat de son assassinat, le fit arrêter sur le champ. . . . La veuve Levasseur ne demande pas . . . qu'il fût fait mourir, mais qu'il soit puni d'une manière à ce qu'il n'en commette pas d'autres, que puisque cet individu est un des plus riches de Belleville, qu'il fût condamné à payer une somme quelconque pour aider sa malheureuse veuve et 6 enfants orphelins réduits à mendier leur pain, ainsi que pour leur malheureuse mère qui est infirme, hors d'état de gagner sa vie. . . .' The Minister wrote in the margin of the petition: 'Je vous préviens, Citoyenne, qu'aucune autorité ne peut annuler la déclaration d'un jury légalement formé qui acquitte un prévenu, il m'est donc impossible de rien faire sur votre pétition. . . .'

On the subject of the two girls accused of stealing potatoes, see below, p. 228, n.D.

Chapter 2

(A) We have only scattered figures for crimes committed *sur le pourtoir de Paris* during the Thermidorian Reaction and the Directory. If we take the period November 1794 to July 1799, we arrive at the unimpressive total of

39 murders in 57 months. But if we stop at the end of 1798, the score would be 37 murders in 48 months: on either count, this represents less than one murder a month, though in many of the cases quoted more than one person was murdered in each separate affair, sometimes as many as five. This is not then an unusually high rate of criminality, comparing quite favourably with the figures we have obtained for Paris itself, *intra-muros*, for a total period of 27 months (21 March 1796–18 August 1796; 21 December 1797–20 June 1800) with 34 murders. At first sight, these figures would appear to invalidate the claim that crimes of violence were more frequent outside Paris than within the city, and that the highroads through woodland and forest were much more dangerous than the city streets, whether by day or by night. But it must be called to mind that the Paris figures quoted for the two periods are *total*, and must be related to a population numbering about 800,000, if we are going to include the *habitants de garnis*; secondly, that the figures for the Seine-et-Oise, the Seine-et-Marne, the Eure, the two rural Districts of the Département de Paris have, on the contrary, no global value, given the archival sources from which they have been drawn. They only represent the tip of the iceberg. We have no overall picture for the year III. But 17 murders for 1796 and 11 for 1797 tell their own story eloquently enough. 1798 witnessed a marked improvement in the effectiveness of government.

There are 17 murders out of 40 or so under survey, in the area immediately surrounding Paris (Argenteuil, Belleville, Bondy, Clichy, Asnières, Saint-Denis, Versailles, Neuilly-sur-Marne, Vincennes). 14 murders are recorded in the Brie, nearly all of them along the great highroads from Paris to Lyon and Paris to Strasbourg.

(B) See A.N. BB 18 283 (Ministère de la Justice, Dyle, le général de division Songis, au Ministre de la Justice, 10 frimaire an IV [1 December 1795]): '. . . Les ennemis de la Révolution, qui fourmillent à Bruxelles et dans les pays conquis . . . avoient semé sur la forêt de Soignies des bruits qui avaient alarmé le gouvernement; à les entendre, un rassemblement considérable de brigands bien armés remplissait la forêt et la rendoit inabordable, c'étoit enfin une seconde Vendée. . . . je me suis convaincu que ces brigands . . . n'étoient autre chose que des gens sans état. . . . j'ai fait partir de Bruxelles, dans la nuit du 5 au 6, 2,000 hommes [qui] . . . les prirent presque tous dans leurs chaumières, 2 ou 3 qui voulurent résister payèrent de leurs vies cette résistance. . . . près d'une centaine. . . . sont en notre pouvoir. . . .'

See also A.N. BB 18 619 (Justice, Ourthe, Jugement rendu par le conseil militaire de Bruxelles, 18 nivôse an IV [8 January 1796]). The following are condemned to death for 'brigandages commis en forêt de Soignies':

'1. *Henri Stembaskliers*, dit *Froonens*, 33 ans, né à Linbeek;
2. *Théodore Vanisterdael*, dit *Poste*, 26 ans;
3. *Jean-Baptiste Michiels*, père, dit *Patard*, 59 ans;
4. *Henri Michiels*, fils, 24 ans;

5. *Jean-Baptiste Vanderkelen*, 26 ans, tous trois nés à Rodes.
6. *François Debue*, 21 ans;
7. *Joseph Vanderborght*, 18 ans;
8. *Michel Demunster*, 24 ans, tous trois nés à Uccle.'
   They were all executed the same day.

Chapter 3

(A) A report dated 1er Prairial year IV [20 May 1796] refers to such popular fears: '. . . Ils voyent renaître souvent ces longues années de famine qui ont rendu si célèbres les années de 1709, 1725, 1741 . . .' (A.N. F11 1185). '. . . On eut à craindre,' states a report from the Gers, dated 29 July 1812, 'l'année suivante une mortalité semblable à celle dont l'histoire conserve le souvenir et qui fit de si grands ravages l'année qui suivit la famine de 1709' (A.N. F11 710). An English family, the Garveys, living in Rouen, 'a rendu des services importants à la France; en 1752, 1769 et 1789, ils ont fait venir des quantités considérables de grains de l'étranger, et ont préservé la commune de Rouen de la disette. . . .' (A.N. D III 273 (292), Robert Garvey à la Convention, 3 ventôse an II). Finally, a report addressed to the Committee of Public Safety on 1 Pluviôse year III states '. . . On se rappelle même qu'en 1785 on craignit une disette de bestiaux et que le Gouvernement qui existait alors se vit obligé d'envoyer dans la Souabe, la Franconie, le Birkenfeld et autres contrées de l'Allemagne des agents chargés d'y opérer des achats de bestiaux pour alimenter les marchés de Sceaux et de Poissy, depuis le mois de novembre jusqu'au mois de juillet suivant, époque à laquelle l'ancienne province de Normandie commence à ouvrir ses engrais. . . . A combien plus forte raison a-t-elle besoin de ce secours pendant la guerre? . . .' (A.N. F11 292). See also A.N. F11 277 (projet de rapport de la Commission d'agriculture, au Comité de salut public, s.d. prairial an II): '. . . Il existe dans les herbages du ci-devant Charolais [et] de la ci-devant Normandie environ 130 à 140,000 bêtes à cornes destinées à entrer dans la consommation. . . . Ces herbages approvisionnaient autrefois Paris et les grandes communes qui l'avoisinent depuis le commencement de juillet jusques vers la fin de novembre. . . .' 1709, 1725, 1741, 1752, 1769, 1785, 1789, 1794–6, 1801, 1812, 1816: these are the years that would stand out the most in terms of popular memory to the inhabitants of the Seine valley. Indeed, as Brice or his successors remind us, the two votive pictures by the de Troy, father and son, in the church of Sainte-Geneviève, depict, the one, the end of the long freeze of 1709, the other, the longed-for break in the rain clouds of 1725.

(B) The population of Saint-Denis in 1794 was 6,000 (A.C. Saint-Denis, 1d1 4, 29 vendémiaire an III). That of Vincennes and Saint-Mande was estimated at 4,000, including only 100 farmers. (A.C. Vincennes 1D3, 24 prairial an II). Versailles had a population of 35,000 in 1795; 5,000 of these were described as *indigents* in October 1794 (A.N. F15 260). That of Boulogne was 3,600, 'et dont la plus grande partie sont des journaliers et des petits cultivateurs, tous pères de famille . . .' (A.N. F11 1476B, pluviôse an II). Choisy had 1,800 inhabitants, one third of whom were wage-earners (A.C. Choisy D 4, 12 septembre 1793). 'La commune [de Meudon] est composé de plus de 4,000 habitans, dont les travaux sont consacrés presque uniquement à la culture de la vigne . . .' (A.N. F9 79, 7 vendémiaire an III). In 1810, the *curé* refers to 'the immense population' of Montreuil (A.N. F8 77). In 1810, the population of Clichy totalled 1,691 (434 hommes mariés; 395 femmes mariées; 382 garçons; 435 filles; 17 veufs; 21 veuves). In April 1831, it had gone up to 3,050 (A.C. Clichy, Grand Registre). The population of Saint-Germain-en-Laye was estimated, in 1793, as 12,117 (3,099 votants, 552 aux armées, 43 sans droit de voter [domestiques?], 4,807 femmes et filles, 1,806 enfants femelles, 1,821 enfants mâles au-dessous de 21 ans). In Prairial year III, the municipality was to comment: '. . . 13,000 âmes, plus de 9/10 sont dans une indigence absolue, et les autres ne sont que de petits rentiers dont les rentes fort arriérées sont insuffisantes pour les faire exister' (A.C. Saint-Germain, D15). In Nivôse year III, the population of Viroflay was said to be 1,000 (dont 100 indigents) (A.C. Viroflay D 1).

(C) A.D. Oise, 8me registre du directoire du District de Clermont (séance du 7 prairial an II): '. . . Considérant que la loi du 6 octobre 1793 (v.s.) laisse aux corps administratifs le droit de fixer la hauteur des eaux nécessaires à l'usage des moulins, afin d'éviter des dommages auxquels leur trop grande élévation pourroit donner lieu . . . vu . . . le mémoire présenté par Antoine Budin, cultivateur et meunier, demeurant à Ronquerolles, commune d'Agnetz . . . concernant à une difficulté existante entre . . . Budin et Pinchenez, relativement à la visite et nivellement de la rivière de Brêche sur laquelle sont construits les moulins de l'exposant et celui dud. Pinchenez, afin de constater le reflu d'eau dont s'est plaint ce dernier, led. mémoire tendant à obtenir . . . le point d'eau qu'il doit avoir. . . considérant qu'il est évident . . . que la rivière a été curée à vif fond, et que rien ne s'oppose à ce que Budin obtienne son point d'eau . . . [le directoire passe outre].'

(D) A.P.P. A/A 62 (commissaire de police de la Section des Arcis, 15 fructidor an III): 'Anne Petit, 24 ans, marchande d'amadou et Catherine Cochet, 22 ans, brodeuse de souliers . . . pourquoi elles vont la nuit dans les champs voler la propriété d'autrui plutôt que de faire leur état dans Paris, ont répondu qu'elles y avaient été pour prendre des pommes de terre pour manger. . . . la fille Cochet a dit qu'il y avait 2 jours qu'elle était sans ouvrage. . . . demandé à la citoyenne Petit s'il y avait longtems qu'elle connaît la fille Cochet, a répondu qu'elle la connaît depuis 3 jours, qu'elle en a fait connaissance dans les rues, mais qu'elles se sont trouvées hier sur le pont au change, qu'elles ont été ensemble toute l'après-dîner, qu'elle ne s'est point couchée, ni sa camarade, qu'elles ont été ensemble voler les pommes de terre. . . .' In other words, bridges offer an easy rendez-vous at which decisions can be taken. Furthermore, in an enterprise of this kind, it is better to be two than one. Anne Petit was a provincial, from Champigny, near Châtillon-sur-Seine.

See also ibid. (7 vendémiaire an IV): 'Amainte Durand, 21 ans, native de Monistrol [Haute-Loire], travaillant en linge: . . . à lui demandé ce qu'elle faisait sur les 11 heures *au bas du pont Notre-Dame*, a dit qu'elle allait au charbon avec une de ses camarades . . . Alexandrine Lelerge, 16 ans, native de Corbeil. . . .' As the two girls had parents to vouch for them, and as Amainte Durand was able to prove that Alexandrine had been entrusted to her care, they were both released, with a warning from the *commissaire* not to hang about near the bridge.

(E) The case is quoted in my *Quelques aspects de la criminalité parisienne*.

It was possibly for this or similar reasons that extreme mobility was regarded as an indication of criminal activities. See, for instance, the case of 'Victoire Robin, 30 ans, native d'Orléans, à Paris depuis un an', questioned by the *commissaire* of the Section des Arcis, 7 Frimaire year III (27 November 1794]: '. . . elle a demeuré 1. chez Le Roy, logeur; 2. chez Tartif, menuisier; 3. chez Raymond, limonadier, rue Jean Denis; 4. enfin au Gros Caillou. Elle est prévenue d'avoir volé une vieille couverture de chez une logeuse et qu'elle a cachée sous sa jupe et qu'elle voulait vendre pour s'acheter un bonnet. Elle se rendait à l'hôpital pour se guérir de la galle. Elle n'a jamais été arrêtée . . .' (A.P.P. A/A 61, commissaire de police de la Section des Arcis, 7 frimaire an III). She was probably out of work, as people with that highly contagious skin disease would be excluded from the company of those still unaffected. A man of 19, Denis Saunier, a Paris-born shoemaker, and a boy of 12, Alexandre Viton, a Swiss in Paris for the previous two years, 'faisant des commissions et couchant dans les écuries de la rue Nicaise', both suspected of theft, are cross-examined on 29 Vendémiaire year IV [20 October 1795]. Saunier is asked if he is working, 'a dit que non, *depuis qu'il a eu la galle, les ouvriers ne veulent pas le souffrir*, et qu'il fait ce qu'il peut pour gagner sa vie . . .' (A.N. F111 1183).

See also A.P.P. A/A 99 (commissaire de police de la Section de la Butte-des-Moulins, commissaire près la 2me administration municipal, au commissaire, 6 ventôse an IV [25 February 1796]): 'Je vous prie . . . de prendre tous les renseignements que vous pourrez sur le compte et la moralité d'un nommé *Charles-François Cauchie*, qui, dans un passeport qu'il a pris, à la Section de la Butte-des-Moulins, s'est donné la qualité de maître-d'armes et qui se dit actuellement marchd. de vin. En floréal dernier il demeuroit rue d'Argenteuil, no. 224. Vous voudrez bien vous informer quelle étoit son existence à cette époque, s'il étoit logé dans ses meubles et s'il faisoit beaucoup de dépenses. . . .'

(F) A.P.P. A/A 99 (procès-verbal dressé par le commissaire de police de la Section de la Butte-des-Moulins d'une visite faite à l'entresol du No. 23 des galéries du Palais-Royal): '. . . Avons été raccroché sous les galéries . . . par une vieille femme qui nous a offert de nous prostituer une jeune fille qu'elle tenait à son bras et de nous conduire chez elle. . . . nous avons feint d'accepter . . . et fûmes montés à l'entresol. . . . [elle] . . . nous a offert d'aller chercher une seconde fille [qui] . . . a dit se nommer *Lucille Decuchesne*, de Tepauline [*sic*] en Hollande, se disant couturière en robes. . . . [une 3me] . . . a dit se nommer *Marie-Françoise Woichiechosky*, âgée de 17 ans, native de Nancy, ouvrière en modes . . . [et] qu'il est à sa connoissance que ladite Martin [the old woman] a cette jeune fille chez elle depuis 3 ou 4 jours . . . laquelle a dit se nommer Marie-Anne Bertet, âgée de 16 ans, native de Paris, y ayant ses père et mère au Gros-Caillou, rue Dominique, no 195. . . . nous a dit qu'il y avoit environ un mois qu'elle avoit quitté ses parens qui la maltraitaient et qui n'avoient pas le moyen de lui donner son nécessaire, et que depuis cette époque elle a fait le métier de femme publique . . . qu'en effet depuis environ un mois qu'elle fait ce métier, elle donne la moitié de ce qu'elle a gagné en se prostituant à ladite Martin . . . qu'elle peut avoir gagné depuis qu'elle va chez ladite Rosine environ 20,000 livres. . . .' La Martin was clearly something of an amateur, as she had not recognised the *commissaire de police* of her own Division; she said that she had been in the trade for under a year. The three girls were released with a caution. It was natural for a teen-age girl from the Gros-Caillou running away from her parents, to have gravitated towards the Palais-Royal. It is also of interest to note that, no doubt as a result of the formation of *la Grande Nation*, Paris prostitution had begun to recruit Dutch, as well as Belgian girls (see above, chapter 5 p. 153). The presence of a girl with a Polish name from Nancy may be explained by the former presence there of the court of Stanislas Lesczynski.

(G) A.P.P. A/A 98 (commissaire de police de la Section de la Butte-des-Moulins, au Bureau central, 21 messidor an III). On the morning on which the body of the murderer was found, the father of the victim received a letter, written by Tournay and posted early in the morning: 'Je vais donc terminer ma vie et mes maux, votre infâme fille m'a forcé à la vengeance. Que n'ai-je pu réunir dans le même instant l'homme, qui a servi à me rendre malheureux, cet homme impudent ose (étant couché près de moi) chanter à mi-voix *Nuit charmante, nuit sois propice à l'amour &ca*. Je vous recommande mes enfants. Le C. Lâllemant, demeurant rue Neuve des Petits Champs, vis à vis la rue Chabanais, a reçu ce qui revient de mes rentes. Ils aideront à la subsistance des enfants. Adieu, je vais mourir. Je vous ai entendu hier au soir chez votre fille, j'ai évité de vous parler, ma femme ne me faisait pas savoir que vous

étiez chez elle, et m'ayant entendu rentrer.' A neighbour, Bleau, was to state
that he had seen Tournay the night before, at 10.30; they had talked together;
Tournay 'donna au déclarant le journal du soir en lui disant: *tenez, Bleau,
lisez le journal*, sans que lui comparant s'aperçut que ledit Tournay eut l'air
agité. . . . que dernièrement il a entendu Tournay dire à son épouse *Ma bonne
amie, nos affaires seront bientôt terminées, je fais arranger mon appartement
faubourg Saint-Germain, je te débarrasserai d'un enfant que je mettrai en pension*. . . .'

(H) A.P.P. A/A 99 (Bureau central, au commissaire de police de la Section
de la Butte-des-Moulins, 28 germinal an IV [17 April 1796]): 'Le Ministre
de la Police Générale nous a informés . . . que dans la nuit du 16 au 17 de ce
mois, des quidams se sont introduits dans la maison du C. Rumel, au hameau
de Sermaise, commune de Bois-la-Nation, près Fontainebleau; y ont assassiné le C. Rumel, sa femme, une domestique et 2 domestiques mâles, que
ces brigands ont volé ensuite toute l'argenterie, les bijoux, les papiers mon-
noye, et une jument sous poil bai, taille de 4 pieds, hors d'âge, à tous crins, et
sellée d'une selle à l'angloise garnie de boutons argentés. Comme il seroit
possible que ces scélérats fûssent venus à Paris, nous pensons que la petite
jument pourroit servir à les découvrir. Nous vous invitons en conséquence
. . . à vous transporter sans délai dans toutes les auberges de votre arrondissement où se trouvent des écuries, ainsi que chez les marchands de chevaux,
et autres personnes qui tiennent des chevaux. . . .'

(I) A report to the Minister of the Interior, dated 5 Fructidor year V [22
August 1797], on the subject of a petition by the authorities of La Chapelle,
illustrates with great clarity the point of view of the higher authorities: '. . .
ils soutiennent que de tems immémorial les veaux se sont vendus à La Chapelle . . . à la vérité depuis quelques années, et notamment depuis la suppression des droits d'entrée, il s'y est établi [à La Chapelle] une espèce de marché
aux veaux [Note the *espèce de*, with its undertones of contempt, the very
vocabulary of Parisian insolence], mais ce marché n'est autre chose qu'une
réunion d'agioteurs et de mercandiers. . . . vous savez qu'il existe à Paris
une halle qui offre toutes les facilités convenables pour le commerce des
veaux, indépendamment des commodités d'un établissement aussi utile,
l'administration est plus à portée de surveiller les ventes et d'y exercer une
police active. . . . D'ailleurs, le concours de la marchandise offre le spectacle de
l'abondance qui, à son tour, produit une diminution sensible sur les prix . . .
(A.N. FF11 1177, Bureau Central au Ministre de l'Intérieur, 5 fructidor an V).

(J) Probably because many of them had originally been recruited there; a
return to the faubourg Saint-Marceau would be an admission of defeat, and
one all the more humiliating in that it would be witnessed by many who had
known the girls at an earlier stage, before they had departed for the centre.

boasting perhaps of future success. See Restif, *Le Palais-Royal*, p. 25: '. . .
Elles sont chez une femme, qu'on nomme la Restauratrice . . . qui a plus
de 40 jeunes filles de cet âge [15], prises dans les fauxbourgs & dans les provinces; car rarement elle se fournit au centre de la ville. . . . Rosalie & Fan-
chette sont 2 cousines, prises à l'extrémité du Fauxbourg Saint-Antoine.
Elles ont été achetées par Madame Janus, à l'âge de 4 ans, d'une femme qui
les conduisait, après la mort de leurs parens, à l'hôpital général. . . . l'une
était fille de ce malheureux jeune homme du Fauxbourg, qui aimait sa soeur,
& qui l'avait poignardée; c'est Rosalie. . . .'

On the other hand, prostitutes of the lowest order would come in from the
perimeter to the centre, to ply during the day: 'Une troupe de malheureuses,
logées à l'extrémité des fauxbourgs, viennent chaque soir au centre de la ville,
communiquer leur corruption à ces hommes utiles et robustes, que leur peu
de fortune a rendu les serviteurs de l'humanité . . .' (Restif, *Le Pornographe*,
p. 123). He is referring to Limousin building labourers. The presence in the
centre of women of this condition must have further contributed to Parisian
prejudices on the subject of the *communes* of the southern and eastern perimeter and of their inhabitants.

See also, for a much later period, Balzac's *La Cousine Bette:* '. . . Au commencement du mois de décembre 1845, Adeline prit pour fille de cuisine, une
grosse Normande d'Isigny . . . bête comme une pièce de circonstance, et
qui se décida difficilement à quitter le bonnet de coton classique dont se
coiffent les filles de la Basse-Normandie. Cette fille, douée d'un embonpoint
de nourrice, semblait près de faire éclater la cotonnade dont elle entourait son
corsage. . . . On ne fit naturellement aucune attention dans la maison à
l'entrée de cette fille appelée Agathe, la vraie fille délurée que la province
envoie journellement à Paris. Agathe tenta médiocrement le cuisinier, tant
elle était grossière dans son langage, car elle avait servi les rouliers, elle sortait
d'une auberge de faubourg. . . .'

(K) The *commissaire* attached to the Dyle court, who knew his area well
and who, in this instance, had clearly taken a careful look at the map, before
writing to the *Grand Juge* states in a letter dated 30 Pluviôse year XII [20
February 1804]: 'Je crois devoir m'empresser de vous faire connaître la
bonne conduite et l'intelligence avec laquelle mon substitut est parvenu à
trouver les traces d'un vol considérable de marchandises commis dans un
Département voisin [Jemappes]. . . . Instruit par les bruits publics qu'un
vol considérable avait eu lieu dans la commune de Braine-le-Comte . . . il
présuma que les voleurs seraient tentés de venir vendre à Nivelles le produit
de leur vol, il donna en conséquence ordre aux commissaires de police et à la
gendarmerie de parcourir les rues de Nivelles et de conduire devant lui tous
ceux qui colporteroient des marchandises à vendre, il a été bien secondé par ces
fonctionnaires subalternes, puisque le 26 courant ils lui conduisirent deux
filles, l'une d'Arquennes [a village on the road from Braine-le-Comte to

Nivelles], l'autre de Seneffe [on the highroad from Nivelles to La Louvière]
qui colportoient diverses marchandises à vendre . . . et par l'interrogatoire
qu'il fit subir à ces deux filles il parvint à découvrir où étoit le restant des marchandises provenant de ce vol et quels en étaient les auteurs au nombre de
12 à 15, il a déjà fait effectuer l'arrestation de 10 de ces brigands. . . . Ce
même substitut vient encore de faire effectuer une arrestation bien import-
ante. Instruit encore par les bruits publics qu'un vol considérable d'argent
monnoyé et d'effets précieux avait eu lieu à Lans [?] près de Liége, département de l'Ourthe, il donna tout de suite les ordres les plus sévères dans tout
son arrondissement d'arrêter tout étranger qui serait dépourvu de passeport,
ainsi que tous autres qui seraient rencontrés sur les routes détournées et
inusitées. Cette mesure lui a parfaitement réussi. On a arrêté à Jauche, petit
village des confins du département qui avoisinent l'Ourthe, deux individus
sur lesquels on a trouvé plusieurs des effets volés et une grande quantité
d'argent monnoyé.

J'ai cru, C. Grand Juge, vous faire plaisir en vous fesant connaître la
bonne conduite de mon substitut à Nivelles. Il serait à désirer que tous les
magistrats de sûreté fûssent animé du même zèle: si de proche en proche on
se fait des mêmes précautions que lui, lorsque des délits se commettent dans
les environs de leurs arrondissements, on parviendroit bientôt à rétablir
l'ordre social partout. . . . il serait bien important pour ce Département [la
Dyle] que l'on en agît dans les Départements voisins, et surtout dans celui
des Deux-Nèthes [Antwerp], car j'ai la certitude que la plupart des délits qui
ont lieu dans celui-ci sont causés par des individus qui viennent de ce département ou vont s'y refugier. . . .' (A.N. BB 18 402, Justice, Jemappes).

(L) Some idea of the relative poverty of the different Sections of Paris may
be derived from a table drawn up for the Minister of the Interior on 25
Fructidor year IV [11 September 1796]:
'*Nourrissons recevant le pain des indigents:*
  Champs-Elysées—*500*; Roule—*222*; Vendôme—*175*; Tuileries—*125*;
Le Peletier—*97*; Faubourg-Montmartre—*332*; Montblanc—*148*; Buttes-
des-Moulins—*100*; Contrat-Social—*243*; Brutus—*96*; Poissonnière—*255*;
Mail—*97*; Halle-au-Bled—*200*; Gardes-Françaises—*177*; Marchés—*134*;
Muséum—*300*; Bonne-Nouvelle—*220*; Faubourg du Nord—*331*; Boncon-
seil—*237*; Bondy—*315*; *Gravilliers—440*; Lombards—*364*; Temple—*255*;
Amis de la Patrie—*266*; Arcis—*246*; Droits de l'Homme—*347*; Homme
Armé—*140*; Réunion—*170*; *15/20—508;* Indivisibilité—*248*; Popincourt—
340; *Montreuil—415; Fidélité—657;* Fraternité—*190*; Arsenal—*300*;
Cité—*326*; Ouest—*360*; Fontaine de Grenelle—*200*; Invalides—*225*;
Unité—500; Théâtre-Français—*250*; Thermes—*267*; *Luxembourg—419;*
Pont-Neuf—*110*; Panthéon—*326*; *Jardin des Plantes—433; Observatoire—
433; Finistère—409.*' (A.N. F11 1183). The two faubourgs, the riverside
Sections, and the Gravilliers show the highest figures.

Chapter 4

(A) A.D. Seine D 4AZ 590 (Huet, habitant de Belleville, à la municipalité de Belleville, 25 vendémiaire an II): '. . . Depuis que l'on s'occupe à Paris de la taxe des objets de première nécessité, les débitans des campagnes, les habitans eux-mêmes qui vont à Paris, ne peuvent sortir de marchandises. Sous peu de jours, les débitans qui n'achètent ordinairement à Paris qu'au prorata de leur débit dans leurs villages, n'auront plus aucune marchandise, l'agriculteur, cette classe si intéressante, va donc se trouver manquer de nombre d'objets de première nécessité. Les débitans des campagnes qui achètent au prorata de leurs débits chez les marchands de Paris, où pourront-ils se fournir de marchandises que leurs faibles moyens ne leur permettent de prendre qu'en petite quantité? Si par le maximum arrêté par la municipalité de Paris, il n'en peut rien sortir, non seulement les débitans des campagnes se trouveront sans état, mais encore les agriculteurs, cette classe qui mérite des égards se trouvera manquer de quantité d'objets qui sont d'une très grande nécessité, tant pour la nourriture que pour le vêtement. J'ai tout lieu d'espérer que la municipalité pèsera dans sa sagesse ma juste observation, et qu'elle voudra bien m'appuyer auprès de la municipalité de Paris qui prononcera contre un abus qui pourroit devenir funeste en détruisant l'unité, l'indivisibilité et la fraternité entre tous les républicains. . . . je vous représente aussi, Citoyens, qu'il ne se fait aucun commerce dans le département que dans la seule ville de Paris, qu'il n'y a ni bois ni marché, que l'on ne receuille pas même pour ainsi dire de blé dans son étendue qui est très circonspecte, que les décrets qui concernent la ville de Paris doivent s'étendre par tout le département de Paris. . . .' No wonder Belleville was to get a bad name.

(B) Roger Lévy, 'La rivalité entre Rouen et le Havre', *A.H.R.F.*, 1932.

The argument could also work the other way. There was no question, for instance, of le Havre consenting to the inclusion within its boundaries of the poor villages situated on the periphery of the port, especially that of Ingouville, dominated, from the time of his election as *maire*, by 120 votes out of 180, on 9 December 1792, to his replacement, by Jacques Duval, on 29 September 1793, by the powerful and controversial personality of Musquinet-Lapagne (see *Reactions to the French Revolution*, pp. 107–14). The Havrais regarded Ingouville with fear, both as a centre of crime and as containing a population that was very poor. On 25 September 1793, a few days before his overthrow, the members of the municipality were to pay tribute to the work carried out by Musquinet in the following terms: '. . . il est vrai que le C. Maire . . . en l'absence du juge de paix . . . a arrêté environ 50 scélérats, voleurs ou assassins, qui désolaient tout le canton, des fabricateurs de faux assignats qui avaient établi leur fabrique dans la commune. . . .' In the summer of 1794, it is stated that Ingouville contained 988 *chefs de famille*,

1,300 *feux*, with an effective population of 4,782, 3,500 of whom were dependent on the bakers for their daily supply of bread, a striking testimony to the extreme poverty of the mass of the population. (A.C. Ingouville, D1 19, séance de la municipalité du 17 thermidor an 11). In the following year, the *comité de législation* was to write to the Thermidorian Committee of Public Safety: '. . . La seule commune d'Ingouville contient 5,500 habitans à ma connaissance depuis la Révolution, près des deux tiers des criminels qui ont été exposés sur l'échafaud, avaient leur domicile à Ingouville . . .' (A.N. D III 270, d. 40, 28 ventôse an III [18 March 1795]). On Messidor of the same year [8 July 1795] the public prosecutor of le Havre was to comment: '. . . Cette commune [Ingouville] . . . est habitée en grande partie par des gens sans aveu, des femmes publiques, on n'y fait pas 20 pas sans rencontrer des cabarets, c'est l'asile des mauvais sujets, des échappés des galères, des déserteurs, la police y est fort mal tenue et, maintes fois, il a été question de réunir cette commune et celle de Lheure, autre mauvais lieu, à celle du Havre, mais le municipalité du Havre craint et appréhende cette réunion. . . . c'est à mes yeux un noyau de chouannerie, l'association aura bientôt une caisse formée de ces vols. . . .' And he went on to say that robberies had been particularly numerous on all the outskirts of le Havre in the course of the previous three months, that is from Germinal (A.N. D III 271 d 19).

The case of Ingouville could be taken as that of many of the villages on the perimeter of Paris, and the unwillingness displayed by the Havrais authorities to take over such an alarming place, even if it would have greatly improved repression and the activities of the police, is equally characteristic of the attitude of successive Parisian officials towards villages like Vincennes. Ingouville, Lheure, Graville, and Sanvic were not to be included within the city limits of le Havre till the present century.

(C) Another example of this kind of person comes from Dourdan: François Guillaume, a founder member of the local *société populaire* at its opening in January 1791, aged 29, *garçon perruquier*, then *perruquier* in his own business, which he had set up on his arrival in Dourdan in 1787. He had left his parents at the age of 15 and seems to have lived in Paris till his arrival in Dourdan. He quickly acquired an ascendancy in the Dourdan club, as a result of which he was elected *officier municipal* in Pluviôse year II [Jan.–Feb. 1794]. He remained in these functions for the next fifteen months; during the Thermidorian Reaction, he was sent by the municipality to Paris in order to take a course of instruction in the manufacture of saltpetre. His next move was to use the skills thus acquired to get himself appointed *chef de l'atelier de salpêtre* in Rambouillet. From there he was recalled to Dourdan, towards the end of the year III, on being appointed a member of the local *gendarmerie*. This is the last we hear of him. The president of the neighbouring club of Cernay, in the year II, was Vincent Prévost, who, before the Revolution, had been *cocher de fiacre* in Paris, 'et depuis vivant de son revenu'. He had come to Cernay in 1790 (A.D. Seine-et-Oise Lm11m Dourdan 30, sociétés populaires du District de Dourdan). Referring no doubt to similar personalities, the *comité révolutionnaire* of Fontainebleau was to complain, in Pluviôse year II: '. . . des refugiés de Paris et autres lieux . . . font tous leurs efforts pour influencer partout . . .' (A.D. Seine-et-Marne L 886).

(D) On 11 Prairial year II [30 May 1794] the Committee of Public Safety, in an order signed by Robespierre, Collot-d'Herbois, and Billaud-Varenne, had entrusted Rousseville with the specific task of looking into the affairs of the *commune* of Neuilly and of discovering the 'partisans' of Bonnard. On the same day, a second *arrêté*, signed by the same three members of the great Committee, had ordered Rousseville to go to Neuilly to arrest the former marquis de Canizy, seigneur de Vassy. The order was carried out on 13 Prairial by the *comité de surveillance* of Neuilly. But on 19 Prairial, the *comité révolutionnaire* of the Section du Bonnet-Rouge, in Paris, was to denounce Canizy to the Committee of General Security. There are thus elements of a conflict of powers between the two Committees of Government, a conflict that has often been referred to by historians as a factor contributing to the breach between them and to the 9 Thermidor. Rousseville can be seen as acting as the personal agent of the Committee of Public Safety, without the knowledge of the police Committee. There is, of course, nothing to suggest that he was in any way a protégé of Robespierre, Collot and Billaud being likewise responsible for his repressive missions during these crucial days following the Admirat affair (A.N. F7 4632 d 3, Canizy). Canizy was actually living in Villiers-la-Garenne at the time of his arrest. On the fourteenth a third order, signed this time Robespierre, Couthon, and Carnot, entrusted Rousseville with the arrest of Larivoire, former *curé* of Fontenay-sous-Bois (A.N. F7 4631 d 2 Caille).

(E) Or even earlier, for already in March the municipality was being blamed by the Paris Jacobins for having victimised an inhabitant of Belleville, Chevillard, *maître maçon*. A member of the *comité de correspondance* of the Jacobins wrote to the local club, on 8 March 1793: 'La Société des Jacobins, à laquelle vous vous étiez adressés pour mettre d'accord votre Municipalité avec un citoyen nommé Chevillard, maître maçon, a chargé son Comité de Correspondance d'examiner cette affaire et le Comité . . . m'a chargé de lui en faire le rapport. En attendant une pièce principale qui est, je crois, une nouvelle dénonciation de la municipalité de Belleville, j'ai examiné celles qui m'ont été remises par le C. Chevillard: j'ai confessé ce Citoyen, j'ai cru remarquer en lui un homme d'une probité rare; mais ce qui m'a singulièrement surpris, c'est le ménagement avec lequel il parle d'adversaires qui le poursuivent depuis le mois de 9bre avec un acharnement sans exemple; j'ai conclu de cette douceur dans le caractère, de la lettre écrite le 17 9bre à la municipalité de Belleville par le Ministre Pache, de celle du commissaire adjoint au Ministre de la Guerre actuel &c &c &c que la municipalité de Belleville, qui s'est déjà attiré le mépris du Ministre ou du moins de son adjoint pour la 5me Division, finira par s'attirer celui des Jacobins et le vôtre; il est sans doute de votre intérêt, frères et amis, de lui éviter ce désagrément . . . si . . . je ne me suis pas trompé sur le compte du C. Chevillard, vous engagerez la Municipalité à se départir d'un système qui la déshonore, vous m'en donnerez avis avant que j'aie fait mon rapport afin que cette affaire rentre dans le néant dont elle n'aurait jamais dû sortir. Je suis votre frère Pollet, commis à la trésorerie nationale, rue du Ponceau, no. 49.' The Municipality and Gilbert, *commandant en chef du canton de Belleville*, it seems, had accused Chevillard of having deserted from his regiment, an accusation that was vigorously denied by the *adjoint à la 5me Division*. The *maire*, Thiébault, had sided with Gilbert. Both sides had appealed to the local club.

(F) A.D. Seine 4 AZ 590 (femme Sibillot à la société, 20 ventôse an II): 'Vous savez tous que le C. Sibillot, mon mary se trouve impliqué dans une affaire malheureuse et d'autant plus accablante qu'elle est éloignée de son coeur et des principes que vous luy connaissez. Ma situation et mes forces ne me permettent pas d'entrer dans de longs détails, je me bornerai . . . à prier ses collègues et ses frères d'armes de vouloir bien suspendre leur jugement et leur opinion jusqu'à ce qu'il aît établi sa justification, de vouloir bien à cet effet luy accorder des défenseurs officieux qui présenteront à l'adhésion de la Société le tableau de toute sa conduite, dans la carrière de la révolution, et l'assurance des principes de liberté et d'égalité et de fraternité qu'il n'a cessé de professer. Femme Sibillot.'

(G) *Louvain*, 27, *marchand de vin*, member of the club since 20 July 1792; Jacques Eméry *Ozéré*, 29, *employé à la Commission du Commerce*, member since 1 July 1791: 'né à Paris, Paroisse Saint-Roch, en 1766 . . . lors de la réélection de la municipalité au mois de novembre 1791 . . . fut nommé secrétaire de la municipalité. . . .' On 7 April 1793, he was appointed to the local *comité de surveillance*. In an undated *Mémoire*, he outlined his services to the commune, adding: 'il demande votre justice et votre bienveillance. On l'accuse d'être un *intrus* et un *banni*. . . .' His crime no doubt was to have been born in Paris. *Bodson, ex-perruquier aux gardes françaises*, member since 14 April 1791, which seems to have been the date of the foundation of the club; Bodson should not be confused with the militant of the same name from the Section du Pont-Neuf. Other members of the 1791 vintage were *Thiébard*, 41, *chirurgien*; *Serrez*, 49, *chirurgien*; *Bouchez aîné*, 42, *cordonnier*; *Favart*, 49, *artiste*; *Huet*, 41, *droguiste*; *Pérouze*, 53, *ancien militaire*. The club must have been one of the first to have been formed in the Paris area (A.D. Seine D 4AZ 590 (*détails biographiques de quelques membres* . . .)).

(H) The *société*, in its session for 3 Germinal [23 March], was especially

careful, when appealing to the municipality to establish an equitable system
of meat rationing, at least to render lip service to the prime needs of the
capital, as well as to those of Belleville: '. . . Vous avez entendu, Citoyens,
quelles sont les demandes de vos frères, vous allez sans doute les peser dans
votre sagesse, vous allez promptement aviser aux moyens de les satisfaire,
votre sollicitude s'étendra tout à la fois sur le malade, . . . sur tous les
habitans de cette Commune, pauvres ou riches sans préférence, sur ceux de
la Commune du Pré Lepeletier, enfin sur ceux de Paris qui viendroient icy
chercher des secours. . . . Les Parisiens respectent les arrêtés de leur Commune, ils respecteront les vôtres, ils verront sans peine l'ordre des distribu-
tions tellement établi parmi nous, que chacun n'aît également qu'une petite
portion de subsistances afin qu'elles puissent suffire pour tous et s'étendre
même jusqu'à eux. La satisfaction dès lors sera générale, vous aurez fait pour
vos voisins ce que vous pouvez, et pour tous les habitans ce que vous leur
devez, l'harmonie se rétablira. . . .' (A.D. Seine 4 AZ 590).

(I) A.D. Seine 4 AZ 719 (serment civique): 'Nous promettons au Patriote
Palloy d'être les Tyrannicides des Brigands couronnés, de plonger le fer
dans le sein des despotes, des Royalistes, des fanatiques ennemis de la patrie,
de défendre avec le courage qui nous anime, pour soutenir la République
une et indivisible, faire partout respecter la Constitution sanctionné par le
Peuple; c'est d'après cette profession de foi que nous avons reçu dud. patriote
la médaille comme étant un gage du civisme qui doit animer tous les français
et tous les amis de la Liberté et de l'Egalité, dont reconnaissance patriotique
le 19me Jour du 1er mois de l'an II . . . Bunel, commissaire au comité de
surveillance de la section brutus; François Grégoire, député de l'assemblée
populaire des liégeois.' Palloy was to have plenty of opportunities to carry
out the first part of this programme!

(J) A.D. Seine D 4AZ 719 (Delaunay à Palloy, 1er germinal an II): 'Citoyen,
j'ai appris avec autant de satisfaction que de plaisir l'heureux moment où la
Convention a ordonné ta sortie de la Force. La justice et l'oeil vigilant des
représentants du peuple ont reconnu ton patriotisme, et je crois que c'étoit
le seul crime dont tes persécuteurs cherchoient à tirer parti afin de te calom-
nier, et couvrir ton républicanisme du voile de l'hypocrisie; ton triomphe
est d'autant plus grand que tes dénonciateurs se sont couverts d'oppobres
et doivent être voués à l'infamie; voilà le sort qui les attend, qu'ils rentrent
dans le néant, ces êtres malfaisants, dont l'âme crapuleuse et vile n'a jamais
connu ce que c'étoit que la vertu; pour toi, cher patriote, ton innocence fait
ton triomphe, puisse-tu en jouir en paix en dépît de tes ennemis et sois per-
suadé de l'intérêt que je prends à tout ce qui peut être agréable et crois-moy
en vray Républicain ton amy Delaunay.' He is presumably referring to the
hébertistes.

(K) Huet, the member of the Belleville club whom we have quoted earlier on this very subject, makes the point very clearly: '. . . Je vous représente aussi Citoyens . . . que si chaque municipalité faisoit la taxe des marchandises selon sa localité, l'on verroit une atteinte à l'unité et l'indivisibilité de la république, il est aisé de s'en convaincre; une municipalité d'après sa taxe faite la regardera comme personnelle et ne voudra pas que les marchandises sortent de son local, alors il existe autant de républiques que de municipalités. J'ajoute même que déjà à Paris plusieurs marchands ont refusé de vendre à des personnes parce qu'elles étoient d'une autre Section. Ces abus pourroient devenir très funestes.' This is exactly the point made by Jean Jaurès, in his *Histoire socialiste*, when describing the ultimate logic of the *hébertiste* position: 'Cela aurait consisté à réduire la France en une myriade de petites républiques, diétines à la polonaise, égoïstes et sanguinaires. . . .' Jaurès was, of course, a 'centralist'. Kropotkin had a much clearer understanding of the nature of the problem of 'communalism'.

(L) Among the *sociétés* known to have been affiliated with the Cordeliers, we should note the special case of that of *La Vertu Sociale*, the rival to the Jacobin-inclined and more respectable, because much older, *les Droits-de-l'Homme*, in Versailles, dissolved in Ventôse year II as suspected of *hébertisme*, as well as those of Gentilly, Montrouge, Sèvres, Vaugirard, Issy, and, perhaps the most important, Gonesse (A.D. Seine-et-Oise L11m Gonesse). The Belleville club, on the other hand, as we have seen, had received recognition from the Jacobins; it does not seem to have sought affiliation with the Cordeliers. That of Vanves, as we noted earlier, approached it, on 27 Frimaire year II, in order to request affiliation with Belleville, as a first step towards recognition by the Jacobins. In its address, it pointed out that it was already affiliated with the Vaugirard club, hardly a recommendation to a club so respectable and so prudent as that of Belleville. The *société* of Bagnolet, possibly under the influence of Rousseville, who presumably still enjoyed some local standing, was so eager to obtain the official approval of the Belleville club that it approached it on four occasions, in addresses dated 8 Pluviôse, 15 Ventôse, 30 Ventôse, and 5 Germinal year II. Such insistence cannot be unconnected with the realisation that non-recognition by the Jacobins might lead to dangerous accusations, judging from the dates of the last two addresses (A.D. Seine 4 AZ 652, société populaire de Bagnolet). In the case of Vanves, the members were clearly anxious to play safe, by getting approval both from the Jacobins and the Cordeliers, as well as from Vaugirard and Belleville. A great many more no doubt attempted to take the same precaution. And no doubt a great many more still, so tenuous and obscure was their brief existence, even at the height of the Terror, were never recognised by either club and only owed their rather nominal existence to the intervention of *apôtres* from the nearest *chef-lieu de District*. The remarks made by the members of the District d'Étampes, in a reply to an inquiry, dated 9 Nivôse year III [29

December 1794] on the subject of the club set up in the village of Boissy, could certainly have been applied to scores of these rural *communes*: 'Il sera probablement inutile de vous adresser la liste des membres [de la société de Boissy] . . . puisque depuis le 10 messidor [28 June] elle ne subsiste plus . . . la moisson étant survenue, elle fut le prétexte de la dissolution de la société. . . . la moisson étant finie, elle n'a pu se reformer; l'insouciance en est la seule cause. . . .'

(M) Among children arrested for theft on 24 Brumaire year IV [14 November 1798] we note: 'François Blanchard, commissionnaire, 15 ans, natif de Versailles; demeurant rue des Martyrs dans une auberge; Barthélémy Morel, 10 ans et ½, natif de Saint-Germain-en-Laye; Barbier, 12 ans, natif du Mesnil-Aubry; demeurant chez une logeuse, rue de la Tannerie; Jean-Pierre Mathieu, 14 ans, natif de Montmartre; Antoine Mégnot, 14 ans, natif de Versailles' (A.N. BB 18 760, Justice, Seine).

See also A.P.P. A/A 99 (rapport du commissaire de police de la Section de la Butte-des-Moulins, du 13 ventôse an IV [3 March 1796], sur une visite faite, 93, Maison-Égalité): '. . . Nous avons trouvé dans l'une d'elles les nommées *Nicole Laurence*, qui s'est dite brodeuse, âgée de 16 ans, et *Manette Bazile*, se disant couturière en linge, âgée de 17 ans, toutes logées depuis trois jours dans ladite chambre sans avoir été portées sur le livre de la police . . . dans une autre chambre occupée par la citoyenne *Rosalie Didier-Rossignol*, qui n'avait pas couché chez elle et qui se trouve enregistrée nous y avons trouvé couchées les nommées *Madeleine Delile*, ouvrière en linge, âgée de 16 ans, *Anne-Françoise Choulagnet*, brodeuse, âgée de 24 ans, et *Marie-Rosalie Labrétèque*, sans être portées sur le livre de police, laquelle était couchée avec la nommée *Babet Doré*, qui n'était pas enregistrée, ladite Marquoy nous a dit être dans cet endroit depuis environ 4 mois et payer au C. Broule à raison de 30 l. en numéraire par chaque mois quoiqu'elle n'aît point d'état. . . .'

In the same box, the *commissaire* reports on: '*Anne Bazin*, 17 ans, native d'Orly, se disant brodeuse, demeurant 93 maison-égalité. . . . *Rose Bertrand*, 16 ans et ½, native de Nogent-sur-Seine, se disant fleuriste et avoir des personnes qui lui font du bien' (9 ventôse an IV [Sunday 28 February 1796]).

There is also an account of a runaway girl from Paris itself, in a statement made on 12 Ventôse year III [2 March 1795] to the *commissaire de police* of the Section des Arcis: '. . . que depuis environ 9 mois la citoyenne *Suzanne Guyot*, sa belle-sœur, âgée de 16 ans, taille d'environ 5 pieds, visage rond, yeux bruns, nez carré, bouche petite & les dents blanches, les cheveux noirs coupés en Jacobin, étoit demeurante chez elle, qu'elle s'étoit toujours bien comportée et n'avait [*sic*] jamais sorti sans la comparante ou son épouse, mais que ce jourd'hui matin [a Monday, to make it worse] il a été fort étonné . . . d'apprendre qu'elle était disparue sur les 6 heures du matin avec ses habits et linges . . .' Chapter one, in fact, on the road to the Palais-Royal (A.P.P. A/A 61).

See also A.P.P. A/A 61 (commissaire de police de la Section des Arcis, 27 brumaire an III [17 November 1794]) *Nanette Fratte*, aged 15, native of Sèvres, where her father was still living, as a *vigneron*, 'demeurant chez une logeuse', was accused of having helped a prisoner to escape from the *gendarmes* as he was being taken out of the Châtelet.

(N) There is a sadly repetitive chronicle of children and young people leaving or unwilling to return home because they had been ill-treated by their parents, in the papers of the Paris *commissaire de police*. Thus *Geneviève Fleury*, 19, native of Paris, 'marchande à la Grève', prostitute 'chez Lamy, logeur: à elle demandé si sa mère a connaissance de sa mauvaise conduite, a dit que non, à elle demandé si elle est en état de se faire réclamer par sa mère, a dit qu'elle ne veut pas que sa mère sache cela' (A.P.P. A/A 62, 9 vendémiaire an IV). This is also an example of what might be described as popular jansenism in a purely Parisian milieu. See also the case of *Elisabeth Lenoir, femme Revon, chapelier*, native of Longwy: 'Si elle peut se faire réclamer par son mari? A dit qu'elle préfère aller en prison que de se faire réclamer de son mari . . .' (ibid. 11 vendémiaire an IV). *Marie-Françoise Heno*, '12 ans, native de Boulogne, demeurant chez son père, porteur d'eau à la Petite Pologne'; she had been thrown out by her father two months before: 'Elle a vécu comme elle a pu d'un tas de ramassés et qu'elle a toujours couché dans les rues: si elle veut qu'on envoye chercher ses père et mère, a dit qu'elle le veut bien . . .' (ibid. 29 vendémiaire an IV). She, clearly, had had enough of the life of the street. See also: '. . . Le C. Michel Bureau, charpentier & concierge de la pompe Notre-Dame . . . [qui] nous a dit que vers les 4 heures il a vu un enfant avec un bonnet de coton blanc sur la tête descendre dans la pompe, qu'il a demandé à coucher. . . . pourquoi? . . . que cet enfant lui a dit que son père l'avait jeté à la porte avec sa soeur, que le comparant lui a dit . . . qu'il allait le reconduire chez son papa, que l'enfant lui a dit qu'il aimait mieux aller se noyer que d'aller chez son papa parce que son papa lui avait dit qu'il lui donnerait cent coups de bâton . . . que son papa était tellement méchant qu'il avait jeté dans l'eau sa petite soeur de 2 mois que sa mère nourrissait. . . .' Brought before the *commissaire de police* of the Section du Muséum, 'cet enfant . . . lui a dit qu'elle était fille et que c'était son papa qui l'avait toujours laissée s'habiller en garçon, et que son papa lui avait donné un assignat de mille livres en le mettant à la porte. . . . elle a dit se nommer *Marguerite Manon Bourdet*, âgée de 13 ans et ½, native de Paris, demeurant à la place du Chevalier du Guet. . . . son père . . . est tailleur . . . qu'elle n'a qu'une belle-mère. . . . à elle demandé où elle veut que nous la conduisions, a dit où nous voudrons, pourvu que ce ne soit pas chez son père. . . .' The child was then sent before the *juge de paix* of this riverside Section (ibid. 7 nivôse an IV). '. . . Les citoyennes Adélaïde Victoire Carpentier et Alexandrine

Marie Noël Carpentier, ses belles soeurs, demeurant ordinairement à Vaucresson . . . sont arrivées ce soir chez lui [le commissaire de police de la
Division de la Butte-des-Moulins] en lui disant que leur soeur *Marie
Charlotte Eléonore* étoit partie ce matin de la maison paternelle, que n'étant
âgée que de 15 ans et ½ au plus . . . et d'après les lettres qui lui ont été adres-
sées par le C. Jadin, marchand bonnetier, rue des Bons Enfans . . . elles
présument que ce dernier l'a retirée chez lui pour en abuser et profiter de
son jeune âge. . . .' Jadin had in fact acted honourably, finding the girl a
room with a laundrywoman until he had had time to write to her family.
Asked why she had left home, Eléonore replied: 'parce qu'elle ne s'y plaisait
pas à cause des mauvais traitemens qu'elle recevait de tems en tems de la
part de sa belle-mère. . . .' (ibid. A/A 95, 16 frimaire an III). *Ibert*, son of a
public letter-writer from Marly, aged 13 'est parti depuis 2 jours parce que
son père voulait le frapper . . .' (ibid. A/A 98, s.d. an III). '*Prot Lafrance*,
âgé de 8 ans, natif de Moulins, ne faisant rien, n'ayant point de domicile
depuis bien longtems . . . qu'il n'a ni père ni mère, qu'il demande l'aumône
pour vivre et qu'il couche tantôt dans la rue, tantôt dans le corps de garde
. . .' Later he was to state: 'n'ayant pas de père et n'ayant pas voulu dire où
demeuroit sa mère . . .' (ibid. 18 brumaire an IV). Finally: '*Marie Anne
Bertet*, âgée de 16 ans, native de Paris, y ayant ses père et mère au Gros
Caillou, rue Dominique No. 195 . . . il y avait environ un mois qu'elle
avait quitté ses parens qui la maltraitaient et qui n'avaient pas le moyen de
lui donner son nécessaire, et que depuis cette époque elle a fait le métier . . .'
(ibid. A/A 99, 5 germinal an IV).

(O) A.N. F7 4782 (séance du comité de surveillance de Fresnes, du 21 germinal an II): '. . . Un membre a dit qu'il avait aperçu, le lendemain du jugement d'Hébert et de ses complices plusieurs mendians valides inconnus qui
s'étaient présentés dans cette commune et qui y ont mendié d'un air insolent,
qu'avant cette époque il s'était écoulé plusieurs semaines sans qu'il en parût
aucun, qu'il semblerait que ces individus ont fui la surveillance des autorités
constituées de Paris, qu'il pourrait se faire qu'ils fûssent entrés dans le complot, et que, le voyant manqué, ils se soient soustraits à la recherche . . . il
propose . . . que chaque membre du comité sera tenu de surveiller les mendians qui se présenteront dans cette commune. . . .' A stricter control should
be made on passports, valid beggars must show their papers. The reaction
of the Committee of this village is entirely characteristic. When in doubt,
blame the beggars. Faced with a political crisis in Paris, close the ranks against
strangers, especially poor ones unable to justify the means of their existence.
Fresnes in any case, was too near Bicêtre for its inhabitants to be easily reassured. Almost exactly a year later, a few days before the *journées de germinal*, we encounter a similar propensity to keep a wary eye out for valid
beggars, in times of political crisis, this time on the part of the Paris authorities, the *commissaire de police* of the Section de la Butte des Moulins reporting,

on 8 Germinal year III: '. . . L'agent national . . . vient de nous informer que les mendians reparaissent depuis quelques jours . . .' (A.P.P. A/A 96). Perhaps this is why the revolutionary authorities became so obsessed with the recurrence of political crises in the *Spring*; for it did not need any great detective skill to assume that beggars would appear once more in force and in the open, with the return of sunshine and warmth. They would be as much part of spring as the blossom and love. During the winter, crouching in cellars or in doorways, they would have been less visible.

(P) Nothing good could be expected of an *habitant de garni*. See, for instance, A.N. F7 4627 d 1 (Buisson). Étienne Buisson had been elected captain in the company of the Paris Revolutionary Army of the Section de la Réunion. He is denounced to the Revolutionary Committee, by the *commissaire de police*, Martin, in the following very revealing terms: '. . . Il nous a dit que ledit Buisson était incapable de posséder aucun grade . . . qu'[il] était un homme qui n'avait rien fait pour la Révolution, qu'il y avait tout au plus 3 mois qu'il avait une carte de citoyen, que bien qu'il soit garçon chapelier, il n'a pas depuis 6 mois travaillé de son état un mois de suite parce qu'aucun fabricant ne veut lui confier aucune marchandise, attendu son inconduite, qu'en conséquent il ne peut produire aucun moyen de subsistance assuré qu'il loge et a toujours logé en chambre garnie, et qu'il n'a aucun domicile fixe et ne présente aucune responsabilité pour occuper une place, que d'ailleurs ledit Buisson a été amené devant le déclarant comme soupçonné d'un vol de chapeaux dont il ne s'est pas parfaitement lavé. . . .' The Revolution had not been made for the Buissons of this world. Nor could such a man ever be allowed into the hallowed and virtuous precincts of *la sans-culotterie*.

The *commissaire de police* of the Section de la Butte-des-Moulins would be equally suspicious of the *habitants de garnis*, for there were 155 *maisons garnies* in his Section (A.P.P. A/A 96, 24 ventôse an III). There is much more to be learnt about the lives of these disinherited non-citizens in other reports of the *commissaires*: 'Les C. Pierre Lecointre, Jacques Guy, Jean Laurent Legrand, tous 3 couvreurs, et François Youf, militaire invalide, tous 4 demeurant ensemble dans une même chambre, rue Jean-de l'Epine, No 9' (A.P.P. 61, Muséum, 13 prairial an III). '. . . Le C. François Fontaine . . . demeurant rue de la Tannerie, No 12 . . . et 7 autres de ses camarades couchant ensemble dans une même chambre. . . .' There were in fact nine people living in this room (A.P.P. A/A 61, 20 prairial an III). '. . . Dans ladite chambre y avons remarqué 6 lits, qui sont loués à différents ouvriers, au bas d'un des lits un cadavre de sexe masculin nu en chemise . . .' (ibid. 24 messidor an III). It was only by dying that the poor man, a fifty-eight year old *journalier* from Coutances, would ever have come to the attention of the authorities.

We can glimpse briefly in these sad reports a closely-knit, secret masculine world, of single men, driven into co-habitation by poverty, constantly exposed to theft, often at the hands of one of their sleeping companions, yet still clinging together, strangers in the city, and spending their few hours of leisure in bouts of frantic drinking that would often end in violent fights and punch-ups and even in accidents resulting in death. The *commissaire* of the Section du Muséum is informed, on 9–10 Floréal year III [28–9 April 1795] that a man has just been thrown from the floor of a lodging-house, 4, rue de la Vieille Lanterne, through a window, landing in the courtyard where an *officier de santé* declares him to be dead. The victim is André Vélu, *oiseleur*. The man who threw him down is Jean-Baptiste Gessiont, 33, a Parisian-born *tabletier*. He is still completely drunk when questioned by the *commissaire* and is unable to recall the cause of their quarrel. They had been drinking all day, which, as a *décadi*, was a holiday. Gessiont when a little soberer, was to state that they had up till then lived in harmony, sharing everything that they possessed. He thought that they may have had an altercation on the subject of who had paid for most of the drink, on reaching the landing of their room. Revolutionary feast days could be as dangerous as religious ones, in this world of the very poor.

See also A.P.P. A/A 98 (commissaire de police de la Section de la Butte-des-Moulins, à la Commission administrative, 21 thermidor an III): '*Félix Houlier*, garçon marchand de vin, natif d'Angervilliers (Calvados), logeant avec un autre garçon marchand de vin, tombé par la fenêtre de la cour à 5 heures du matin, après avoir passé une partie de la nuit à boire avec ses camarades chez un traiteur des Champs-Elysées.' The date, 8 August 1795, was, predictably, a Saturday.

(Q) Three years later, at the time of the formation of the nine Belgian Departments, we hear of similar gatherings in the canton of Fontaine-l'Évêque (Jemappes). On 19 Messidor year V [7 July 1797] the *administration munici-pale* of this canton wrote to the Directory: '. . . il résulte que le peuple dud. canton se voit privé des secours et de la consolation de la religion dont ils professent, se plaint amèrement et abandonne en foule ses foyers les jours des dimanches et des fêtes pour aller entendre la messe en d'autres lieux et cantons quelquefois fort éloignés, attendu cette privation ainsi que ce déplacement occasionnent des plaintes et des murmures, troublent la tranquillité publique qui régnoit dans ce même canton et sont de nature à la troubler davantage encore par une plus longue continuation . . .' (A.N. BB 18 400, Justice, Jemappes, administration municipale du canton de Fontaine-l'Évêque, au Directoire, 19 messidor an V).

See also A.N. BB 18 619 (Ourthe, administration centrale du département de l'Ourthe, au Ministre de la Police générale, 28 nivôse an V): 'Dans le mois de floréal de l'an IV l'administration municipale du canton de Hodimont dé-fendit au curé de Petit Rechain de faire une procession qui avait lieu tous les ans le mardi de la Pentecôte, dans la vue d'éviter des rixes auxquelles elle donnoit lieu périodiquement. Ce curé ayant reclamé, nous approuvames l'arrêté de la municipalité . . . fondé sur celui du représentant . . . Giroust en date du 4 thermidor an III, qui interdit toutes les processions religieuses hors l'enceinte des temples. . . .'

There is a similar report from the Sambre-et-Meuse in July 1797: the commissaire attached to the court of Marche, Langrand (see below, p. 249), informs the Minister: '. . . Le curé de cette commune . . . s'est permis d'aller avant-hier 28 [messidor; Sunday 16 July 1797] en l'église des ci-devant Carmes . . . célébrer publiquement la fête du Carmel, avec deux autres ecclésiastiques, dont un curé de Roye, on y prêchoit, dit-on, *que l'on avait chassé de ce lieu les enfans d'Élie, mais qu'ils y rentreroient*, je ne suis pas certain de ce fait. . . .'

On 19 Prairial year VI [7 June 1798] a procession was held, followed by a mass, in Blasvel, canton de Willebroeck, near Antwerp, on the occasion of the *Fête-Dieu*. A week later, on 15 June, mass was celebrated in the parish church of Serick (A.N. BB 18 564, Deux-Nèthes).

(R) Such panic fears, especially on the part of women, were not, however, confined to the countryside. There is a very sad case of an over-zealous domestic servant from the Section de la Butte-des-Moulins (A.P.P. 95, commissaire de police, 4 frimaire an III). The *commissaire* reports that a girl had fallen into a courtyard, rue des Moulins: Jacques Geoffroy, *peintre-doreur* 'déclare que *Marie-Anne Lâche*, étoit sa fille de confiance depuis 3 jours, et que les deux premiers jours qu'elle a été chez lui, elle s'est levée longtems avant le jour et est venue sonner et frapper à sa porte pour demander ce qu'elle avait à faire et qu'il lui répondit qu'il falloit qu'elle se couchât, qu'il n'étoit pas tems de se lever, qu'il croit que cette fille avoit toujours peur de ne pas faire son devoir, car elle s'est levée toutes les nuits depuis qu'elle est chez lui, qu'elle étoit seule dans sa chambre. . . .' He thought that she must have fallen out of a window while sleep-walking, or that she had lost her balance while not fully awake. She was brought to the Hôtel-Dieu, semi-conscious and with terrible internal injuries. When questioned by the staff there, the girl could not remember what had happened. But what is clear in this lamentable episode is the poor girl's anxiety, as a newly-employed maid, an anxiety so insistent that she had got up each day, well before dawn, and had, furthermore, knocked up the master of the house, for fear of over-sleeping and of thus failing in her duties and being dismissed without a reference. The whole incident is a fearful commentary on the insecurity of the easily-replaced female domestic servant. It is a fear more permanent and more explicable than that of the unknown dangers of the rural night.

(S) There were civil dangers, too, in failing to give death the respect that was its traditional due. In a petition to the Thermidorian *comité de législation*, an inhabitant of Étampes, Sedillon, pointed out: 'Les cloches, en annonçant autrefois la pompe funèbre des défunts, prévenaient leurs créanciers, ou ceux ayant droit à leur succession, qu'elle était ouverte, et les officiers publics de veiller aux droits de tous. Aujourd'hui qu'il n'existe plus de cloches, les créanciers, les héritiers et les officiers publics . . . les ignorent: de là, spoliation . . .' (A.N. D III 279 (1) (54), Sedillon au Comité de Législation, 26 vendémiaire an III [17 October 1794]). A similar complaint was voiced by the Ministry of the Interior, on the subject of the famous *maison de santé* of Dubuisson, which, like so many other undesirable institutions, was situated on the edge of Paris, near the barrière de Montreuil, in the Section of the same name. During the Terror, Dubuisson had taken in a number of well-to-do suspects, bankers, and noblemen, on the pretext that they had been suffering from generally unspecified illnesses, thus, on many occasions, saving them from the attentions of Fouquier-Tinville. In the year IV, the ingenious doctor is reported as failing to inform the municipal authorities of the number of deaths in his establishment, in order to retain, for the use of himself, his family, and the surviving inmates, a larger meat ration (A.N. F11 1178, 9 Pluviôse year IV [29 January 1796]). This is not the last one hears of the establishment, for it was from here that Malet, at the time under treatment, walked out, in December 1812, to stage his second conspiracy. There was a danger, too, so it was felt, in the anonymity of death, as it applied to the very poor, the very old, the disinherited. A *commissaire de police* of a Paris Section reports on the death of a seventy-five year-old, found dead in his room in a lodging-house: 'sur les noms, âge et lieu de naissance dudit *Perpignan*, il nous a dit que ce nom était celui de son pays, qu'il ignorait son véritable nom. . . .' (A.P.P. A/A 96, 2 pluviôse an III [21 January 1795]).

(T) On 2 Germinal [22 March], that is at the height of the political crisis, the Directoire du District de Franciade was to report severely on the 'fanaticism' of several more rural *communes* to the north and north-east of Paris. Writing to the Committee of General Security, the Directoire states: '. . . Les communes de *Romainville* et de *Noisy-le-Sec* . . . sont celles qui ont conservé le culte le plus longtems. La présence des prêtres dans ces communes ayant paru peu propre à calmer les esprits. . . . le C. Crassous . . . m'a donné ordre le 6 [ventôse, 24 February] de faire arrêter les ecclesiastiques. . . . j'ai fait arrêter le C. Maurel, ex-vicaire de Noisy-le-Sec, et le nommé Moulin, curé de Romainville. . . .' The same official writes about the disturbances that had just taken place in Aubervilliers: '. . . Je vous ai rendu compte . . . de la conduite scandaleuse tenue par plusieurs citoyens dans l'assemblée populaire d'Aubervilliers, des propos injurieux adressés à quelques membres qui avaient voulu chanter des hymnes patriotiques et des pierres même qui leur avaient été jetées, les auteurs n'ont pu être reconnus. . . .'

Earlier, the *comité révolutionnaire* of the Section de l'Homme Armé had written to the comité de surveillance du Département, 15 Nivôse year II [4 January 1794], to denounce the village of Nogent-sur-Marne, to the east of Paris: '. . . Un fait que vous aurez sans doute peine à croire . . . c'est qu'*aux portes de Paris* [and this somehow made it worse] c'est-à-dire à deux lieues, dans la commune de Nogent-sur-Marne, il existe encore, au mépris de la loi, de la Raison, et du besoin urgent que nous avons de canons, 4 cloches bien sonnantes de ladite commune servant à appeler journellement, non seulement les fanatiques de l'endroit, mais encore ceux de toutes les communes circonvoisines, tous lesquels sont guidés dans leurs principes outrés du fanatisme, par le curé de ladite commune de Nogent, lequel paraît tellement irascible qu'il dit ouvertement qu'il ne quittera son poste que lorsqu'on l'y contraindra avec le canon, sentiment qu'il paroit avoir si bien insinué dans l'esprit de la majeure partie des habitans de ce canton qu'ils s'y expriment de même . . .' (A.N. F7 4783, Nogent-sur-Marne).

(U) See also A.D. Oise Grande Registre du comité de surveillance de Chaumont, s.d. nivôse an III. A member of the Committee had been sent to the village of Villeneuve-les-Sablons, on the road from Méru to Chaumont, on 3 Nivôse year II [23 December 1793] to remove the bells. His arrival provoked a minor riot and he was threatened with a beating-up by a number of the villagers. An inhabitant, questioned by the Committee, stated: '. . . que les femmes seulement l'ont menacé de lui couper la queue. . . . [il] convient avoir reproché au commissaire d'avoir quitté sa cure et son état, d'être venu les troubler dans un jour aussi saint que le jour de Noël [which in fact fell this year on 5 Nivôse] que cela était un scandale, que le nommé Denis Prieur, tailleur d'habits, a tenu le même langage, ainsi que Laruelle, charpentier, Simon Burel, marchand de peaux de lapin. . . .' The Committee, it would seem, had been doubly imprudent—or perhaps it had acted deliberately—in thus dispatching one of its members so near Christmas, and in choosing for the purpose a man who was the object of additional odium as an ex-priest.

The problem was not confined to the special conditions imposed by the year II. It persisted indeed right up to the Concordat. There is a similar report, concerning Christmas Day 1795, from the Aisne. On 4 Nivôse year IV, the *commissaire près le tribunal* of Saint-Quentin wrote to the Minister of Justice: 'Le projet de sonner la cloche a été mise à exécution hier [that is, on Christmas Eve] 3 heures précises . . . au moment où les ministres du culte catholique allaient chanter les premiers vêpres de Noël. . . . il y avait dans le clocher un rassemblement considérable de femmes et d'enfans qui, pour y parvenir, avaient brisé une forte porte de chêne qui en fermait l'entrée . . .' (A.N. BB 18 92, Aisne).

Again, writing to the same official on 29 Fructidor year VII [15 September 1799] the *juge de paix* of a small village in the Ardennes (Sévigny-la-Forêt, near Rocroi, and close to the old border) informed him: 'le 28 thermidor dernier [15 August 1799], jour anciennement férié de l'Assomption, le garde-champêtre de la commune de Sévigny fit un rapport contre différens individus qui jouaient au jeu de fer ce jour-là, en vue des lieux et voies publics . . .' (A.N. BB 18 130, Justice, Ardennes).

(V) A.D. Seine D 4AZ 590 (Société populaire de Belleville, brouillon d'un discours, s.d.): 'Mayence, Condé, Valenciennes, qui devoient être le tombeau des armées combinées sont, par les infâmes menées d'un Général ci-devant noble [Custine] au pouvoir de nos féroces ennemis! des armées nombreuses, intrépides, les vainqueurs de Jemappes, de Worms, de Spire, ont été les témoins immobiles de revers si funestes. Sous le prétexte si souvent profané d'une aveugle obéissance, d'une sévère discipline, la volonté d'un seul, sa trahison, ont enchaîné le courage de nos braves frères d'armées! Sa tête va rouler sur l'échafaud—mais tout son sang vaut-il une goutte de celui qu'il faudra verser pour réparer sa perfidie?—La trahison seule, dès le commencement de la guerre, a fait la ressource et le succès de nos ennemis; en vain, ne consultant que son coeur généreux, le français, trop longtems, a pu croire au patriotisme que singeoient ces infâmes étrangers, ces nobles si profondément scélérats: tristes jouets de cette caste artificieuse, des républicains ont cru devoir remettre le soin de leur salut, de leur gloire, à ces monstres doublés d'orgueil et de bassesses! que de sang a coûté cette malheureuse confiance! ... plus d'étrangers, plus de traîtres, plus de nobles, à la tête de nos armées ... le peuple est une pépinière de héros, dans six cent mille braves sans-culottes qui sont sur nos frontières, nous trouverons des chefs. ...'

(W) Jacques-Denis Nutin or Noutin, *chirurgien*, of Bonnelles, in the District de Dourdan, is described, in a document dated Pluviôse year II (Jan.–Feb. 1794], as 'homme profondément scélérat, violent, emporté, vindicatif' (A.D. Seine-et-Oise L 11m Dourdan 30, listes des membres des sociétés populaires du District de Dourdan.) The description has a double significance, for in the autumn and winter of 1793 and the spring of 1794, Nutin seems to have been a typical 'ultra-revolutionary' and local wild man. He was a militant member of the *société de la Vertu-Sociale*, the more extreme of the two rival Versailles clubs and one that was linked with the Cordeliers. In the spring of 1794, he acted as *apôtre civique* of this club in the villages of the District of Versailles. He had also been employed by the Committee of General Security on various repressive missions, this time in the District de Dourdan, in the course of the winter of 1793. As an 'ultra' and as an active 'dechristian-iser', he was no doubt the sort of person to have gained the confidence of the more actively atheistic members of the police committee. In Ventôse year II [March 1794], he seems to have come under suspicion, and the *société de la Vertu-Sociale*, which had been the principal vehicle of his ambitions in Versailles, was dissolved, apparently under pressure from Crassous, the *Représentant-en-mission*. Learning of the dissolution of his favourite club, he wrote, angrily, to the *comité de surveillance*: 'Notre club est détruit ... je m'en fous; je me dédommage en allant dans les villages en établir; je m'amuse avec les paysans qui sont enchantés de m'avoir. Je mets les foutus gueux de fermiers à l'ordre, ainsi que les vignerons. ... Mon règne durera longtemps parce que d'abord je suis sans-culotte. ...' A prophecy which, as we shall see, was doubly foolish. Like many 'ultras' who had operated on the periphery during the Terror, Nutin seems to have taken refuge in Paris during the Thermidorian Reaction. He was once more denounced by the authorities of Dourdan and of Bonnelles and on 13 Messidor year III [1 July 1795] he was arrested. He was described at the time as *médicin accoucheur* and was stated to be living in the Section des Piques. He was released on the orders of the Committee of General Security on 27 Vendémiaire year IV [19 October 1795]. Although, then, he had lasted rather longer than the so-called *sans-culottes*, his reign was in fact not to be very long. On 12 Ventôse year XII [3 March 1804] he murdered his sister-in-law, *la femme* Gruau, in Bonnelles. Tried and convicted by the Versailles court, he was guillotined on a public square of Montreuil on 12 Thermidor [31 July 1804]. He thus ended publicly in a *commune* in which he had enjoyed such a public rôle in the course of the Terror. (A.N. F7 4774 58 Noutin; and my *Armées révolutionnaires*, p. 344(163)).

Chapter 5

(A) There might be other advantages too for French citizens prepared to follow in the wake of the armies, and take up posts of a semi-military nature, or in the newly formed civil administrations in the former Austrian Netherlands. As a result of the reorganisation of the courts, and the introduction of the *Codes* and of the French judicial system, it seems likely that the French authorities were unwilling to rely entirely on the co-operation of Belgian law-officers, judges, and public prosecutors. It is often impossible to tell whether a given *directeur du jury d'accusation*, or a *commissaire* attached to a criminal court is in fact French or Belgian, though it is likely that more Belgians were used in the Flemish Departments than in the Walloon ones. We know, for instance, that Baelde was a Fleming, but the public prosecutor of the Antwerp court has a French name (Carré). The need to find officials who were both reliable and loyal to the Directory no doubt offered chances of promotion, or of entirely new careers, to men with no, or little, previous experience of the courts. There is an interesting, and no doubt, characteristic example of such a change of direction in a professional career as a result of the circumstances of revolution and conquest that comes from the Sambre-et-Meuse (Namur). Forwarding to the Minister his *curriculum vitae*, in order to establish his claims to promotion, the *commissaire du Directoire près le tribunal de Marche* gives the following details of his career up to Messidor year V [June–July 1797]:

'*Tableau des différentes places auxquelles le C. Lengrand,
âgé de 39 ans, a été pourvu pendant la Révolution.*

8 octobre 1789: Professeur de Philosophie, Salon (Bouches-du-Rhône), jusqu'au *1er février 1791.*

1er février 1791: secrétaire du canton, Robion [Lengrand places it in the Bouches-du-Rhône, but at the present day it is in the neighbouring Vaucluse] jusqu'au *1er octobre de l'an 1er* [1792].

7 octobre de l'an 1er [*1792*]*:* Principal du Collège de Lille (Bouches-du-Rhône) [I have been unable to identify this commune] jusqu'en *juin 1793*.

12 juin 1793: incarcéré par les ennemis de la Révolution, à la Tour du Bout, à Marseille, 3 mois. Pendant ce tems on a pillé son domicile.

30 août 1793: commissaire du général Carteaux, chef de bataillon, district de Salon, 2 mois, blessé en fonctions.

4 octobre 1793: juge de paix, Lançon (-de-Provence), jusqu'au *2 pluviôse* (*an II*) [21 January 1794]. Démission donnée pour raison de santé.

12 pluviôse (*an II*) [31 January 1794]: secrétaire-général au district de Salon jusqu'au *2 germinal* (*an II*) [22 March 1794]. Appellé à Paris.

1er prairial (*an II*) [20 May 1794]: employé à la commission de la rédaction des lois à la Convention nationale, Paris, trois mois, quitté pour mettre ordre à ses affaires à Valenciennes.

14 fructidor (*an II*) [31 August 1794]: juge militaire: Condé, Maubeuge, Lille, Tournai, & toute la Weste-Flandre, jusqu'au *7 nivôse an III* [27 December 1794].

7 nivôse (*an III*)*:* administrateur de l'arrondissement du Hainaut [the future Jemappes], Mons, 7 mois, mis en réquisition.

7 vendémiaire (*an IV*) [28 September 1795]: juge du tribunal civil de Sambre-et-Meuse, Namur, 6 semaines.

15 nivôse (*an IV*) [4 January 1796]: président du tribunal criminel de Sambre-et-Meuse, Namur, 9 mois.

2 thermidor (*an IV*) [20 July 1796]: confirmé juge civil par le Directoire à Namur, 4 mois.

6 thermidor (*an IV*)*:* Président de la 2me section du tribunal de Namur, 2 mois.

1er brumaire (*an V*) [22 October 1796]: directeur du jury et président de la police correctionnelle à Marche, 6 mois.

12 floréal (*an V*) [1 May 1797]: commissaire du Directoire près le tribunal correctionnel de Marche. En exercice' (A.N. BB 18 793, Justice, Sambre-et-Meuse, s.d. messidor an V).

Lengrand added a comment for the attention of the Minister: that his *états de service* and his republicanism made a strong case for his promotion, though he did not suggest that he wished to return to France. He did not in fact gain promotion, or only promotion on a very small scale, for two years later, in Prairial year VII [June 1799] we find him occupying the relatively unexalted post of *commissaire du Directoire près le tribunal correctionnel de l'arrondissement de Turnhout*, in the Flemish Department of the Deux-Nèthes (A.N. BB 18 654, Justice, Deux-Nèthes).

Lengrand's career was unusual in some respects, especially in his somewhat crablike progress from important posts to less important ones. Yet it must illustrate too the pattern of many careers arising out of the various circumstances of the Revolution. In 1789, he was 31, a teacher, presumably a *doctrinaire*, if not a priest, in Salon. After an incursion into public administration, he returned to teaching, gaining promotion (it must be presumed that if he were a priest or a monk, he must also have been a juror, to have been rewarded with a post of *Principal*) till June 1793. He clearly took the republican side at the time of the federalist crisis of June 1793, so that he was arrested, and imprisoned in Marseille till Carteaux had recaptured the city. He was then a natural candidate for a reward in the republican service, but still in the Bouches-du-Rhône. In the spring of 1794, at the very time of the great political crisis of Ventôse-Germinal came *la montée à Paris*, and indeed a *montée* in the most favourable circumstances then possible, in the very citadel of Jacobin and centralist orthodoxy, in the bureaucracy of the Convention. Like no doubt many more orthodox bureaucrats, he was then rewarded with an appointment as a roving military judge in the wake of the armies, enjoying powers over a very wide area. Even in Mons, he still occupied a very important post in the temporary hierarchy set up before the formation of the Belgian Departments. But once these had been formed, his career seems to have gone into an inexplicable decline. His three posts in Namur are in declining order of importance. He is then shunted off to the comparatively unimportant town of Marche, but one in which there had been a number of pro-Christian riots (see above, p. 245). Two years later, we find him equally modestly placed, in the *arrondissement* of Turnhout, in a Flemish-speaking, and also very anti-French area. His relative lack of promotion may have been due to ill-health; equally, he may have shown especial ability in repression at a local level, always the most delicate area of government under the Directory. For a *commissaire* attached to a *tribunal civil* or *correctionnel* in a *chef-lieu d'arrondissement* would be in more direct contact with the local population then the public prosecutor of a court at the level of a Department. The posts he occupied successively in Marche and in Turnhout were ones that were particularly exposed to the vengeance either of political murder gangs, or of bandits, or of both. Unfortunately, we lose sight of him after the first ten years of the revolutionary period. It seems likely that, having served in the Belgian Provinces for six years, in four different Departments, he would have been retained there under the Empire, returning to France, no doubt disgruntled and embittered, in 1814, aged 56. Perhaps he then retired to the Midi, though, as a former terrorist, he would have been ill-advised to have shown himself anywhere in the neighbourhood of Salon. Or perhaps he sought anonymity in Paris, where he had only spent five and a half months under the Terror.

(B) See A.N. BB 18 401 (Justice, Jemappes, commissaire près le tribunal de Mons, au Ministre, 8 germinal an VI [28 March 1798]): 'Les nommés *Nicolas*

Pierre et *Valentine Pierre*, frère et soeur, furent condamnés à la peine de mort par le tribunal criminel de ce département . . . comme auteurs de l'assassinat commis sur la personne de leur père commun. Ces condamnés se sont pourvus en cassation, leur requête a été rejettée.

J'ai réquis, avant d'en venir à l'exécution, que *Valentine Pierre*, âgée de 17 ans, fût visitée par les gens de l'art qui déclareroient si cette fille étoit enceinte ou non. Leur art ne leur a indiqué aucuns signes de grossesse; mais *Valentine Pierre* leur a déclaré qu'il pourroit se faire qu'elle fût enceinte. . . . En cet état je n'ai pas cru devoir ordonner l'exécution de cette fille. Son frère a subi ce matin la peine de mort. . . .' The Minister's reply was: 'Vous avez agi comme vous le devriez, Citoyen, en faisant suspendre l'exécution de *Valentine Pierre* jusqu'au moment où les officiers de santé auront prononcé positivement sur son état. Mais vous devez prendre toutes les mesures nécessaires pour prévenir l'évasion de cette femme ou sa cohabitation avec un individu de sexe différent. . . .'

(C) See also BB 18 793 (Justice, Sambre-et-Meuse, interrogatoire devant le directeur du jury du tribunal de Namur, 7 germinal an V [27 March 1797]): '. . . à lui demandé à quelle fin il s'était masqué, à répondu pour rire et faire les sots . . . ajoutant que le dimanche Létarc [*sic*] [Sunday 26 March] étant pour ce pays un jour de réjouissance il avait cru pouvoir se livrer à la joie, surtout sa masquarade, n'ayant point eu lieu dans la ville, mais au faubourg. A lui demandé s'il est rentré masqué dans la ville et pourquoi il a été saisi par la garde? A répondu négativement. . . .' The first man questioned is a tanner of 22. Another accused, a cutler of 25, 'a répondu qu'il était couvert de haillons qui ne suffisaient pas pour le déguiser, à lui demandé à quelle fin il s'était déguisé, a répondu pour s'amuser et tourmenter en badinant ses soeurs, sa mère, et ses amis . . . que l'envie de se déguiser lui avait pris en voyant ses amis le faire . . . point d'autre projets que celui de rire et surtout au Letarc, jour de divertissement dans les familles. . . .' A further report states: 'Le rassemblement dont il s'agit a eu lieu le 6 germinal dernier au faubourg de la Plante près de cette ville [Namur] vers les 3 h. de l'après-midi à l'effet de s'y divertir ainsi qu'il a toujours été d'usage dans cette commune tous les ans le jour de létarc . . . Ces jeunes gens, habitués à se divertir dans ce genre sous l'ancien régime un seul jour de l'année, ont cru en agir aujourd'hui avec la même liberté au moins. . . .'

(D) See, for a well-stated case for the military authorities, A.N. BB 18 284 (Justice, Dyle, Ministre de la Guerre, au Ministre de la Justice, 21 thermidor an IV [8 August 1796]): '. . . Il n'est pas inutile de vous observer que Alexandre, chargé de rassembler les denrées nécessaires à la subsistance de l'armée de Sambre-et-Meuse et à l'approvisionnement des places qui en dépendent et d'en faire opérer les versements dans les magasins militaires, a éprouvé de la part des administrateurs des départements réunis tous les obstacles que peut susciter la mauvaise volonté la plus marquée. Après avoir fait parler inutilement les besoins de l'armée, à cette époque réduite à la détresse la plus effrayante [it was the height of the *période de la soudure* in this part of northern Europe], il a été obligé de déployer l'appareil de la force, et ce n'est que par ce moyen qu'il s'est procuré des ressources qui existaient dans le pays, mais dont on avait cherché à lui dérober la connaissance.

Les approvisionnements formés, il a eu les mêmes difficultés à vaincre pour les moyens de transport, toutes les voitures qu'il a demandées lui ont été refusées, et comme il était urgent de faire verser sur tous les points de consommation des denrées que leur entassement dans les magasins de la Belgique exposait à une avarie prochaine, il a été obligé de faire enlever militairement les voitures dont on lui contestait la disposition.

Tout ce que cette mesure peut avoir de vexatoire retombe donc, mon cher collègue, sur les administrateurs qui ne m'ont fourni déjà que trop de preuves de leur indifférence pour les intérêts de la République. . . .' The Minister of War was perhaps being rather unfair, for, to authorities concerned above all to protect their *administrés* from the incessant demands of *commissaires ordonnateurs* like Alexandre, an experienced revolutionary militant from the faubourg Saint-Marceau who had played an important part in the development of 10 August 1792, and who was later to operate in Italy, and to preserve the population of Brussels and of the other large cities from the effects of the famine of 1795, the pressing needs of the French Army would not necessarily take first place. In such a situation, it was a matter of first come, first served. The military had the unique advantage of force; and this they might use effectively for short-term successes. But in the long run, such methods could only increase the hostility of both the local authorities and the civilian population.

(E) 'Informé que dans la commune de Suynaarde, canton de Nazareth . . . il se faisoit au cabaret dit *le Hochepot*, un rassemblement de brigands, ayant pour chef un déserteur autrichien, soutenus par les occupans du cabaret, j'ai chargé le commandant de la gendarmerie nationale de surveiller particulièrement le repaire et de tâcher d'arrêter le chef de bande que l'on m'avait assuré être toujours armé de 2 paires de pistolets à 2 coups. . . . il [le gendarme Dufay] est parvenu à découvrir par les occupeurs dud. cabaret que le déserteur autrichien, nommé de Liven, ci-devant recruteur du régiment de Claerfayt, étoit domicilié à Gand . . . . le mari et la femme du cabaret ont des liaisons avec des officiers autrichiens, prisonniers en France. . . . ils en facilitent l'évasion et correspondent avec eux . . . ' (A.N. BB 18 293, Justice, Escaut, le commissaire près le tribunal criminel de Gand, au Ministre, 29 pluviôse an V).

(F) See, for instance, A.N. BB 18 793 (administration centrale du département de Sambre-et-Meuse, au Ministre, 27 floréal an V [16 May 1797]): '. . . À Marche et à Laroche, quelques habitants, égarés par des fausses nouvelles, et persuadés que la ci-devant province de Luxembourg doit rentrer sous la domination de l'Empereur, se sont rassemblés et ont fait des réjouissances pour célébrer cet événement . . . .'

On 13 Floréal year V [Monday 2 May 1797] there had been a pro-Austrian riot in Namur itself. Two days later, a former judge from Namur writes to a friend in Paris: '. . . Rien n'égale l'audace des royalistes, ils patrouillent dans les rues tous les soirs et font retentir de leurs cris anti-républicains de *vivent les croates, vivent les Kaiserlicks, vive l'Empereur*. . . .'

On 17 Thermidor year VII [Sunday 4 August 1799] there is a similar report from one of the Belgian Flemish Departments, the Deux-Nèthes, concerning the town of Turnhout: 'Un rassemblement de 15 à 16 paysans vient d'avoir lieu dans le canton de Westerloo, 3 gendarmes ont été grièvement blessés, le brigadier a reçu un coup mortel, une affiche incendiaire vient d'être placardée en cette commune.' The French translation of the placard reads: '*Vive l'Empereur des Romains, Vive la Religion Catholique, Extermination des Républicains, mort aux conscrits qui marcheront sous les drapeaux des assassins français, Vive le prince Charles et le général Suvarov, Vive la municipalité*' (A.N. BB 18 564, commissaire près le tribunal correctionnel de Turnhout, au Ministre, 17 thermidor an VII).

The French authorities showed even more concern about what had happened, in Messidor [June] of the same year, in the commune of Boom, an inhabitant of which had painted the tail of his dog, blue, white, and red: '. . . Toutefois, l'on ne peut se dissimuler que l'action de peindre la queue d'un chien aux trois couleurs ne soit une dérision insultante, faite pour jeter du ridicule sur les couleurs nationales . . .' (Carré, accusateur public du tribunal des Deux-Nèthes, à Vanderherreweghe, juge de paix du canton de Boom, 12 messidor an VII).

The former *Représentant en mission* Piorry, an old hand at repression, refers with disgust, in Germinal year VI [March 1799] to the inhabitants of Antwerp and its neighbouring *communes*: '. . . Comment se fait-il qu'Anvers et ses environs soient le receptacle de toute *l'angolmanie*, et que tous les secrets du gouvernement se trouvent éventés ou trahis. . . ?' (ibid. BB 18 564). Finally, in a report on the situation of the Deux-Nèthes, dated February 1798, an unsigned informer of the Minister complains: 'Il est temps qu'un exemple de sévérité apprenne enfin à une poignée d'Anversois qu'ils ne feront pas la loi au Gouvernement français, comme ils se vantent de l'avoir fait à leur ci-devant Empereur. Je demande encore que jamais on ne laisse la ville d'Anvers sans garnison . . .' (ibid. BB 18 564). This was probably a more accurate assessment of the attitudes of the Belgians towards their foreign rulers, both old and new, than those suggesting that they retained an indelible attachment to the Emperor. It might be all right to shout *Vive l'Empereur* in 1798 and 1799: this would be with the benefit of hindsight, and after the experience of four or five years of French rule. The inhabitants of Antwerp had long been noted for their independence, as well as for their drunkenness, and their propensity to brawl. Indeed, for those who have experienced the *Bloed Straat*, and more generally, the quarter of the *Steyn*, it might be said that nothing much has since changed.

(G) The situation was apparently equally deplorable in the neighbouring Ourthe. On 15 Brumaire year V [5 November 1796] the *commissaire* attached to the Liége tribunal writes to the Minister: '. . . il en résulte que le commissaire de St. Vith n'a nul moyen de s'opposer aux entreprises des contrebandiers, il n'existe dans nos départements ni gendarmerie, ni garde nationale, et les citoyens de St. Vith et des cantons voisins sont tous désarmés parce que ci-devant ils faisaient partie de la province de Luxembourg, et pour comble de malheur aucun directeur de jury n'est à son poste, parce que le traitement des juges est arriéré de 6 à 7 mois. . . . chaque jour des vols aussi horribles qu'affreux se commettent à main armée aux portes de Liége et font trembler tous les honnêtes citoyens . . .' (A.N. BB 18 619, Ourthe).

We hear the same dismal reports from a town on the highroad from Paris to Brussels. On 23 Frimaire year IV [14 December 1795] the president of the Soissons court informs the Minister: 'Les évasions de prisons se renouvellent, les assassinats, surtout les vols, se multiplient d'une manière effrayante, tandis que les moyens de surveillance sont presque nuls. Il n'existe à Soissons qu'une seule brigade de gendarmerie . . .' (A.N. BB 18 92, Justice, Aisne).

(H) A.N. BB 18 582 (Justice, Nord). Baret, the highly intelligent president of the Bruges court, in a letter to the Minister dated 13 Nivôse year V [2 January 1797] explains:
'. . . J'ai eu occasion de suivre ces ramifications [de la bande] lorsqu'avant la division des départements j'étais seul accusateur public dans toute la Belgique. Leur fort était toujours dans le département de la Lys, frontière de la Hollande, de l'ancienne France, ayant 16 à 18 lieues de côtes, tous endroits fameux pour la contrebande, pays coupé en tous les sens de canaux et de bois. . . .'
'. . . La bande de Salambier et complices est une bande française, elle a deux rendez-vous, l'un du côté de Lille et de Courtrai, l'autre près de Rouen. Poursuivi pour des faits majeurs dans les départements réunis, ils vont s'établir dans le département de la Seine-Inférieure, et s'ils en sont chassés, ils refluent de nos côtes.
'Je tiens quelques individus d'une autre bande, c'est une bande flamande qui s'étend du Luxembourg, par la forêt de Soignies jusques près de Courtrai, et, suivant les occasions, les deux bandes se donnent la main. . . . leur chef connu sous le nom de *Swaert Pier*, ou le *Noir Pierre*, s'étoit [?] 3 fois de la justice du ci-devant Franc de Bruges. . . .'

(I) Much the same was happening in the winter of 1796 in the neighbouring

Department of the Ourthe. The president of the Liége court writes to the Minister, 1 Frimaire year V [21 November 1796]: 'Dans la nuit du 21 au 22 brumaire dr. un prisonnier [Gérard Enout] s'est évadé de la maison d'arrêt de Verviers. Ce prisonnier est renommé comme un des plus grand brigands qui désolent notre département. Déjà, et peu avant, il s'était évadé des mêmes prisons de Verviers, et un hasard favorable l'avait fait reprendre. . . . Seroit-il donc possible que ces échappés des prisons formâssent cette compagnie de voleurs qui de tems à autre vont en nombre et en armes dans les maisons de campagne, enchaînent les propriétaires et leur monde, volent et pillent tout ce qui tombe sous leur main? Nous avons dans notre département l'ex-emple de plusieurs de ces vols, et les auteurs ont pour eux une organisation complète, des factionnaires sont posés, des veilleurs sont en avant, il y a un mot d'ordre, le *Capitaine* est obéi . . .' (A.N. BB 18 619, Ourthe).

(J) A report from a French official in Antwerp dated 18 Prairial year V [6 June 1797] confirms the fact that there was persistent smuggling in the frontier area: 'La commune d'*Eckren*, située à environ deux lieues du terri-toire hollandais, est depuis longtems l'entrepôt des marchandises prohibées, ou sujettes aux droits . . . par des attroupements tellement nombreux qu'en dernier lieu ils étaient composés de 5 à 600 hommes, l'entrepôt servait à alimenter le commerce de contrebande qui se fait à Anvers à la faveur d'ex-péditions que délivrent les officiers municipaux d'Eckren pour cette destina-tion, et c'est ainsi que sur cette frontière des autorités constituées protègent les abus, les désordres étant devenus très alarmans . . . dans la nuit du 8 au 9 de ce mois . . . [Saturday–Sunday 27–8 May 1797] . . . à 2 h du matin, les préposés ont aperçu une bande innombrable de fraudeurs, chargée de ballots, et qui dirigeait la route sur Eckren . . . ils ont abandonné sur les lieux 28 ballots de sucre et de café . . .' (A.N. BB 18 563, Deux-Nèthes). A report, this time from Turnhout, and concerning the village of Berse, dated 18 Vendémiaire year VI [9 October 1797] notes: '. . . la nuit du 15 au 16 [Friday to Saturday] plus de 400 fraudeurs ont été aperçus par les employés. . . .'

On 25 Messidor year VI [13 July 1798], Piorry, a former member of the Convention, and a regicide, at this time attached to the Antwerp court, writes to the Minister: '. . . Depuis que dans les départements de l'Escaut et des Deux-Nèthes, on se montre si indulgent pour les fraudeurs, il est difficile de vous peindre toute l'étendue de la contrebande, et par conséquent toute l'étendue des marchandises anglaises qui doivent circuler dans l'Intérieur de la République! Les républicains s'indignent de voir, à chaque instant, du jour et de la nuit, des hommes arriver par milliers de l'extrême frontière, le sac sur le dos, le bâton à la main, résister aux préposés par leurs nombres. . . .' (ibid. BB 18 564).

According to the *accusateur public* of the Deux-Nèthes the proximity of the Dutch border had other advantages as well: 'Plusieurs ministres du culte catholique,' he writes on 27 Brumaire year VI [17 November 1797], 'résidant dans les communes de ce département frontière de la Hollande . . . se transportent sur le territoire hollandais, où ils sont suivis par les habitants de leurs communes, et là ils officient librement, après quoi ils reviennent dans leurs communes, se prétendant, au moyen de cette précaution, à l'abri de toute poursuite. . . .'

(K) The closing of the city gates at dusk, which was meant to prevent the entry into a city of suspicious characters, could also be the occasion for serious disorders. On 30 Pluviôse year VI [Sunday 18 February 1798] there was a serious riot in Antwerp, just inside one of the gates, a few minutes after it had been closed by two soldiers from the French garrison: '. . . Je dois préliminairement vous observer que la porte nommée *Kipdorp* qui conduit à la commune de Borgerhout est de toutes celles de la ville la plus fréquentée, principalement les jours de fêtes, et que presque toujours une demie-heure avant sa clôture, la classe des ouvriers s'y rassemble dans l'intérieur pour voir rentrer le monde qui dans ces moments passe en foule. Le peuple était rassemblé de cette manière à cette même porte et dans l'intérieur de la ville le 30 pluviôse dernier à 5h et ½ du soir. . . . la garde . . . . a fermé la porte à 5 h 3/4 . . . en un instant il se trouve au nombre d'environ 400 personnes, tant hommes que femmes et enfans, presque tous de la classe des ouvriers, tous un peu pris de boisson. Au même instant une grêle de pierres se dirige contre les deux chasseurs. . . .' Four French soldiers were gravely wounded in the riot that ensued. The French military police proceeded to search all the numerous inns that were clustered in the vicinity of the *Kipdorp*, looking for individuals who had blood on their clothes, or whose clothes were torn. They started in a café named *la maison verte*, went on to another named *la petite chapelle*. Both were crowded with drunken workmen and their families. They made four arrests, though the only evidence against the artisans arrested was that they had sabre tears on their clothes (A.N. BB 18 564, Deux-Nèthes, commissaire près le tribunal correctionnel d'Anvers, au Ministre, 16 ventôse an VI). There is a splendid account, from a year later, of the unusual conduct of a *huissier*, in charge of a prisoner: '. . . Le citoyen van Engelen, huissier, l'a accompagnée [a female prisoner whom he was supposed to be taking back from court to the central prison] . . . avec sa soeur au cabaret nommé *t'paepenhof* . . ., ils se sont fait conduire en carrosse chez la mère de ces filles. . . . ensuite ils ont remonté en voiture et ont été . . . au cabaret nommé *den enwal*, près de la porte de *Styck* et de la maison d'arrêt. . . . ils y sont restés à boire . . . jusqu'aux environs de 5 h du soir, et alors ils sont tous montés en voiture et sont allés au cabaret nommé *la maison d'anguilles*, hors ladite porte de *Styck*, qu'ils ne sont revenus en ville que vers les 8 heures et ½ du soir . . . ils sont retournés aud. cabaret *den enwal* où ils ont recommencé à boire jusqu'aux environs 10 heures et quart, et que ce n'est qu'à cette heure que Marie Vanderwost a été réintégrée dans la maison d'arrêt

. . .' (A.N. BB 18 564, tribunal correctionnel de l'arrondissement d'Anvers, au Ministre, 4 prairial an VII).

(L) A.N. BB 18 283 (Escaut, commissaire près le tribunal correctionnel du Sas-de-Gand, au Ministre, 29 messidor an V [17 July 1797]): 'Des bandes très nombreuses de fraudeurs armés . . . se portent très souvent sur l'un ou l'autre point de cet arrondissement pour favoriser, soit l'importation des marchandises angloises, soit d'autres. Leur nombre va quelques fois de 2 à 300 individus, ils se rendent le jour isolément et sans armes sur un point indiqué. Des charettes, tantôt à 4, tantôt à plusieurs, s'y rendent également et cachent les armes destinées pour les fraudeurs sous des sacs, dont elles sont chargées . . . il faudroit au moins 3,000 hommes pour s'opposer efficacement à ce brigandage. Cette force devroit être répartie sur toute! lisière des côtes maritimes de la Flandre hollandoise et changée de tems en tems afin de prévenir que les chefs ne se laissent corrompre. . . . Le 10 cour-ant des employés des douanes, des gendarmes et des volontaires avoient rencontré entre Terneuse et le Fort Marguérite un convoi très nombreux qu'ils portent à 58 charettes, aussitôt que l'on aperçut la force armée, des fraudeurs sautent des charettes, se rangent sur la digue et couchent les douan-iers en joue, ces derniers les chargent vivement, les étonnent et les mettent en fuite. Des armes au nombre de 21 sont ramassées sur la route, 11 individus et 13 charettes pris dans l'affaire sont amenés au Sas-de-Gand. . . . ' See also: rapport des douaniers du Sas-de-Gand du 11 messidor an V: '. . . le jour d'hier 10 messidor [28 juin 1797] à 6 h. du matin led. détachement s'est porté sur les chemins qui aboutissent aud. fort Marguérite, près Terneuse. . . . nous avons . . . remarqué . . . une très grande quantité d'hommes armées . . . et parmi lesquels plusieurs d'entre nous ont parfaitement reconnu le nommé *Grégoire*, de Selzaete, entrepreneur de la fraude et organisateur de ces brigand-ages, ainsi que *Louis Vanpeteghem*, de Selzaete. . . . nous avons couru dessus à toute bride ayant foncé sur eux avec nos chevaux avec toute l'impétuosité possible, nous les avons aussitôt étonnés, renversés et mis en déroute, de manière que la plupart, abandonnant leurs armes, se sont jettés dans les fossés, et dans les bleds, d'autres se sauvent avec leurs fusils à travers les bleds . . . ne leur ayant trouvé aucun passeport ni certificat, nous leur avons demandé s'ils en étoient munis et ils ont répondu négativement. . . .'

(M) In the operation against the farm of Michel Bréda, at Hubernez, near Flobecq, on the night of 20–1 December 1795, 'ils lui prirent . . . 21 chemises, 40 aulnes de toile blanche et un gris, une jupe de calmande à lignes bleues et vertes, un mantelet brun à petites mouches rouges, 3 mouchoirs dont 2 blancs de 6 quarts et l'autre de col . . . une couverte de laine blanche, un frac couleur de bouteille, un autre habit couleur de café, un chapeau fin de 22 escalins, en outre 2 bagues d'or, l'une à 7 pierres et l'autre marqué MIF, qu'ils y volèrent aussi 58 couronnes de France cachées dans une boîte liée d'une corde qui se trouvoit dans la paille de leur lit. . . . In the attack on the *ferme au Bois*, near Bouvignies, on 1–2 March 1796, they got away with: '. . . une jupe . . . un déshabillé de soie avec la jupe de coton, 2 tabliers de coton, 10 chemises de femme, une boucle d'argent de feue sa femme, 4 chemises d'homme, 10 serviettes, 2 draps de lit et 2 taies . . . un habit de drap violet, une culotte de velours jaunâtre. . . . 3 fracs d'enfant, un chapeau, 3 paires de draps de lit et 2 chemises d'enfant . . . 2 capotins et une jupe de coton et un mouchoir de mousseline appartenants à la servante, un bassin d'étain et de plus un pot de beurre d'environ 20 livres qui se trouvoit à la cave. . . . In an attack on the farm of Le Wazoir, near Saradaie, 'ils ont en-levé une pendule et 7 à 8 chemises, (qu') ils ont dû abandonner à cause des voisins qui ont accouru. . . .'

(N) '*Michel Claes*, chef;
Charles Claes, frère de Michel;
Jean Petit, dit *Dragon*, 23 ans, natif de Charo [*sic*], district de Bourges, déserteur du 15me régiment d'infanterie;
Adrien Carlier, dit *Dogue*, 37 ans, marchand d'étoupes, demeurant à Flobecq;
Pierre Moreau, habitant d'Ellezelles;
Pierre-Antoine Foubert, 48 ans, tisserand, demeurant à Everbeek;
Pierre Frénay, 24 ans, natif de Saintes, demeurant à Frasnes, perruquier, déserteur du Régiment de la Cavalerie du Roi [which seems to have been part of the *armée de Condé*; Frénay is described in the indictment as *émigré français*];
Jean-Baptiste Lefebvre, sans occupation, dit *Sans-Doigts*, habitant un fau-bourg de Leuze, sur la chaussée de Renaix;
Michet, marchand d'étoupes;
Louis Proust, dit *Flamand;*
Proust père;
André-Joseph Roland, dit *Brasseur*, tisserand âgé de 25 ans, demeurant à Renaix;
Jean-Michel Bourlet, habitant de Renaix;
Jean-Baptiste Daumont, dit *François Parault*, journalier, 32 ans, demeurant à Flobecq;
François Daumont, 28 ans, ouvrier de bois, demeurant à Flobecq [and pre-sumably the brother of Jean-Baptiste];
Jacques Minon, demeurant près de Leuze, chaussée de Renaix;
Emmanuel Lison;
Jacobus, de Gand;
François Vandamme;
deux marchands de chevaux qu'il [Petit] ne connaît pas;
Picard, juif, *Capitaine;*
Fromme, son frère.

(O) A.N. BB 18 579 (Briffault au Ministre, 6 frimaire an IV): 'Lisez et fré-missez, Citoyen, sur le point physique de l'ancienne démarcation du terri-toire français et de la ci-devant Belgique, un peu au-dessus de Bavey à une portée de fusil de la commune d'Eth, à un endroit appellé la Houlette, on vient d'y assassiner un médicin, un autre homme et sa femme avec 6 enfans dont le plus jeune a à peine 18 mois. . . . on paraît l'attribuer à la rage de l'aristocratie contre les patriotes. . . . on a massacré jusqu'à des enfants de 4 ans et 6 ans, on a trouvé sur une table une potée d'eau de vie et 11 verres. . . . on a volé l'argent . . . et des mouchoirs de soie. . . . l'assassinat s'est commis avec des sabres, épées ou bayonnettes, il ne paraît aucunes traces d'armes à feu. Je ne suis point étonné de voir commettre des vols, car ils sont communs dans ce pays, il existe dans ces contrées une classe d'hommes qui n'ont ni biens ni rentes, et qui ne travaille point, cependant ces gens-là vivent et font de la dépense dans les cabarets, mais d'où viennent leurs res-sources lorsqu'on vole de tout côté? . . . D'autres ont été pris sur le fait et on n'osa ni les arrêter ni les dénoncer. La crainte des vengeances . . . arrête tous ceux qui ont quelque connaissance des crimes. . . . le feu mis à des fermes est une suite de ces vengeances. . . .'

(P) Writing to the Minister on 13 Nivôse year V [2 January 1797], Baret was formally to accuse Salambier of the murder of van der Auwera: '. . . Il a été arrêté en vertu d'une ordonnance de prise de corps . . . rendue par notre tribunal comme accusé d'un assassinat atroce commis dans ce Département et pour lequel 2 de ses complices, Dalâtre et Pérignon [there is no mention of them in the indictment], ont subi ici [à Bruges] la peine capitale. Il est prévenu en outre d'être au vent d'un assassinat commis à Aire il y a environ un an, et, au moment de son arrestation, il a été saisi avec une chaise et 2 chevaux, qu'ils s'était appropriés, en assassinant le maître près de Bruxelles, le 1er frimaire dernier . . .' (A.N. BB 18 8582).

He was, however, less affirmative, in his next letter to the Minister, dated 26th of the same month: '. . . Il y a plus, quoiqu'il nie légalement d'avoir commis l'assassinat près de Bruxelles, quoiqu'il se flatte encore qu'il ne sera pas possible de l'en convaincre, sur l'exposé que je lui ai fait de l'état où se trouvait la famille de la victime, incertaine du sort de son chef, il m'a dit où était le cadavre, sur ma parole que je ne ferais pas usage de cette déclaration contre lui . . .' (ibid.).

In a judgement given by the *cour de cassation* on 18 Pluviôse of the same year [6 February 1797], it is stated: '. . . que dans le fait de Paul van der Auwera, aubergiste dans la commune de Contych en Brabant [il] en est parti le 3 frimaire dernier emportant du numéraire pour acquitter une dette à Bruxelles, conduisant dans son cabriolet Salambier & Heller dit *Berry*, que le 6 du même mois ces derniers ont été arrêtés à Dunkerque, nantis d'un cabriolet & de 2 chevaux, qui ont été réclamés comme ayant été volés à Paul van der Auwera, qui n'a pas reparu depuis son départ de Contych. . . .

son cadavre n'ayant pas été trouvé, rien n'apprend quel est le lieu où le crime a été commis, qu'il peut l'avoir été dans l'arrondissement de l'un des départements où ils ont pu contraindre Paul van der Auwera de voyager avec eux . . .' (ibid.).

According to the *substitut* of Baret, in a report to the Minister dated 5 January 1796:

'Le tribunal [de la Lys] a obtenu la preuve que Salambier et son compagnon de voyage avaient logé à l'auberge dite *le Duc* en Brabant en la commune de Contyck sur la route de Malines à Anvers que le 3 frimaire après . . . le C. Paul van der Auwera, occupant de ladite auberge partit avec son cabriolet et les chevaux . . . pour les conduire à Bruxelles . . . que depuis lors sa famille . . .? dans la désolation . . . l'un d'eux seulement dit, et c'est le complice de Salambier, qu'ayant quitté la voiture à une demie-lieue de Bruxelles, l'aubergiste y étant encore, il ne rejoignit que dans Bruxelles, alors il n'y étoit plus, qu'il a eu toute velléité que Salambier s'était défait de cet infortuné dans le trajet . . . mais cette réticence ne fait pas preuve. . . . avant la disparition de cet aubergiste, ces deux individus s'étoient fait conduire de Contyck à Malines avec la même voiture et les chevaux par le cocher dudit auberge et qu'il les a ramenés sans qu'il lui soit arrivé d'accident, et qu'il est possible que l'idée absolue ne leur soit venue qu'à un certain lieu propre à exécuter leurs infâmes desseins, qu'ils aient fait voyager cet aubergiste malgré lui. . . .'

(Q) A.N. BB 18 582 (Ducrez, directeur du jury de Lille, au Ministre, 13 nivôse an V): '. . . Ce sont la plupart les complices et compagnons du nommé Salambier qui est, lui, bien convaincu de s'être trouvé dans différentes expéditions et de l'assassinat de 6 individus dans l'espace de 7 à 8 mois. . . . il se trouvoit 11 brigands à l'expédition de Lambersart, parmi eux s'en trouvaient 3 coupables d'un assassinat commis quelques jours auparavant près de Poperinge. . . .'

'Nous nous sommes concertés . . . sur les moyens qu'il conviendroit de prendre pour acquérir contre *Guéva* et *Rohart* des preuves de leurs brigandages. Ces moyens consistent à les faire surveiller . . . à leur retour de quelque expédition nocturne . . . car les arrêter sur une simple dénonciation ne nous menerait vraisemblablement à rien. Nous avons actuellement dans la maison d'arrêt de cette commune [Lille] une trentaine de ces Brigands. . . .' Three weeks earlier, on 20 Frimaire year V [10 December 1796], Ranson had written: '. . . Plusieurs desdits habitants [de Longprez] ont à leur égard des renseignemens précieux qu'ils n'osent donner à la justice dans la crainte d'être assassinés ou d'avoir leurs masions incendiées; ils donneraient ces renseignemens s'ils étaient certains de n'être pas connus. . . .'

See also, ibid. (directeur du jury de Béthune, au Ministre, 19 germinal an V): '. . . Il reste encore à traduire de cette maison d'arrêt . . . le nommé Charles-Louis d'Haine, dit *Gros Louis*, prévenu d'une multitude de crimes dans cet arrondissement, et l'un des brigands les plus redoutés de la contrée, d'une stature et d'une force prodigieuse. . . .'

(R) A.N. BB 18 582 (commissaire près le tribunal de la Lys, au Ministre, 19 brumaire an VII).

Also possibly connected with the Salambier group, though he may equally have been a lone flier, is the case of Antoine Joseph Moneuse, a native of Douai, twenty-eight, said to be a *marchand farinier et d'étoffes*, living in the village of Saint-Vaast-lès-Vallée, near Cambrai. He was cross-examined on 27 July 1797 by the public prosecutor of Mons, on the subject of a series of armed robberies committed in the Mons area in the course of 1797 and the previous year: 12 January 1796, at Eugies; February 1796, at the former abbey of Béliant; and, in the same month, at Nouvelles; June 1796, at Mesvin; 28 July 1796, at Dour; 9–10 October 1796, at Ville-Pommeroeul; 23–4 October 1796, at Élouges; 2 November 1796, at Feignies; December 1796, at Wandrez; and 22 January 1797, at Le Petit-Quévy. Moneuse was to deny all the charges, while asking to be brought before the Douai court (A.N. BB 18 400, interrogatoire par devant le directeur du jury d'accusation de l'arrondissement de Mons, 9 thermidor an V).

(S) Frontier areas were also particularly sensitive owing to the presence in them of nationals of more than one state. Just as Parisian soldiers might find themselves the object of rural aggressiveness in the inns on the edge of Paris, especially at weekends or feast days or on the occasion of a christening or a wedding, so any contact between French soldiers and other nationalities was likely to lead to trouble. There is a very good example of this type of dispute in a petition addressed by a French soldier to Barras in Nivôse year IV [January 1796] from the prison of Beauvais (A.N. BB 18 602, Oise): '. . . un frère qui à l'âge de 16 ans se comptait déjà au nombre des défenseurs de la patrie, *Auguste Tillet*, après s'être signalé pendant 2 années dans le 1er bataillon de l'Yonne, passe dans les chasseurs du Hainaut, au bout d'un an il est traduit devant un tribunal militaire qui le condamne à deux ans de prison. Quel est son crime? Direz-vous; son crime est d'avoir avancé que la nation française l'emportait de beaucoup sur la nation allemande, cette assertion, combattue par un Allemand, alors caporal dans le même corps, fait naître une querelle que les deux champions prennent résolution de terminer le sabre à la main; mais, au lieu de donner satisfaction, le caporal va se plaindre à ses officiers. . . .' Tillet came from Sacy, canton de Vermenton, in the Yonne, the village in which Restif de la Bretonne was born.

(T) '. . . J'allois m'occuper de leur affaire lorsque le fameux Salambier, qui avait été d'abord arrêté avec eux, et qui depuis s'était évadé, a été repris et conduit à Bruges. Convaincu de ses crimes, Salambier a fait la déclaration de ses complices parmi lesquels se trouvent 5 Brigands qui avaient été arrêtés avec lui, il y a un an, et d'autres individus que nous avons fait saisir d'après cette déclaration. Il nous a paru conforme aux principes qu'on ne pouvait diviser la procédure, et que Salambier et ses complices devaient être jugés par le même tribunal, c'est même le seul moyen de convaincre les complices de Salambier . . .' (A.N. BB 18 582, président du tribunal criminel de Lille, au Ministre, 25 ventôse an V).

See also ibid. (Baret au Ministre, 24 nivôse an V): '*Salambier* m'a avoué qu'une grosse montre de cuivre dont il étoit porteur lors de son arrestation provient d'un vol commis dans un château près de Douai. Ils s'y trouvaient au nombre de 22 Brigands. Un nommé *Casimir*, détenu à Lille, y étoit avec sa femme qui, par sa conduite, a mérité d'avoir part au butin. Dans ce nombre, on comptoit les nommés *Boutonné*, *Saint-Amand*, *Théodore Leroi*, dit *Berger*, *Derenaud*, *Antoine Calendrin*, *Narcisse Duhamel*, *Lammelin*, dit *Lemaire*. . . .'

Name Index

Note. The names of members, alleged members, and accomplices of the *bande à Salambier* will be followed by the letter [S], and those of the so-called *bande juive*, by the letters [BJ]. Nicknames have been added whenever possible.

Index of Place Names